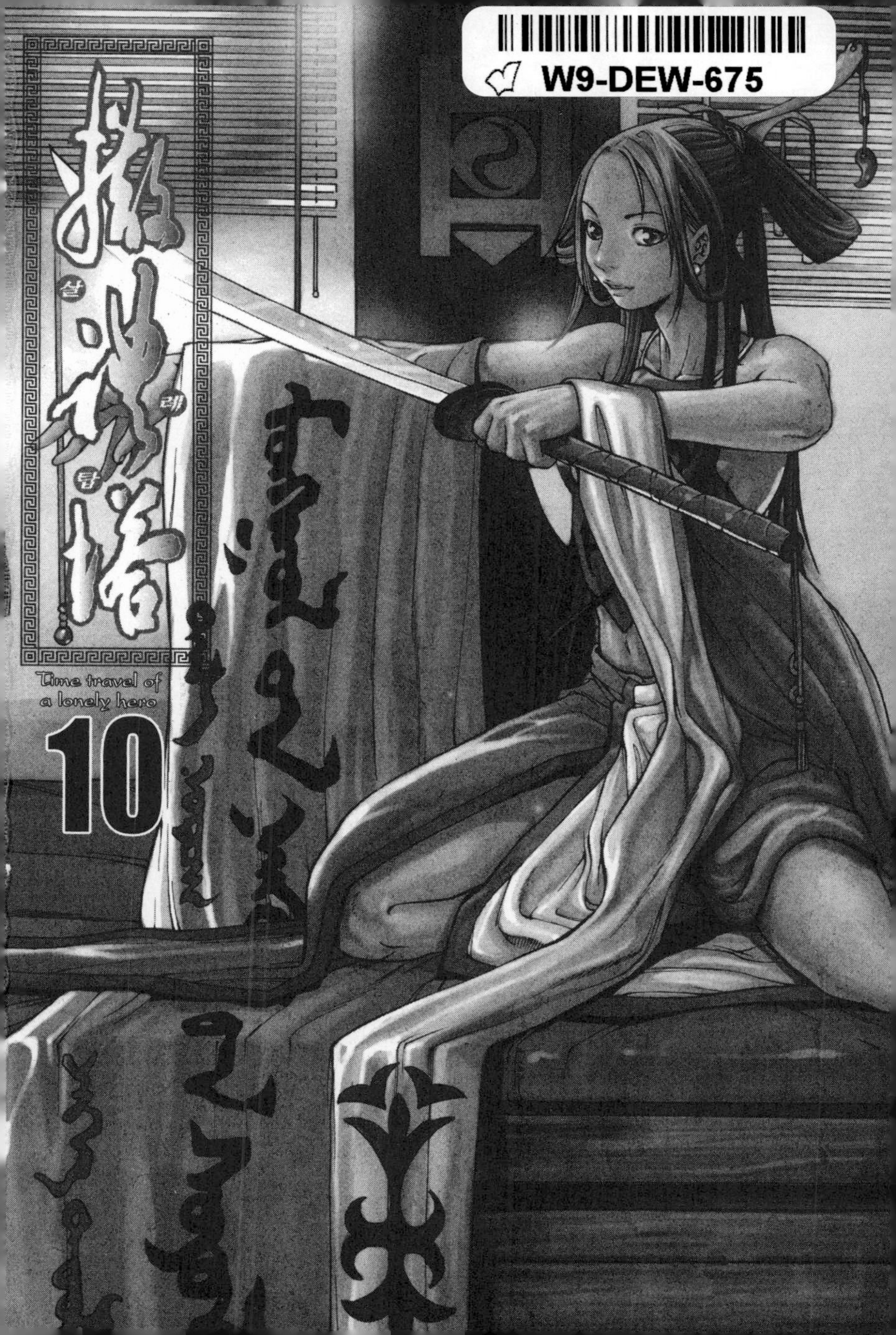
Time travel of
a lonely hero
10

Threads of Time Vol. 10
Created by Mi Young Noh

Translation - Jihae Hong
English Adaptation - Frank Marraffino
Retouch and Lettering - Star Print Brokers
Production Artist - Mike Estacio
Cover Design - John Lo

Editor - Luis Reyes
Digital Imaging Manager - Chris Buford
Pre-Production Supervisor - Erika Terriquez
Art Director - Anne Marie Horne
Production Manager - Elisabeth Brizzi
Managing Editor - Vy Nguyen
VP of Production - Ron Klamert
Editor-in-Chief - Rob Tokar
Publisher - Mike Kiley
President and C.O.O. - John Parker
C.E.O. and Chief Creative Officer - Stuart Levy

A  Manga

TOKYOPOP and  are trademarks or registered trademarks of TOKYOPOP Inc.

TOKYOPOP Inc.
5900 Wilshire Blvd. Suite 2000
Los Angeles, CA 90036

E-mail: info@TOKYOPOP.com
Come visit us online at www.TOKYOPOP.com

ISBN: 978-1-59532-041-4

First TOKYOPOP printing: August 2007
10 9 8 7 6 5 4 3 2 1
Printed in the USA

Threads of Time
搬神搖

Volume 10

By

Threads of Time
TOKYOPOP
Mi Young Noh 1

Threads of Time Vol. 1

High school kendo champion Moon Bin Kim suffers from a recurring nightmare in which he lives as Sa Kyung Kim, the son of a prominent warrior family in 13th Century Korea (Koryo). After a freak accident, Moon Bin falls into a coma, but his modern-day personality resurfaces in the distant past as Sa Kyung revives miraculously after years of unconsciousness. As if being displaced in medieval Koryo wasn't enough, Moon Bin finds the country at the brink of war. Sali Tayi, the most brutal and feared general of the Mongol army, leads the invasion. Opposing him is Moon Bin's 13th Century father, the legendary warlord Kim Kyung-Sohn.

Threads of Time Vol. 2

General Sohn learns that Genghis Khan's granddaughter, Atan Hadas, is gathering intelligence in Koryo and orders her arrest. Unaware that she is a princess and an enemy spy, the impetuous Moon Bin helps her escape capture. Returning to Sali Tayi, Atan Hadas learns that a full-scale invasion of Koryo has begun.

Threads of Time
TOKYOPOP
Mi Young Noh 2

Threads of Time
TOKYOPOP
Mi Young Noh 3

Threads of Time Vol. 3

In an all-out assault, the Mongol army cuts a bloody swath toward Ghu Zhu Palace, the stronghold of Koryo's defense. General Sali Tayi demands Koryo's surrender, but despite facing overwhelming enemy forces, the Koryo palace weathers the Mongol siege. Kim Kyung-Sohn stands against Sali Tayi in personal combat, keeping the hopes of a successful resistance alive.

Threads of Time Vol. 4

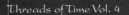

Infuriated by Koryo's resistance, Sali Tayi orders the rape and massacre of Kim Kyung-Sohn's household. Disturbed by the brutality of her fellow soldiers and seeking to repay Moon-Bin's kindness, Atan Hadas warns Moon Bin to save himself. Unable to abandon his 13th Century family, Moon Bin returns home to find everything destroyed...

Threads of Time
TOKYOPOP
Mi Young Noh 4

Threads of Time
TOKYOPOP
Mi Young Noh 5

Threads of Time Vol. 5

Moon Bin dresses as a woman to avoid the murderous clutches of the Mongols. Meanwhile, the Koryo ruler surrenders to the Mongol hordes, much to the shock of General Kim Kyung-Sohn, who fought fiercely for his country only to be betrayed by its leaders.

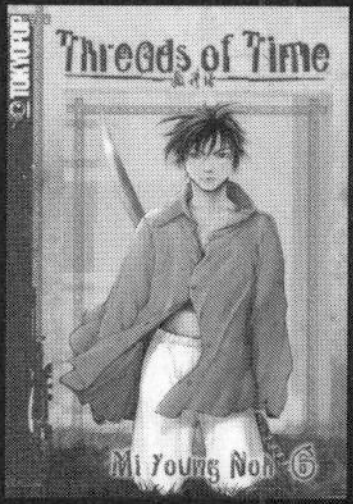
Threads of Time
TOKYOPOP
Mi Young Noh 6

Threads of Time Vol. 6

With the death of General Kim Kyung-Sohn, the last Koryo credible resistance to the Mongol army falls. Moon Bin is captured and placed in the Slave Corps: Koryo citizens who will be trained as Mongol soldiers to fight their own on the battlefield.

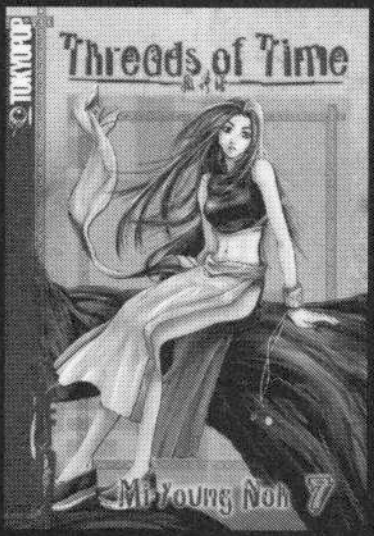
Threads of Time
TOKYOPOP
Mi Young Noh 7

Threads of Time Vol.7

Haunted by the vision of his dead warrior father, Moon Bin awakens in the slave camp with a compulsion to avenge his family's murder. He becomes a cold and fierce warrior and gains the notice of his Mongol commanders who push him up the ranks. Meanwhile, Sali Tayi decides he wishes to marry Atan Hadas.

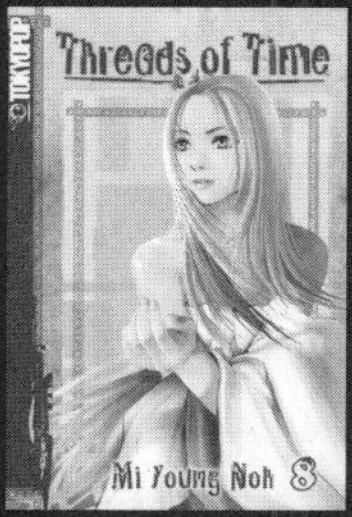
Threads of Time
TOKYOPOP
Mi Young Noh 8

Threads of Time Vol.8

Sali Tayi reminisces about his childhood with Atan Hadas, and how much he loves her now. Meanwhile, Moon Bin comes to believe that retrieving his sword will be the key to returning to his own century. Moon Bin learns that Sali Tayi now possesses the sword...and is betrothed to Atan Hadas.

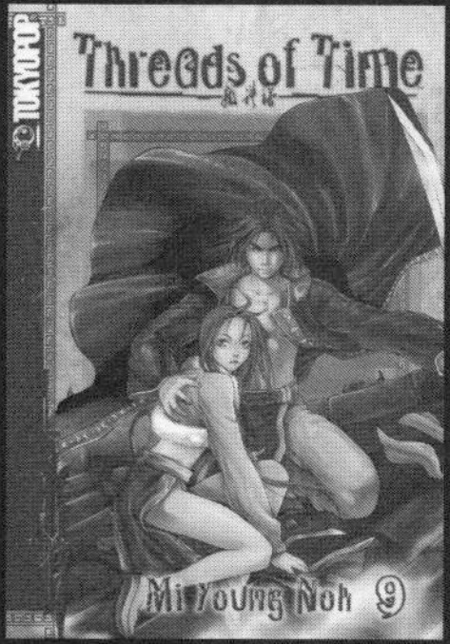
Threads of Time
TOKYOPOP
Mi Young Noh 9

Threads of Time Vol.9

Unwilling to fight against his countrymen, Moon Bin deserts the Mongol army camp, but is attacked by Sali Tayi. During the fight, Sali Tayi is shocked to discover that Moon Bin is Kim Kyung-Sohn's son. Though defeated by Sali Tayi, Atan Hadas helps Moon Bin escape. During his recovery, Moon-Bin resolves to follow his course to its end.

contents

10

Threads of Time

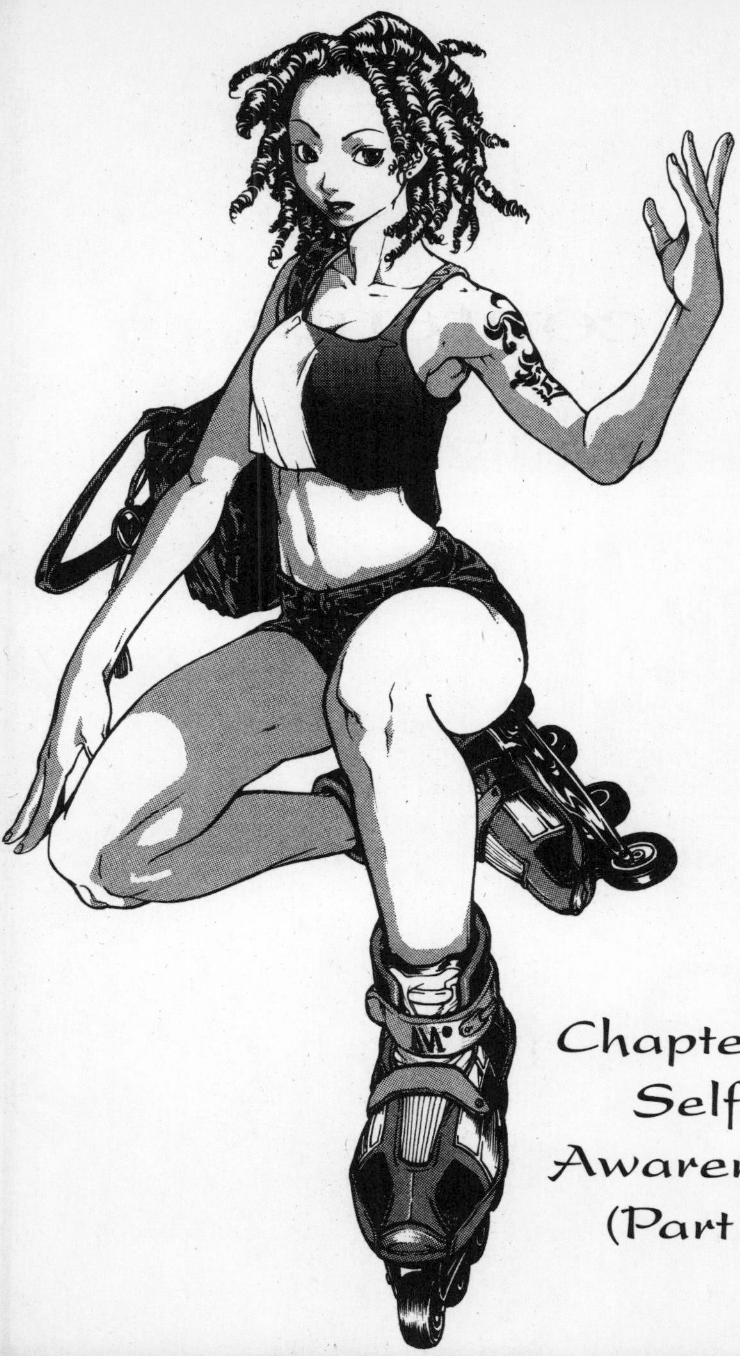

Chapter 41 Self-Awareness (Part 1)

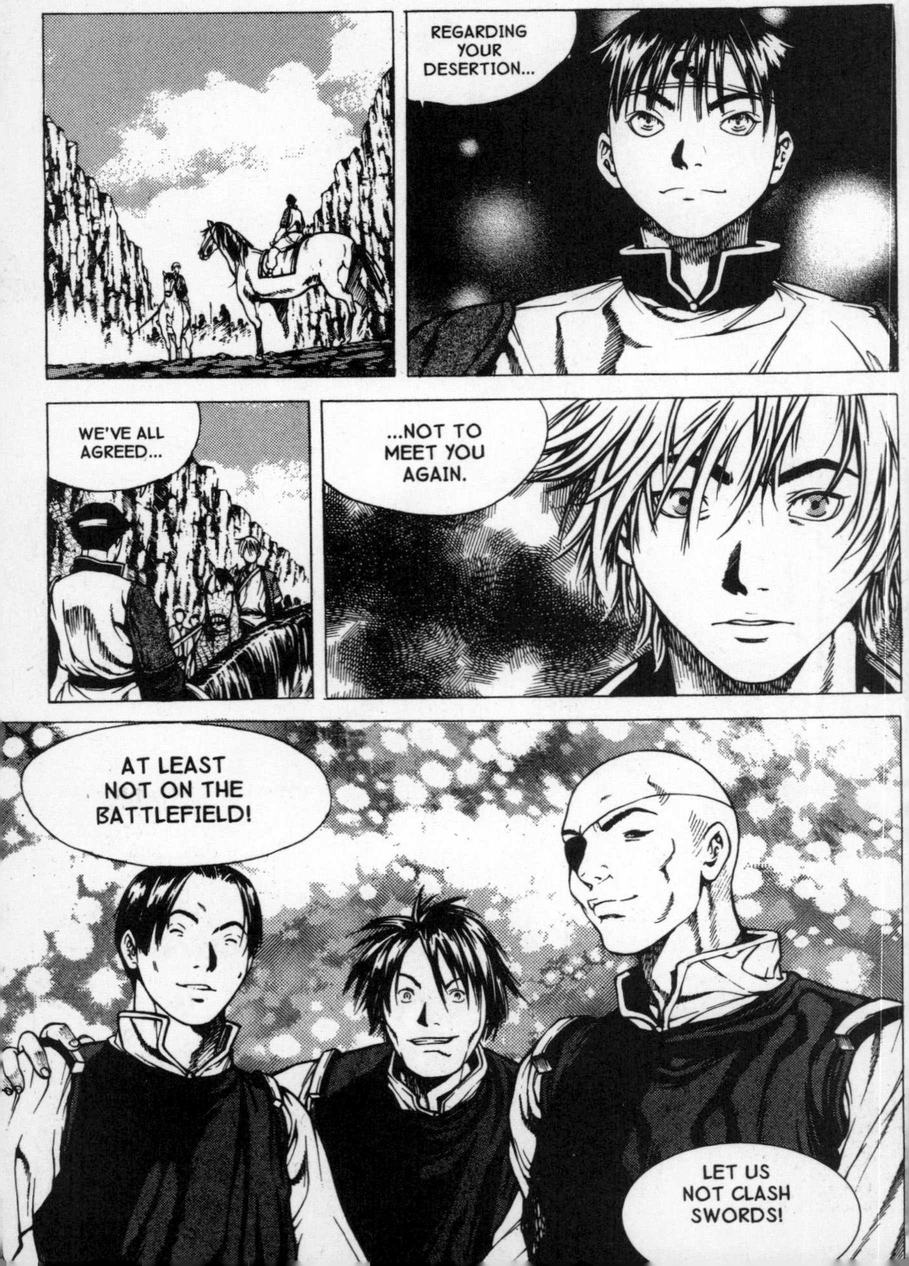
REGARDING YOUR DESERTION...
WE'VE ALL AGREED...
...NOT TO MEET YOU AGAIN.
AT LEAST NOT ON THE BATTLEFIELD!
LET US NOT CLASH SWORDS!

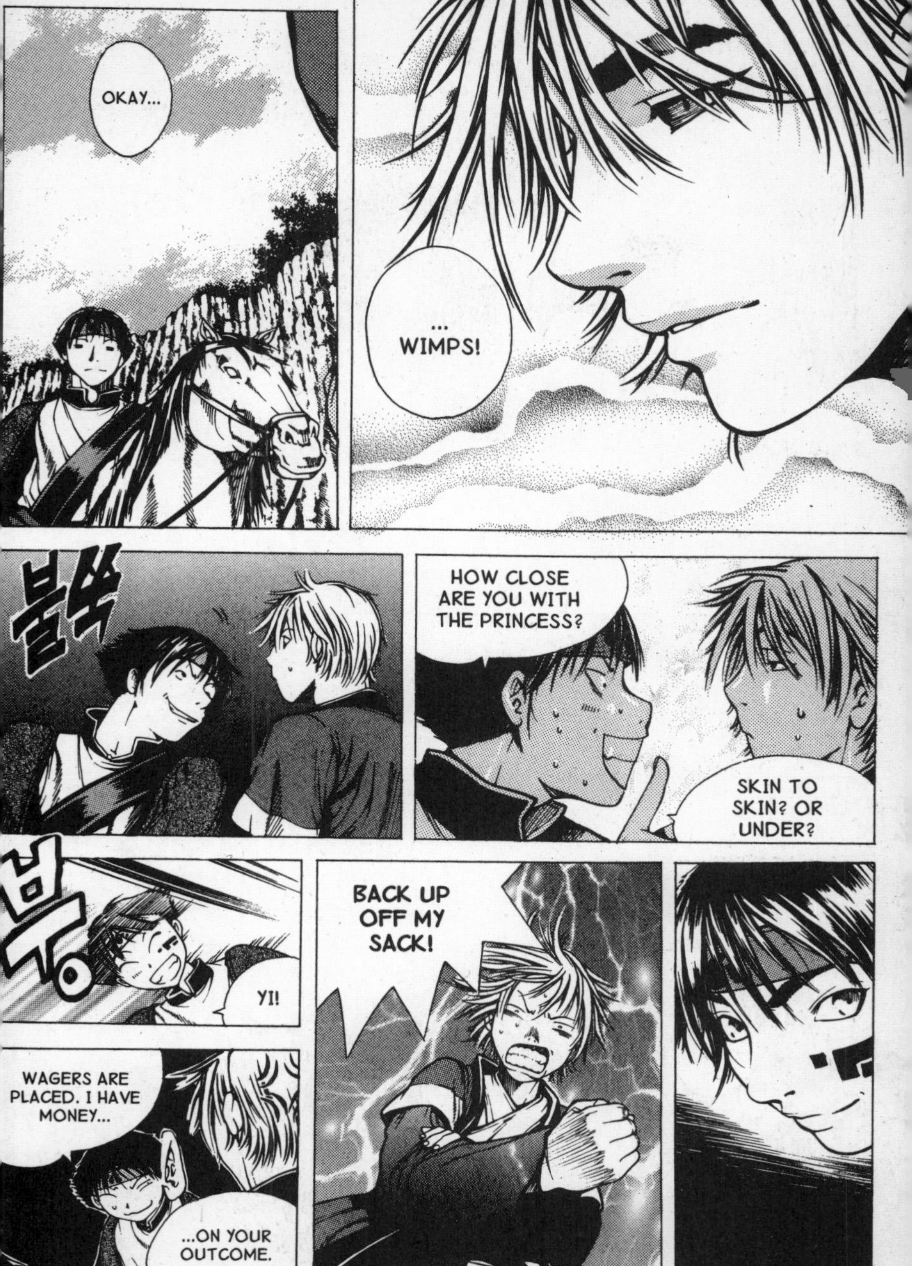
OKAY...
...WIMPS!
불쑥
HOW CLOSE ARE YOU WITH THE PRINCESS?
SKIN TO SKIN? OR UNDER?
YI!
WAGERS ARE PLACED. I HAVE MONEY...
...ON YOUR OUTCOME.
BACK UP OFF MY SACK!

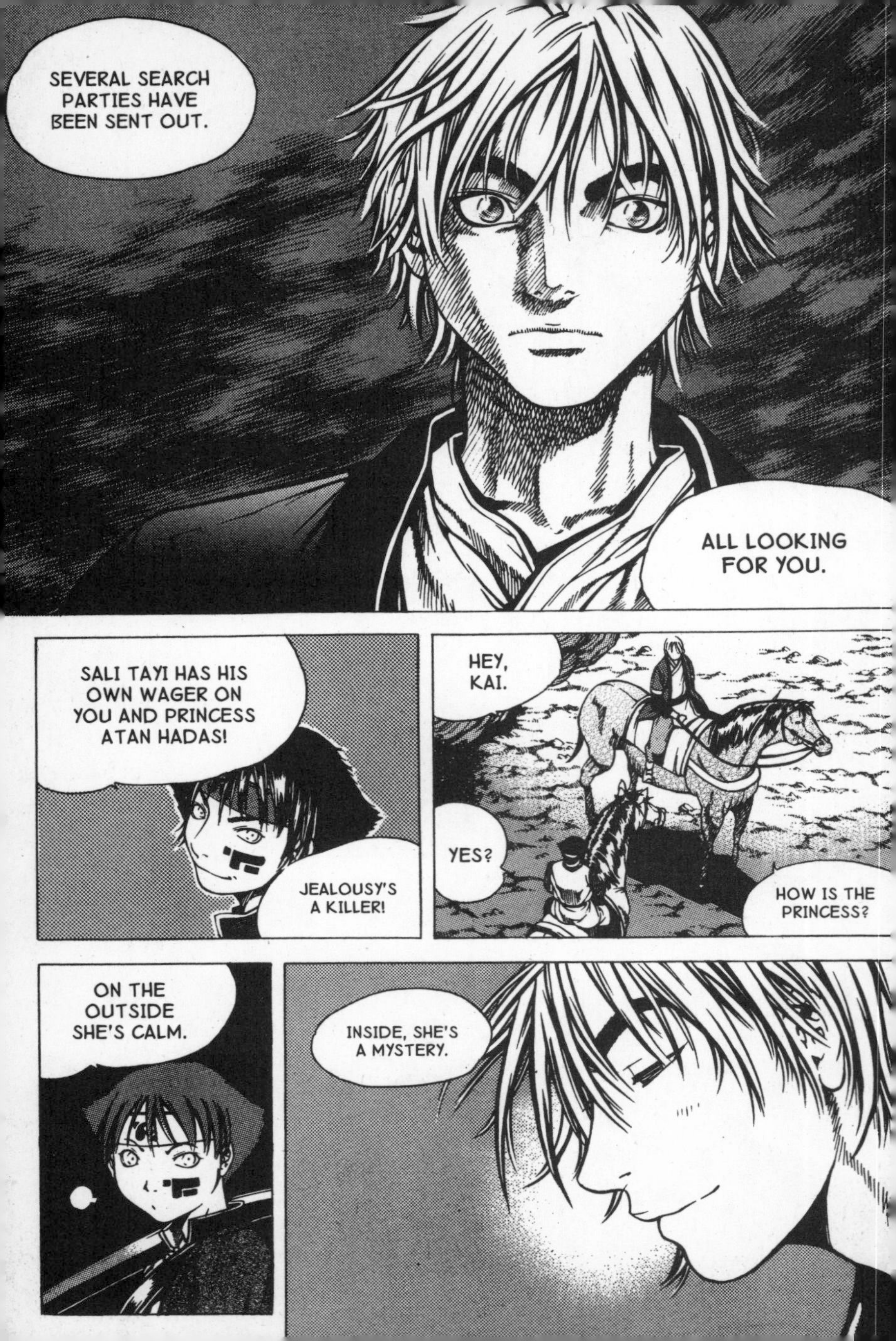
SEVERAL SEARCH PARTIES HAVE BEEN SENT OUT.
ALL LOOKING FOR YOU.
SALI TAYI HAS HIS OWN WAGER ON YOU AND PRINCESS ATAN HADAS!
JEALOUSY'S A KILLER!
HEY, KAI.
YES?
HOW IS THE PRINCESS?
ON THE OUTSIDE SHE'S CALM.
INSIDE, SHE'S A MYSTERY.

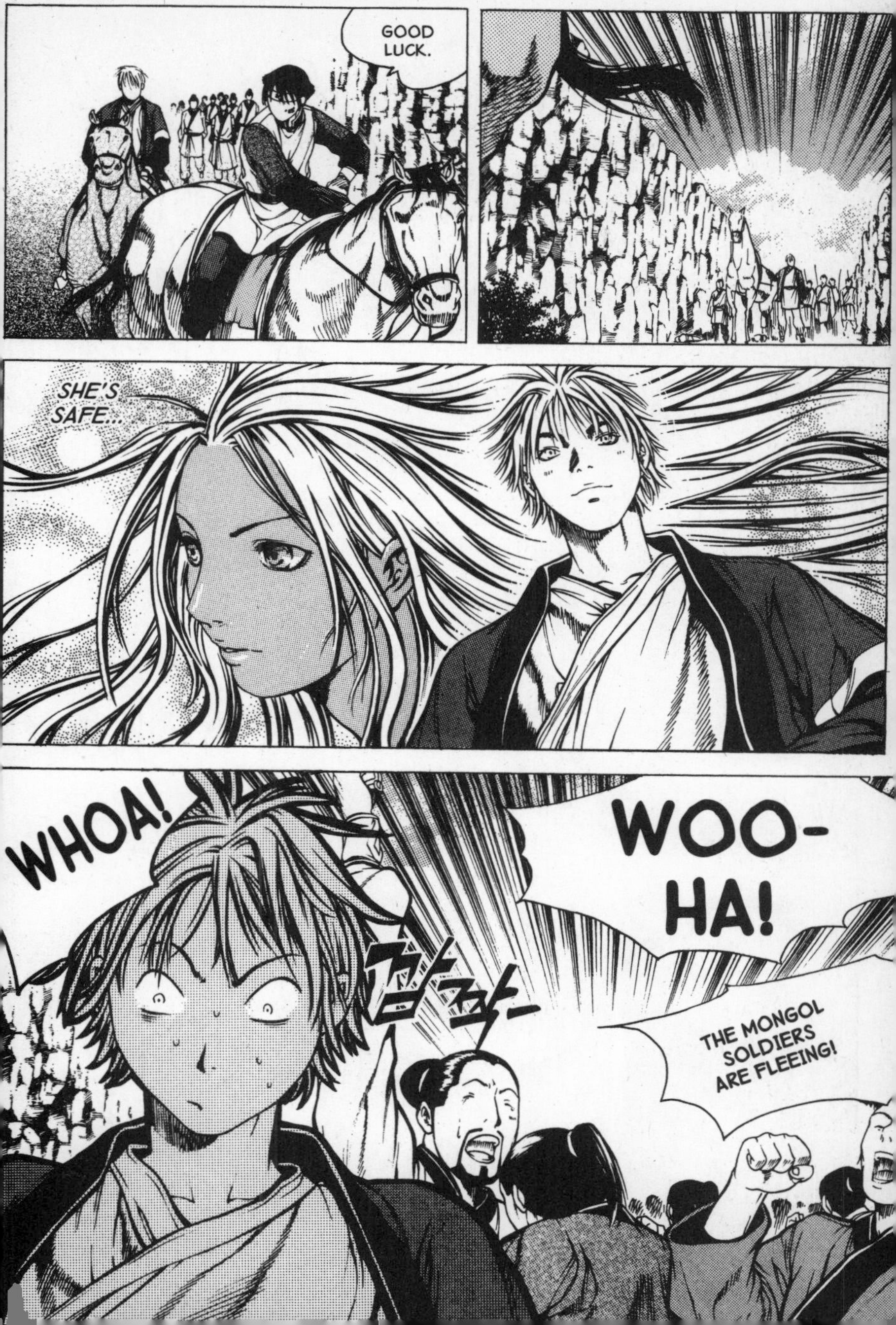
GOOD LUCK.
SHE'S SAFE...
WHOA!
WOO-HA!
THE MONGOL SOLDIERS ARE FLEEING!

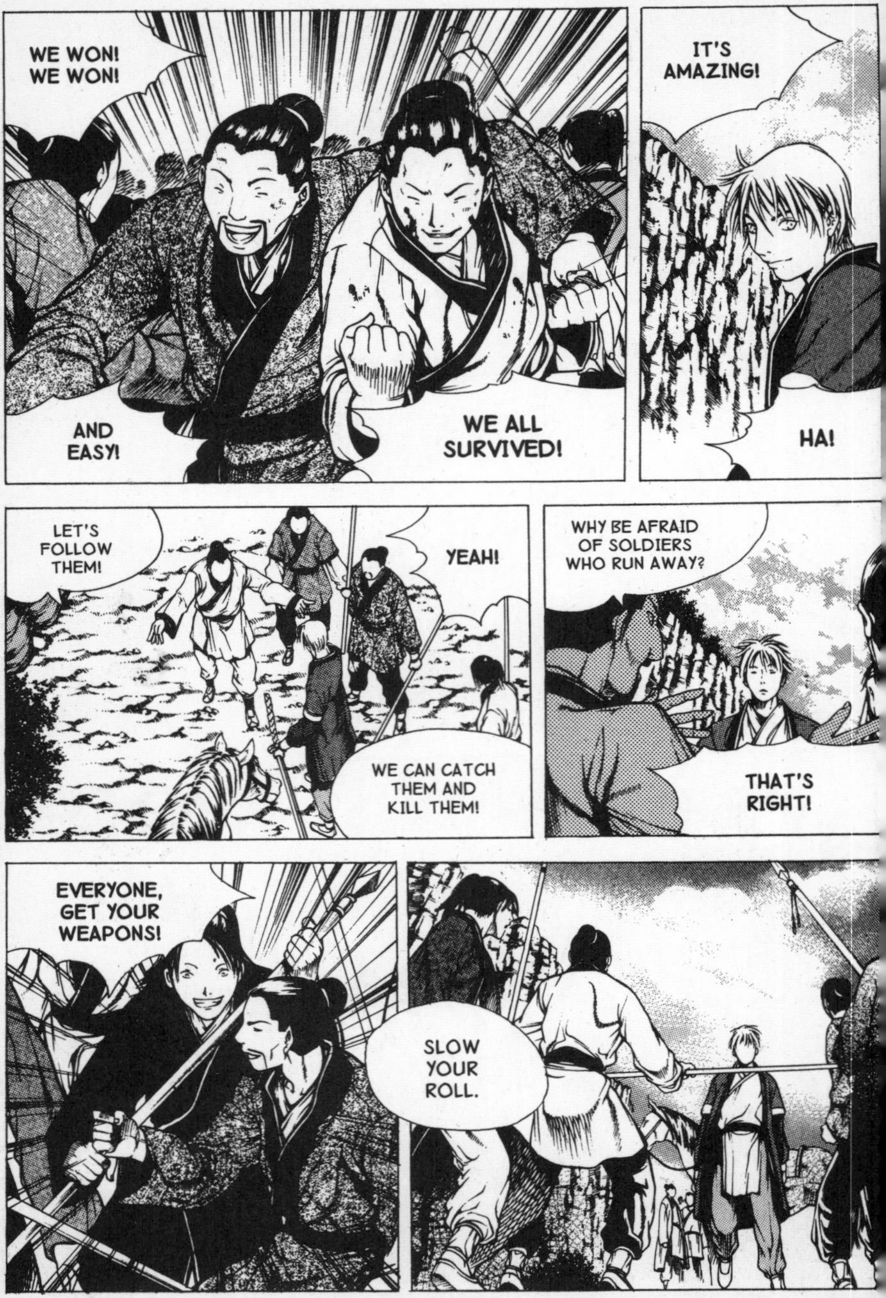
WE WON! WE WON!
AND EASY!
WE ALL SURVIVED!
IT'S AMAZING!
HA!
LET'S FOLLOW THEM!
YEAH!
WE CAN CATCH THEM AND KILL THEM!
WHY BE AFRAID OF SOLDIERS WHO RUN AWAY?
THAT'S RIGHT!
EVERYONE, GET YOUR WEAPONS!
SLOW YOUR ROLL.

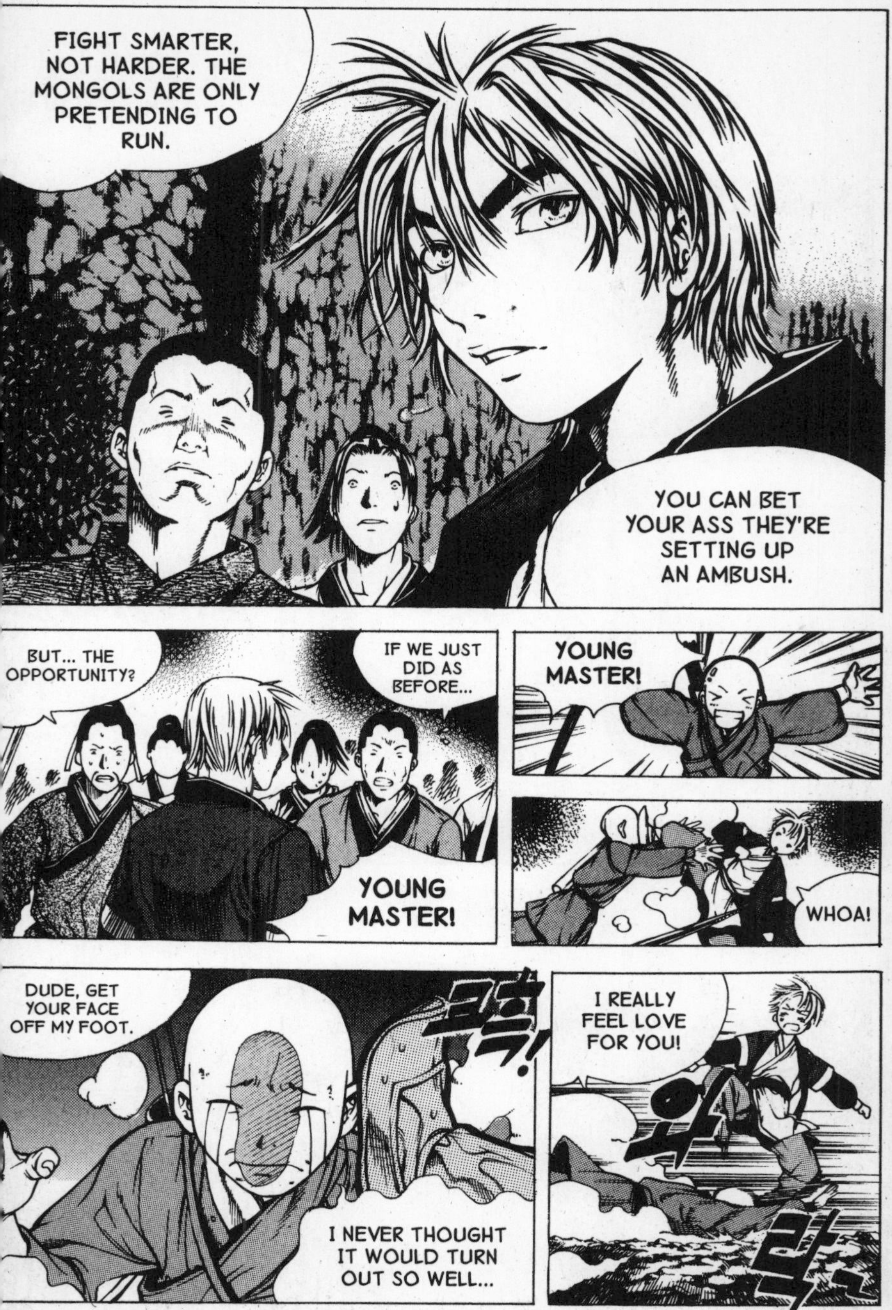
FIGHT SMARTER, NOT HARDER. THE MONGOLS ARE ONLY PRETENDING TO RUN.
YOU CAN BET YOUR ASS THEY'RE SETTING UP AN AMBUSH.
BUT... THE OPPORTUNITY?
IF WE JUST DID AS BEFORE...
YOUNG MASTER!
YOUNG MASTER!
WHOA!
DUDE, GET YOUR FACE OFF MY FOOT.
I NEVER THOUGHT IT WOULD TURN OUT SO WELL...
I REALLY FEEL LOVE FOR YOU!

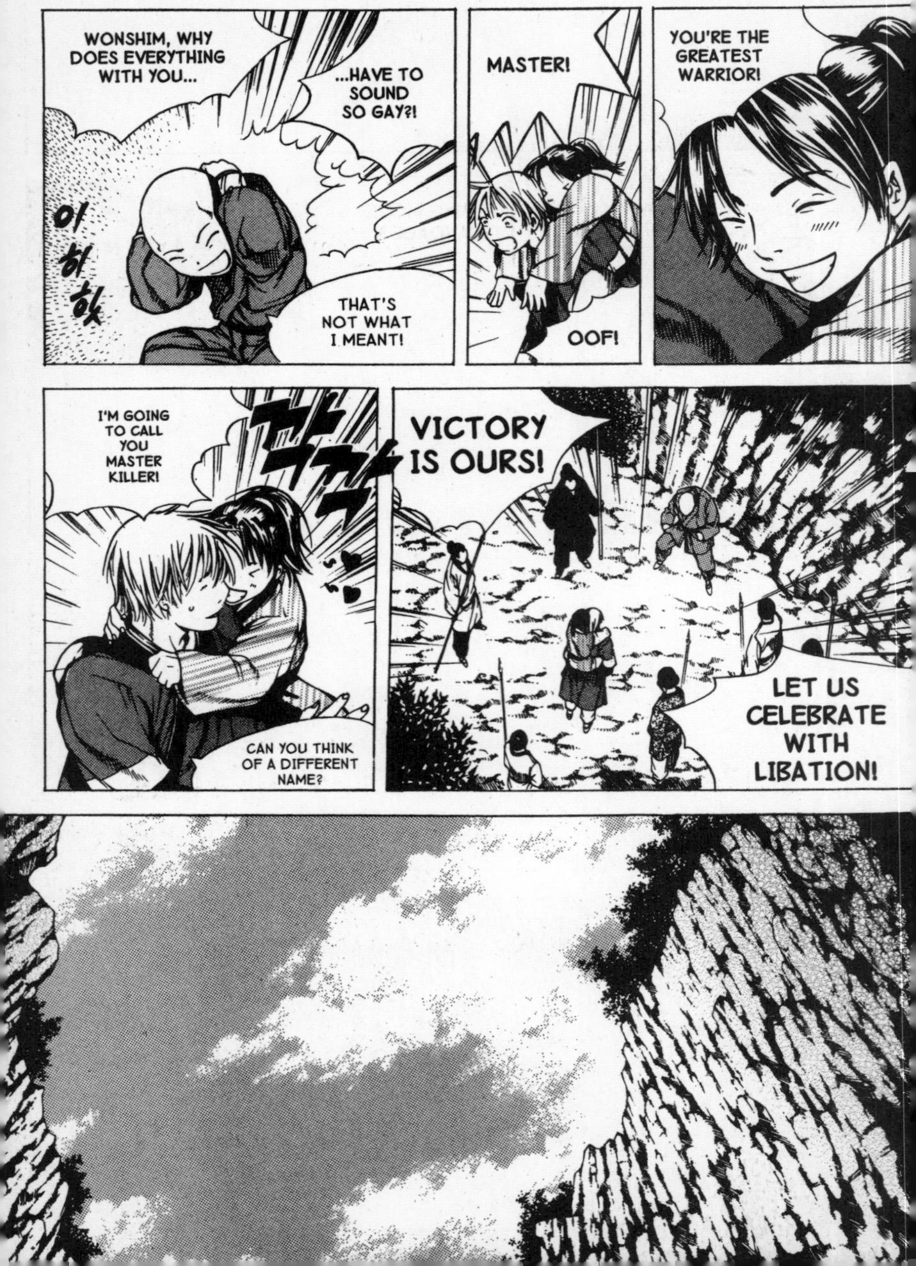
WONSHIM, WHY DOES EVERYTHING WITH YOU...
...HAVE TO SOUND SO GAY?!
아하핫
THAT'S NOT WHAT I MEANT!
MASTER!
OOF!
YOU'RE THE GREATEST WARRIOR!
I'M GOING TO CALL YOU MASTER KILLER!
CAN YOU THINK OF A DIFFERENT NAME?
VICTORY IS OURS!
LET US CELEBRATE WITH LIBATION!

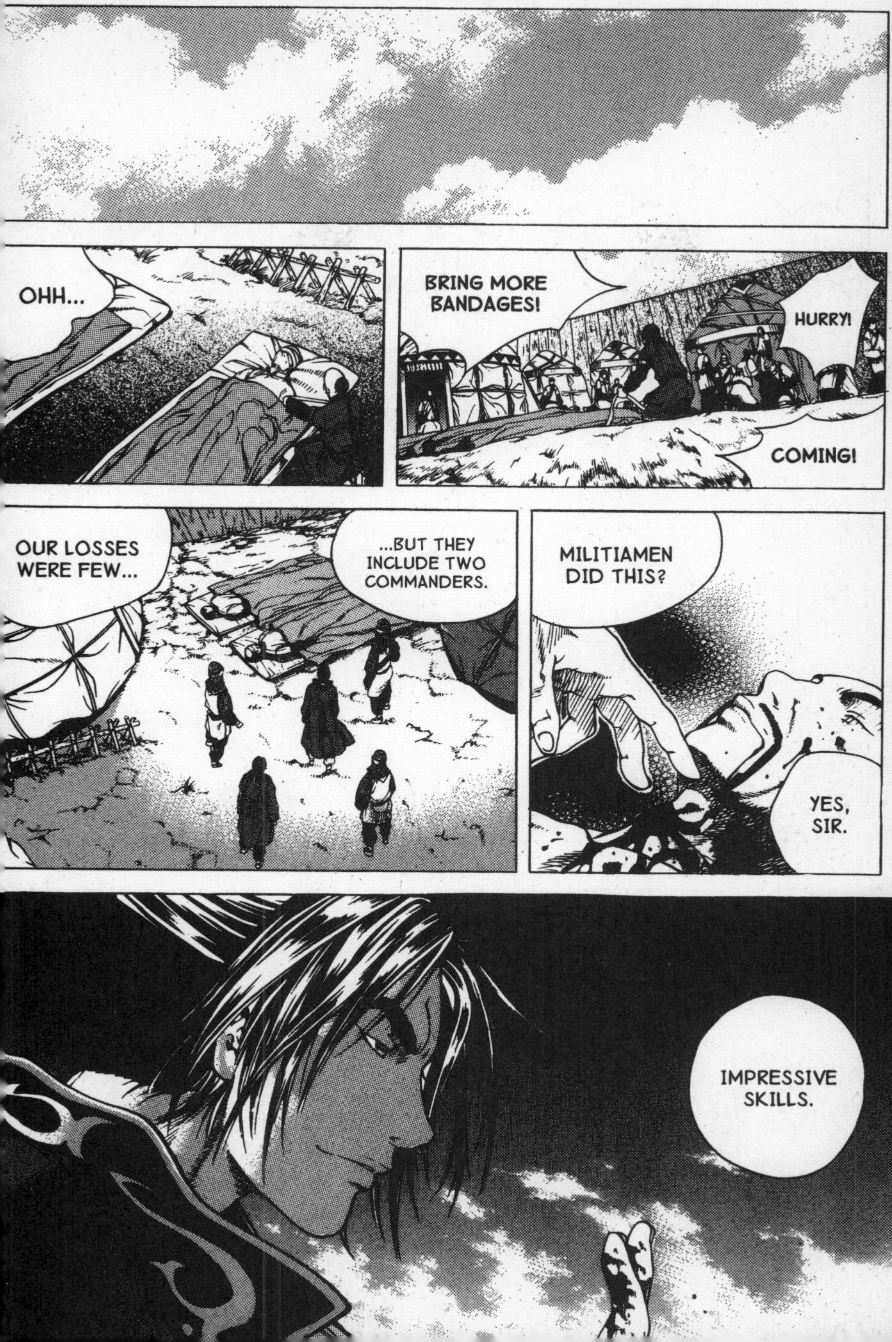
OHH...
BRING MORE BANDAGES!
HURRY!
COMING!
OUR LOSSES WERE FEW...
...BUT THEY INCLUDE TWO COMMANDERS.
MILITIAMEN DID THIS?
YES, SIR.
IMPRESSIVE SKILLS.

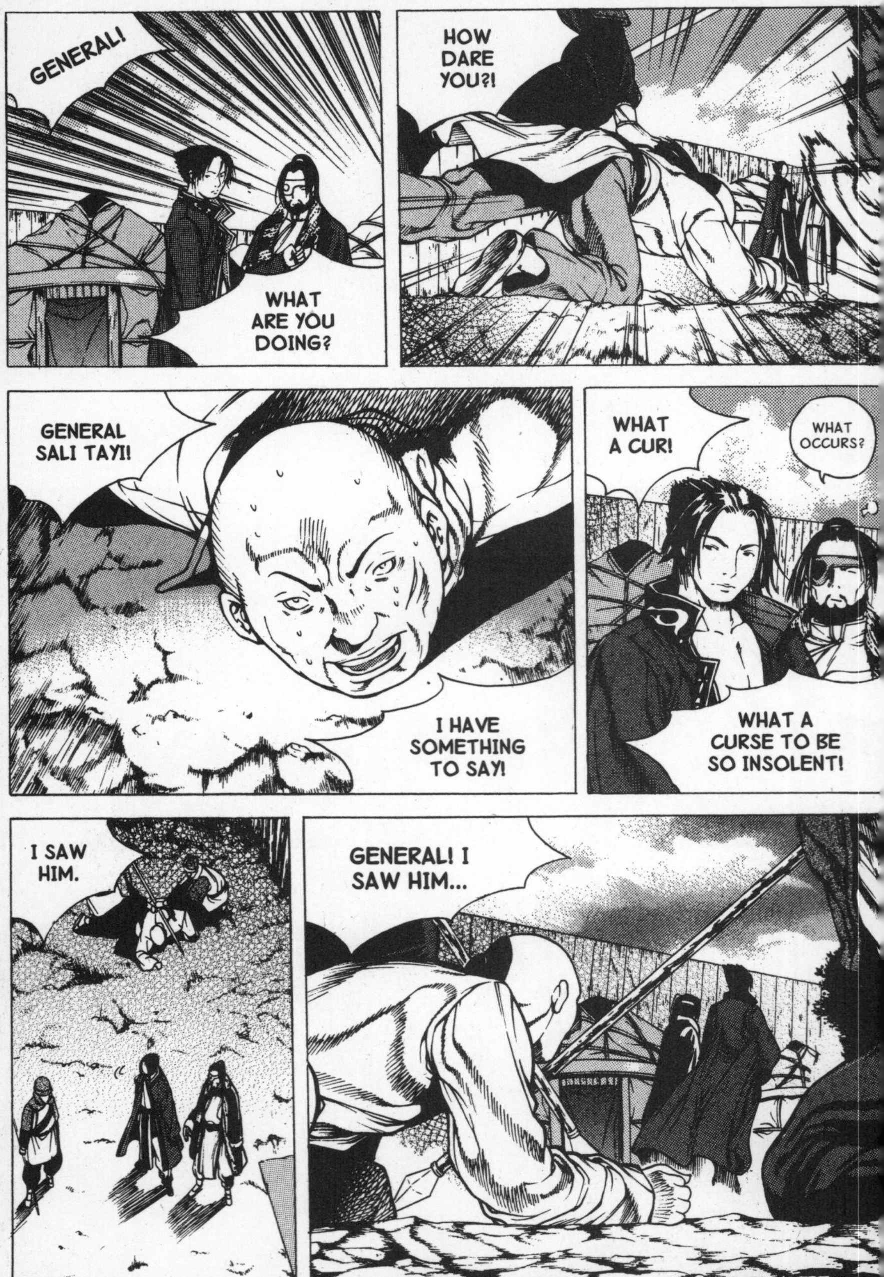
GENERAL!
WHAT ARE YOU DOING?
HOW DARE YOU?!
GENERAL SALI TAYI!
I HAVE SOMETHING TO SAY!
WHAT A CUR!
WHAT OCCURS?
WHAT A CURSE TO BE SO INSOLENT!
I SAW HIM.
GENERAL! I SAW HIM...

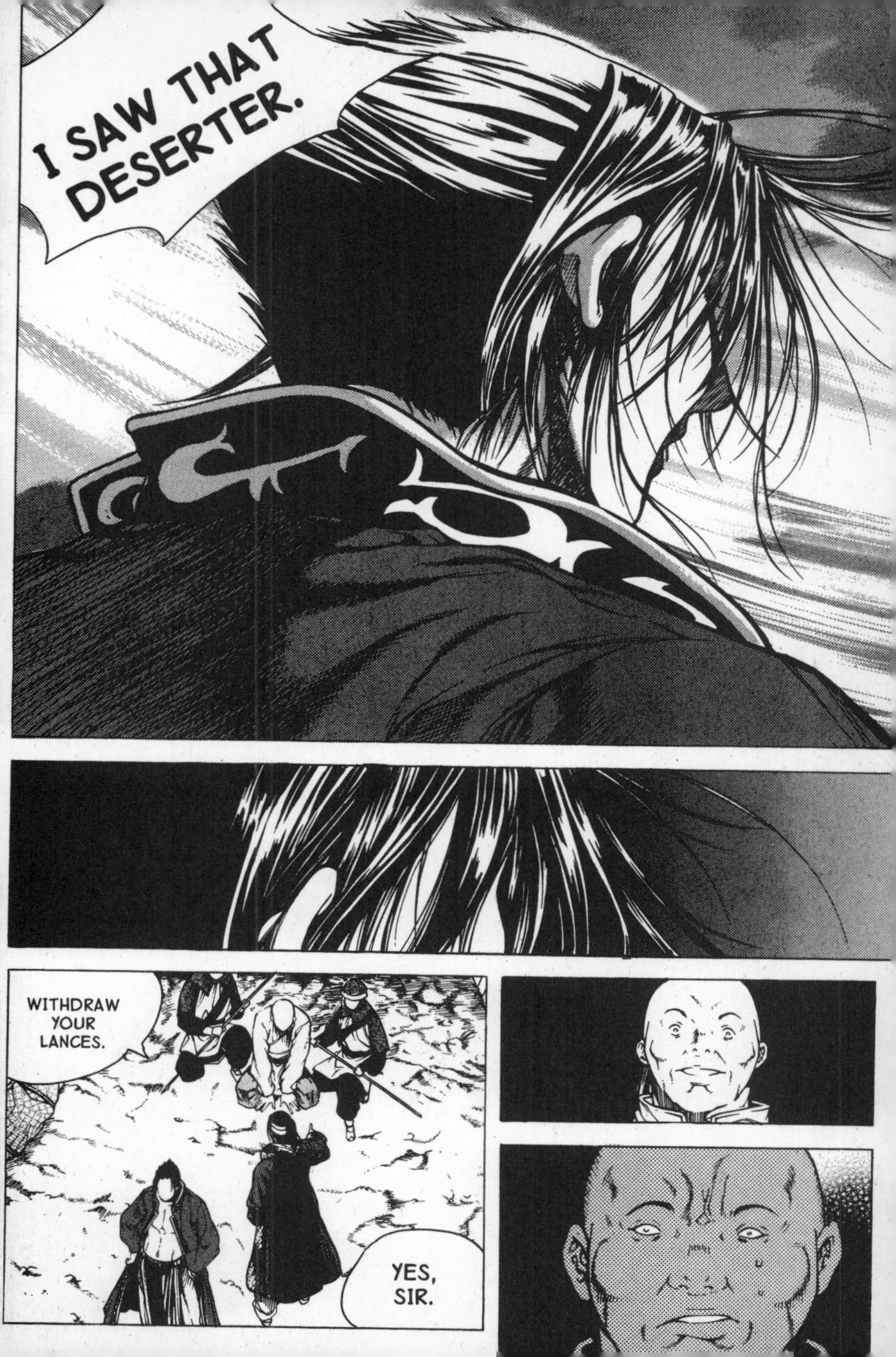
I SAW THAT DESERTER.
WITHDRAW YOUR LANCES.
YES, SIR.

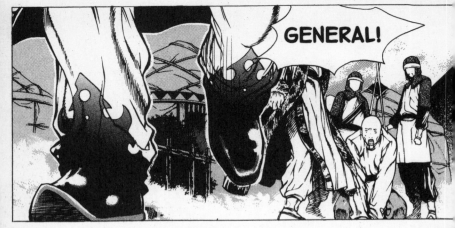

GENERAL!

WELL? GO WITH HIM!

OH! RIGHT!

BUT...

...IF WE FIND YOU'RE LYING, YOUR FAMILIES' LIVES ARE ON YOUR HEAD.

YES, GENERAL.

THAT PIG HAS NO FEAR.

!

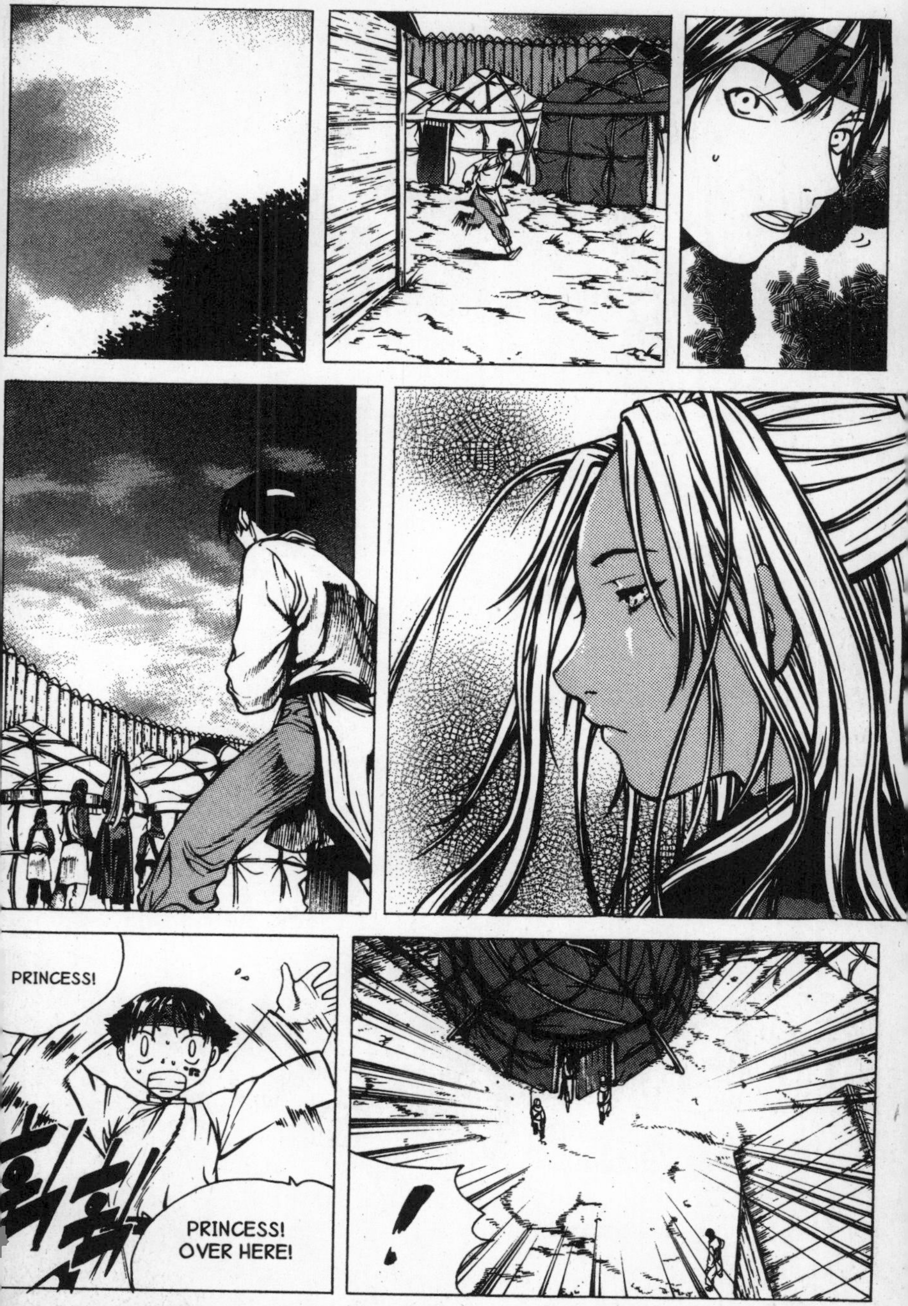
PRINCESS!
PRINCESS! OVER HERE!

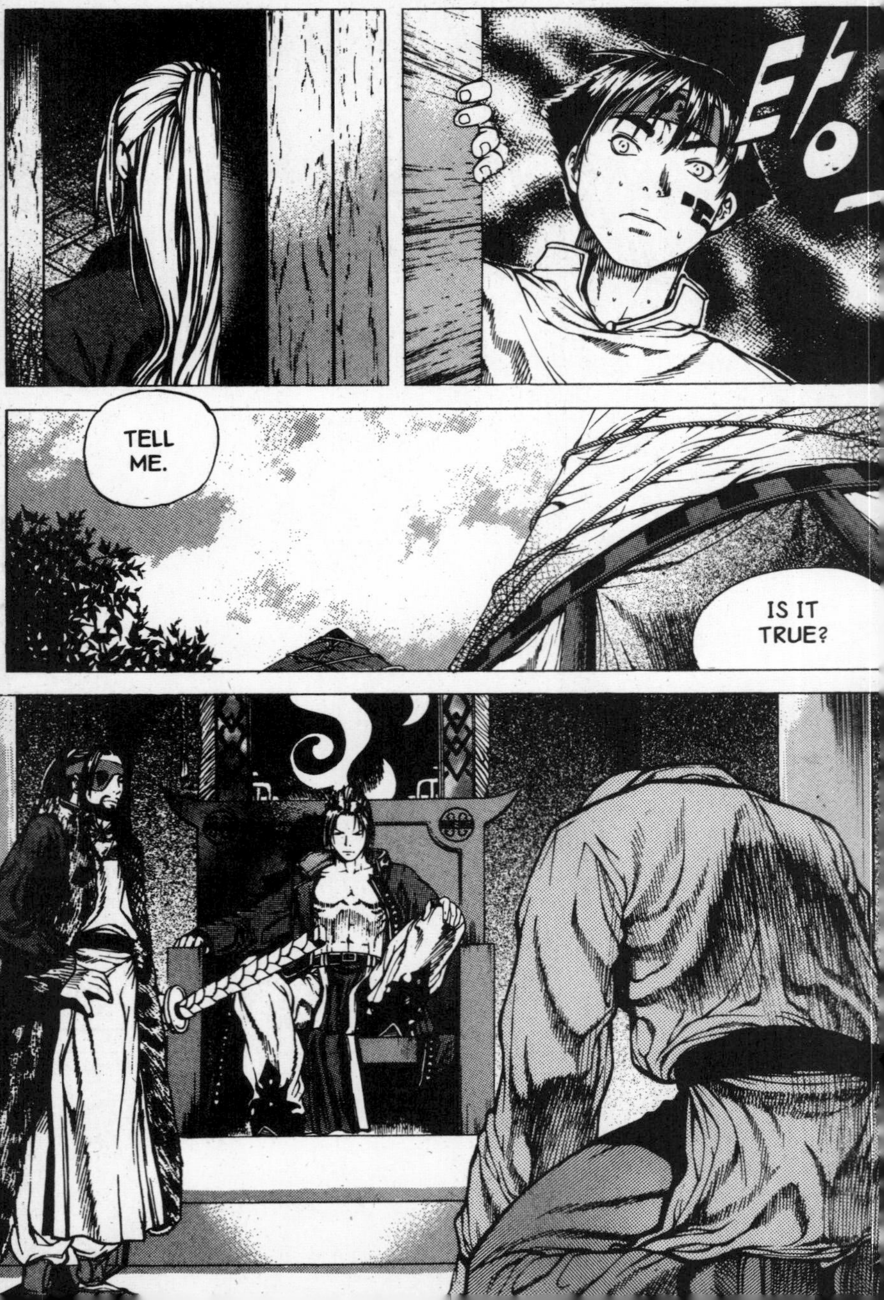
탕—
TELL ME.
IS IT TRUE?

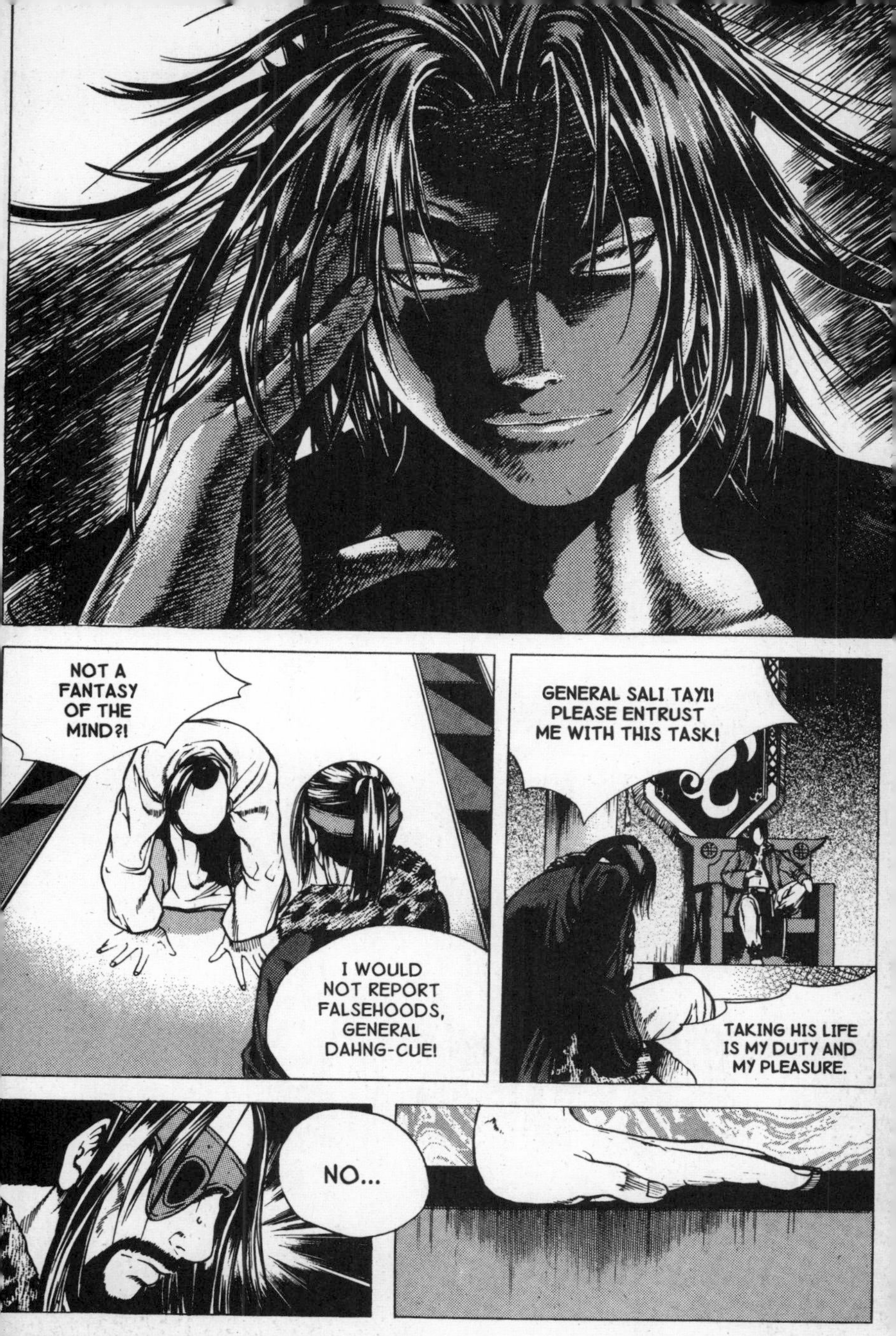
NOT A FANTASY OF THE MIND?!
I WOULD NOT REPORT FALSEHOODS, GENERAL DAHNG-CUE!
GENERAL SALI TAYI! PLEASE ENTRUST ME WITH THIS TASK!
TAKING HIS LIFE IS MY DUTY AND MY PLEASURE.
NO...

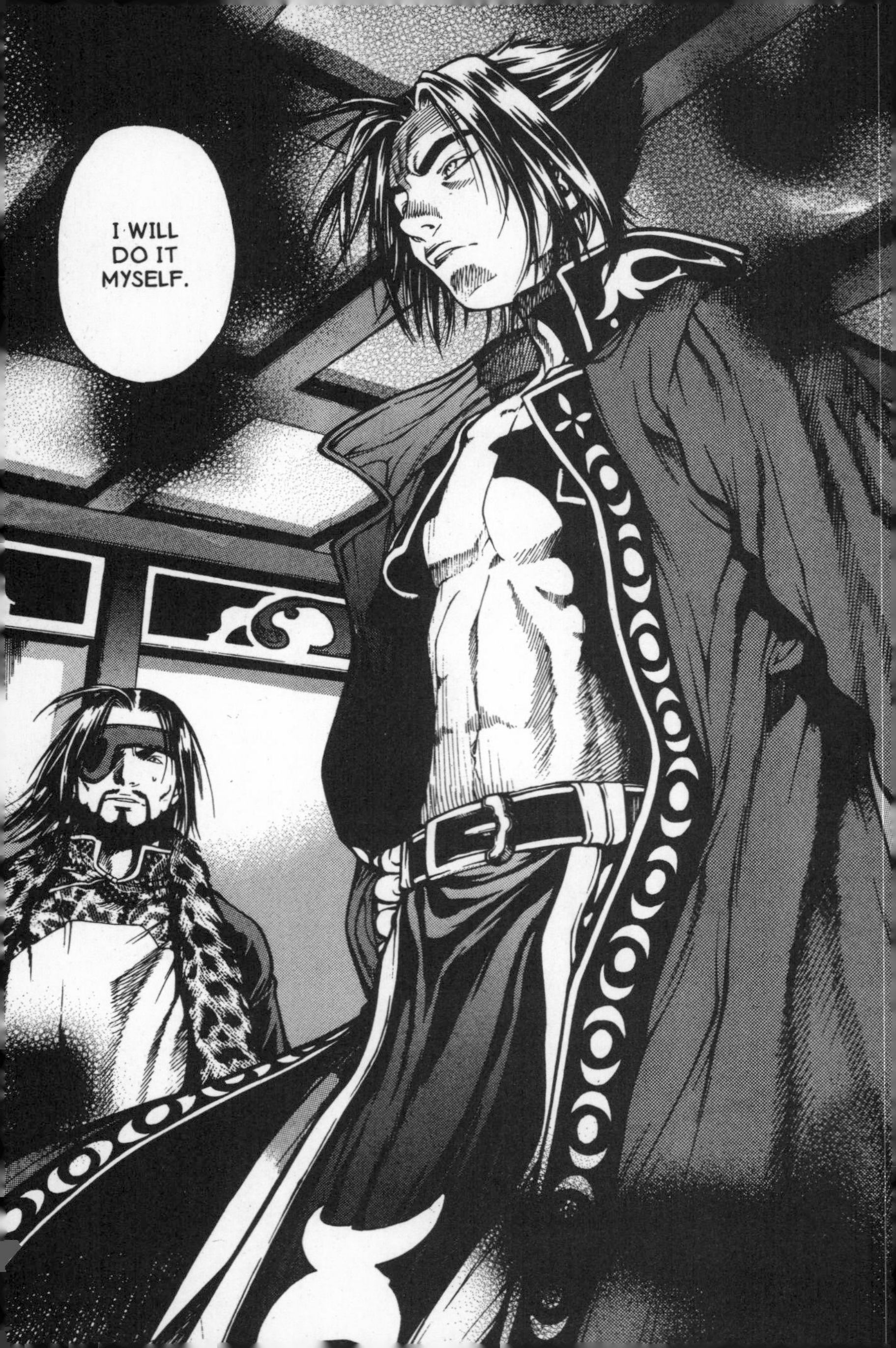
I WILL DO IT MYSELF.

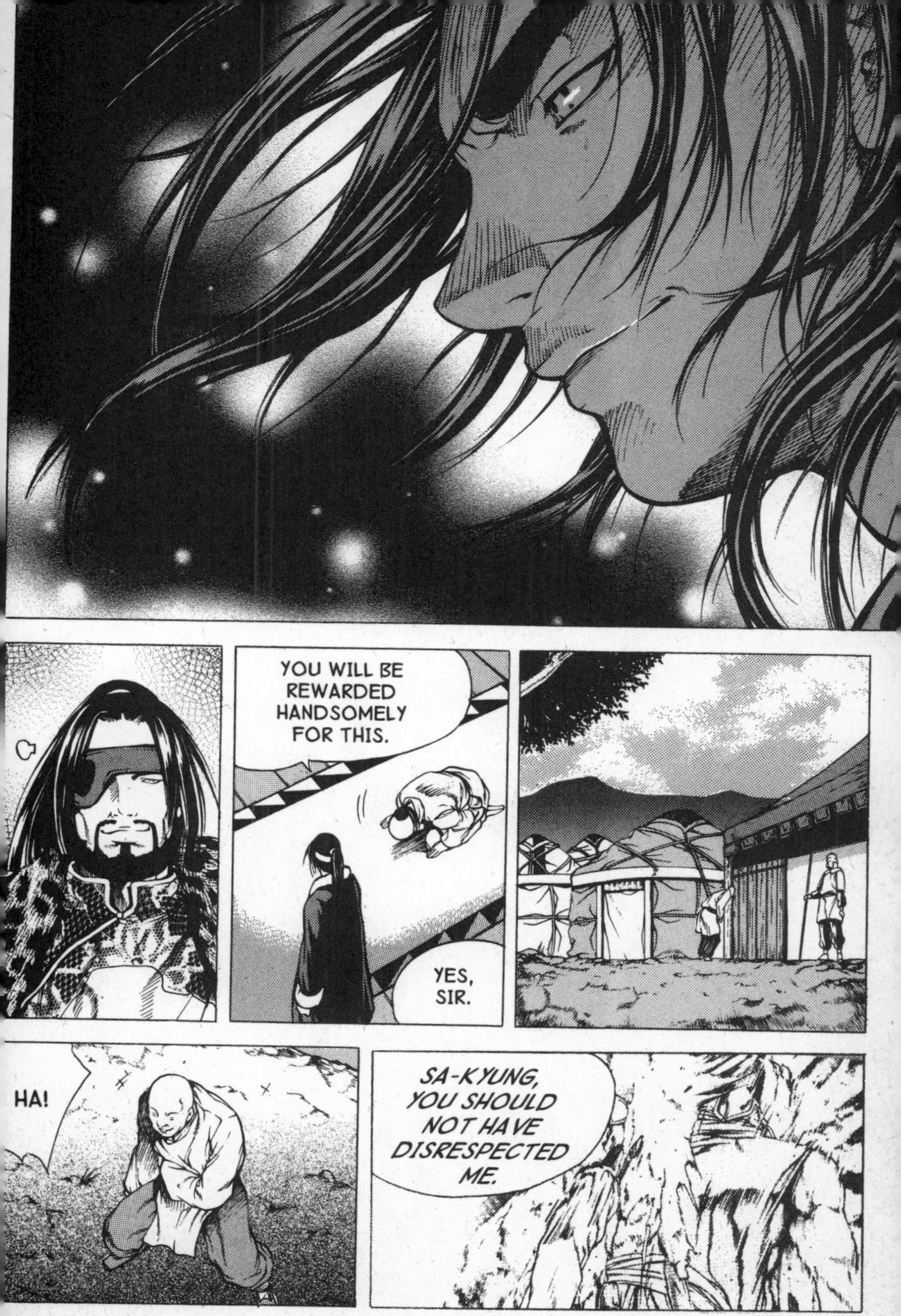
YOU WILL BE REWARDED HANDSOMELY FOR THIS.
YES, SIR.
HA!
SA-KYUNG, YOU SHOULD NOT HAVE DISRESPECTED ME.

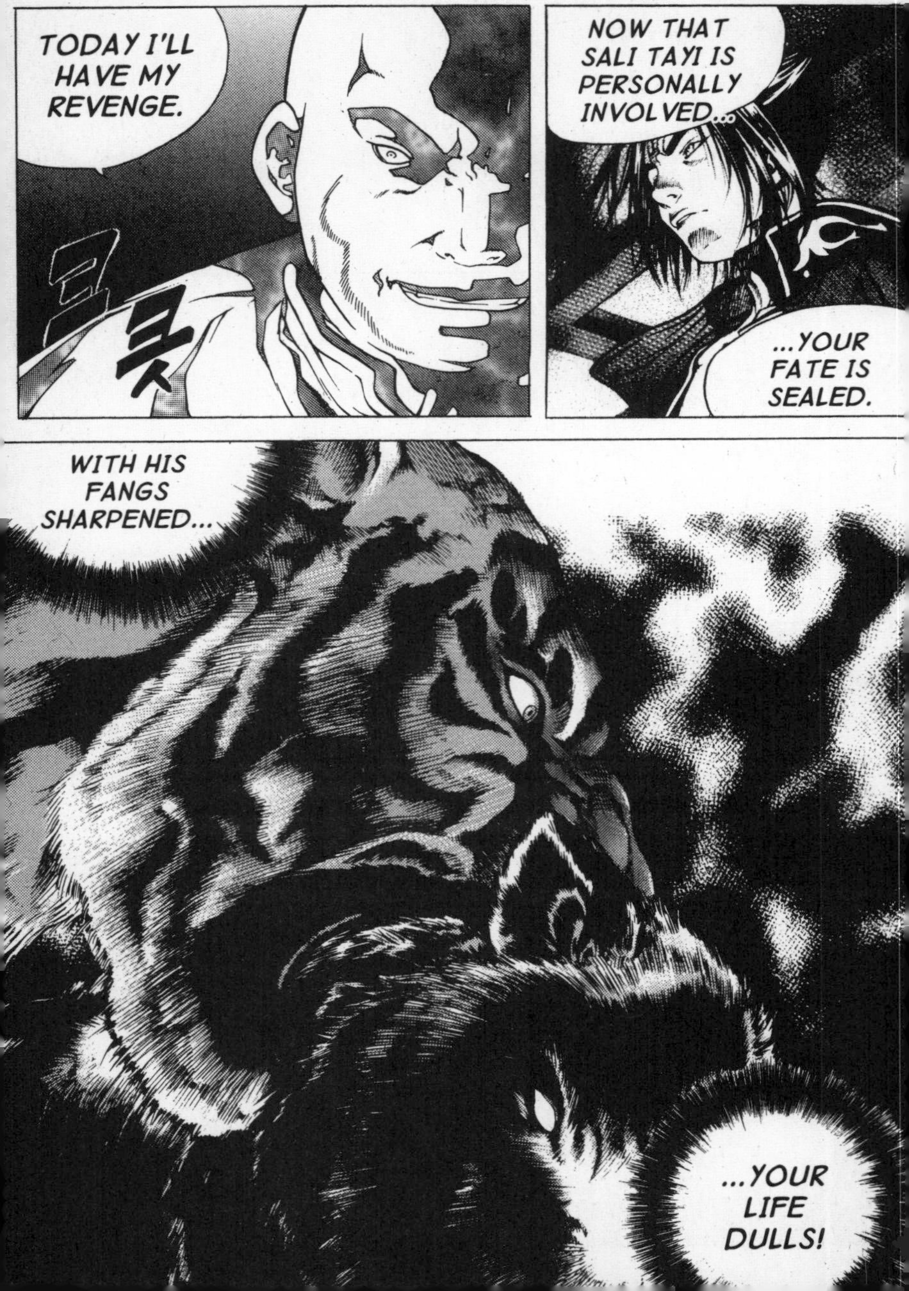
TODAY I'LL HAVE MY REVENGE.
크
크읏
NOW THAT SALI TAYI IS PERSONALLY INVOLVED...
...YOUR FATE IS SEALED.
WITH HIS FANGS SHARPENED...
...YOUR LIFE DULLS!

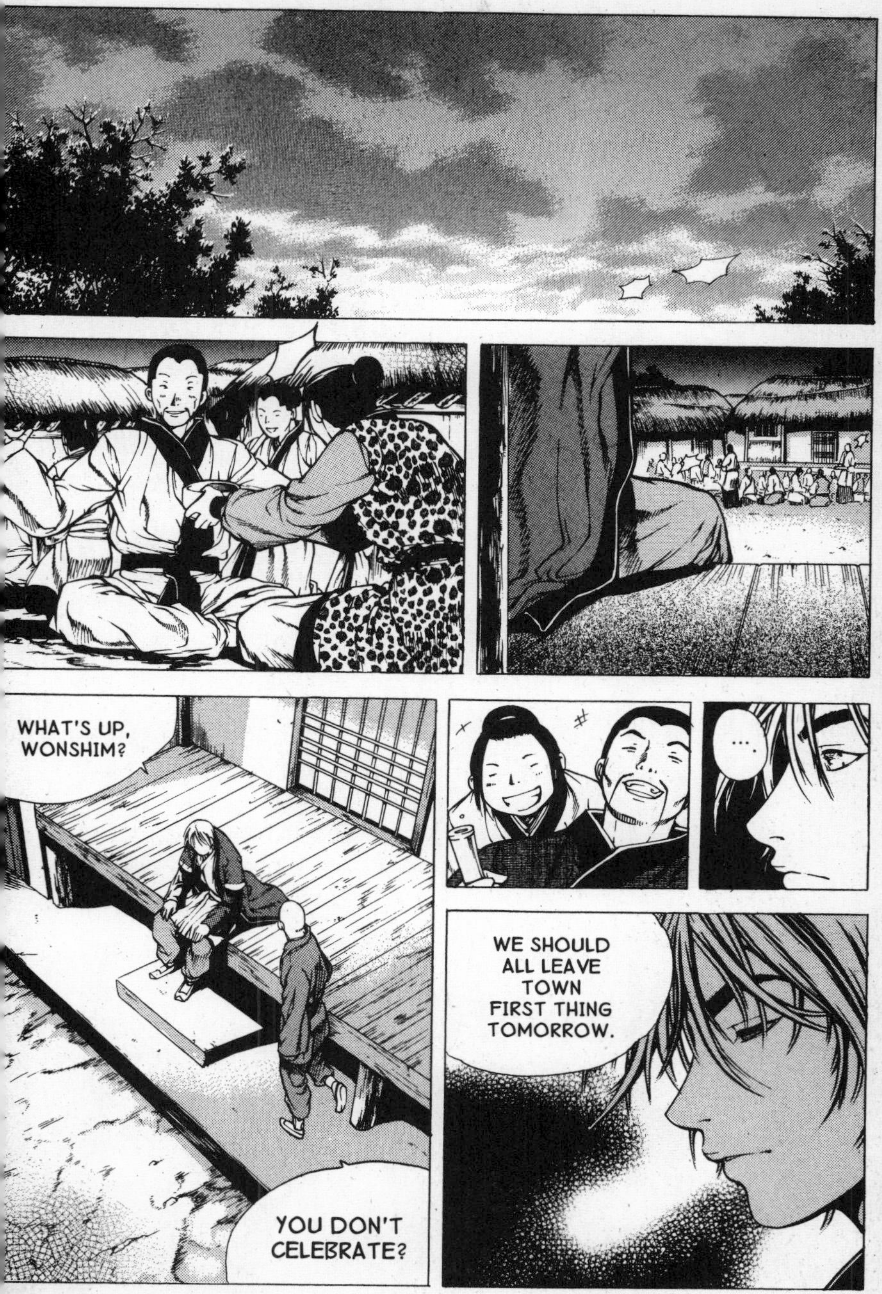
WHAT'S UP, WONSHIM?
YOU DON'T CELEBRATE?
...
WE SHOULD ALL LEAVE TOWN FIRST THING TOMORROW.

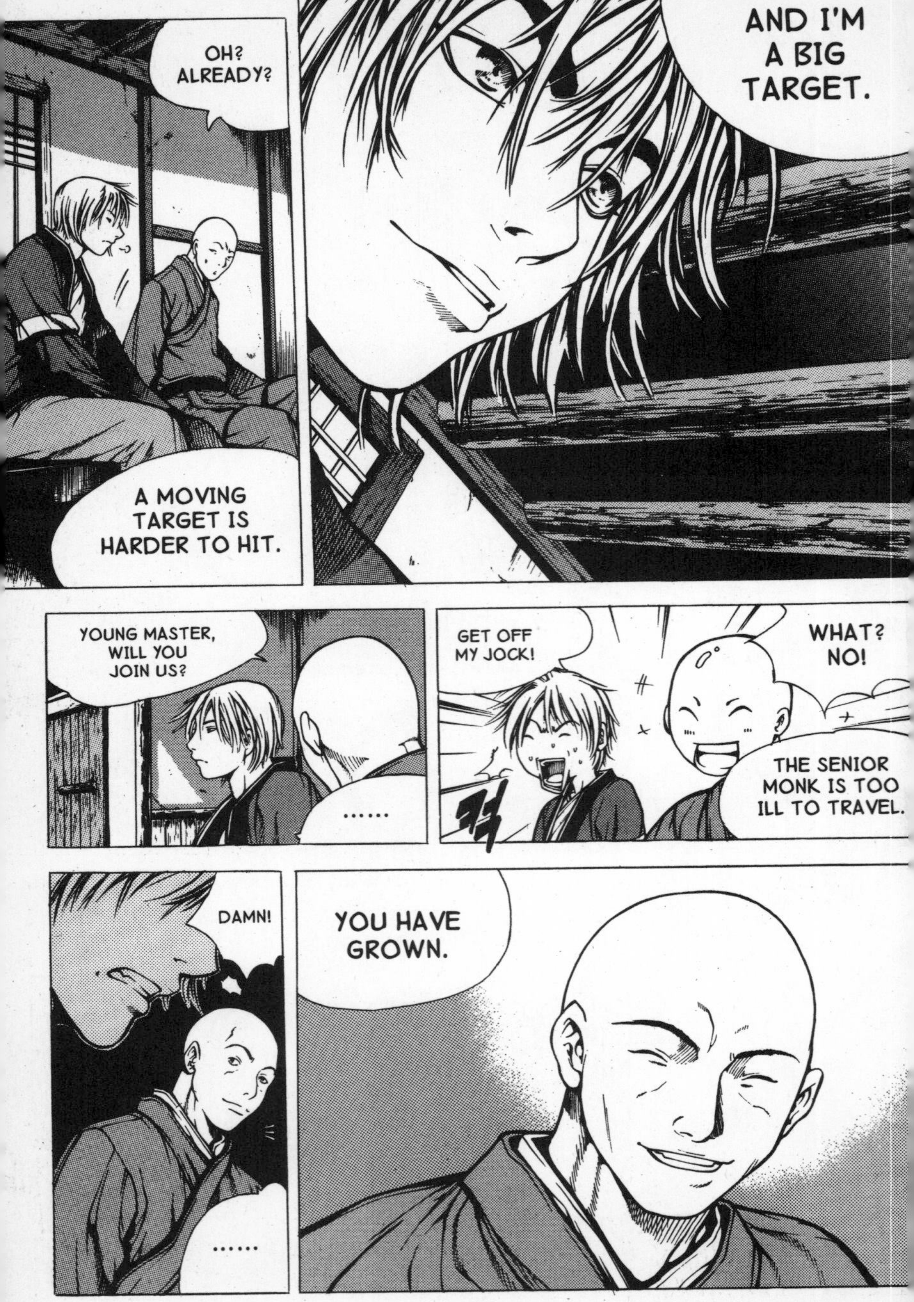
OH? ALREADY?
A MOVING TARGET IS HARDER TO HIT.
AND I'M A BIG TARGET.
YOUNG MASTER, WILL YOU JOIN US?
......
GET OFF MY JOCK!
WHAT? NO!
THE SENIOR MONK IS TOO ILL TO TRAVEL.
DAMN!
......
YOU HAVE GROWN.

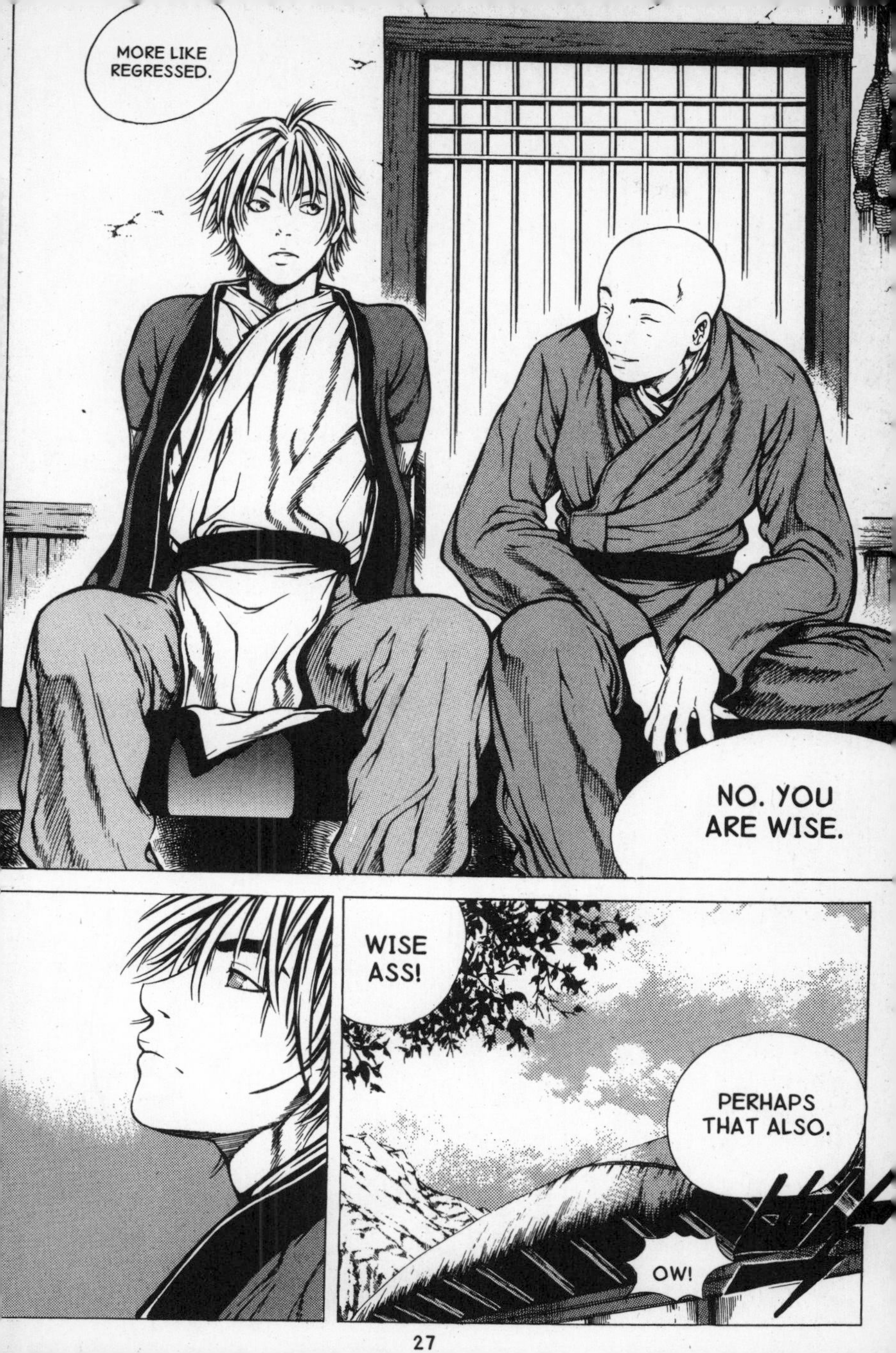
MORE LIKE REGRESSED.
NO. YOU ARE WISE.
WISE ASS!
PERHAPS THAT ALSO.
OW!

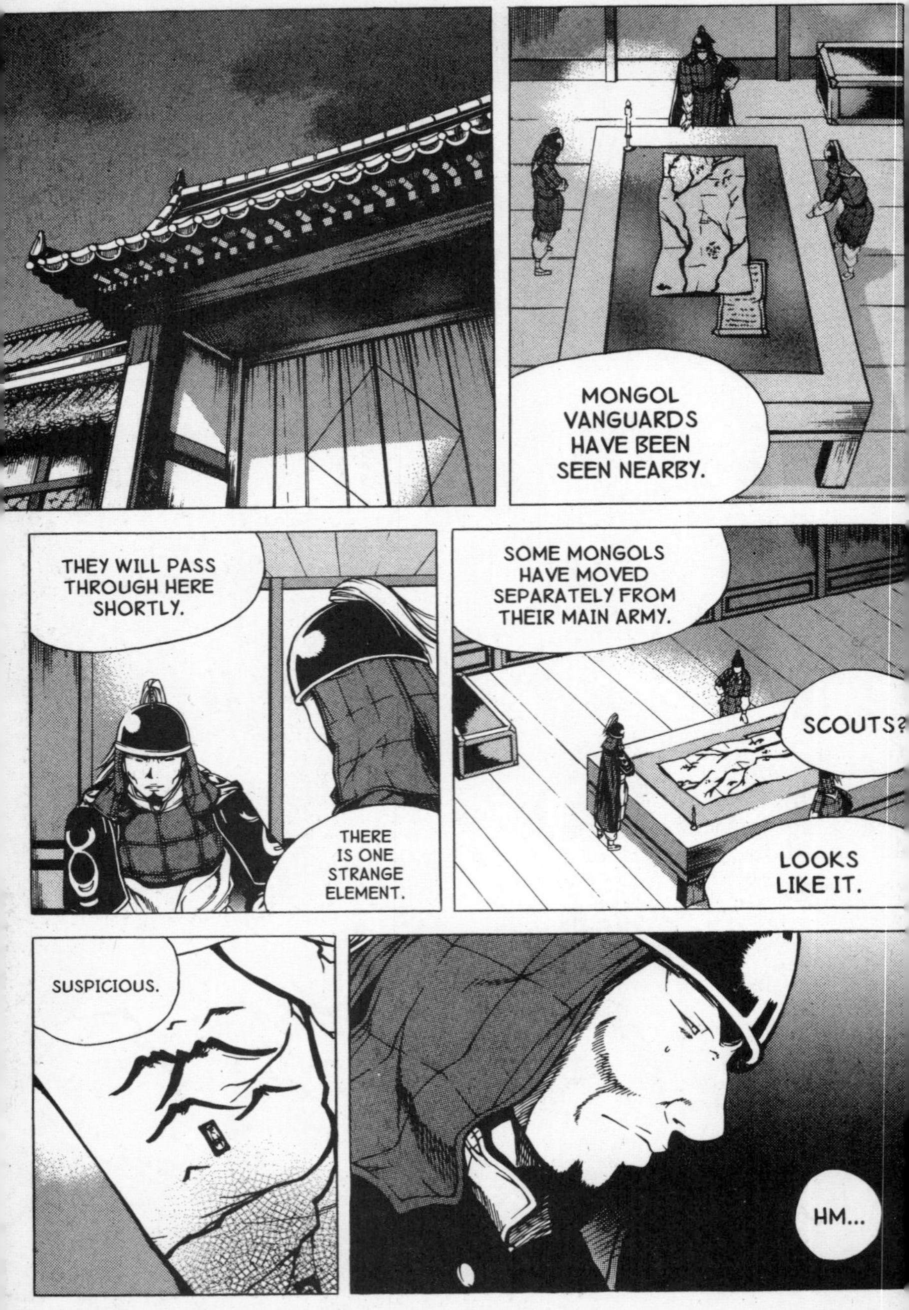
MONGOL VANGUARDS HAVE BEEN SEEN NEARBY.
THEY WILL PASS THROUGH HERE SHORTLY.
THERE IS ONE STRANGE ELEMENT.
SOME MONGOLS HAVE MOVED SEPARATELY FROM THEIR MAIN ARMY.
SCOUTS?
LOOKS LIKE IT.
SUSPICIOUS.
HM...

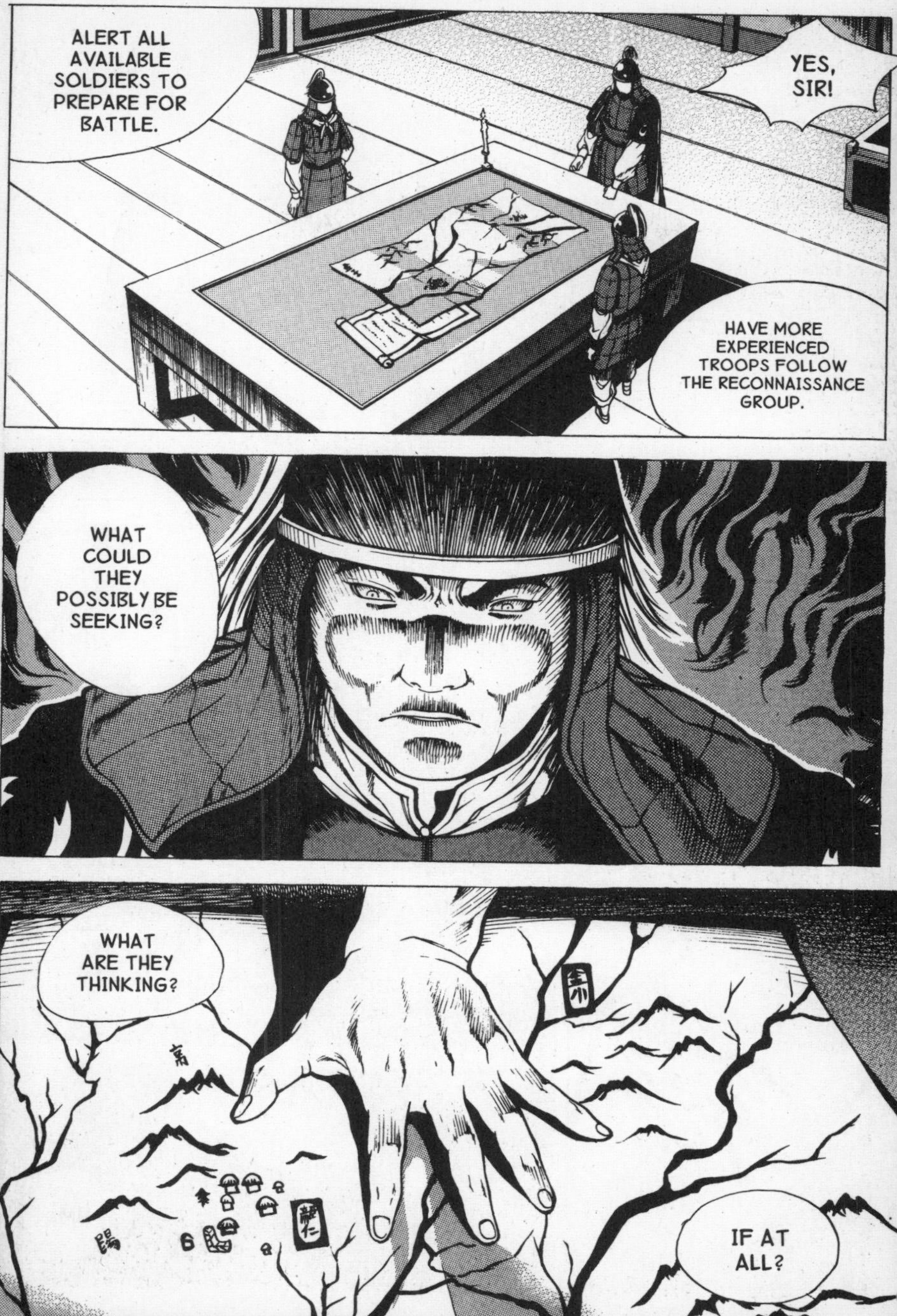
ALERT ALL AVAILABLE SOLDIERS TO PREPARE FOR BATTLE.
YES, SIR!
HAVE MORE EXPERIENCED TROOPS FOLLOW THE RECONNAISSANCE GROUP.
WHAT COULD THEY POSSIBLY BE SEEKING?
WHAT ARE THEY THINKING?
IF AT ALL?

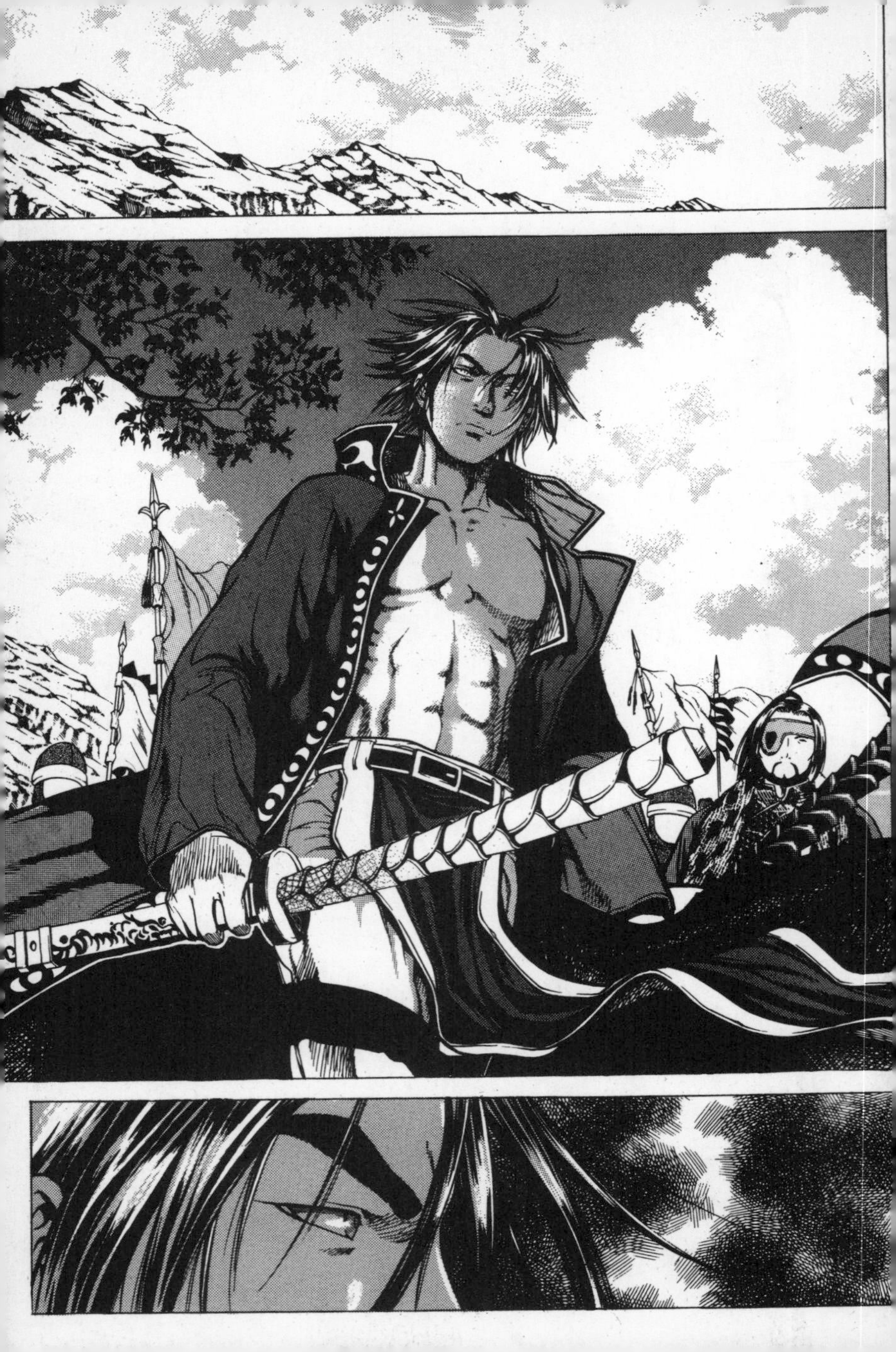

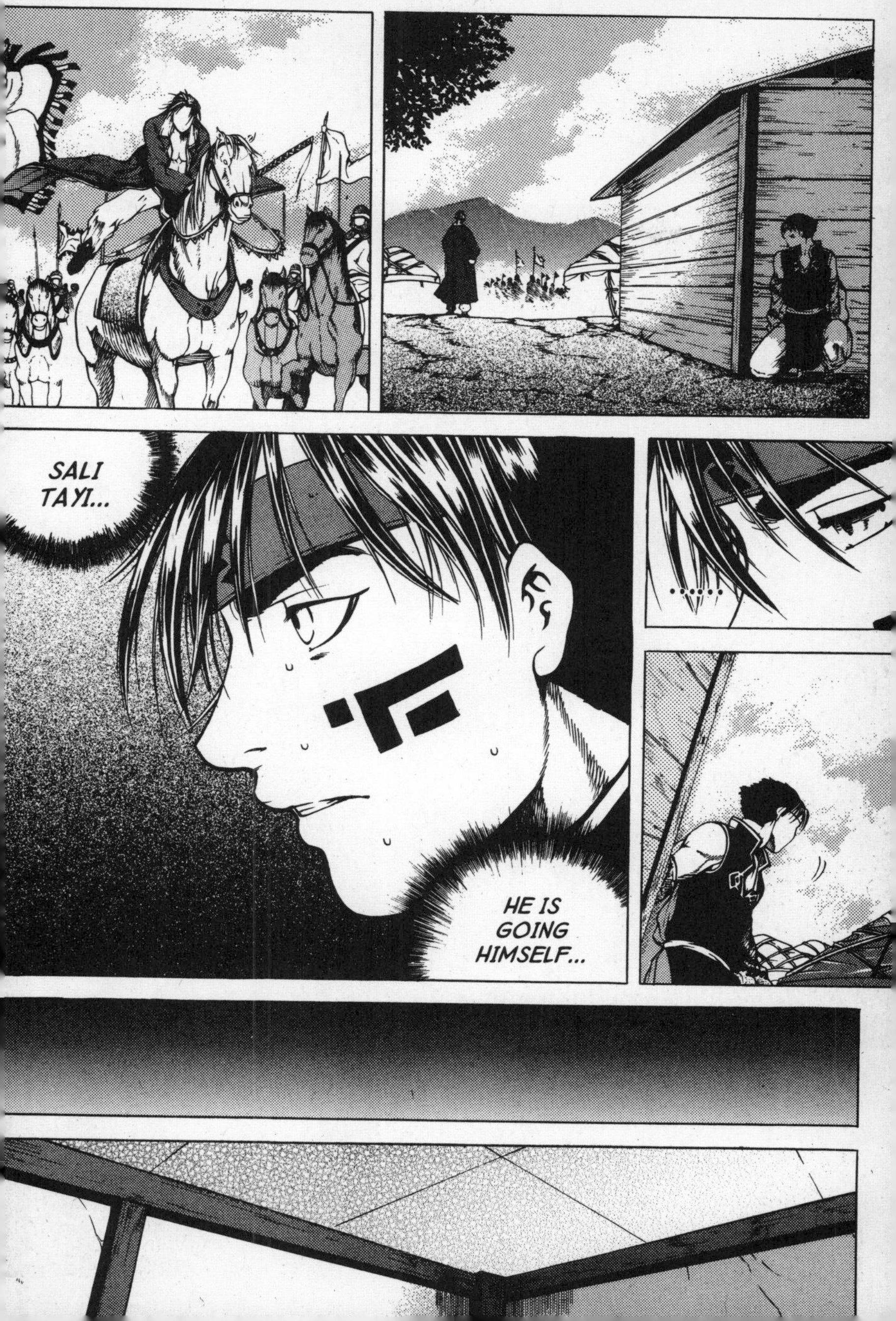
SALI TAYI...
HE IS GOING HIMSELF...
.....

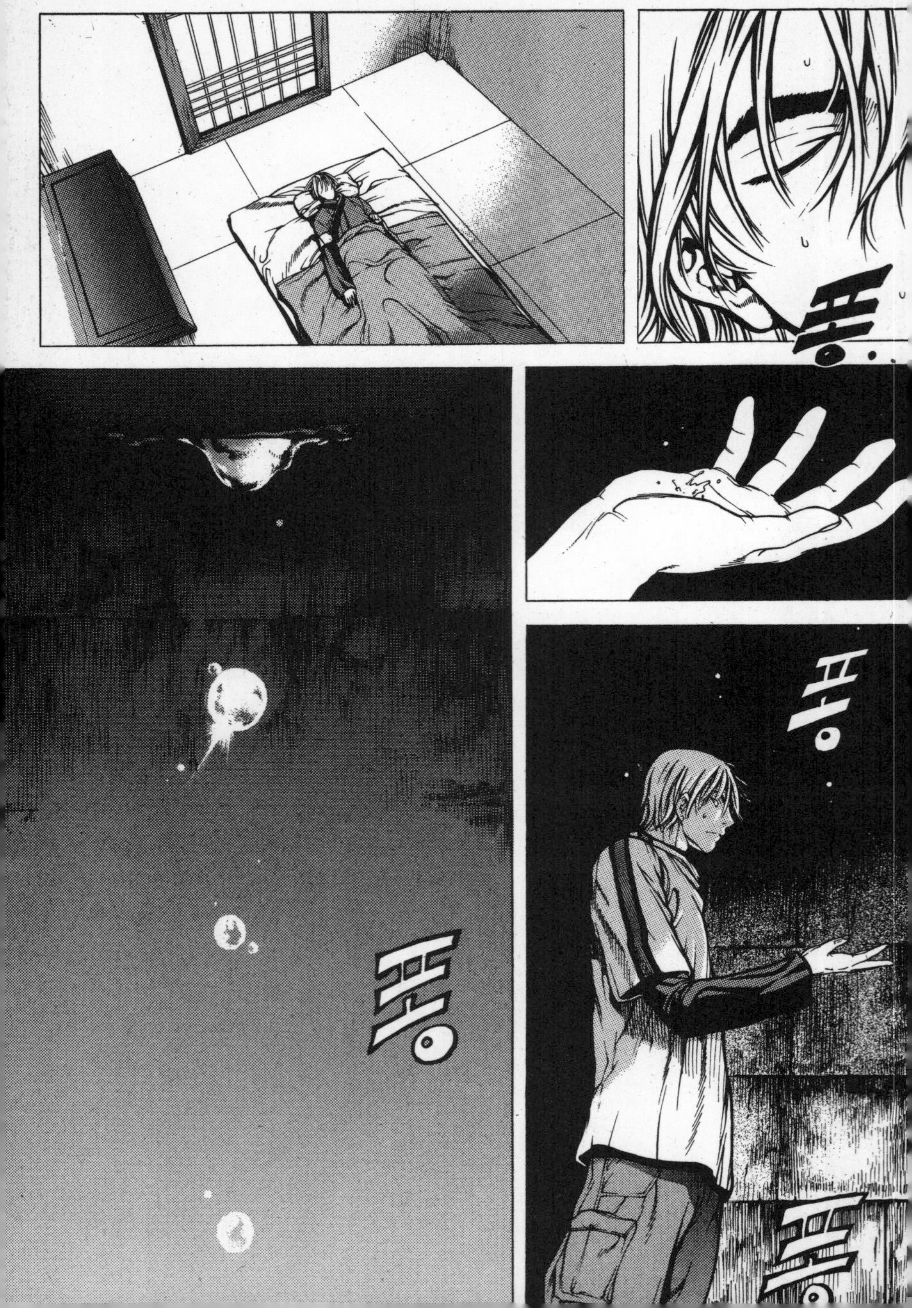

퐁..
퐁
퐁
퐁

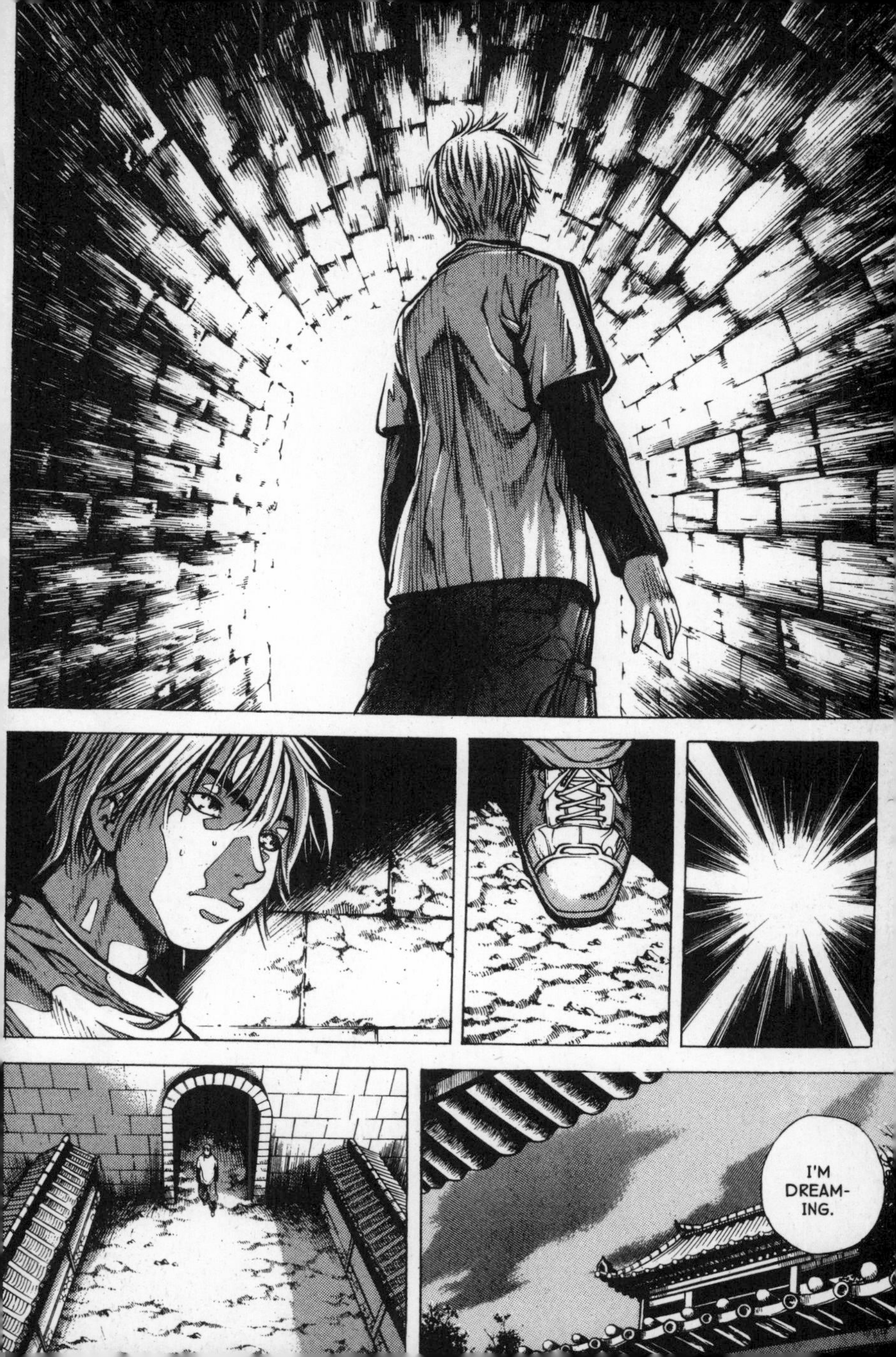
I'M
DREAM-
ING.

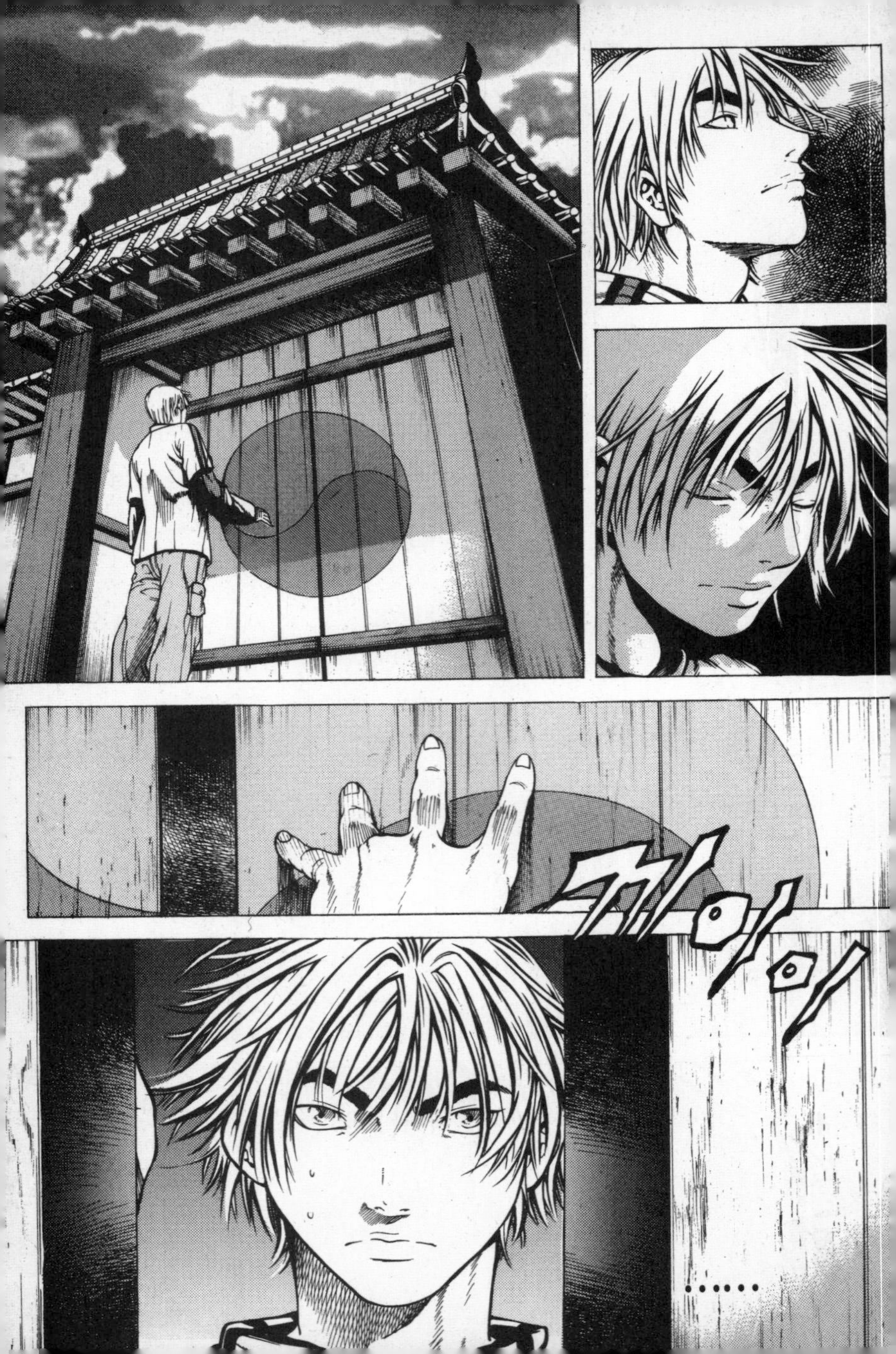
끼이이
……

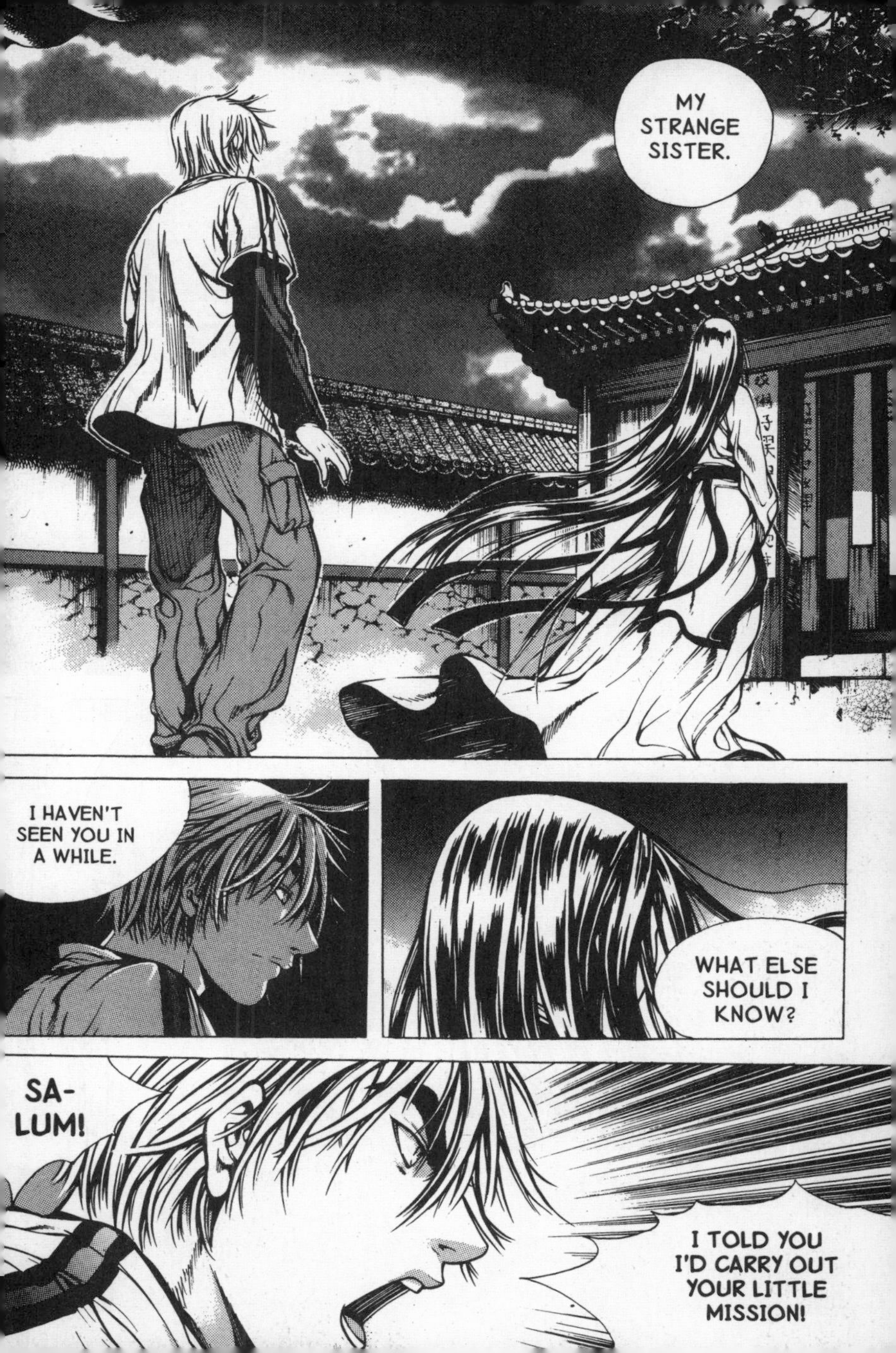
MY STRANGE SISTER.
I HAVEN'T SEEN YOU IN A WHILE.
WHAT ELSE SHOULD I KNOW?
SA-LUM!
I TOLD YOU I'D CARRY OUT YOUR LITTLE MISSION!

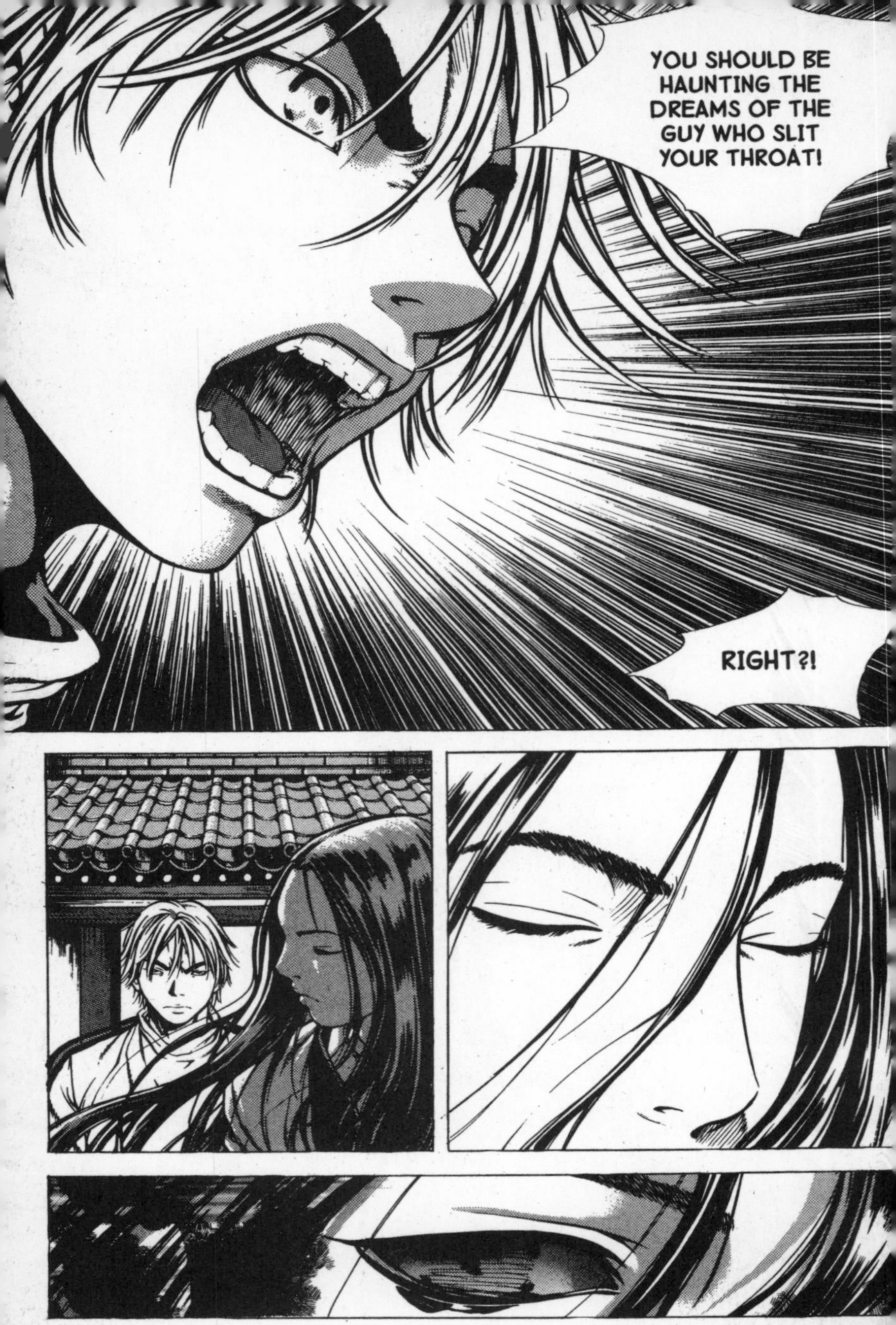
YOU SHOULD BE HAUNTING THE DREAMS OF THE GUY WHO SLIT YOUR THROAT!
RIGHT?!

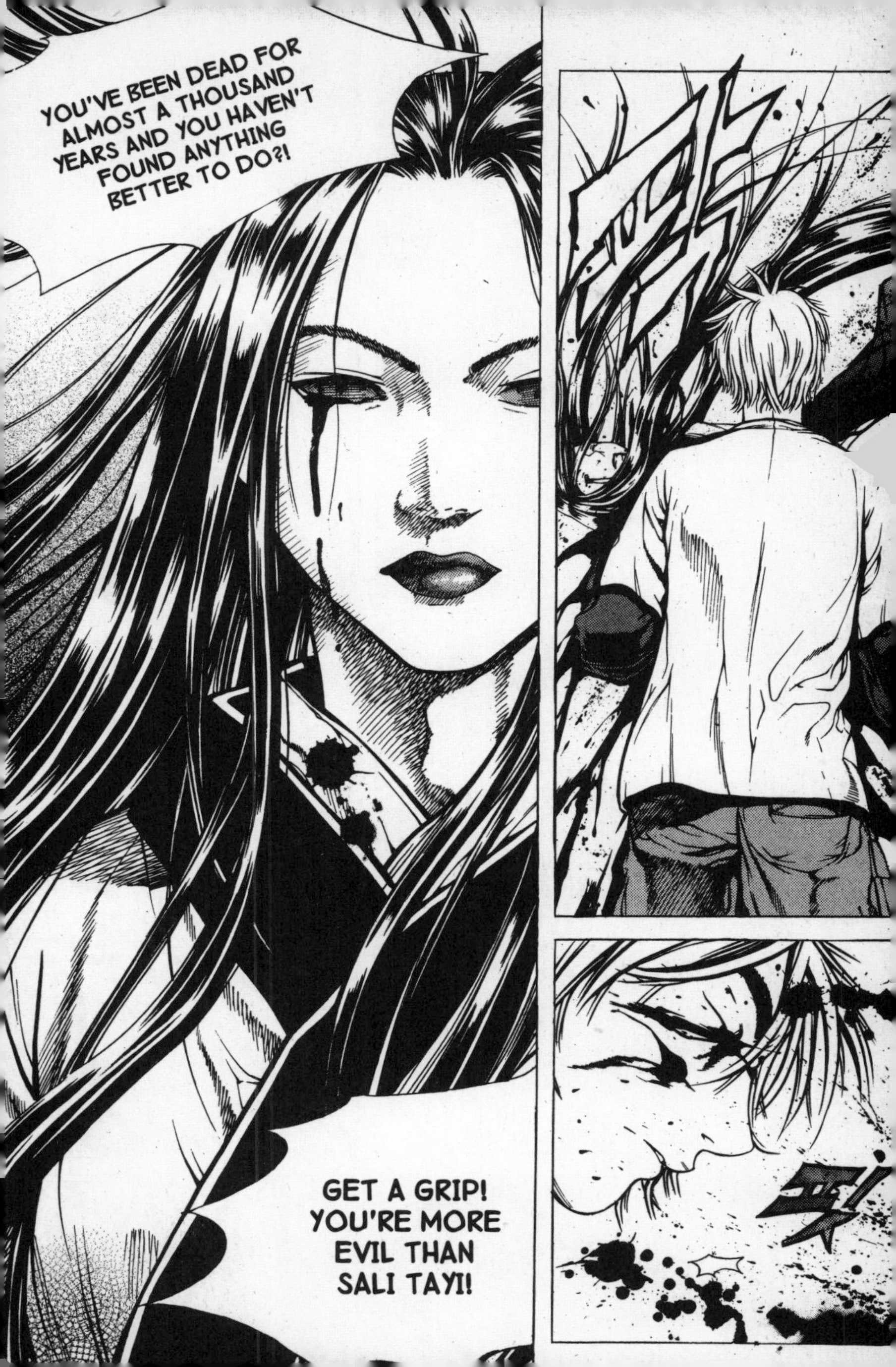
YOU'VE BEEN DEAD FOR ALMOST A THOUSAND YEARS AND YOU HAVEN'T FOUND ANYTHING BETTER TO DO?!
GET A GRIP! YOU'RE MORE EVIL THAN SALI TAYI!

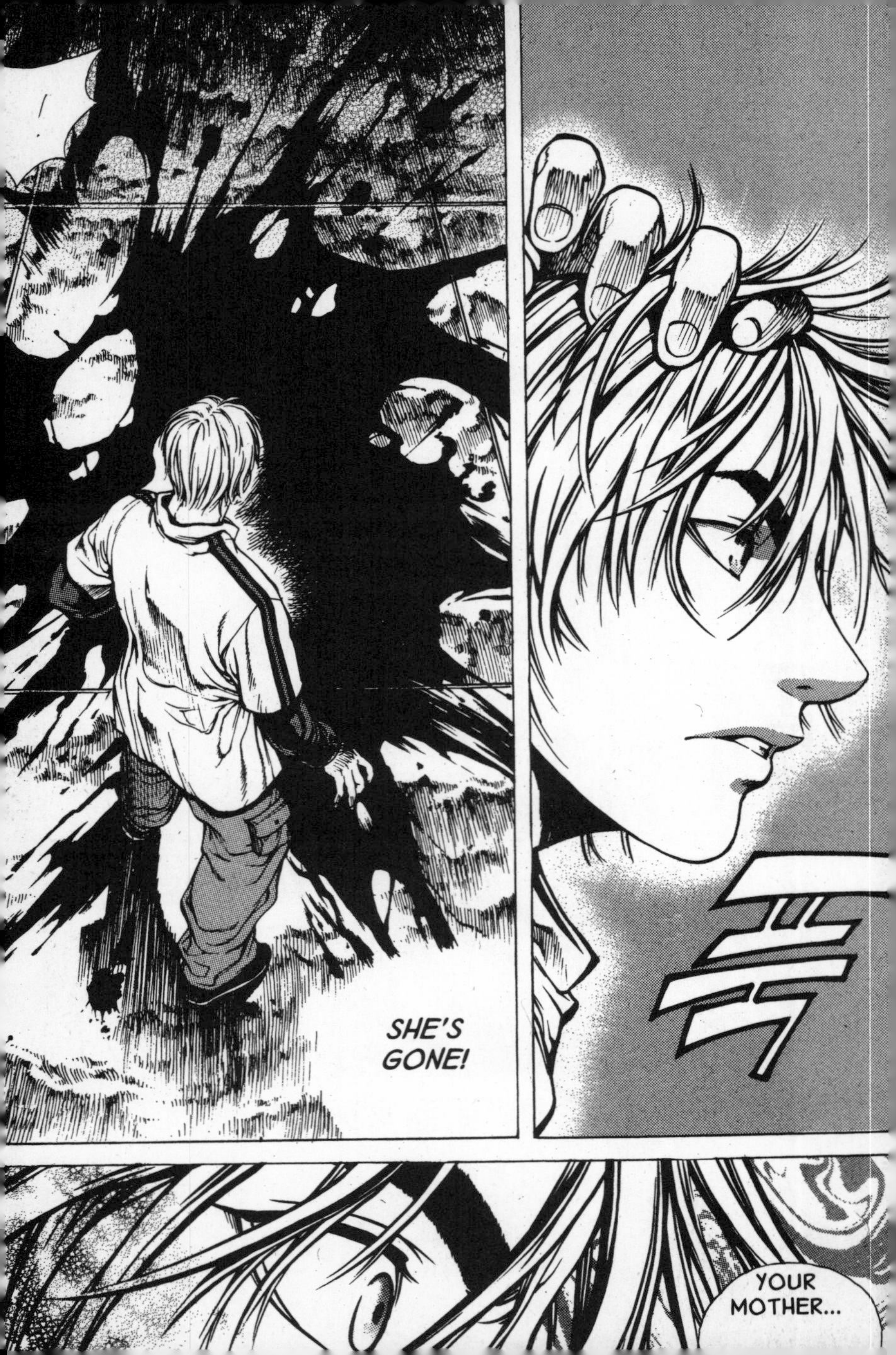
SHE'S GONE!
YOUR MOTHER...

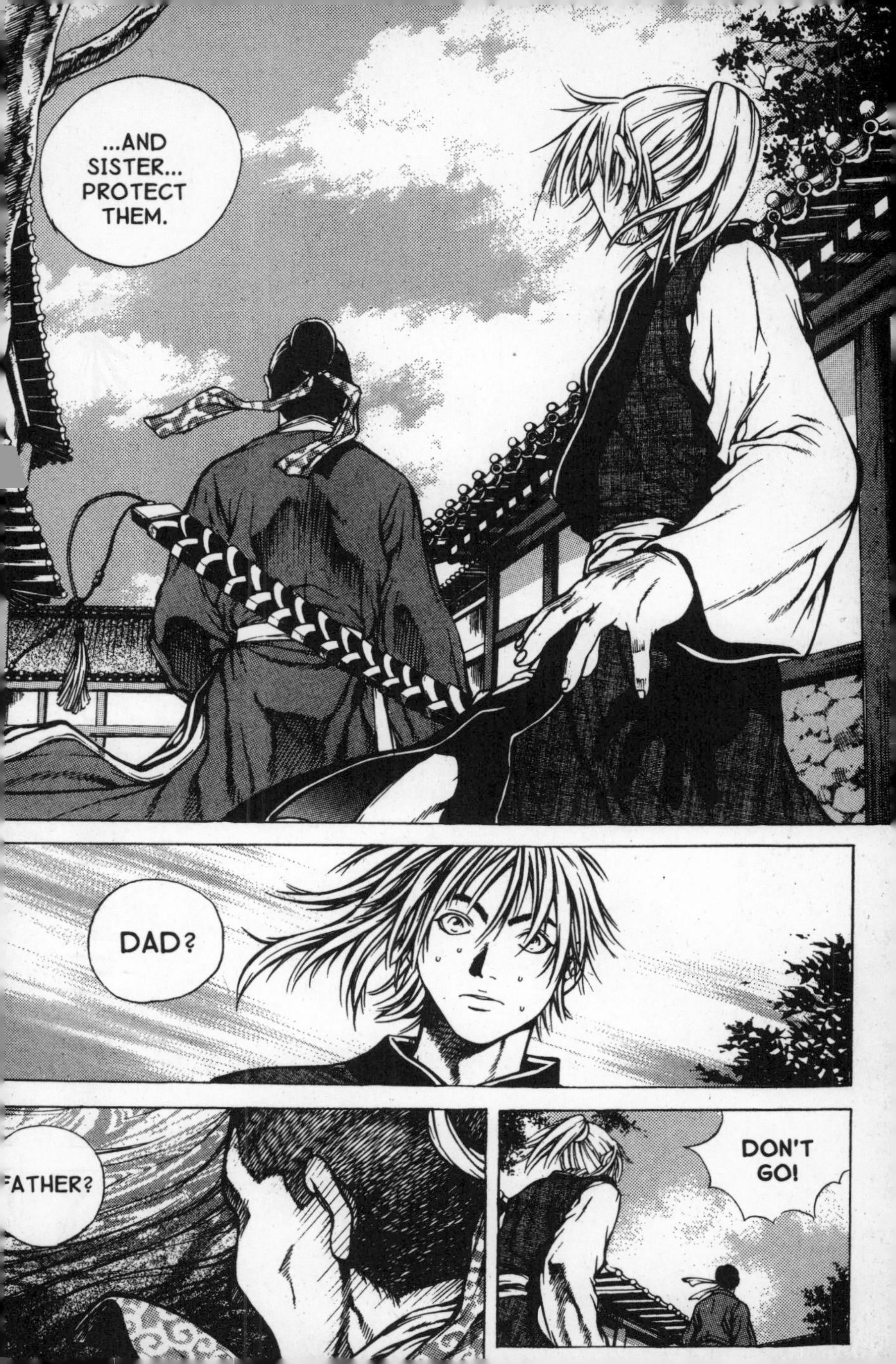
...AND SISTER... PROTECT THEM.
DAD?
FATHER?
DON'T GO!

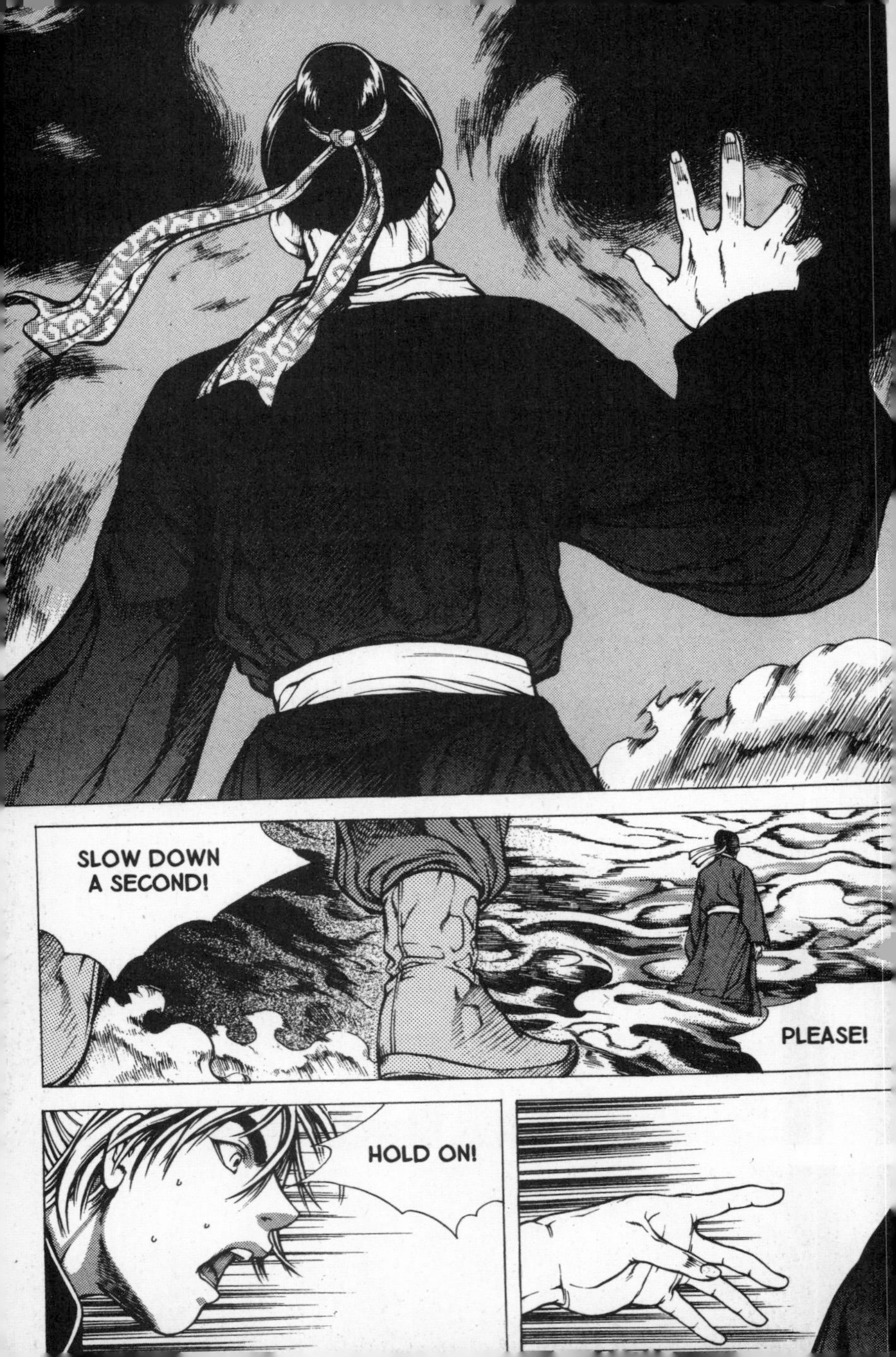
SLOW DOWN A SECOND!
PLEASE!
HOLD ON!

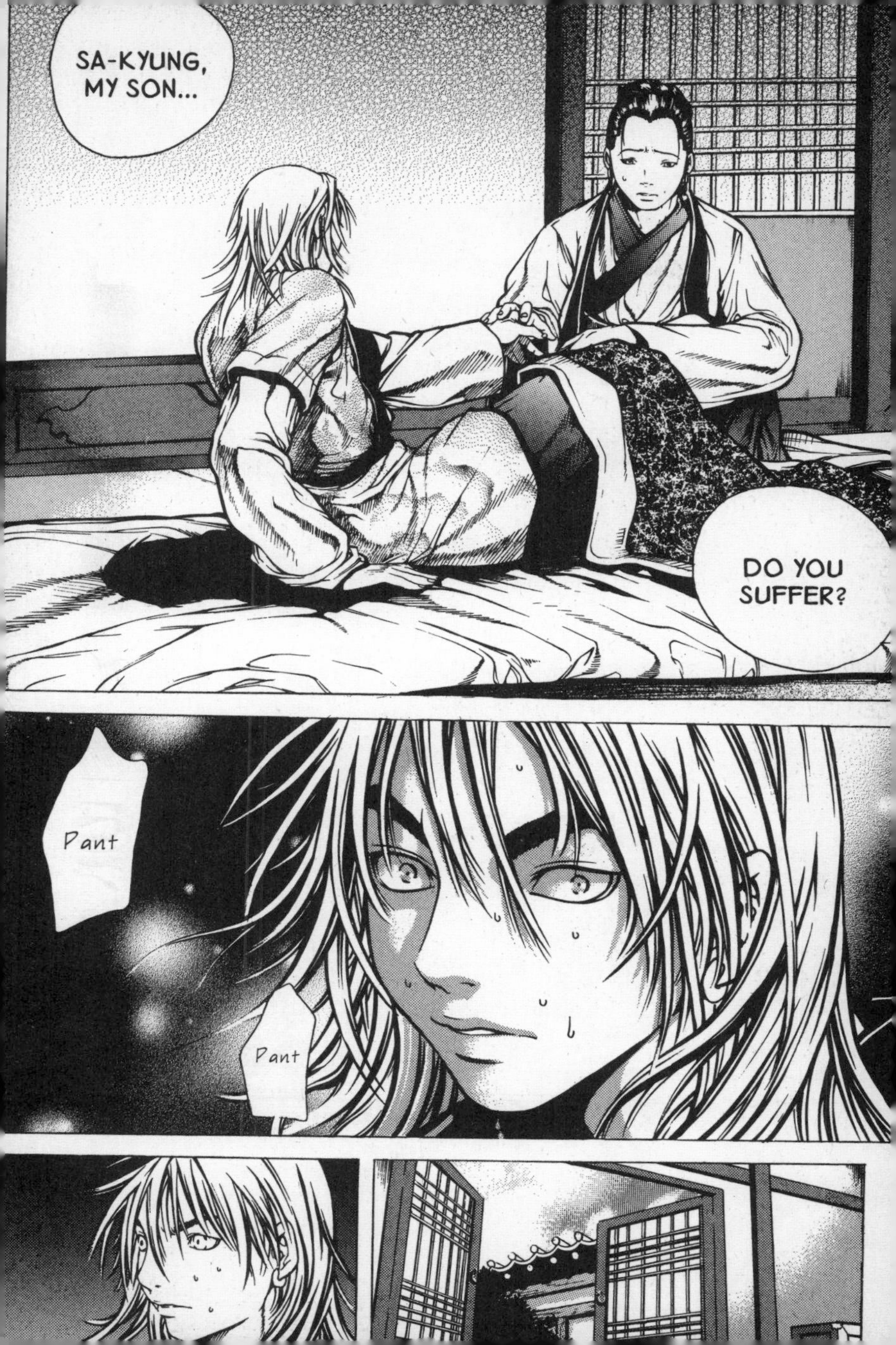
SA-KYUNG, MY SON...
DO YOU SUFFER?
Pant
Pant

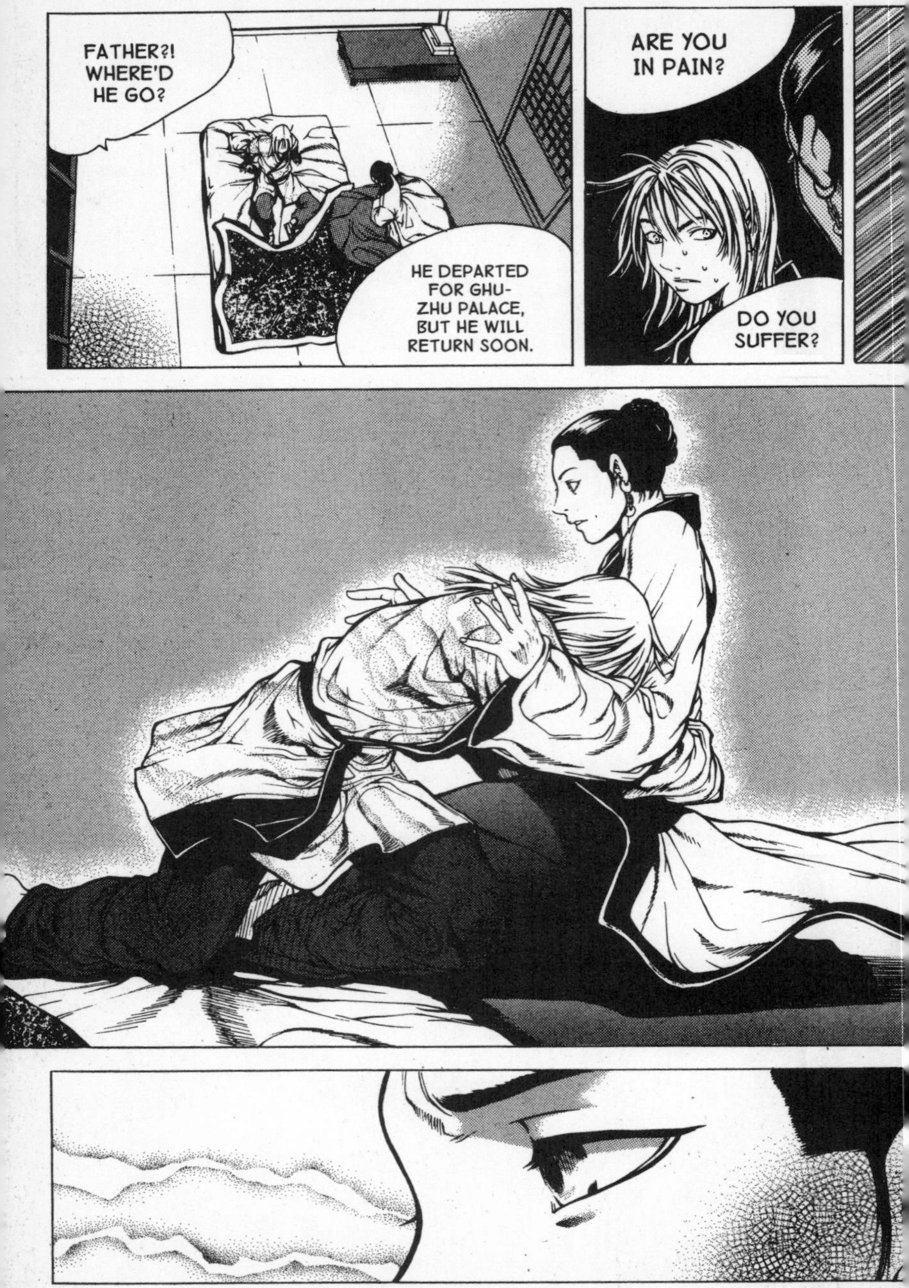
FATHER?! WHERE'D HE GO?
HE DEPARTED FOR GHU-ZHU PALACE, BUT HE WILL RETURN SOON.
ARE YOU IN PAIN?
DO YOU SUFFER?

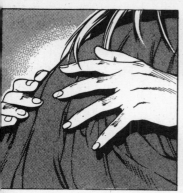

MY REAL MOTHER IS SO COLD...

MAYBE SHE WAS LIKE THIS LONG AGO.

BUT WHAT GOOD IS IT?

MOTHER AND FATHER...

ZHANG-BO... CHUNG-WAR... EVERYONE HAS PROTECTED ME...

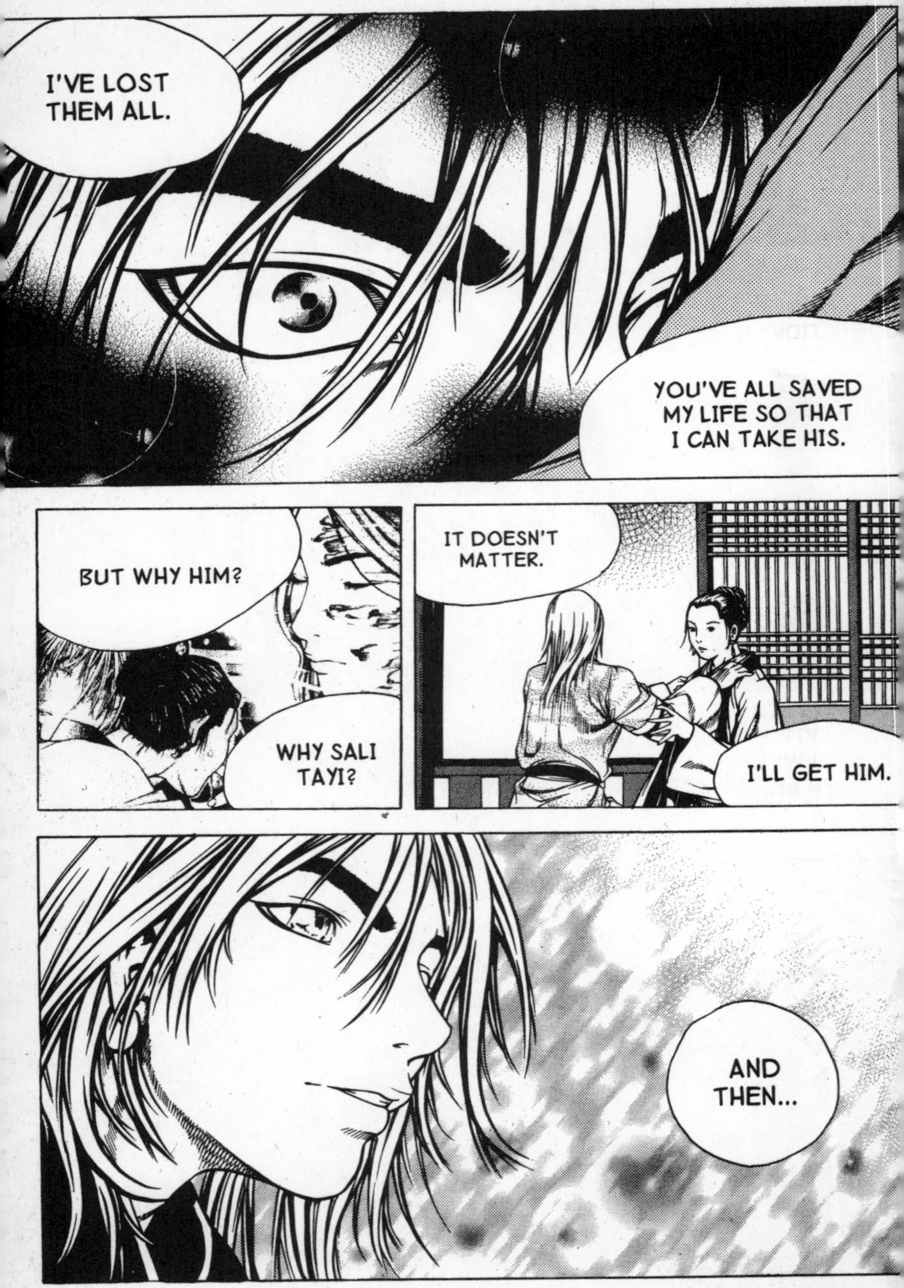
I'VE LOST THEM ALL.
YOU'VE ALL SAVED MY LIFE SO THAT I CAN TAKE HIS.
BUT WHY HIM?
WHY SALI TAYI?
IT DOESN'T MATTER.
I'LL GET HIM.
AND THEN...

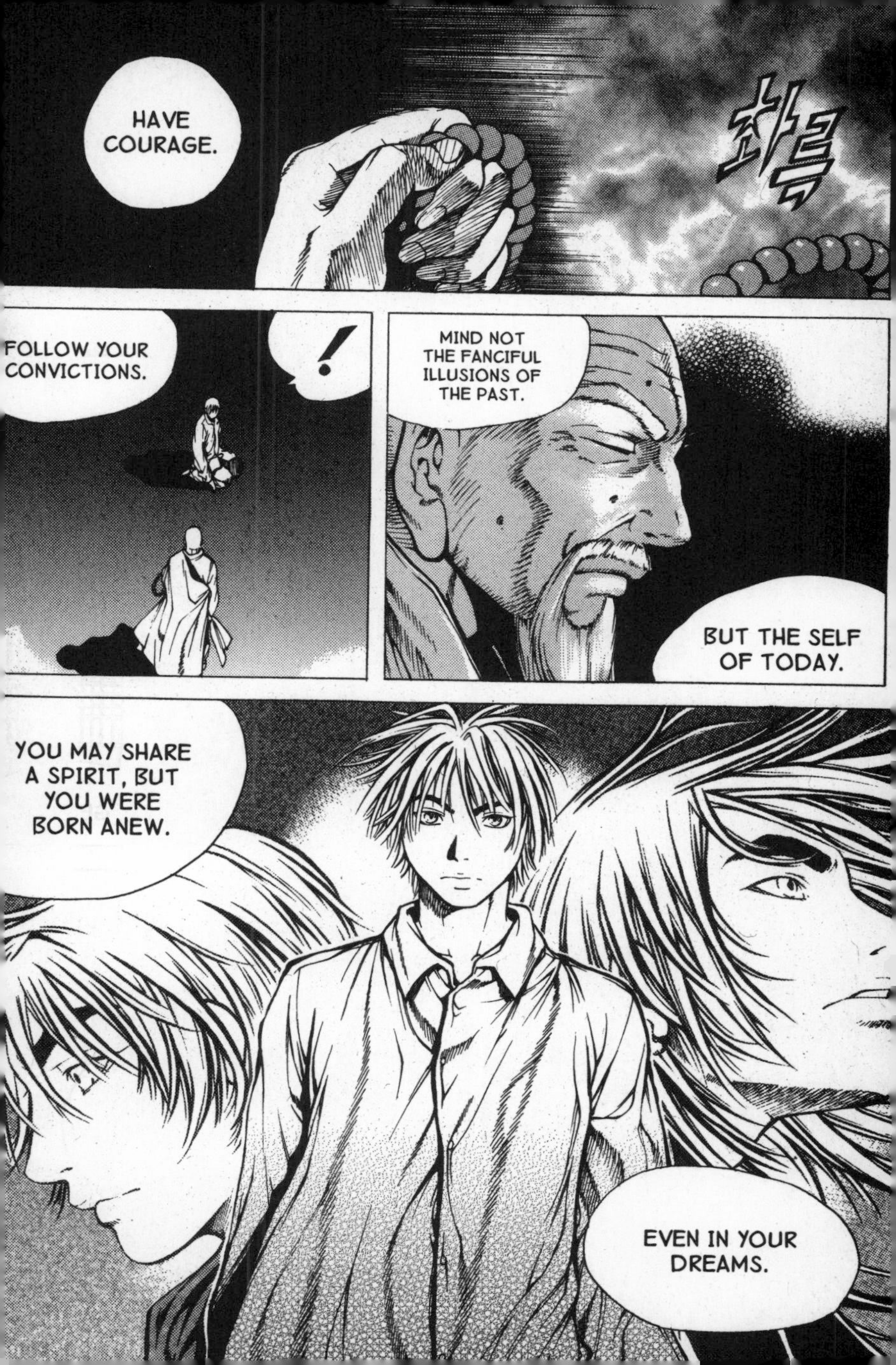
HAVE COURAGE.
촤륵
FOLLOW YOUR CONVICTIONS.
!
MIND NOT THE FANCIFUL ILLUSIONS OF THE PAST.
BUT THE SELF OF TODAY.
YOU MAY SHARE A SPIRIT, BUT YOU WERE BORN ANEW.
EVEN IN YOUR DREAMS.

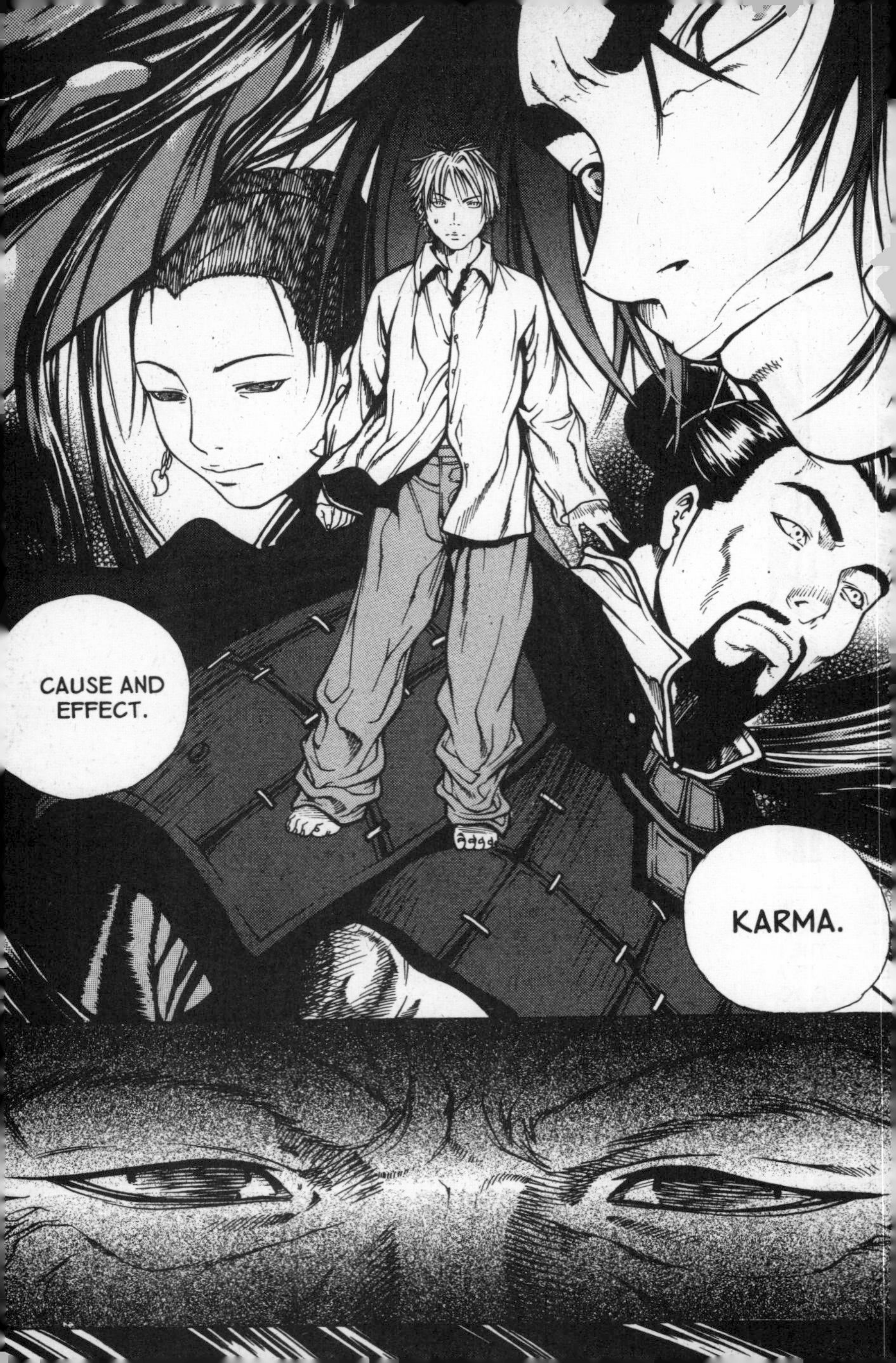
CAUSE AND EFFECT.
KARMA.

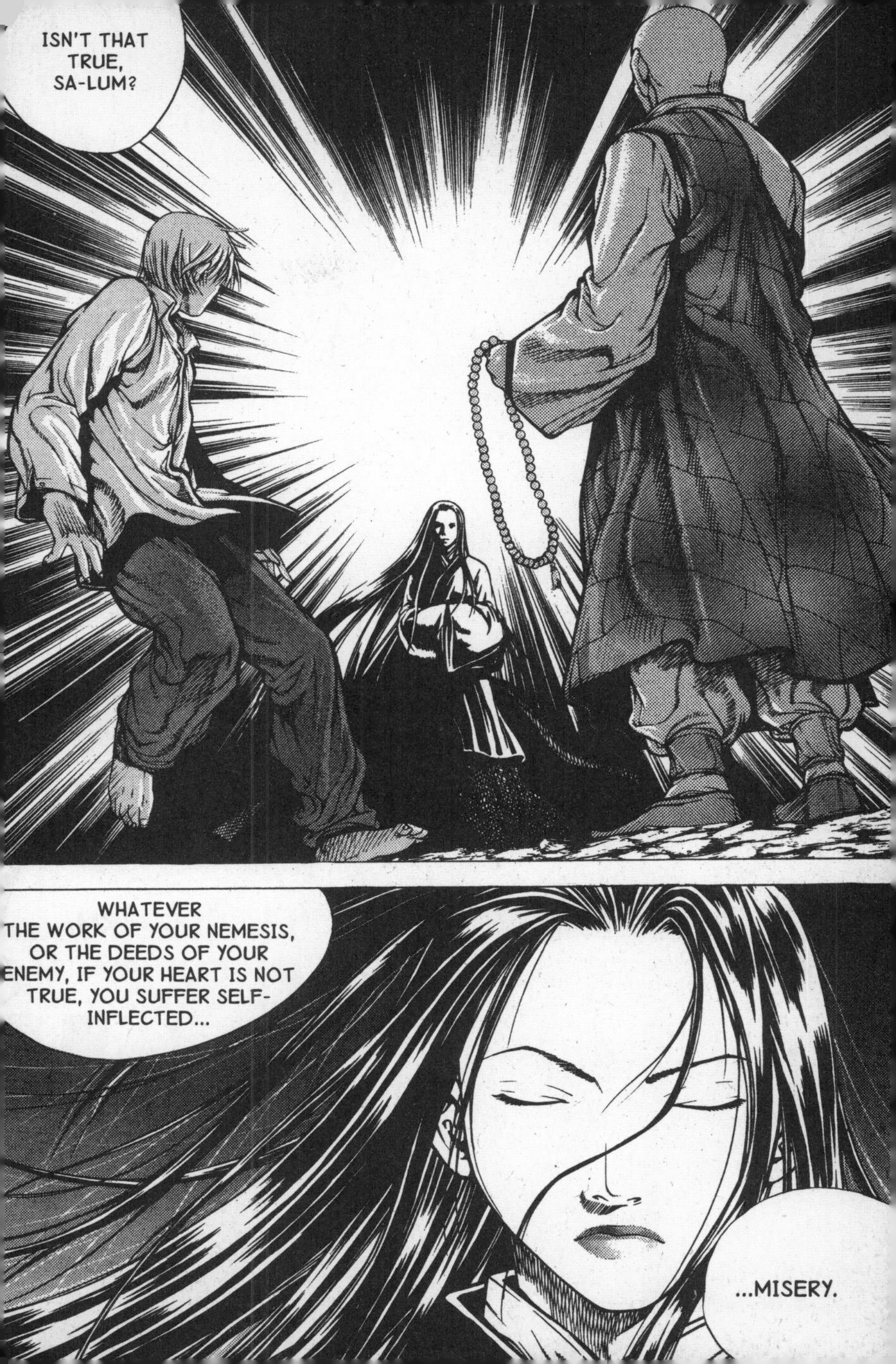
ISN'T THAT TRUE, SA-LUM?
WHATEVER THE WORK OF YOUR NEMESIS, OR THE DEEDS OF YOUR ENEMY, IF YOUR HEART IS NOT TRUE, YOU SUFFER SELF-INFLECTED...
...MISERY.

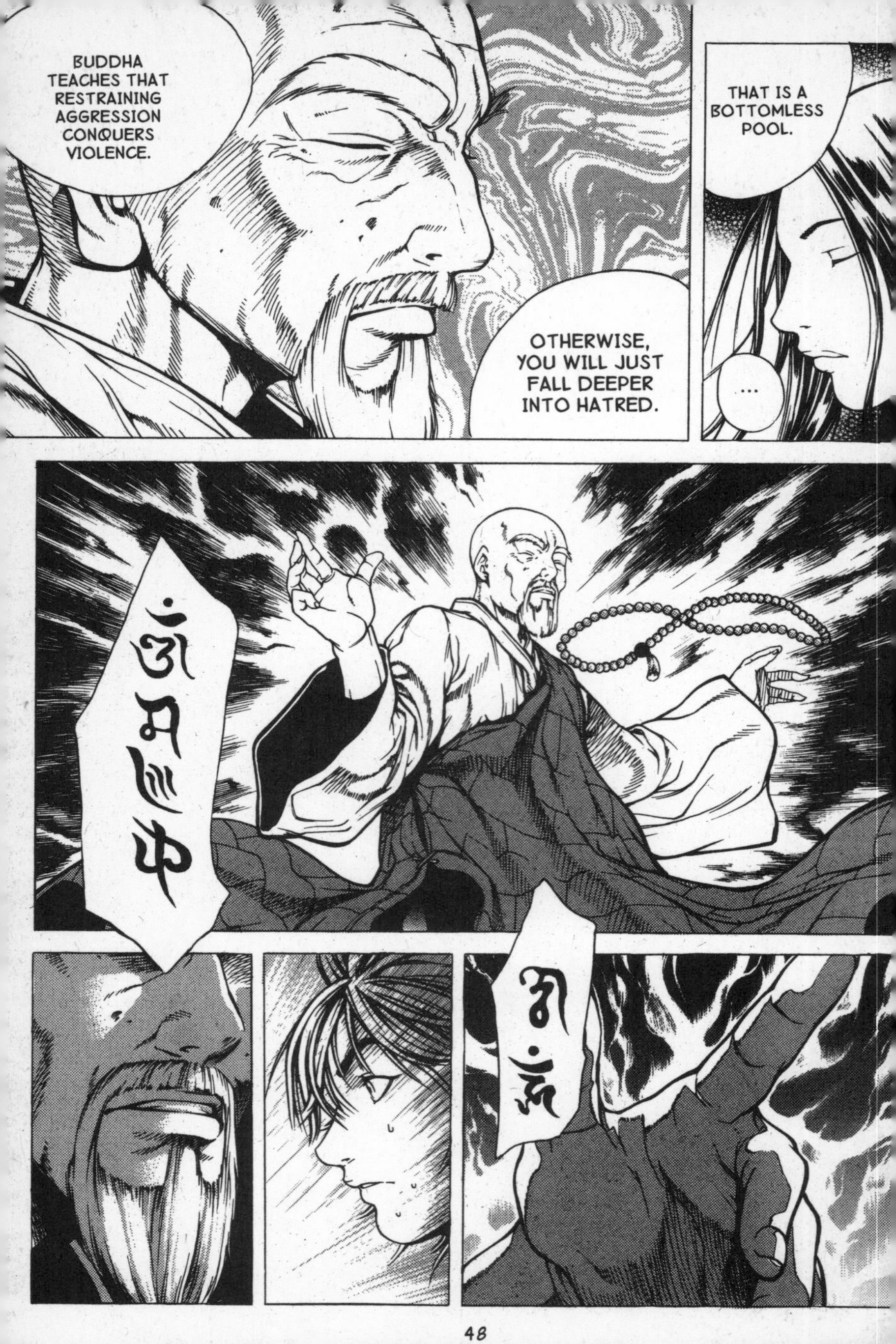
BUDDHA TEACHES THAT RESTRAINING AGGRESSION CONQUERS VIOLENCE.
OTHERWISE, YOU WILL JUST FALL DEEPER INTO HATRED.
THAT IS A BOTTOMLESS POOL.
...

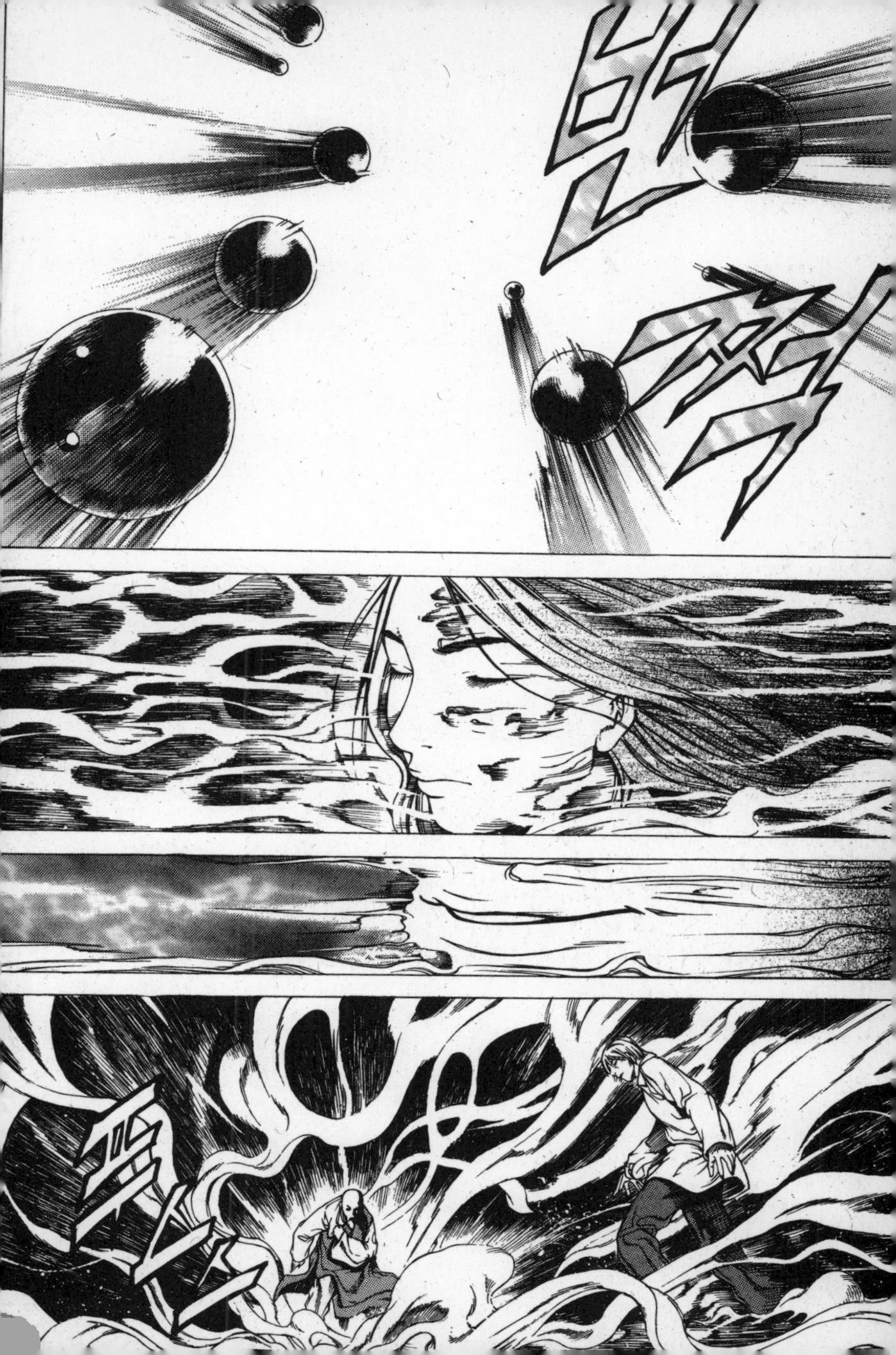

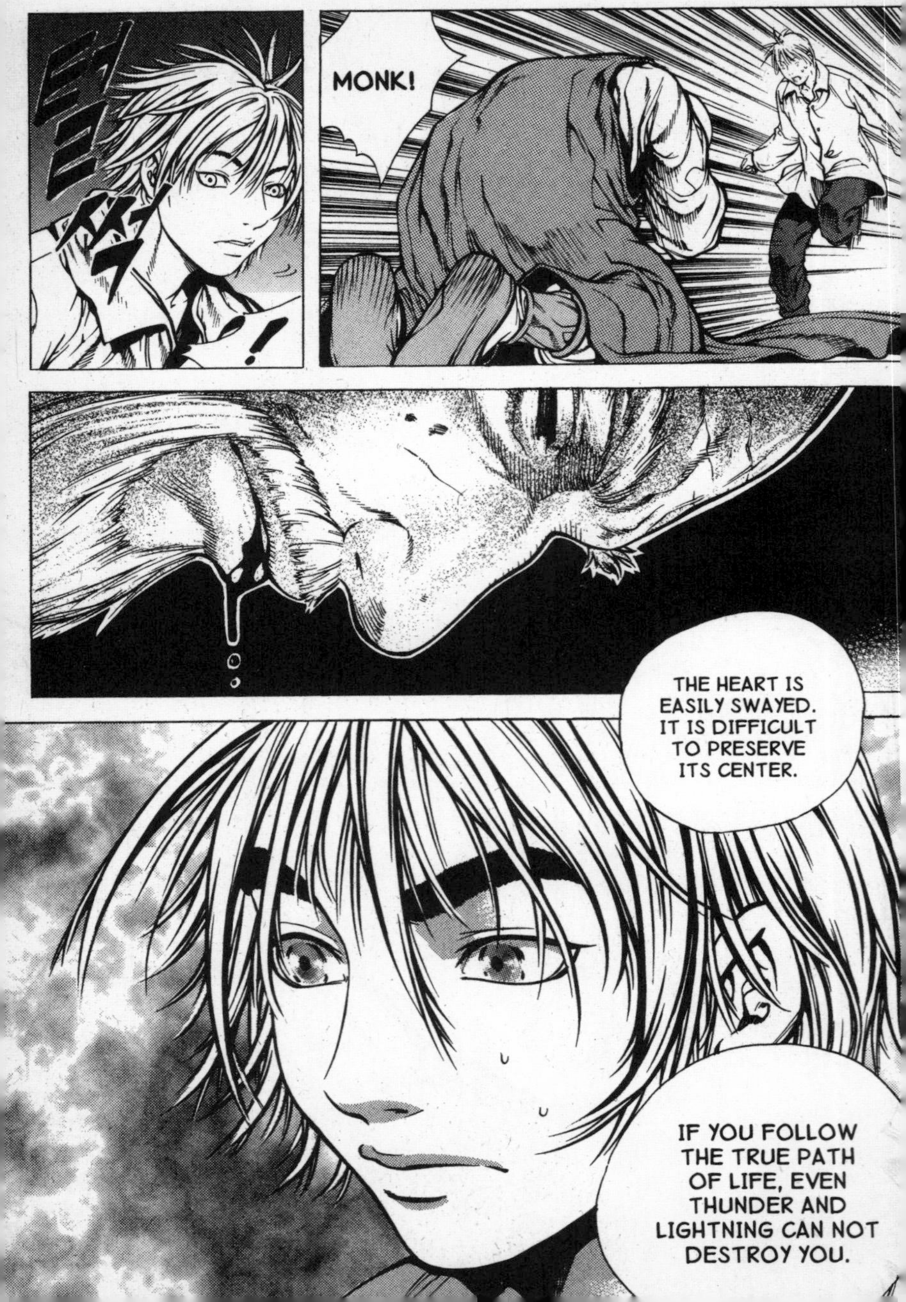
MONK!
THE HEART IS EASILY SWAYED. IT IS DIFFICULT TO PRESERVE ITS CENTER.
IF YOU FOLLOW THE TRUE PATH OF LIFE, EVEN THUNDER AND LIGHTNING CAN NOT DESTROY YOU.

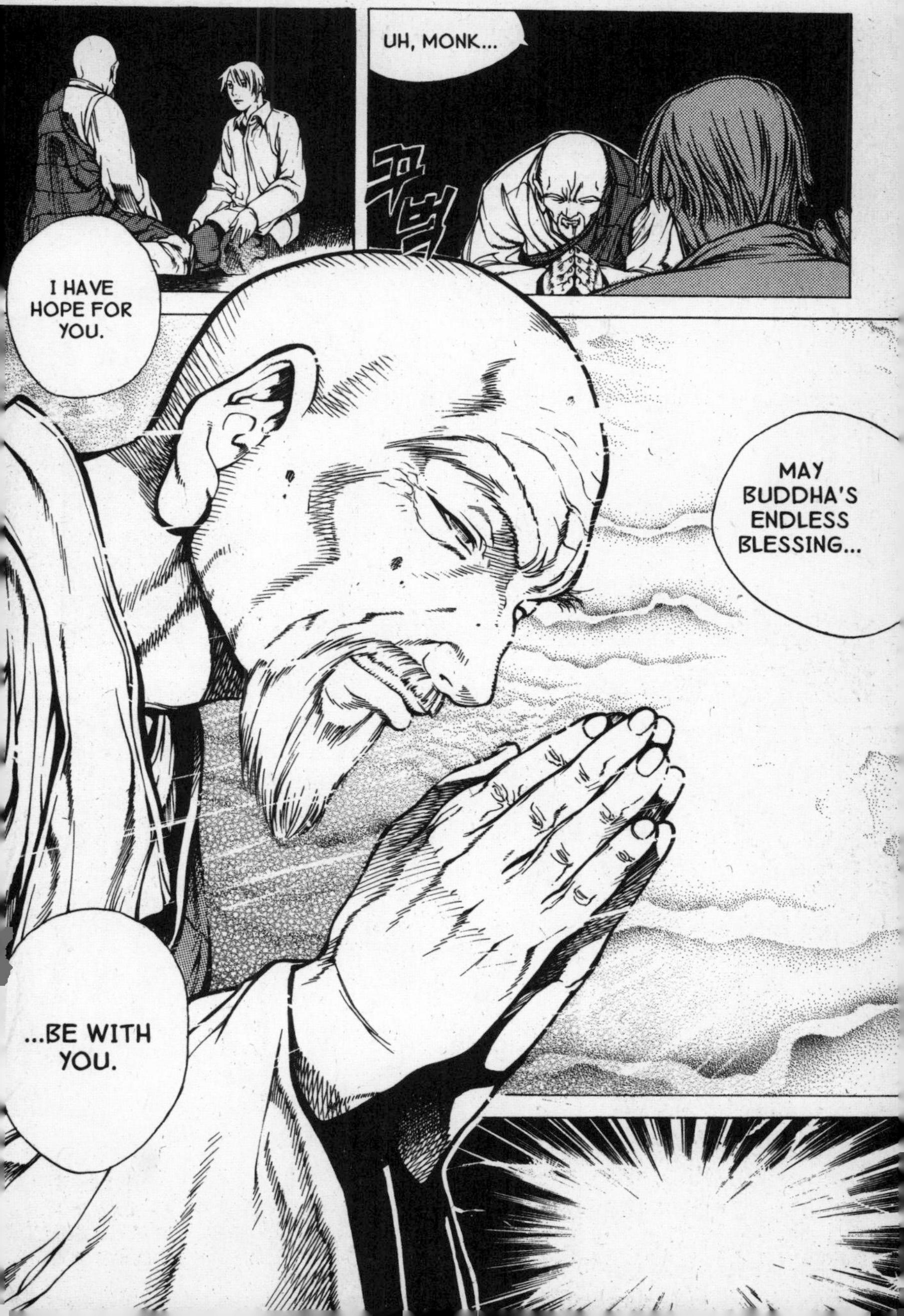
UH, MONK...
꾸벅
I HAVE HOPE FOR YOU.
MAY BUDDHA'S ENDLESS BLESSING...
...BE WITH YOU.

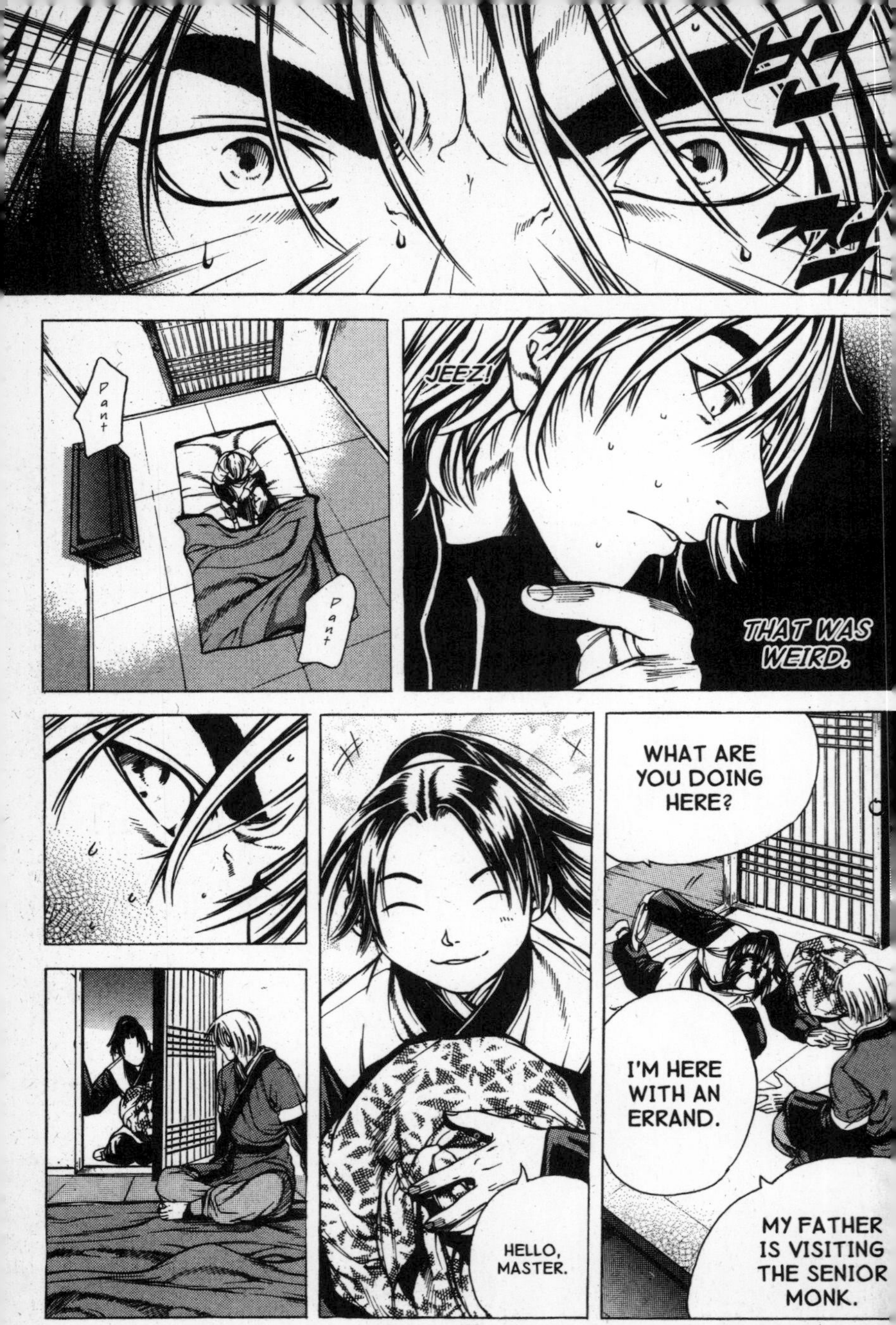
Pant
Pant
JEEZ!
THAT WAS WEIRD.
HELLO, MASTER.
WHAT ARE YOU DOING HERE?
I'M HERE WITH AN ERRAND.
MY FATHER IS VISITING THE SENIOR MONK.

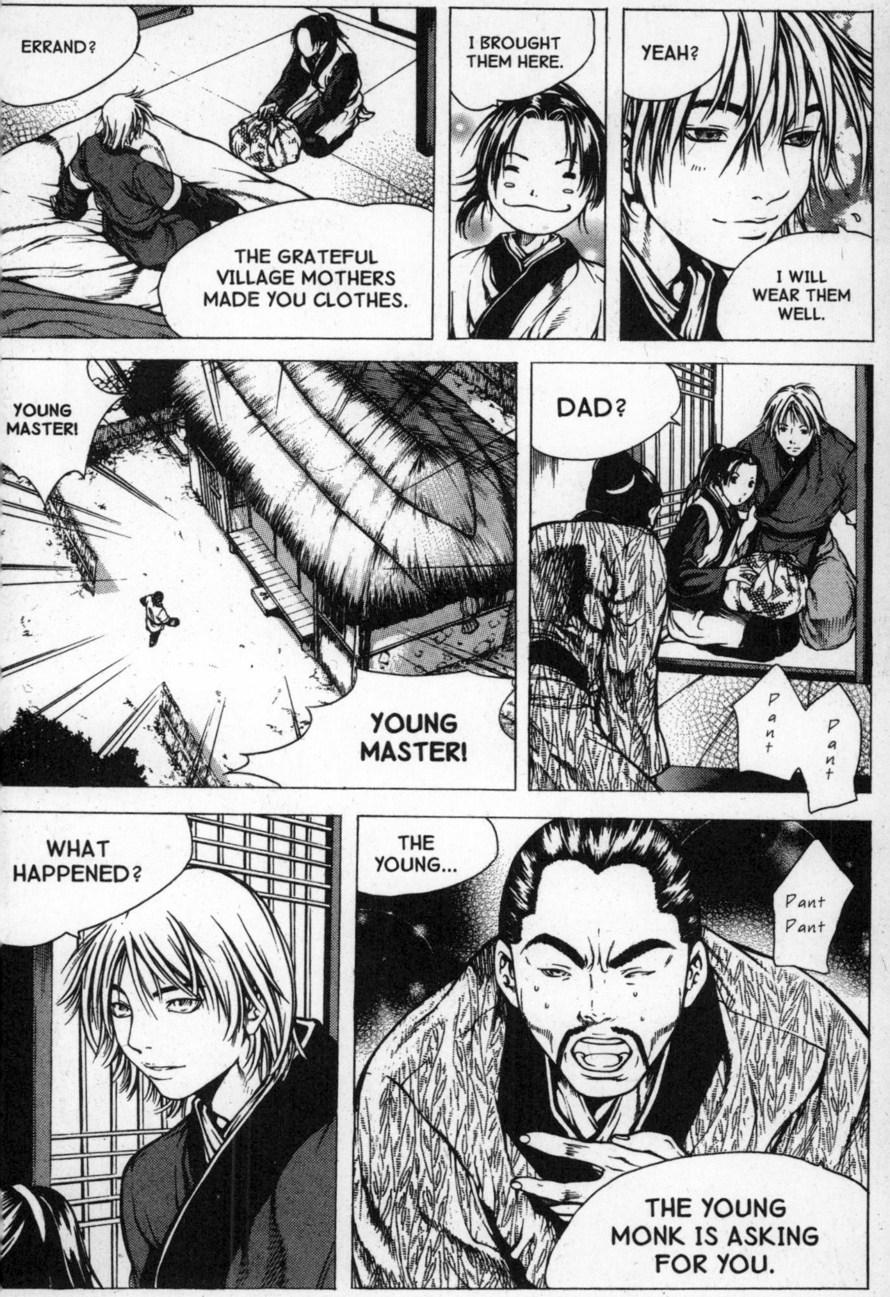
ERRAND?
THE GRATEFUL VILLAGE MOTHERS MADE YOU CLOTHES.
I BROUGHT THEM HERE.
YEAH?
I WILL WEAR THEM WELL.
YOUNG MASTER!
YOUNG MASTER!
DAD?
Pant Pant
WHAT HAPPENED?
THE YOUNG...
Pant Pant
THE YOUNG MONK IS ASKING FOR YOU.

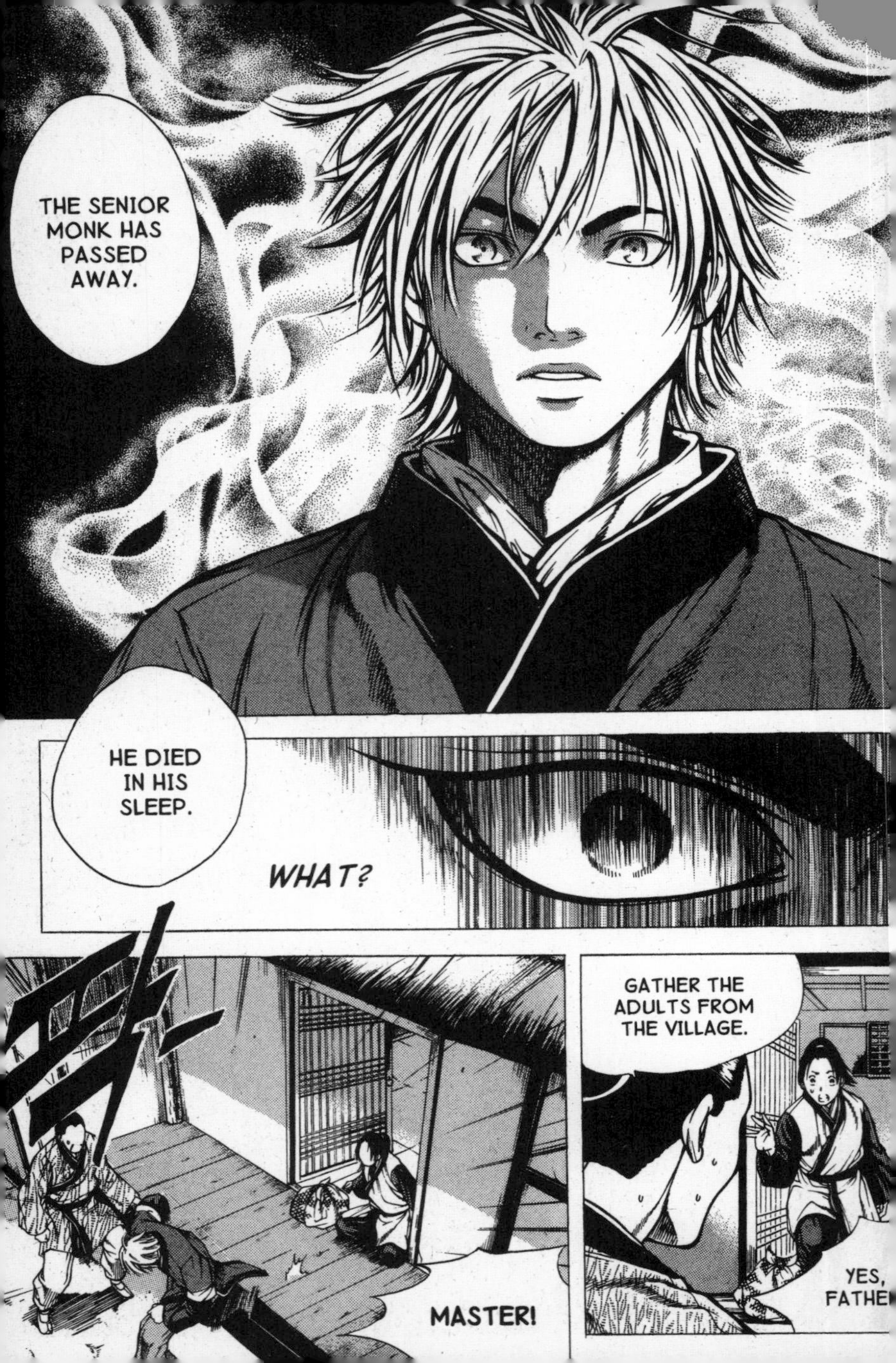
THE SENIOR MONK HAS PASSED AWAY.
HE DIED IN HIS SLEEP.
WHAT?
MASTER!
GATHER THE ADULTS FROM THE VILLAGE.
YES, FATHE

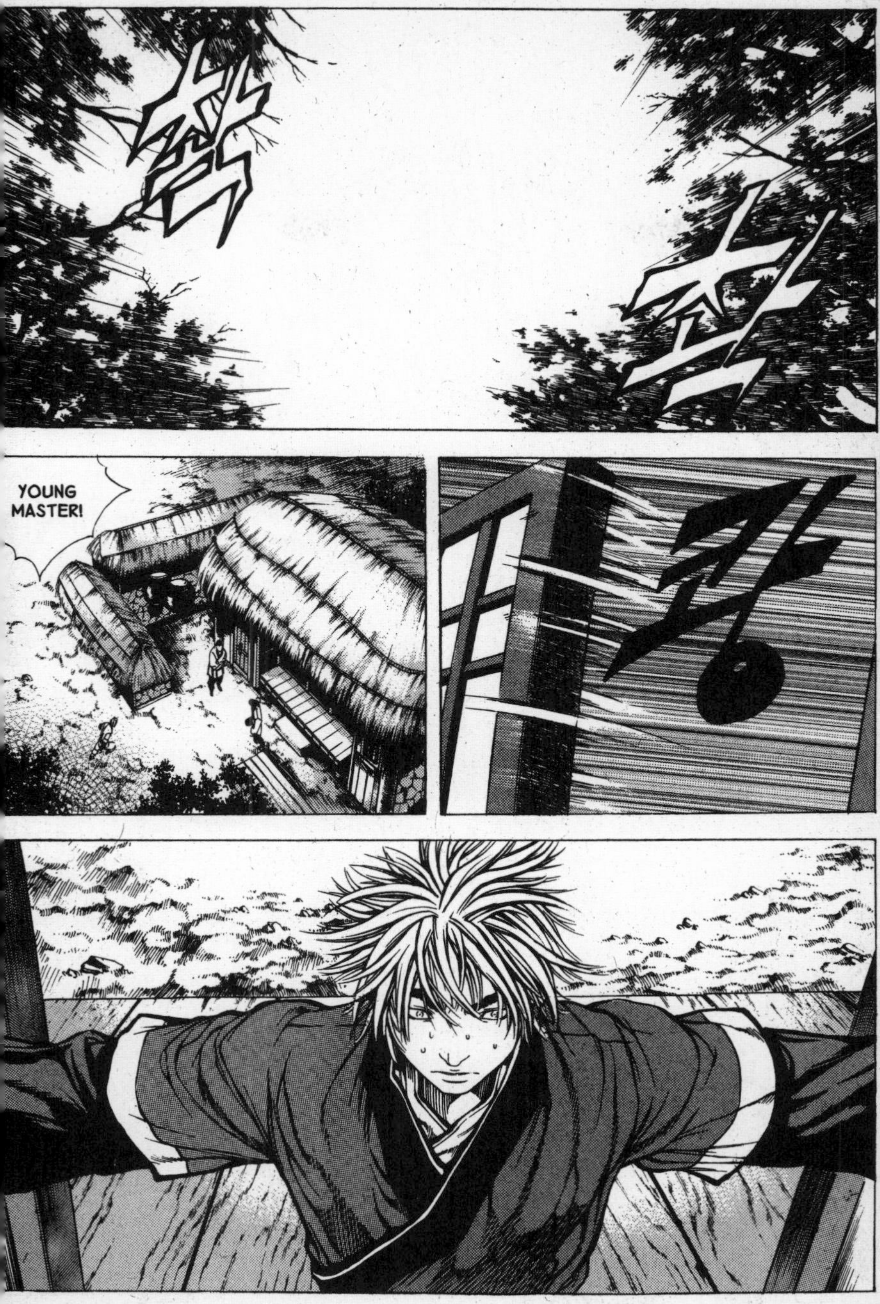
YOUNG MASTER!

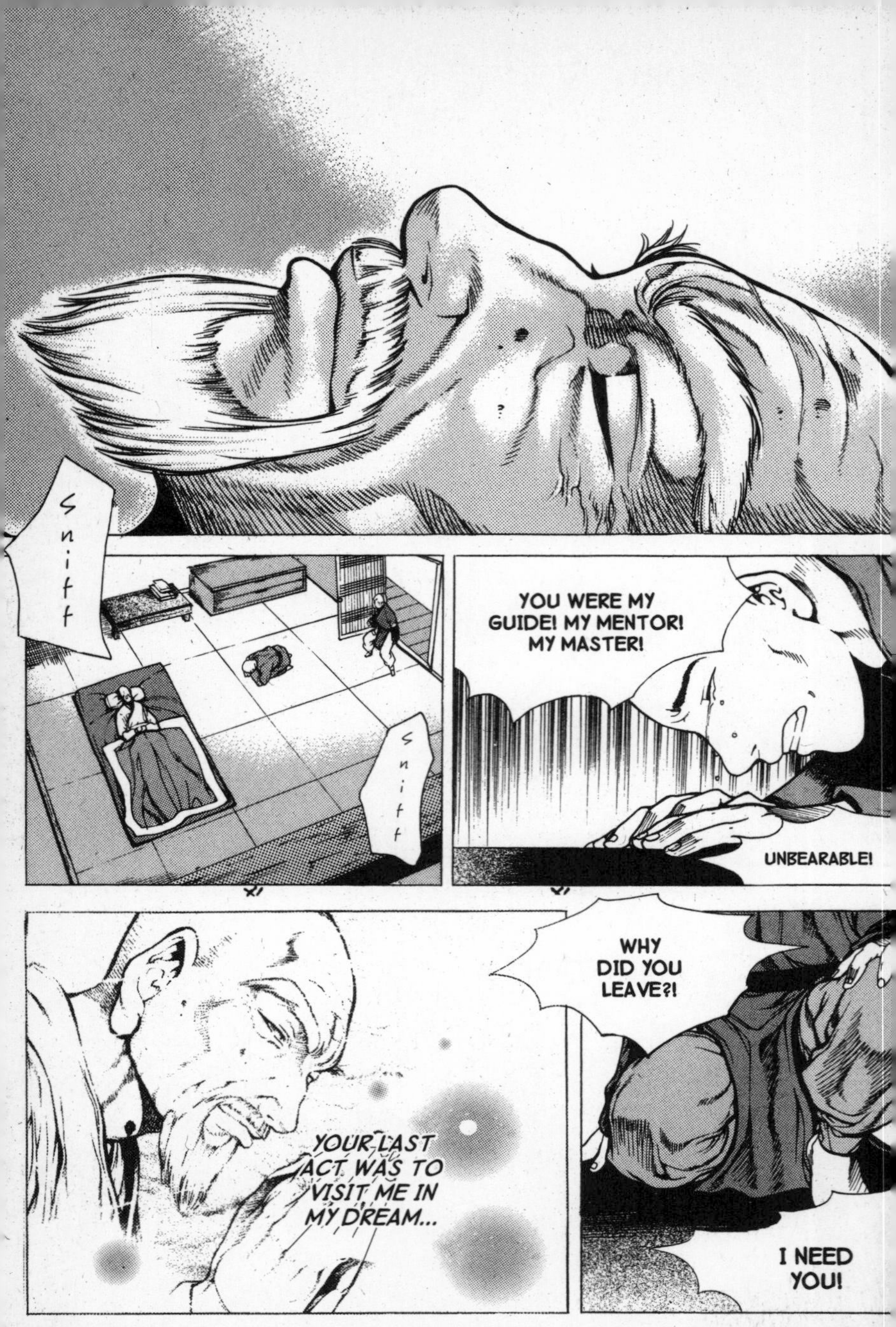
?
Sniff
Sniff
YOU WERE MY GUIDE! MY MENTOR! MY MASTER!
UNBEARABLE!
YOUR LAST ACT WAS TO VISIT ME IN MY DREAM...
WHY DID YOU LEAVE?!
I NEED YOU!

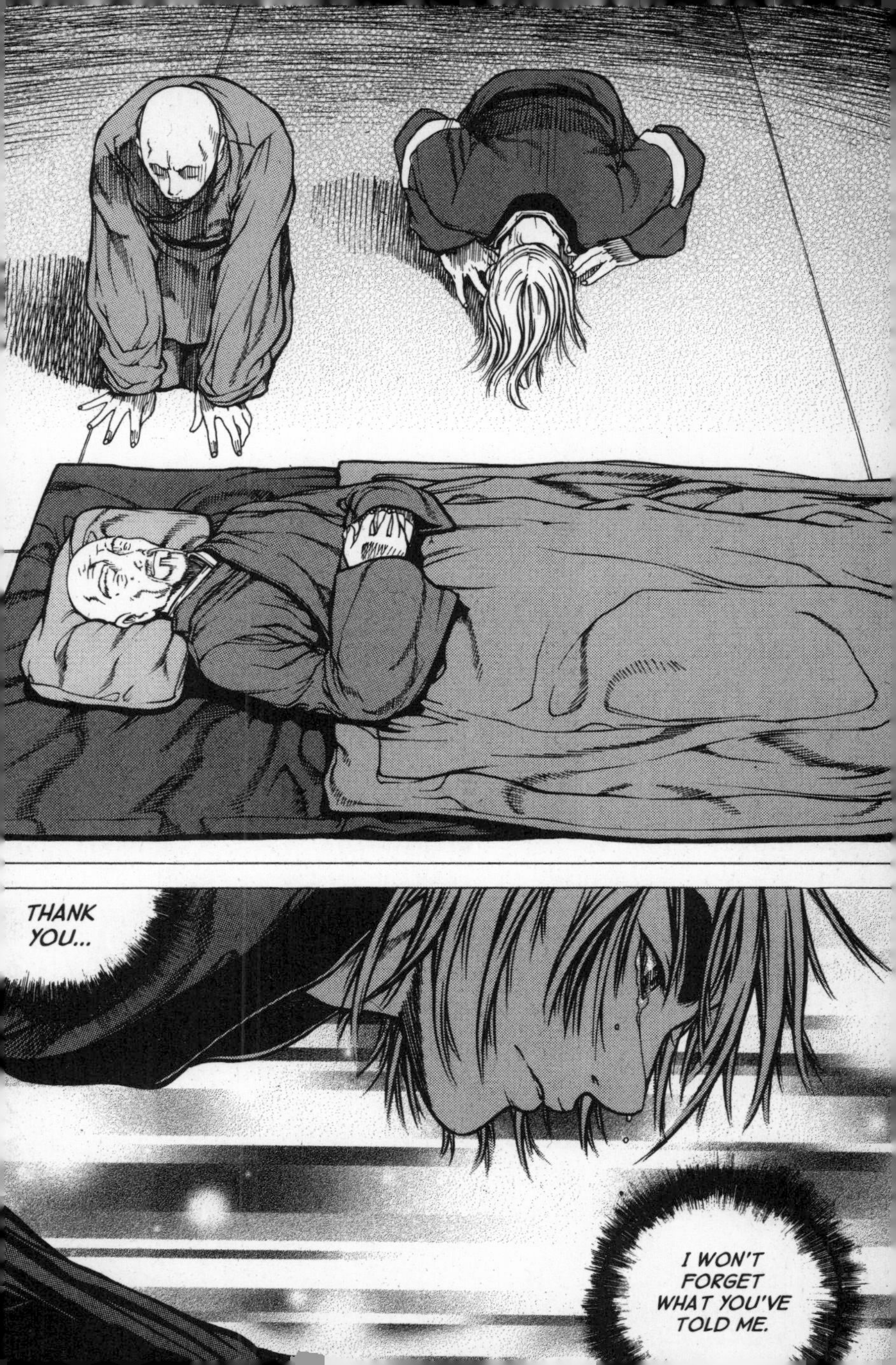
THANK YOU...
I WON'T FORGET WHAT YOU'VE TOLD ME.

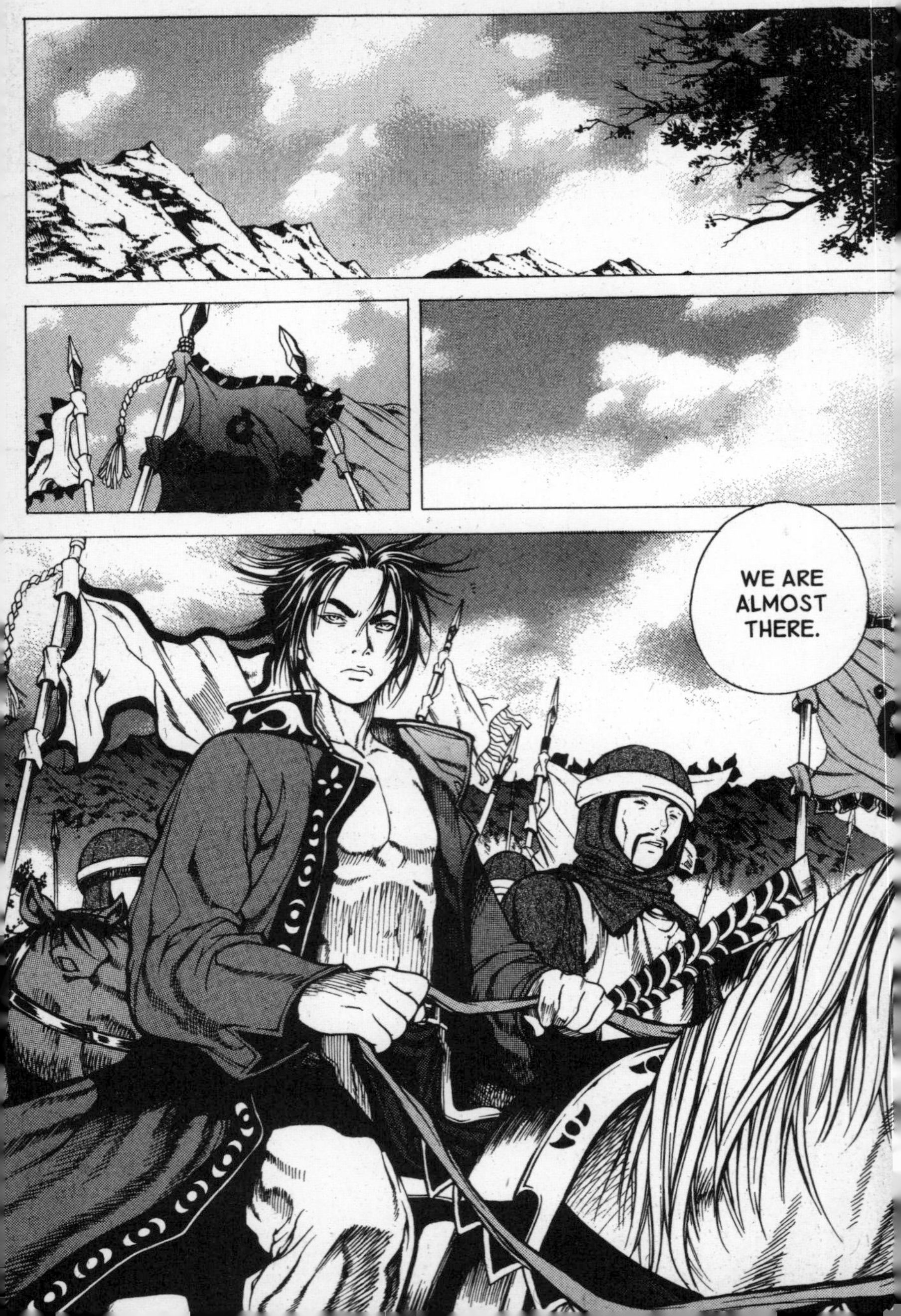
WE ARE ALMOST THERE.

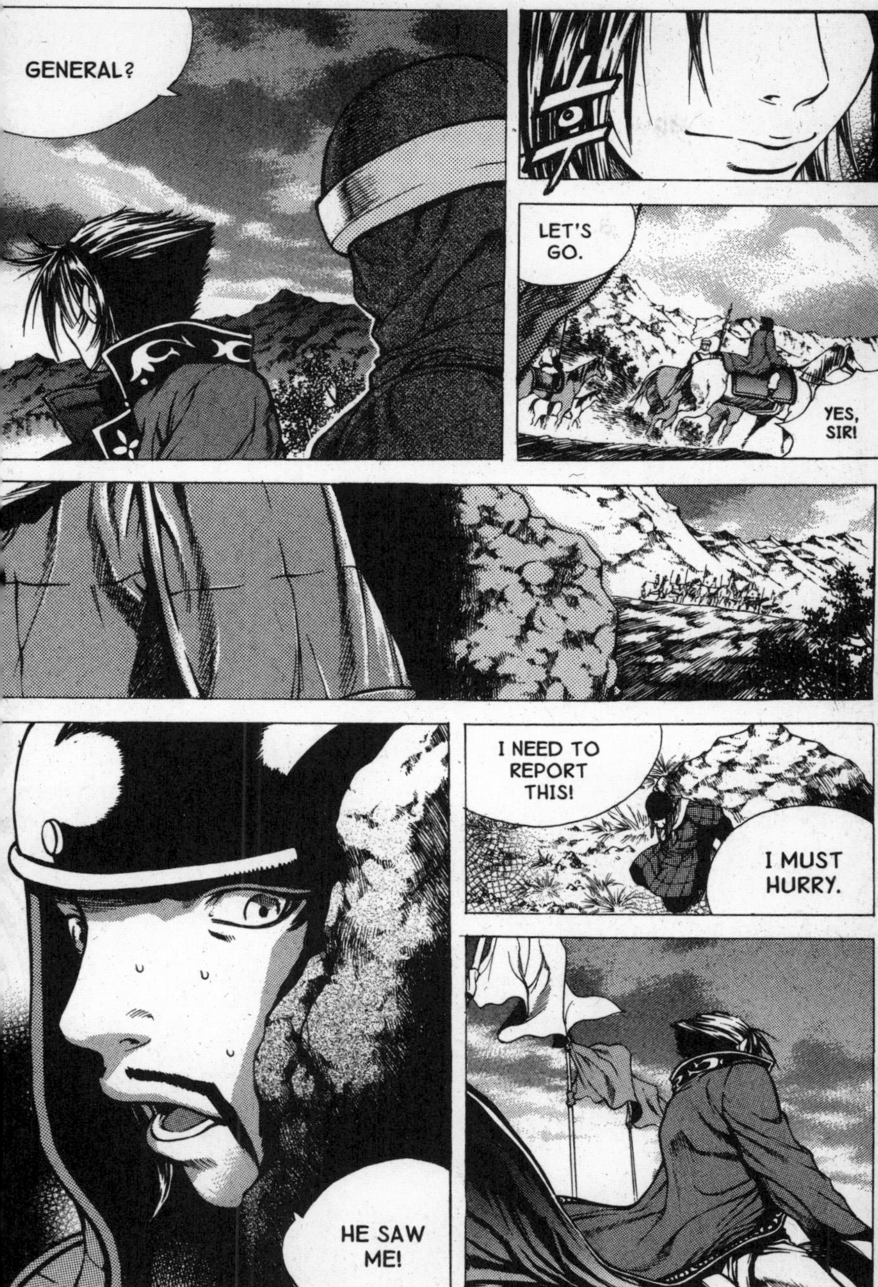
GENERAL?
LET'S GO.
YES, SIR!
HE SAW ME!
I NEED TO REPORT THIS!
I MUST HURRY.

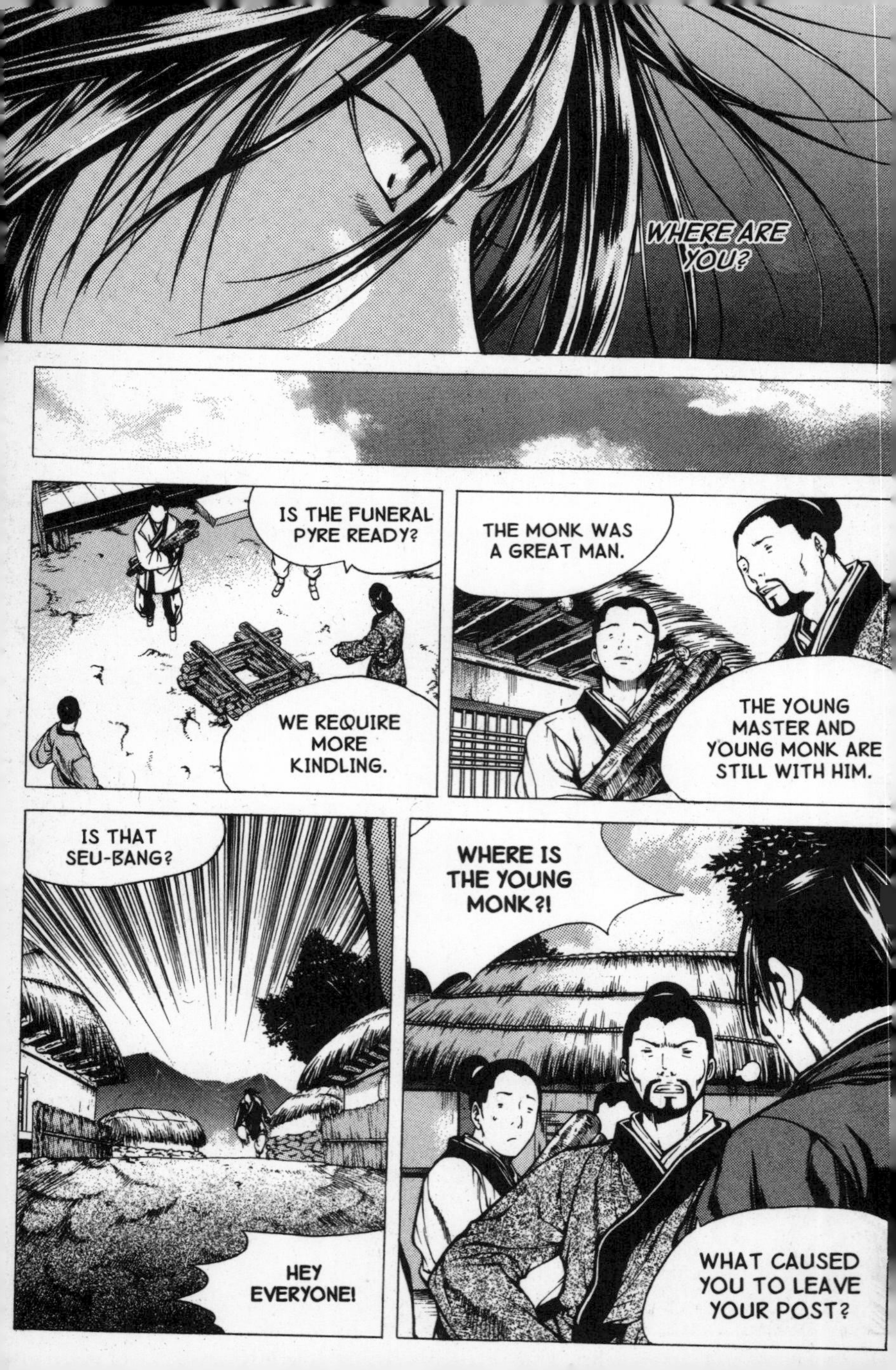
WHERE ARE YOU?
IS THE FUNERAL PYRE READY?
WE REQUIRE MORE KINDLING.
THE MONK WAS A GREAT MAN.
THE YOUNG MASTER AND YOUNG MONK ARE STILL WITH HIM.
IS THAT SEU-BANG?
HEY EVERYONE!
WHERE IS THE YOUNG MONK?!
WHAT CAUSED YOU TO LEAVE YOUR POST?

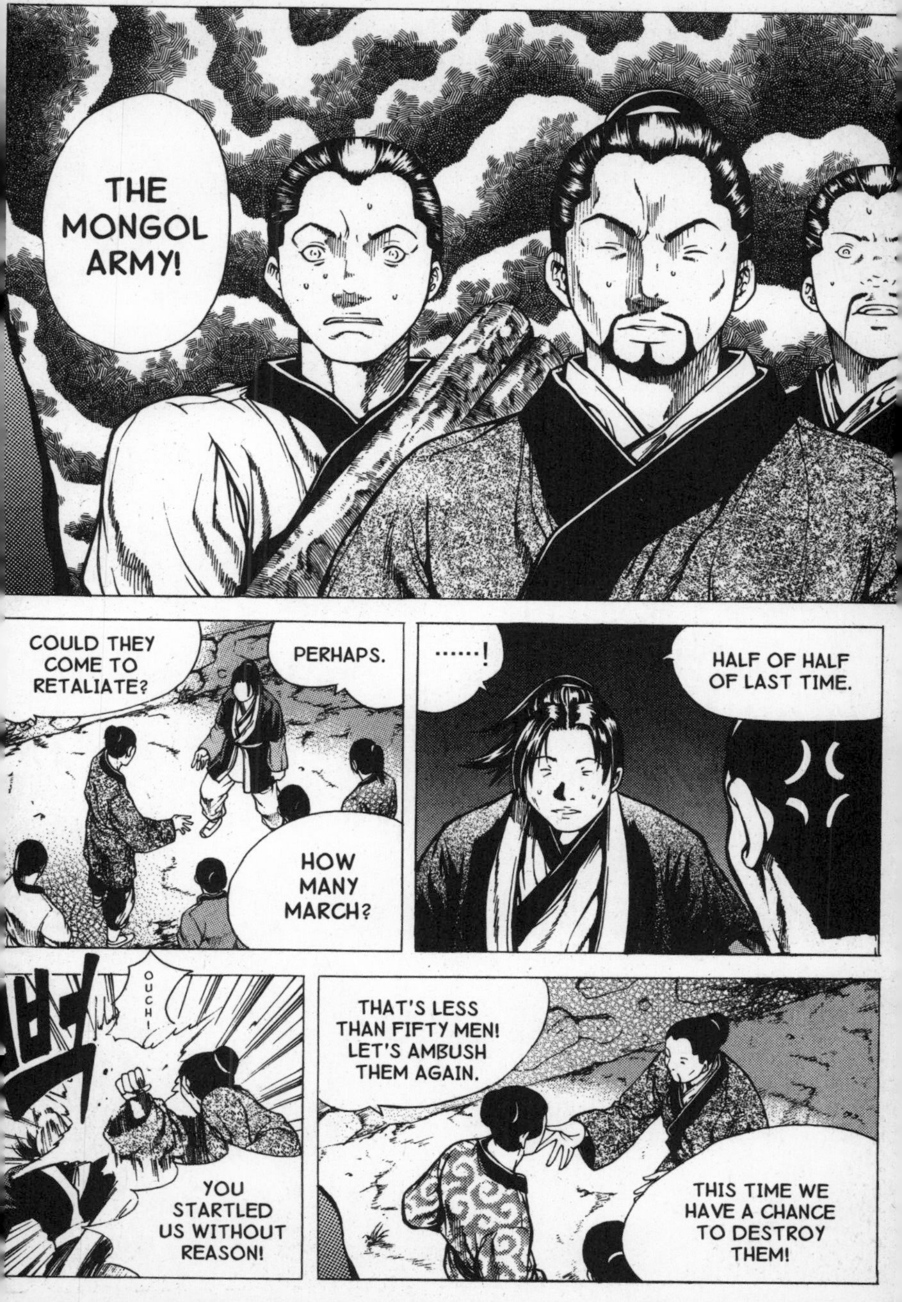
THE MONGOL ARMY!
COULD THEY COME TO RETALIATE?
PERHAPS.
HOW MANY MARCH?
......!
HALF OF HALF OF LAST TIME.
OUCH!
YOU STARTLED US WITHOUT REASON!
THAT'S LESS THAN FIFTY MEN! LET'S AMBUSH THEM AGAIN.
THIS TIME WE HAVE A CHANCE TO DESTROY THEM!

WAIT!

I WILL LET THE YOUNG MONK AND YOUNG MASTER KNOW.

DO NOT INTERRUPT THEIR MOURNING. THEY NEED TIME.

RIGHT.

DO YOU BOW-HUNT?

ONLY WHEN HUNTING MONGOLS!

DAD, CAN I GO TOO?

IT'S DANGEROUS JUST WATCH FROM THE CLIFF.

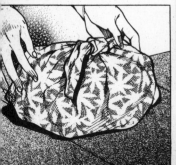

IF IT IS ONLY FIFTY, THIS WILL BE OVER QUICKLY.

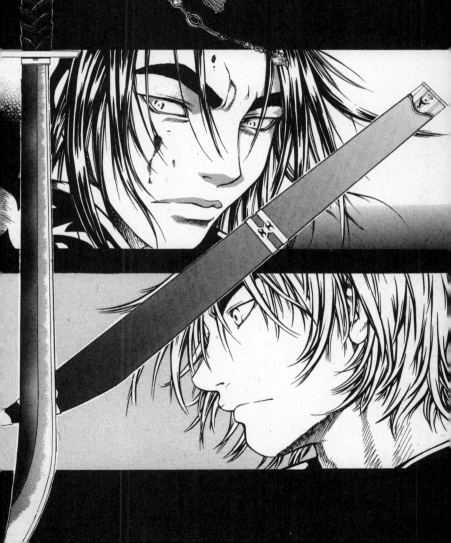

Chapter 42
Self-Awareness (Part 2)

THEY'RE CLOSE, GENERAL.

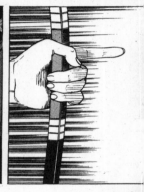

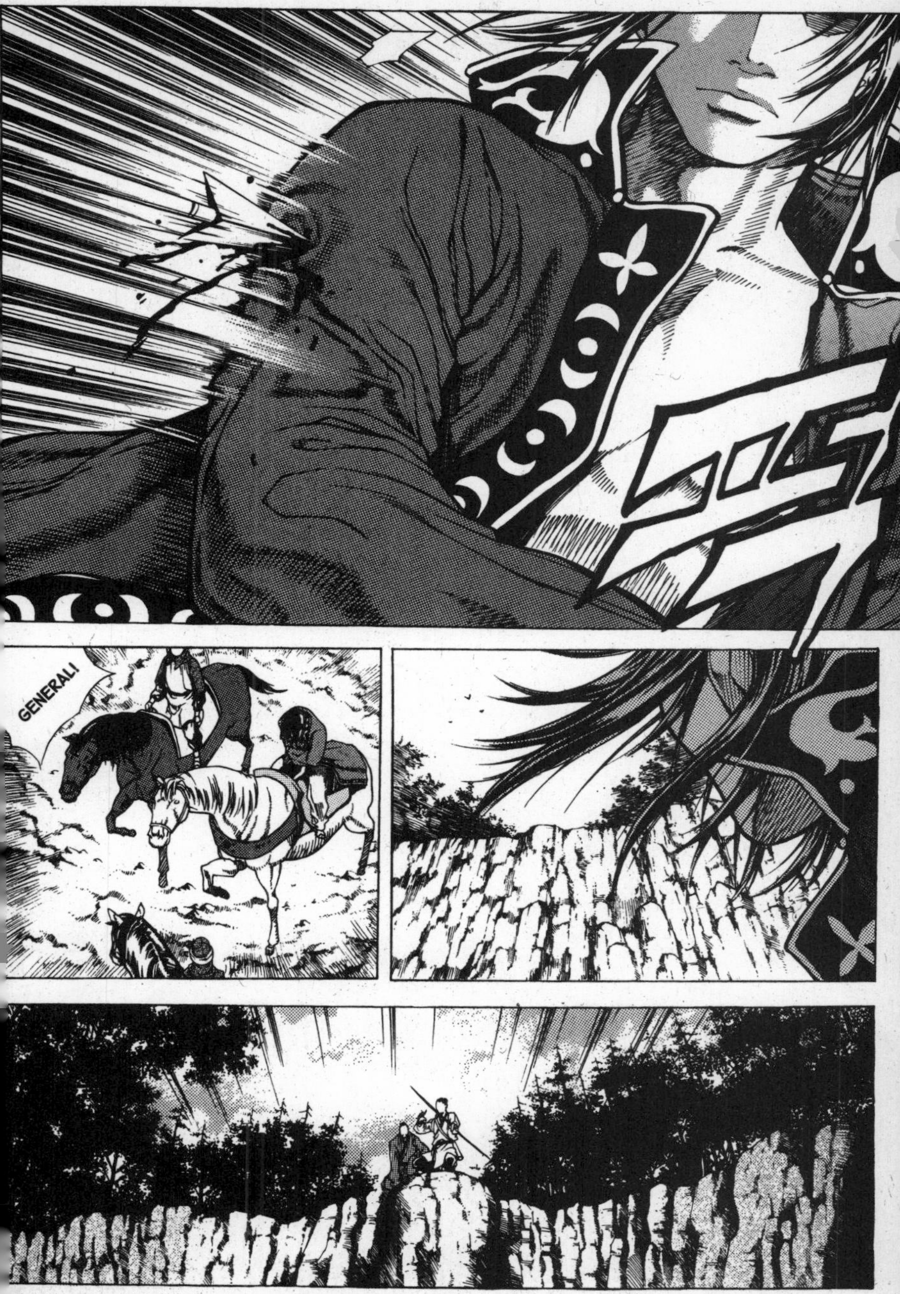
GENERAL!

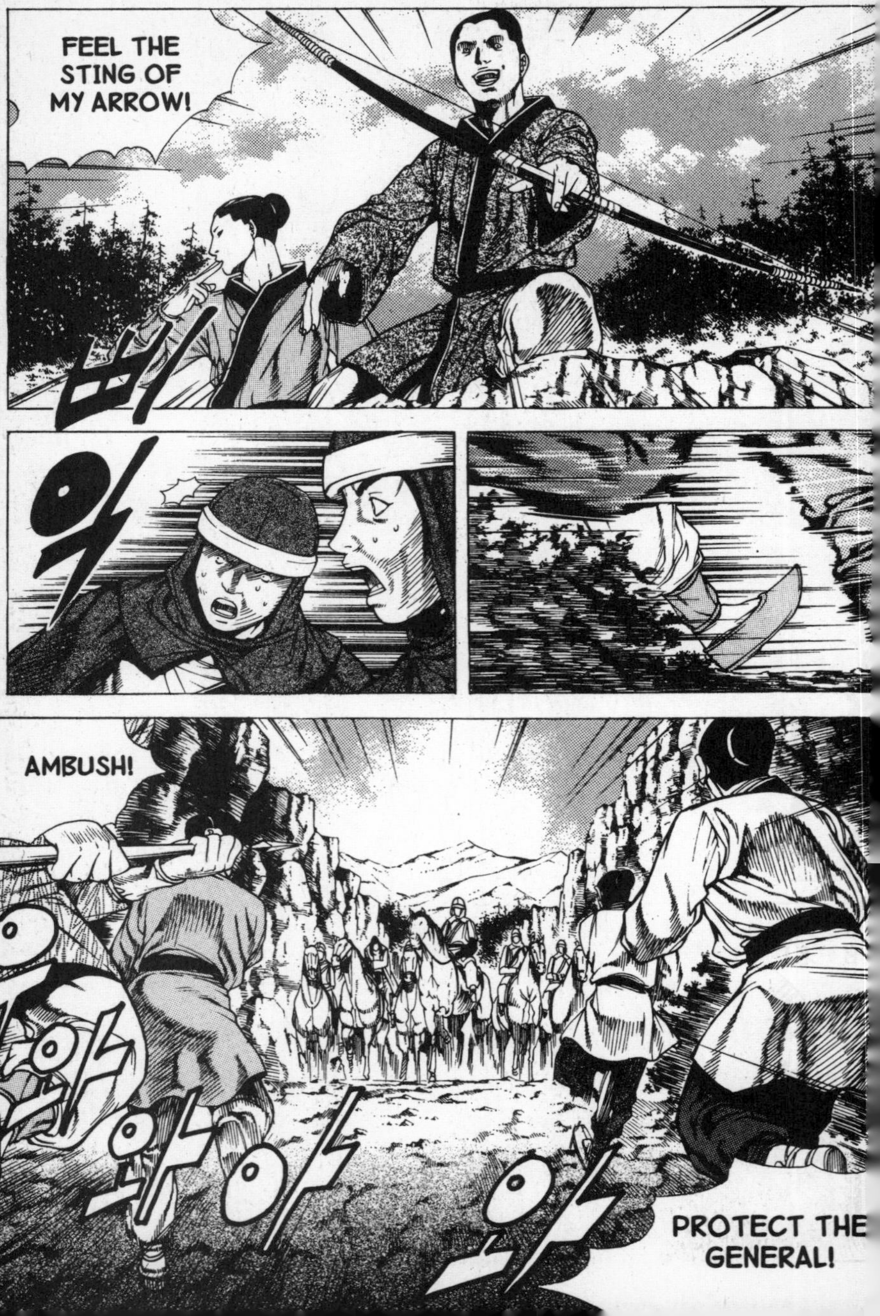
FEEL THE STING OF MY ARROW!
AMBUSH!
PROTECT THE GENERAL!

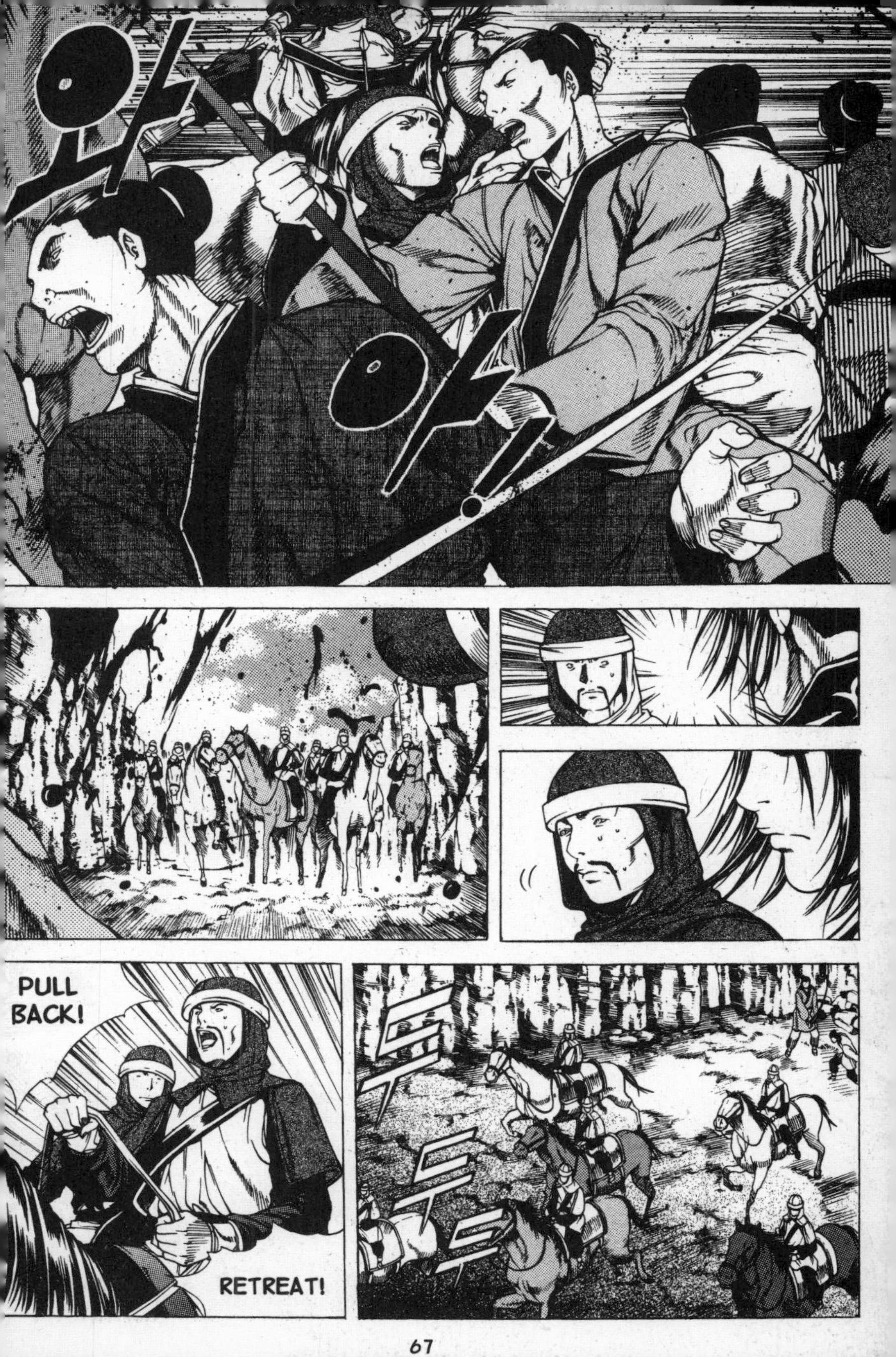
PULL
BACK!
RETREAT!

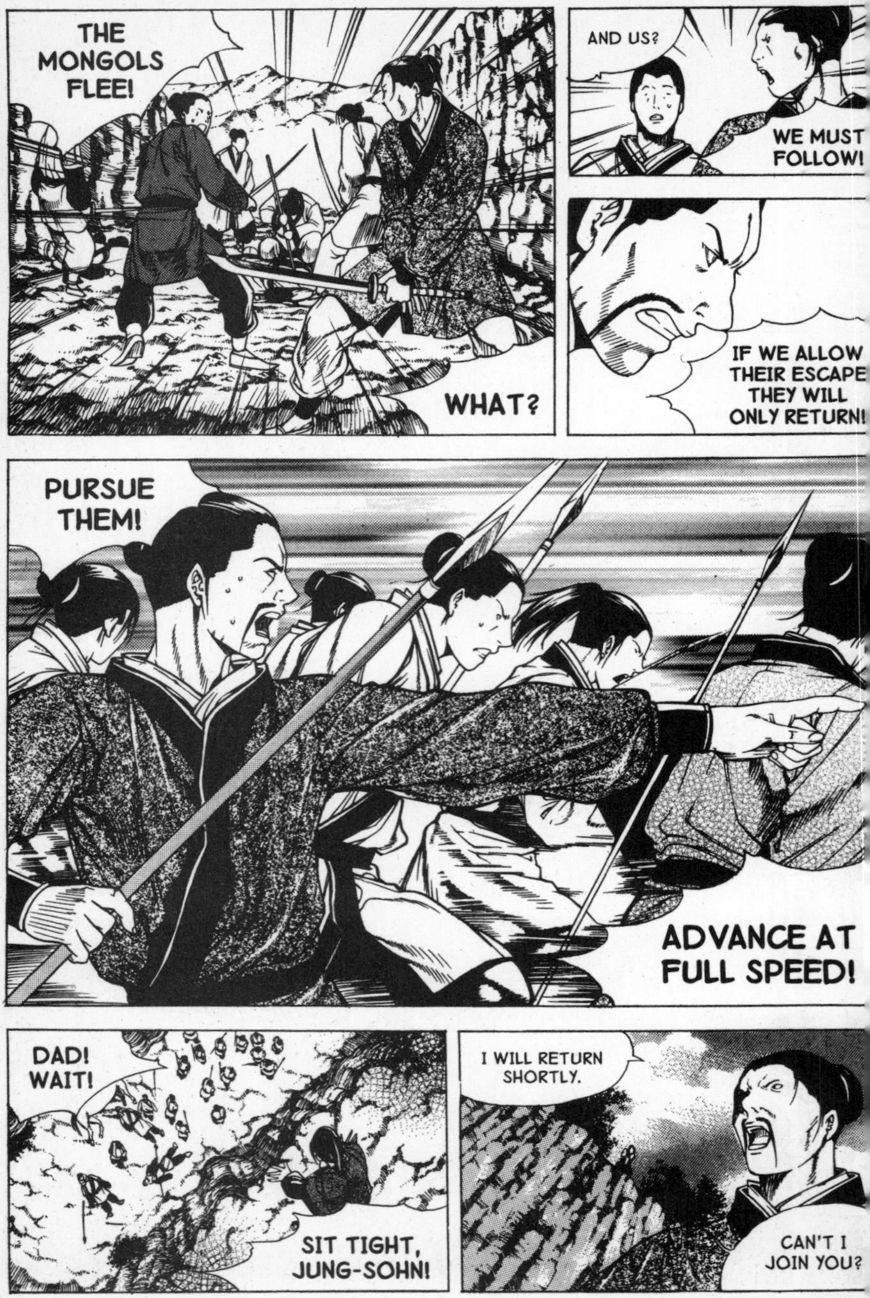
THE MONGOLS FLEE!
WHAT?
AND US?
WE MUST FOLLOW!
IF WE ALLOW THEIR ESCAPE THEY WILL ONLY RETURN!
PURSUE THEM!
ADVANCE AT FULL SPEED!
DAD! WAIT!
SIT TIGHT, JUNG-SOHN!
I WILL RETURN SHORTLY.
CAN'T I JOIN YOU?

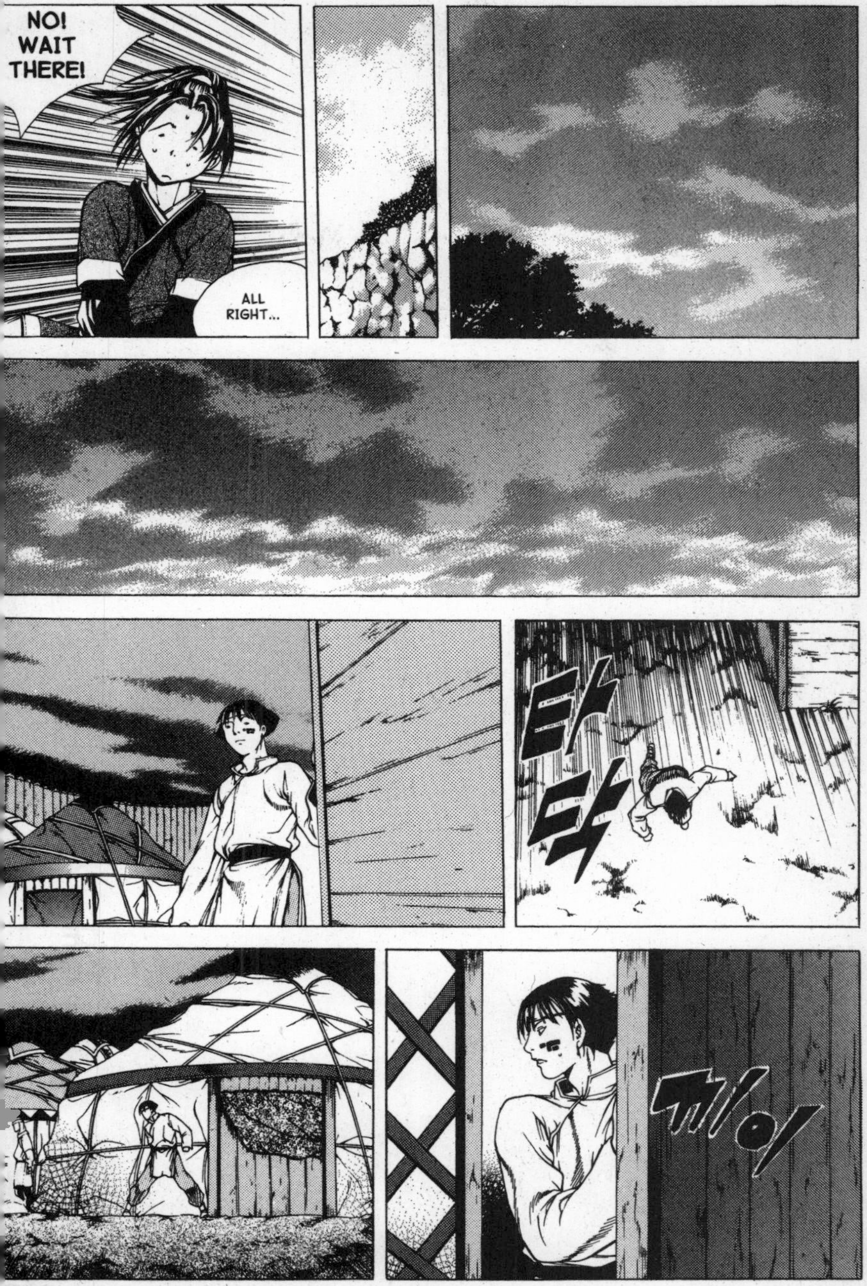
NO! WAIT THERE!
ALL RIGHT...
타닥
끼이

OOPS! IT'S ONLY YOU?

I'M GLAD IT SLIPPED.

IT SLIPPED?

YES. I AIMED AT YOUR HEAD.

THANK HEAVENS, RIGHT?

YOU APPEAR PLEASED WITH THE WHOLE THING!

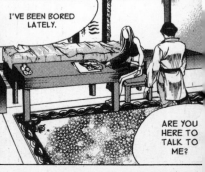

I'VE BEEN BORED LATELY.

ARE YOU HERE TO TALK TO ME?

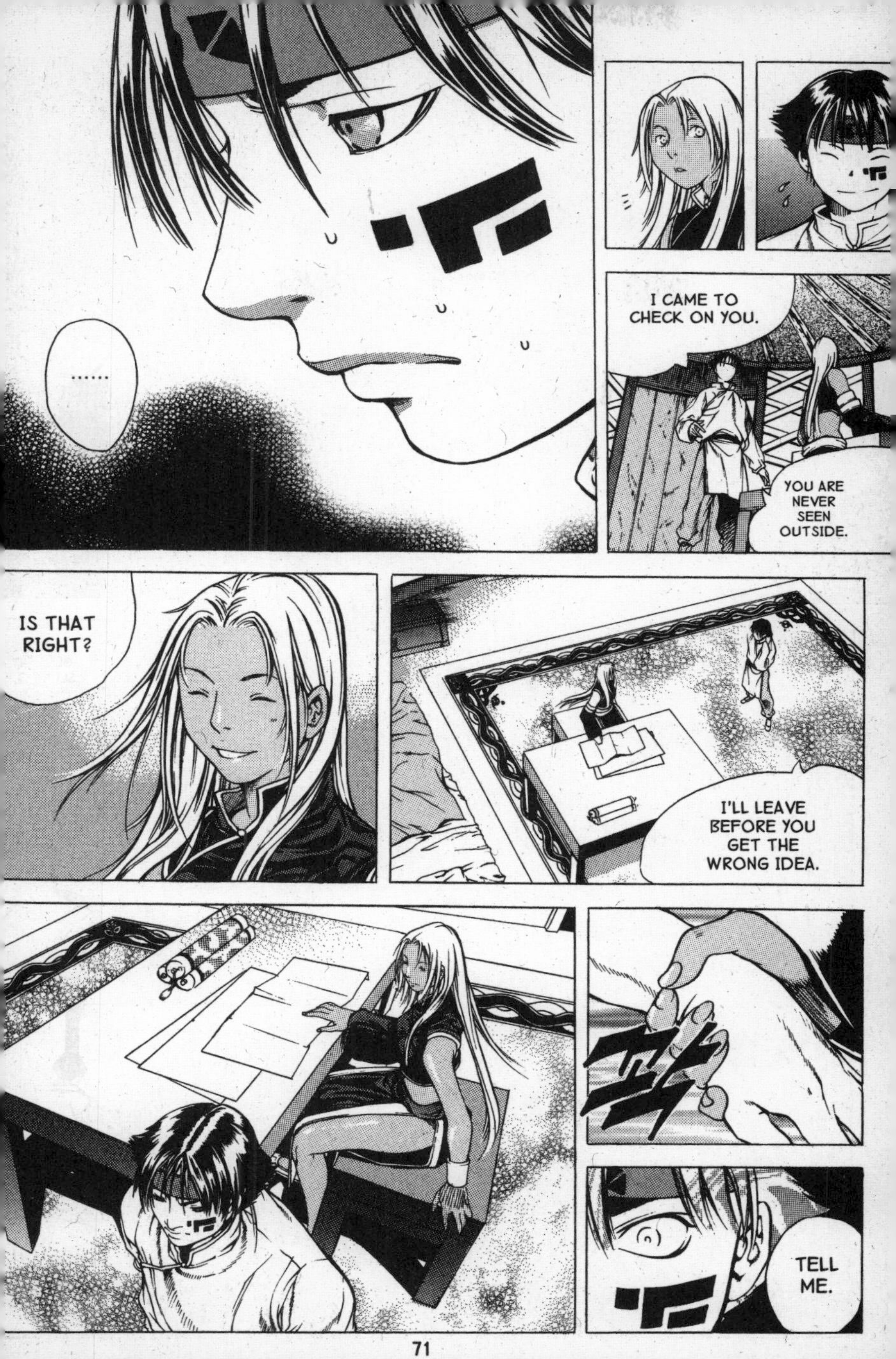

......
I CAME TO CHECK ON YOU.
YOU ARE NEVER SEEN OUTSIDE.
IS THAT RIGHT?
I'LL LEAVE BEFORE YOU GET THE WRONG IDEA.
TELL ME.

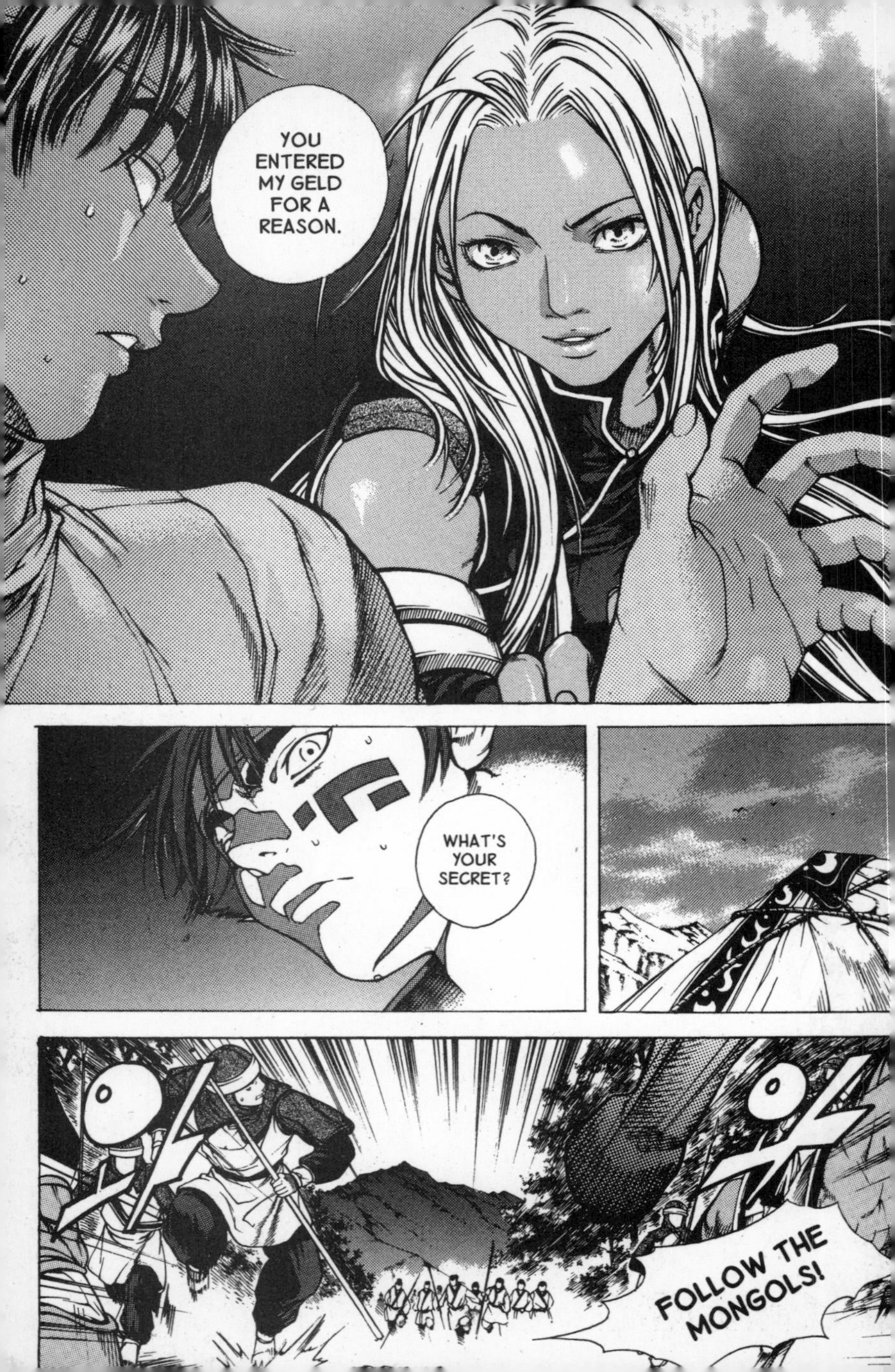
YOU ENTERED MY GELD FOR A REASON.
WHAT'S YOUR SECRET?
FOLLOW THE MONGOLS!

WE ARE ALMOST UPON THEM!

!

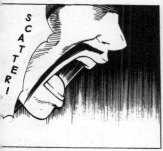

SCATTER!

!

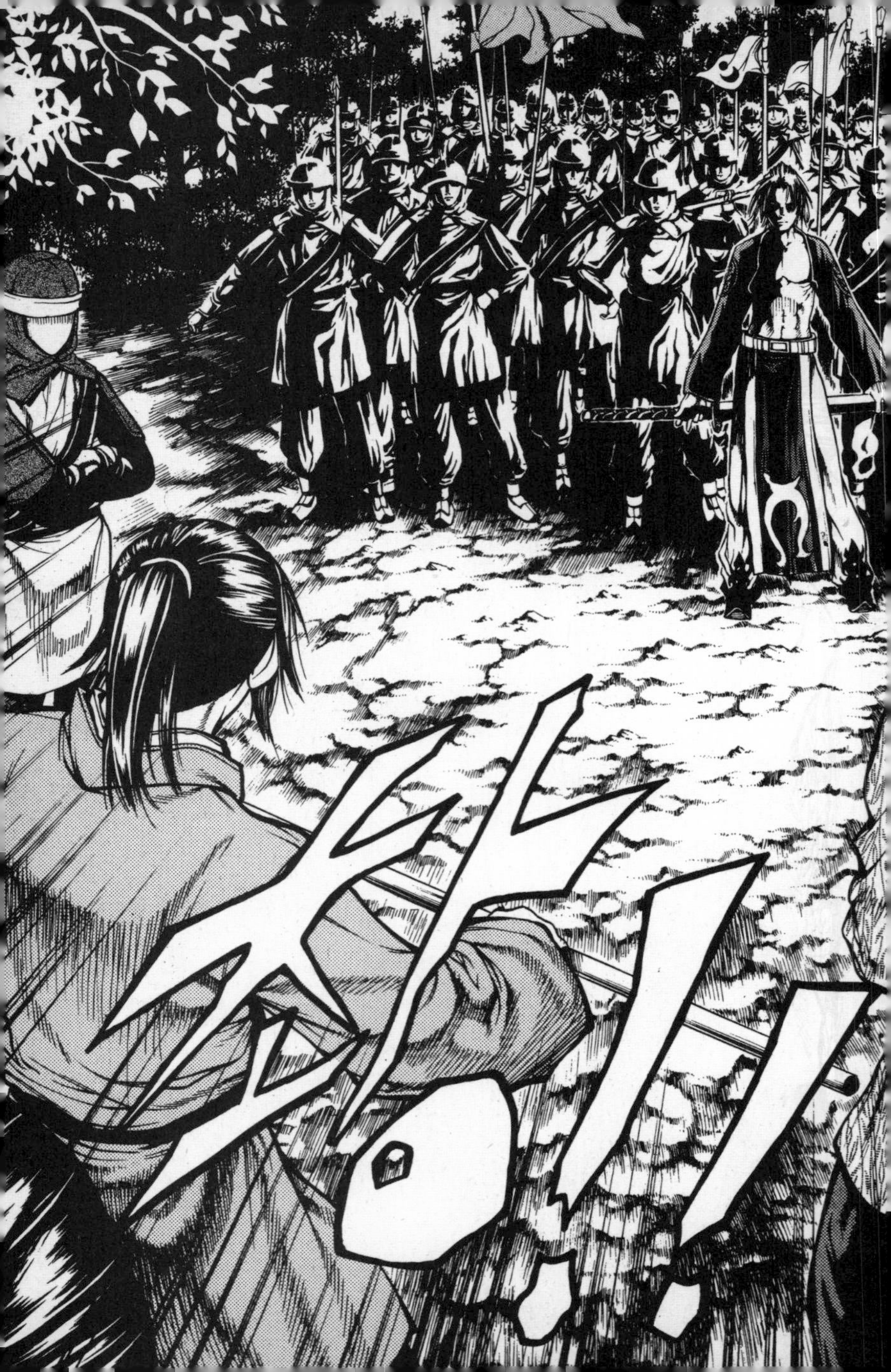

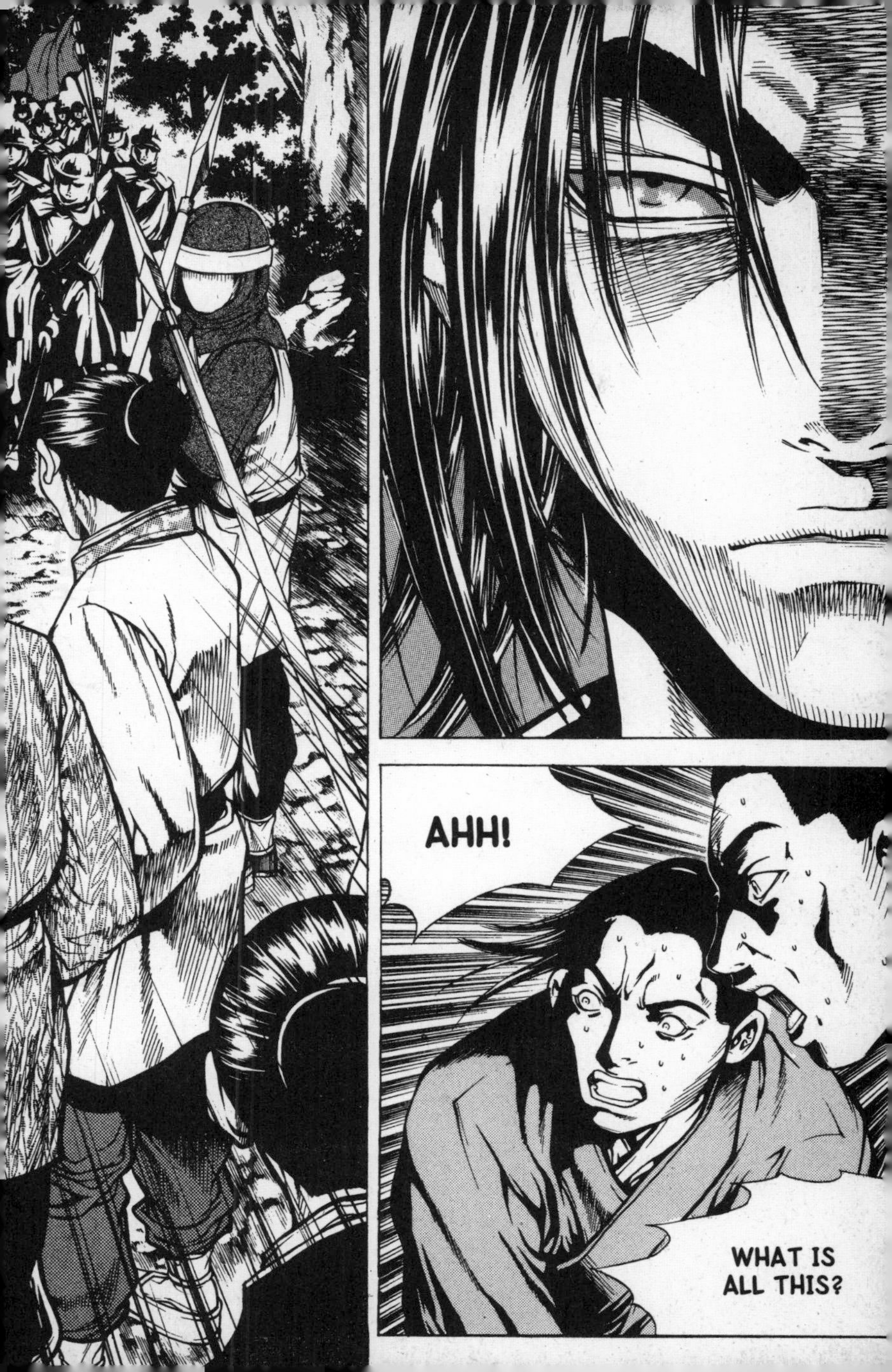
AHH!
WHAT IS ALL THIS?

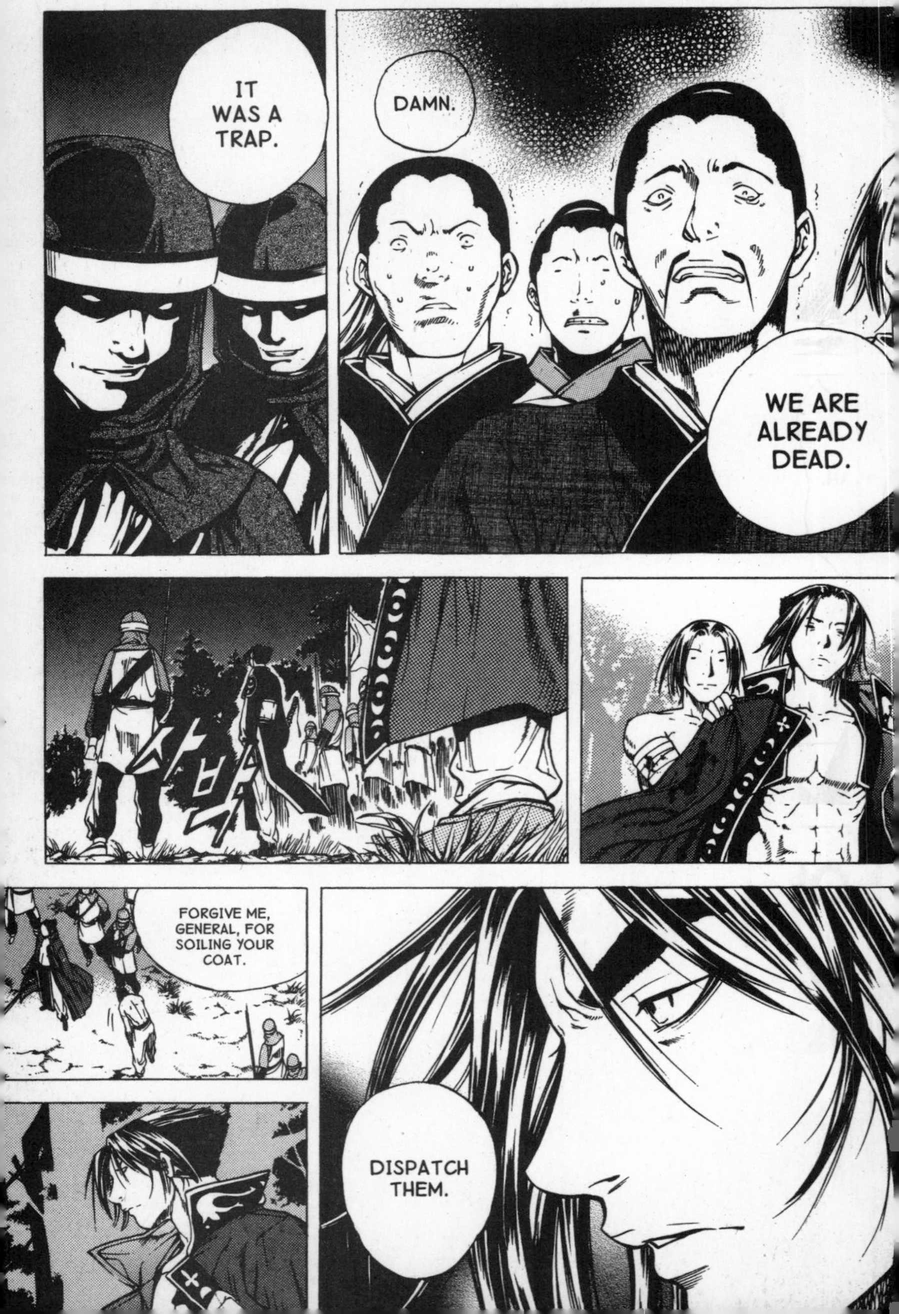
IT WAS A TRAP.
DAMN.
WE ARE ALREADY DEAD.
FORGIVE ME, GENERAL, FOR SOILING YOUR COAT.
DISPATCH THEM.

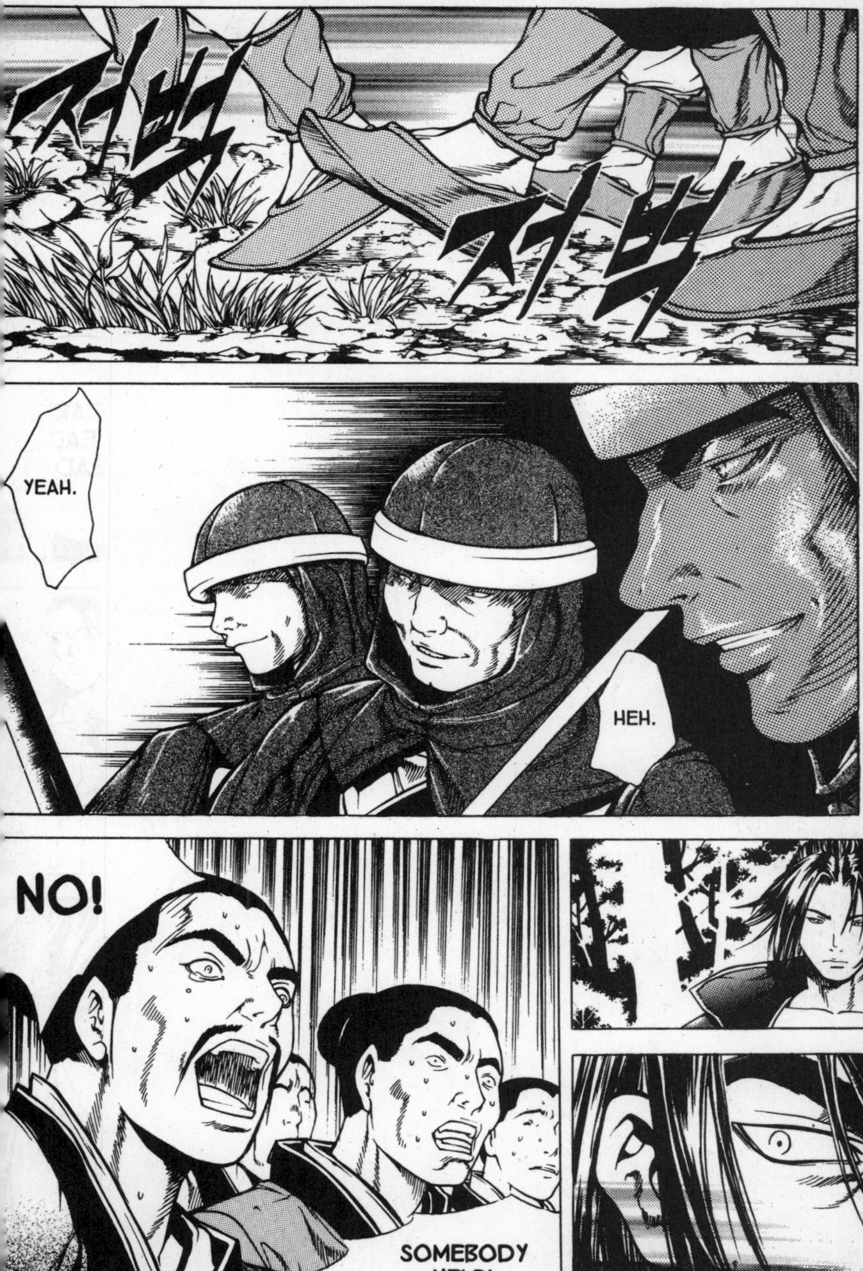
저벅
저벅
YEAH.
HEH.
NO!
SOMEBODY HELP!

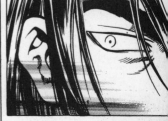

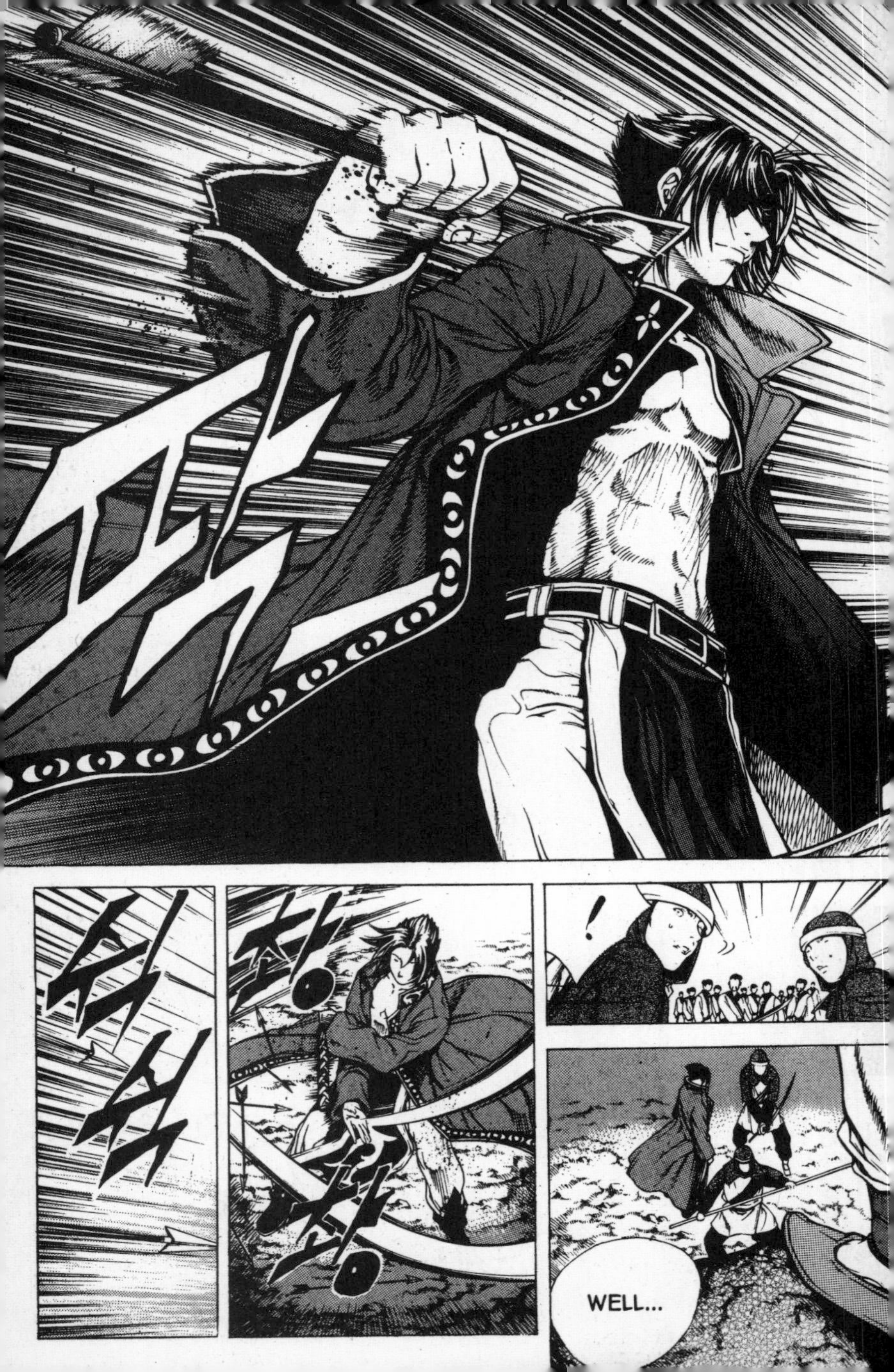
!
WELL...

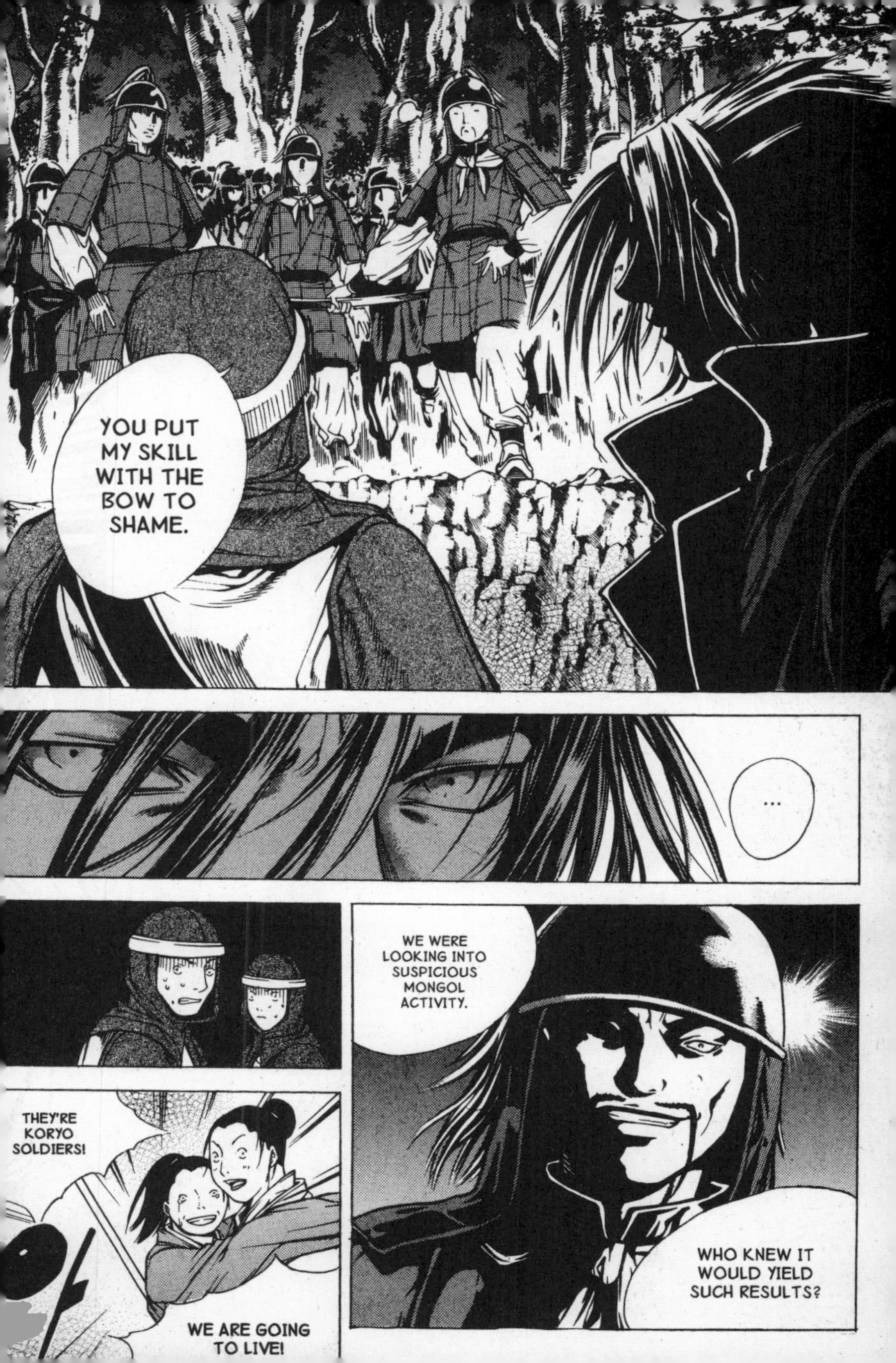
YOU PUT MY SKILL WITH THE BOW TO SHAME.
...
WE WERE LOOKING INTO SUSPICIOUS MONGOL ACTIVITY.
WHO KNEW IT WOULD YIELD SUCH RESULTS?
THEY'RE KORYO SOLDIERS!
WE ARE GOING TO LIVE!

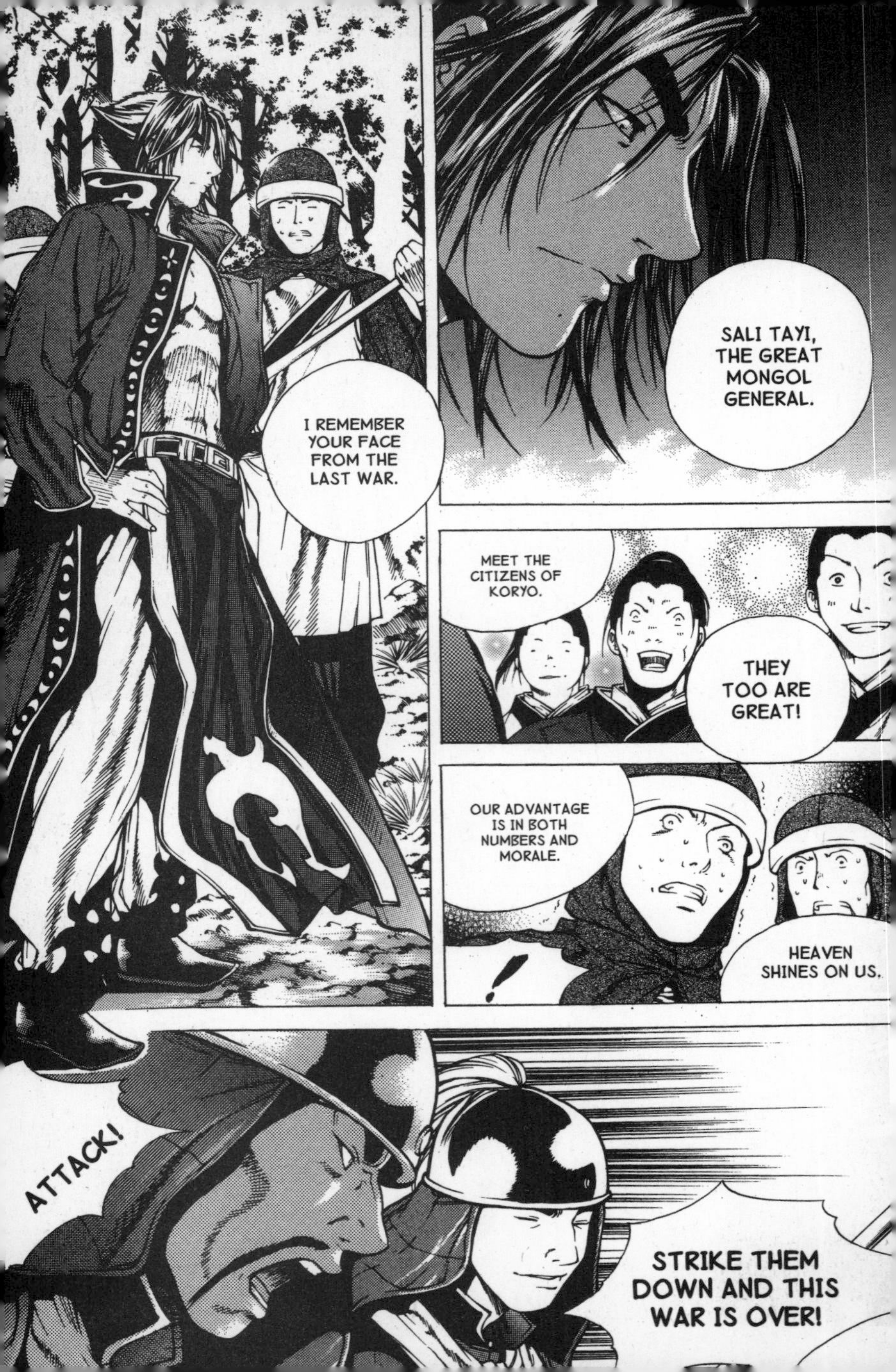
I REMEMBER YOUR FACE FROM THE LAST WAR.
SALI TAYI, THE GREAT MONGOL GENERAL.
MEET THE CITIZENS OF KORYO.
THEY TOO ARE GREAT!
OUR ADVANTAGE IS IN BOTH NUMBERS AND MORALE.
HEAVEN SHINES ON US.
!
ATTACK!
STRIKE THEM DOWN AND THIS WAR IS OVER!

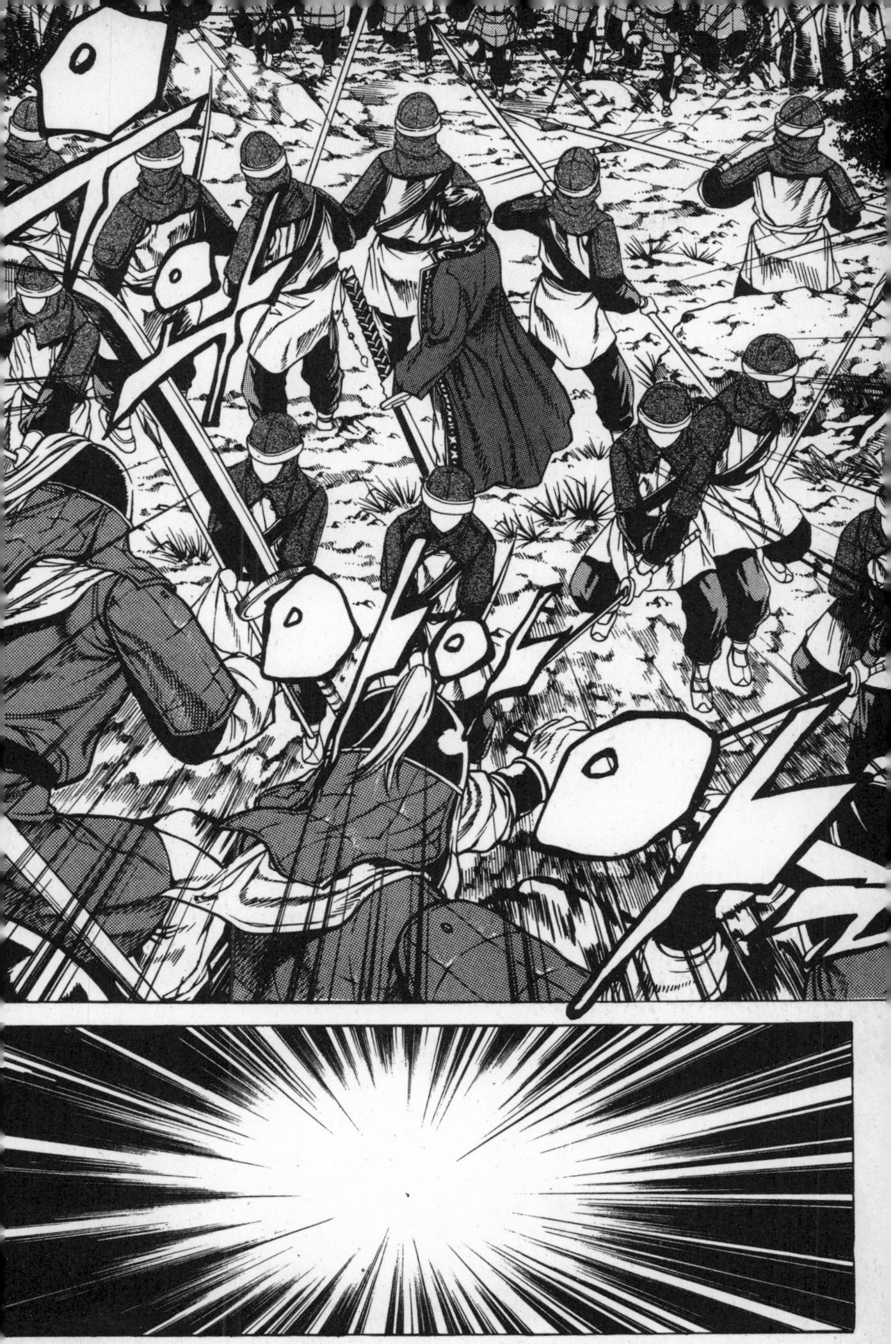

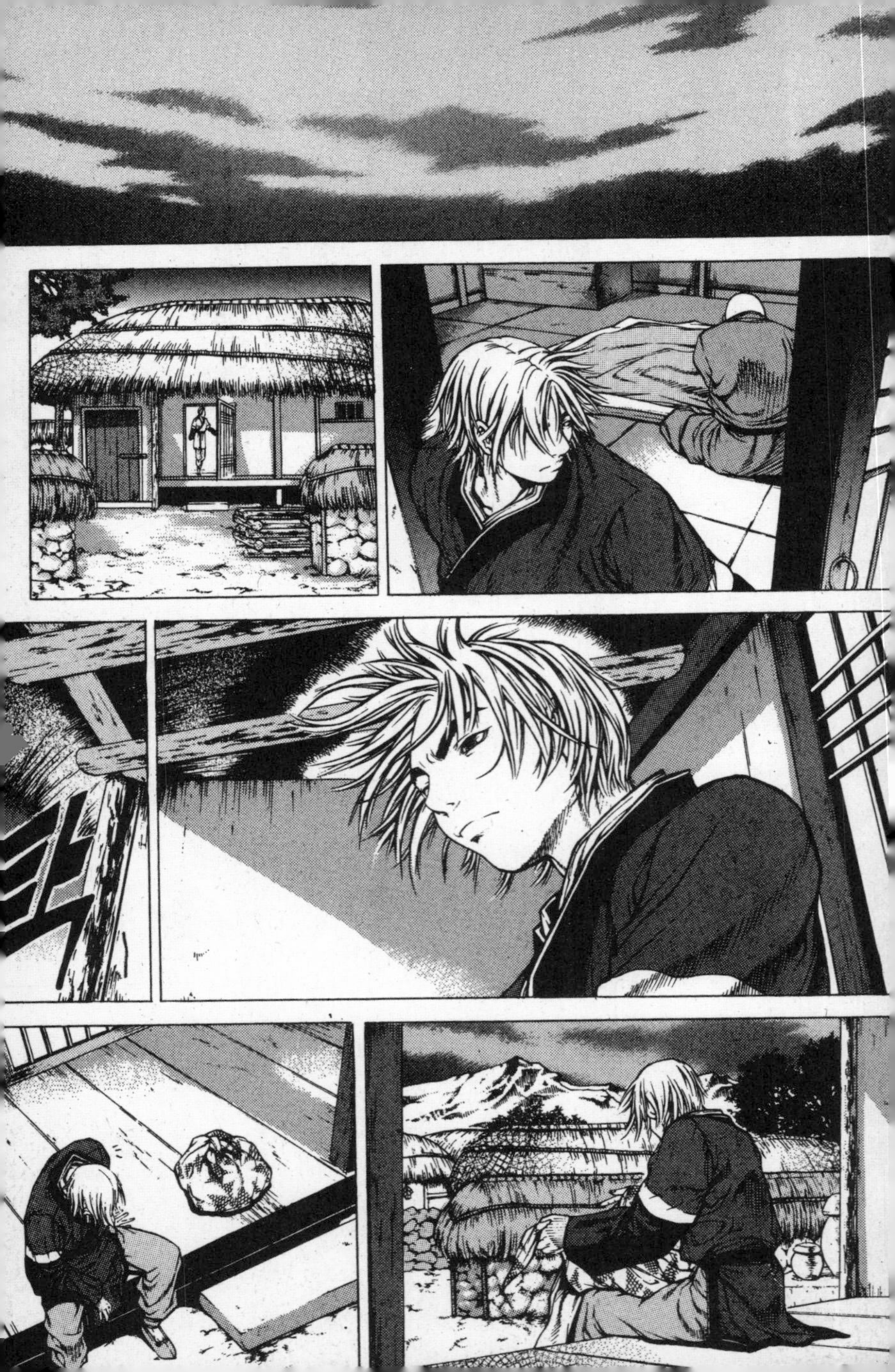

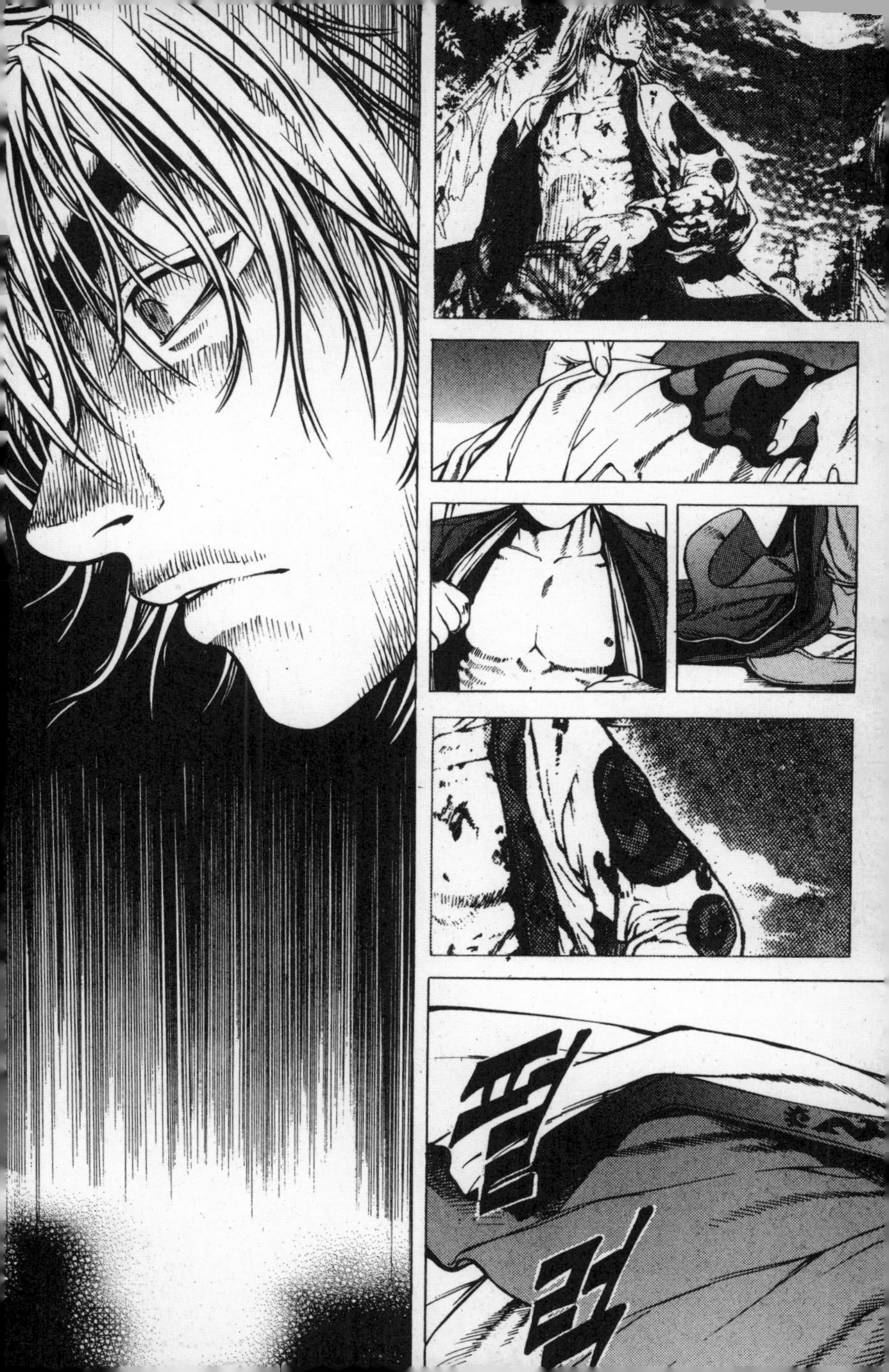
펄럭

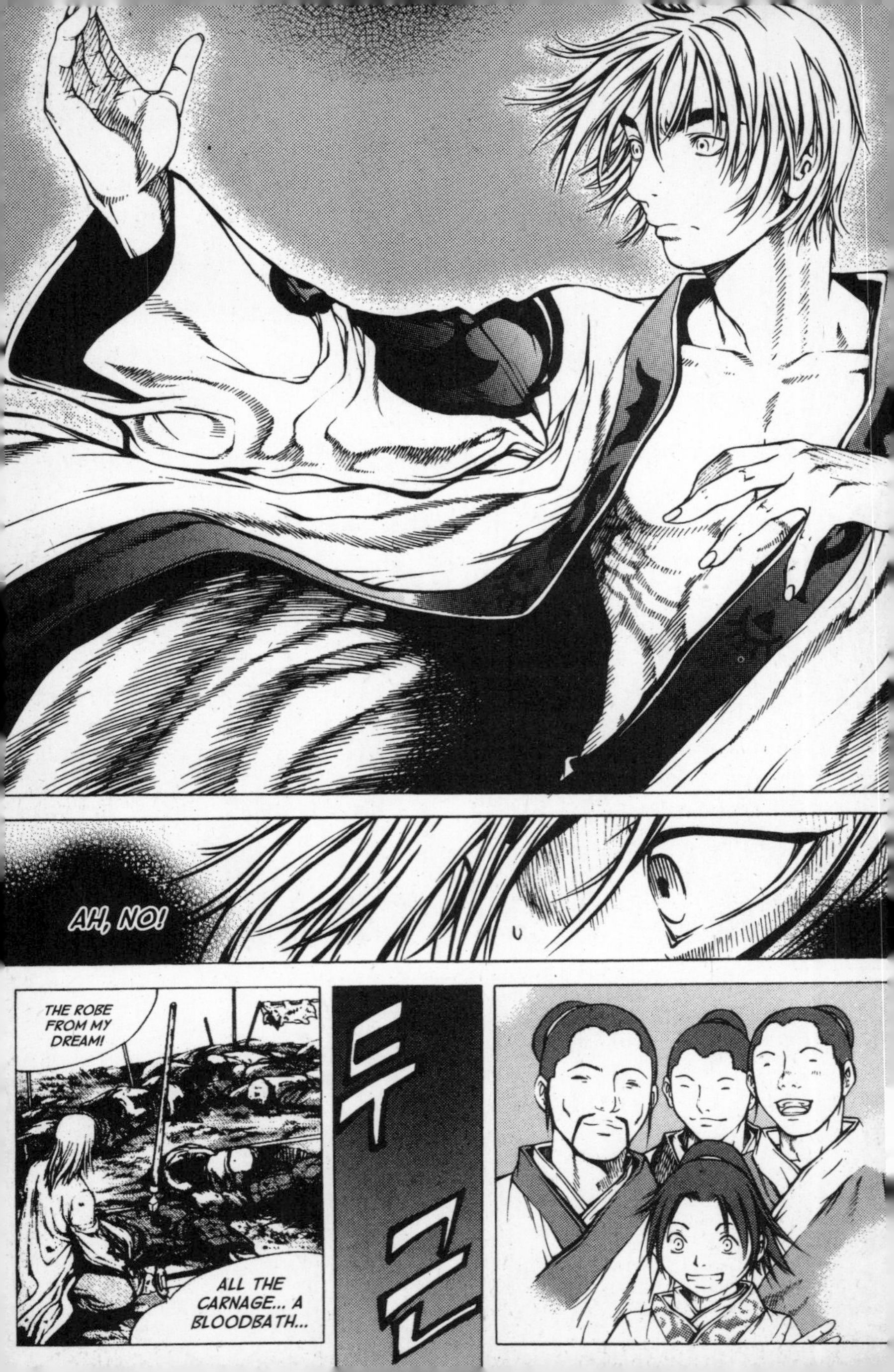
AH, NO!
THE ROBE FROM MY DREAM!
ALL THE CARNAGE... A BLOODBATH...

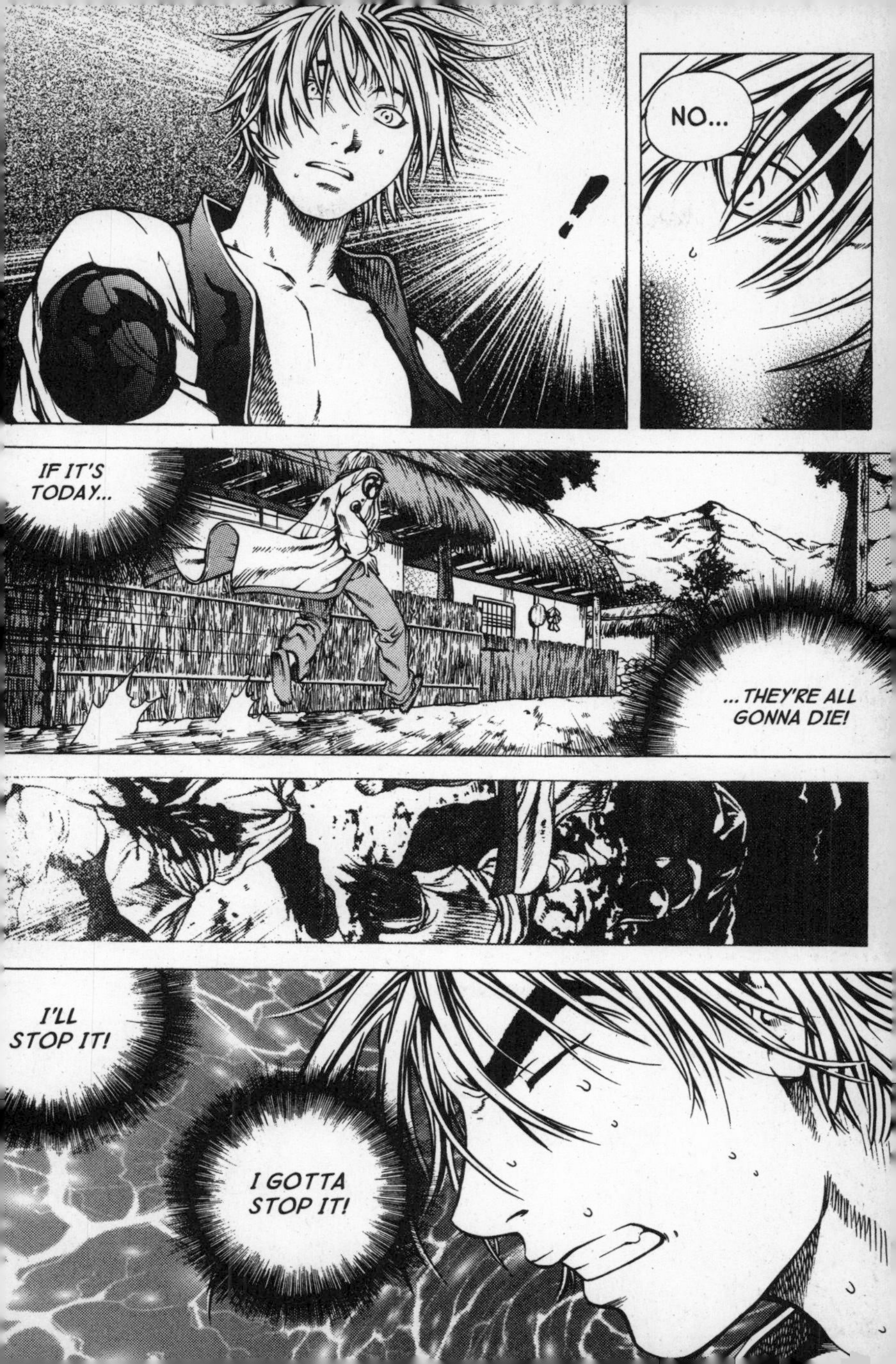
NO...
IF IT'S TODAY...
...THEY'RE ALL GONNA DIE!
I'LL STOP IT!
I GOTTA STOP IT!

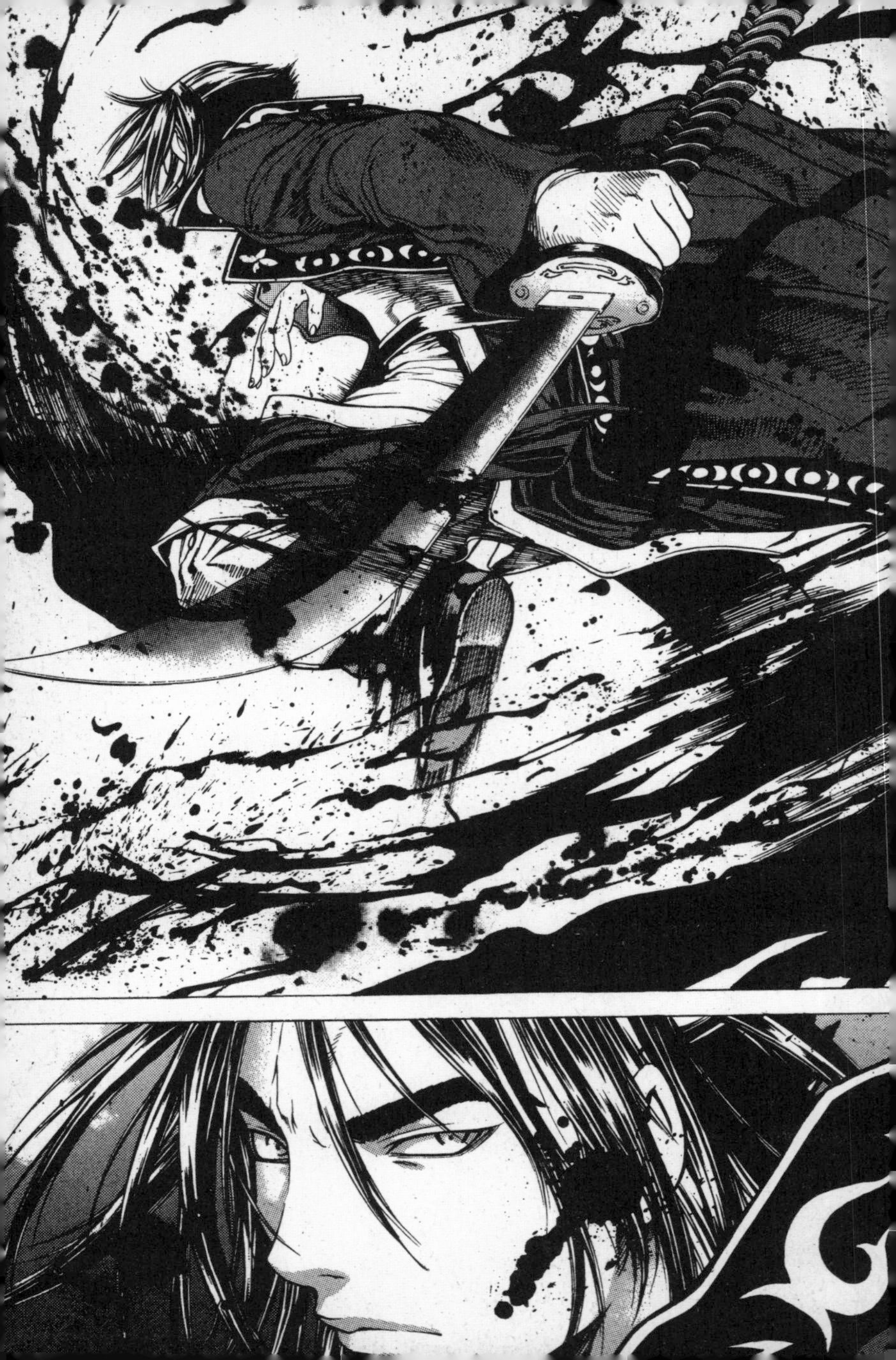

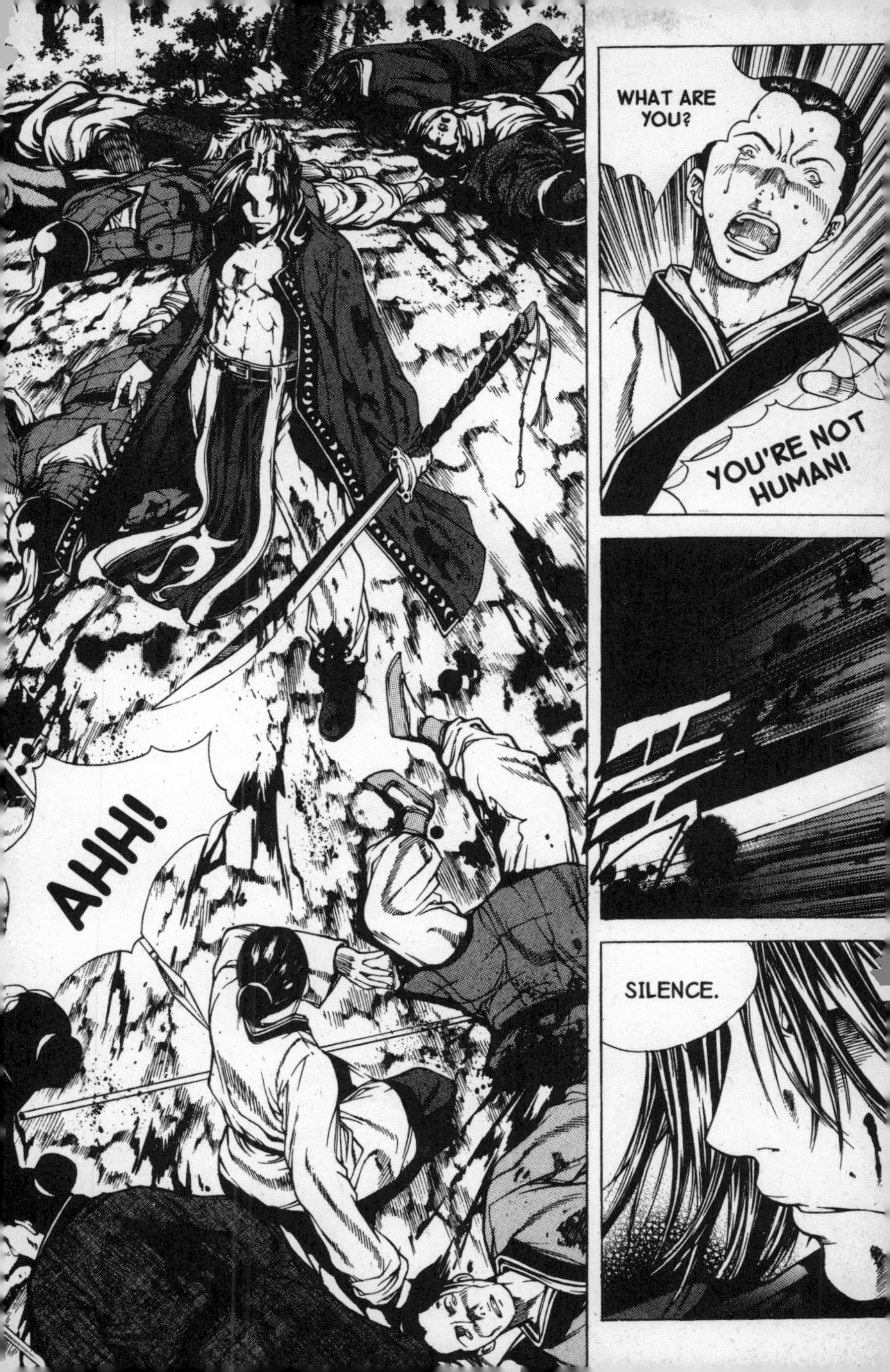
AHH!
WHAT ARE YOU?
YOU'RE NOT HUMAN!
SILENCE.

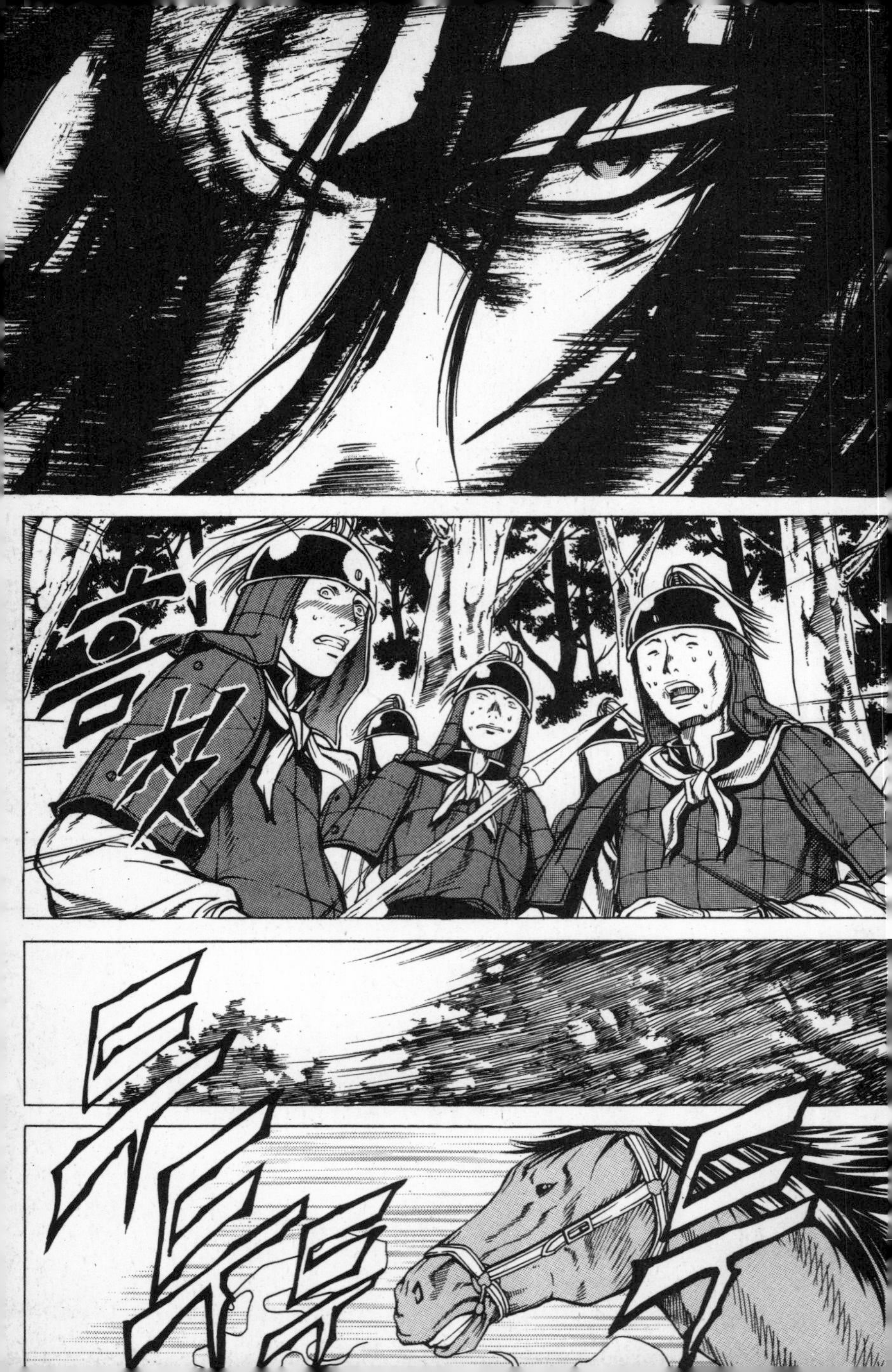

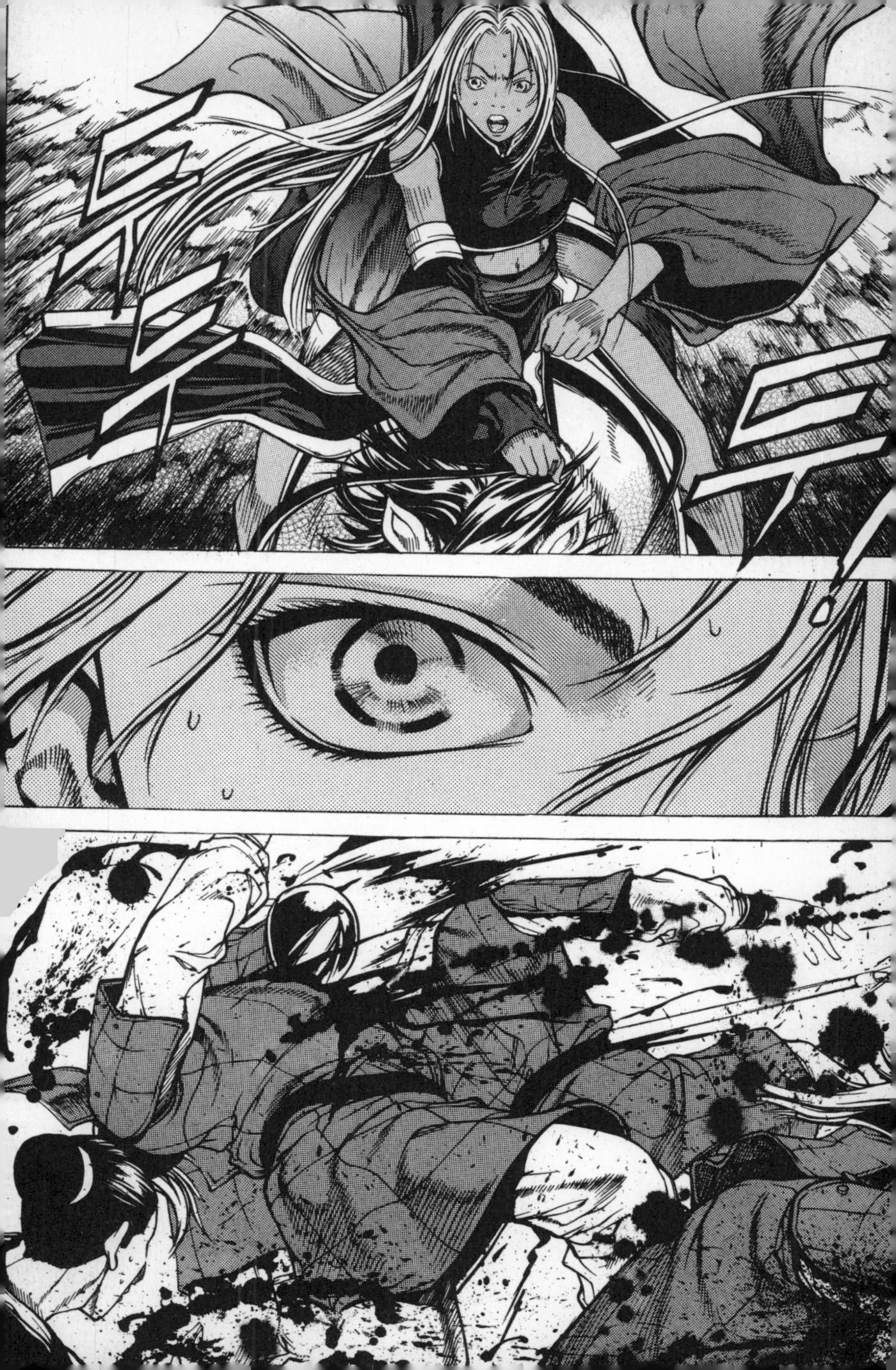

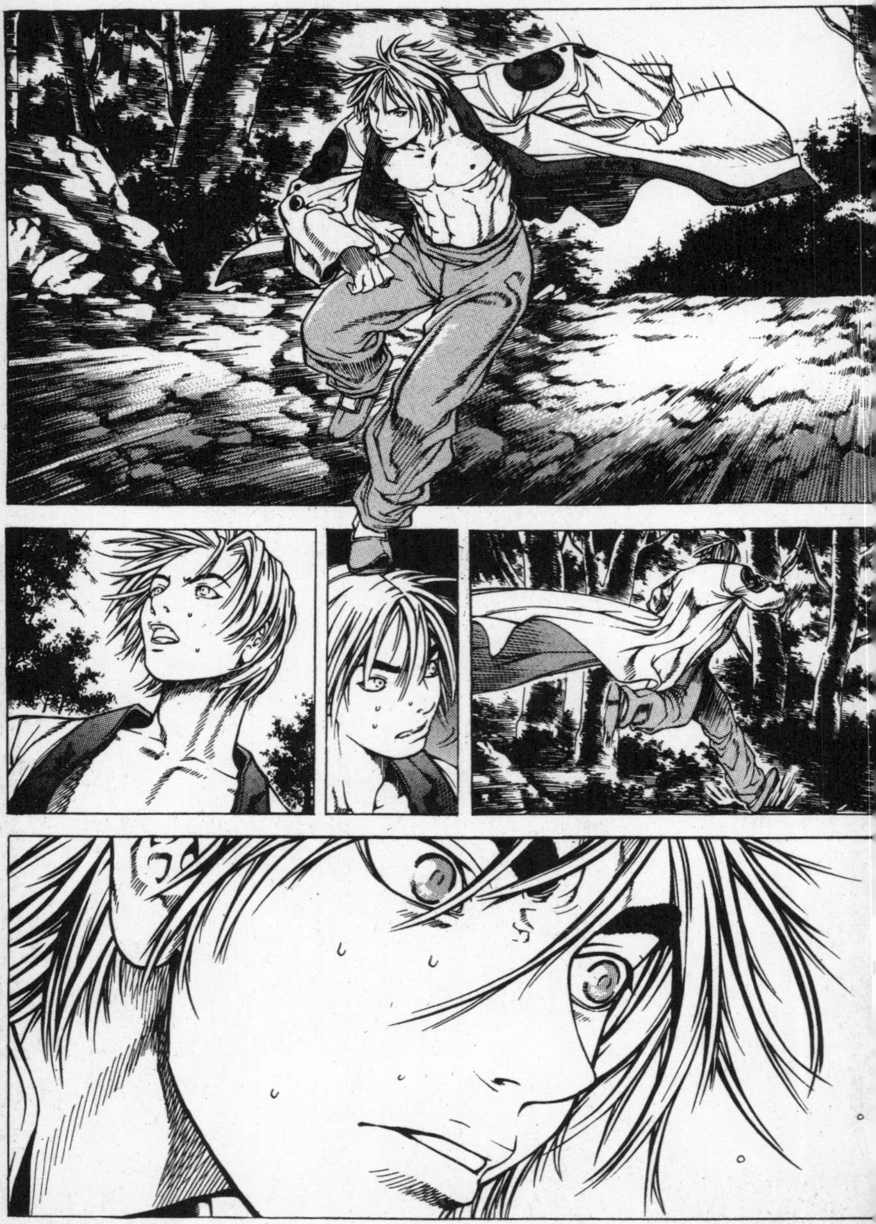

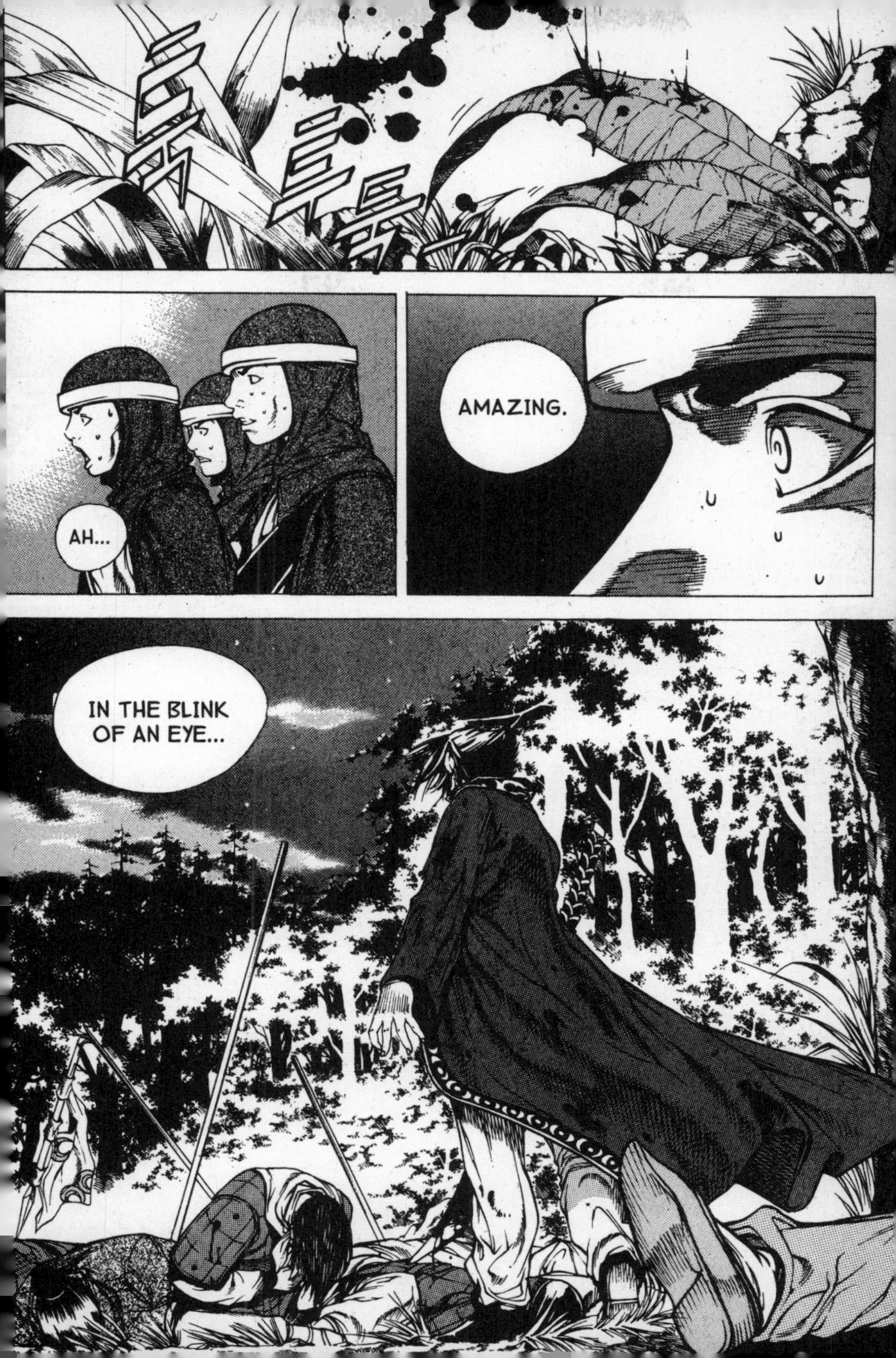
AH...
AMAZING.
IN THE BLINK OF AN EYE...

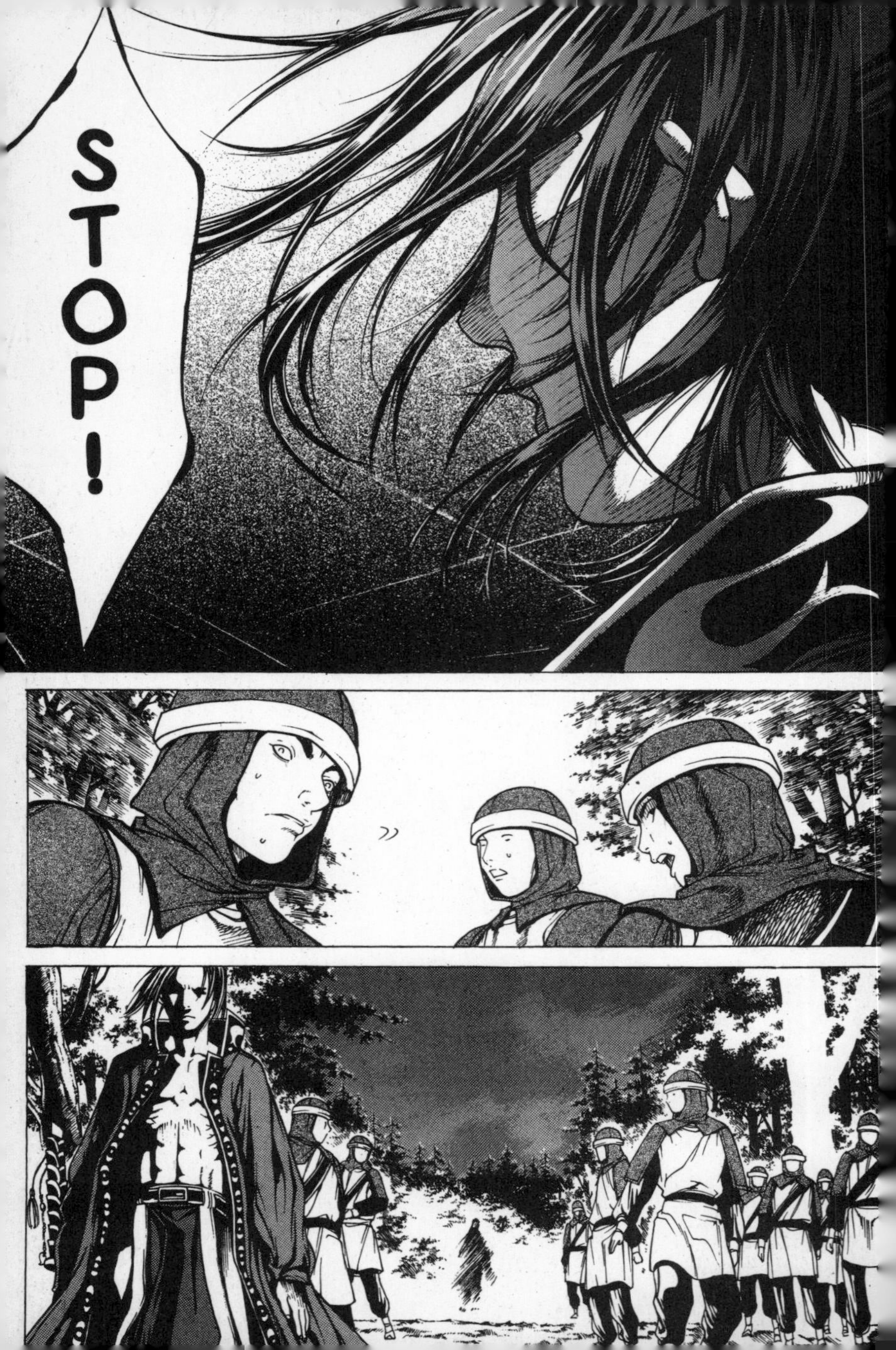
STOP!

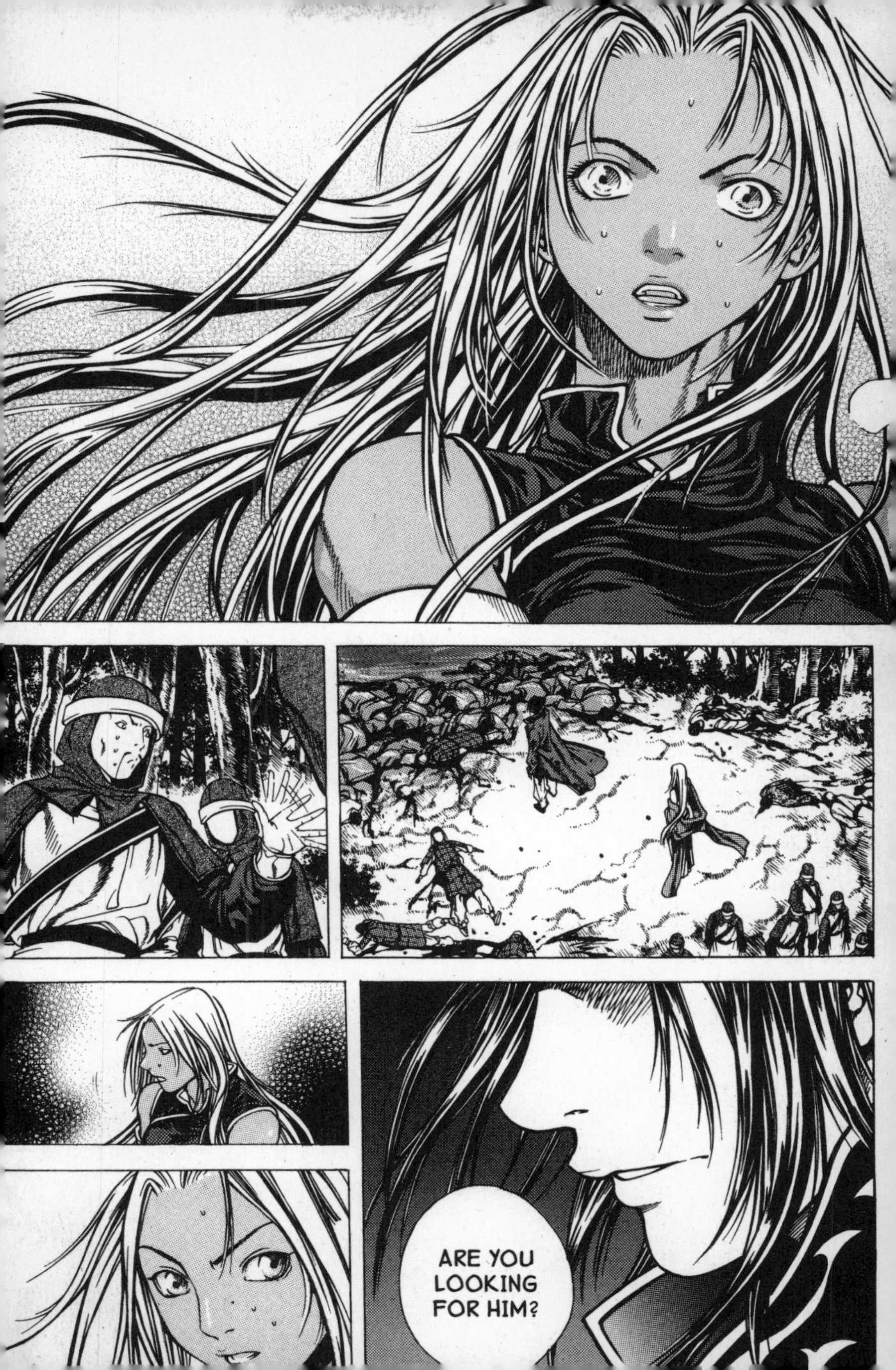
ARE YOU LOOKING FOR HIM?

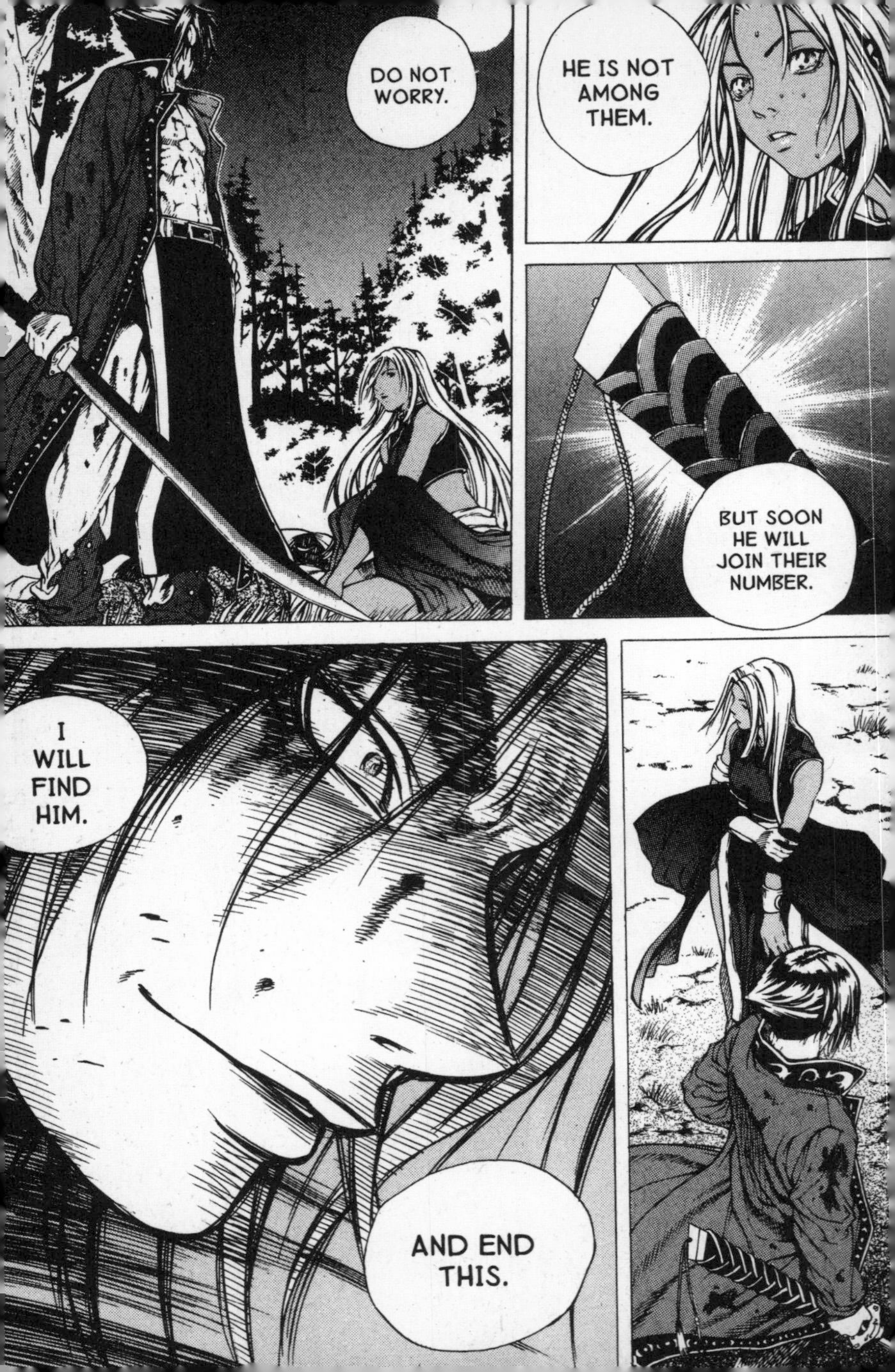
DO NOT WORRY.
HE IS NOT AMONG THEM.
BUT SOON HE WILL JOIN THEIR NUMBER.
I WILL FIND HIM.
AND END THIS.

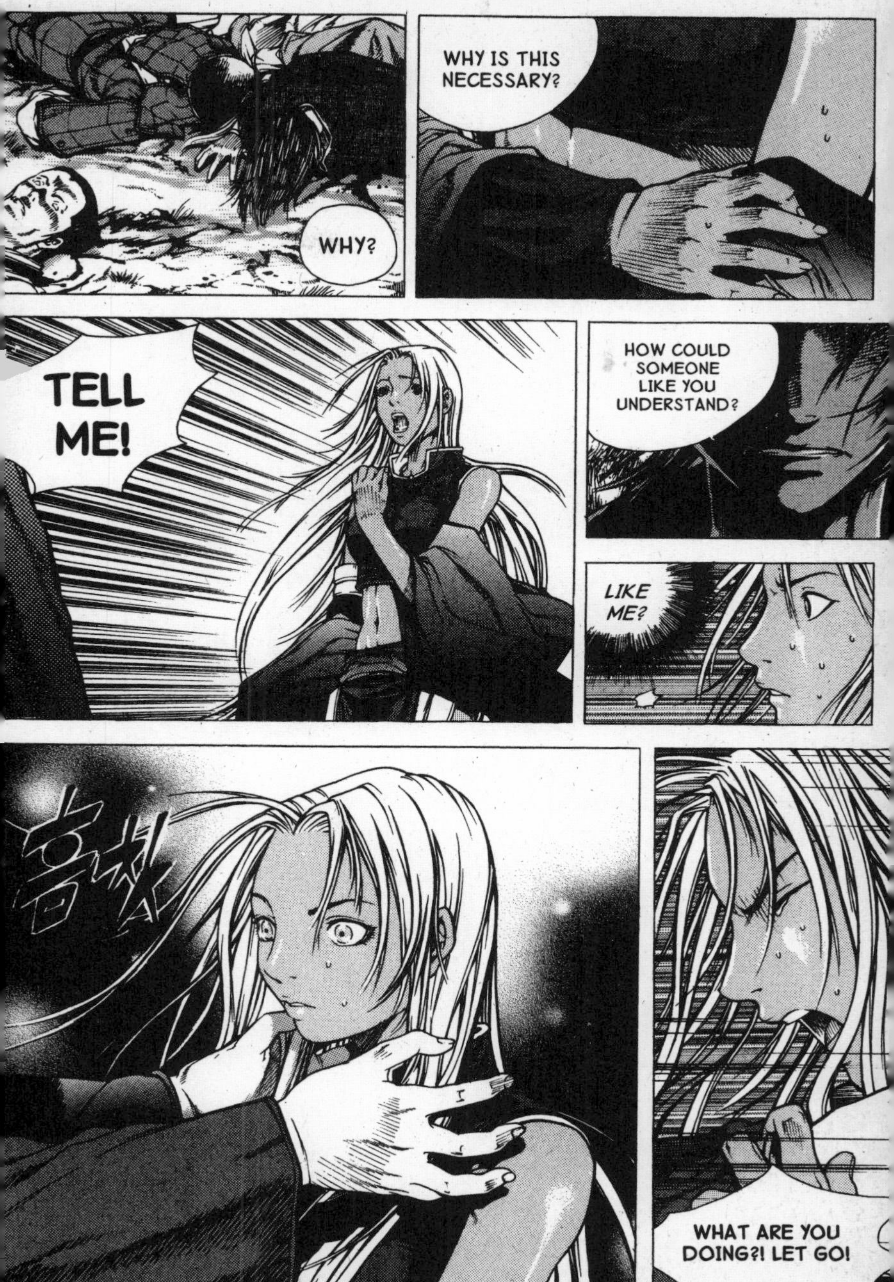
WHY?
WHY IS THIS NECESSARY?
TELL ME!
HOW COULD SOMEONE LIKE YOU UNDERSTAND?
LIKE ME?
WHAT ARE YOU DOING?! LET GO!

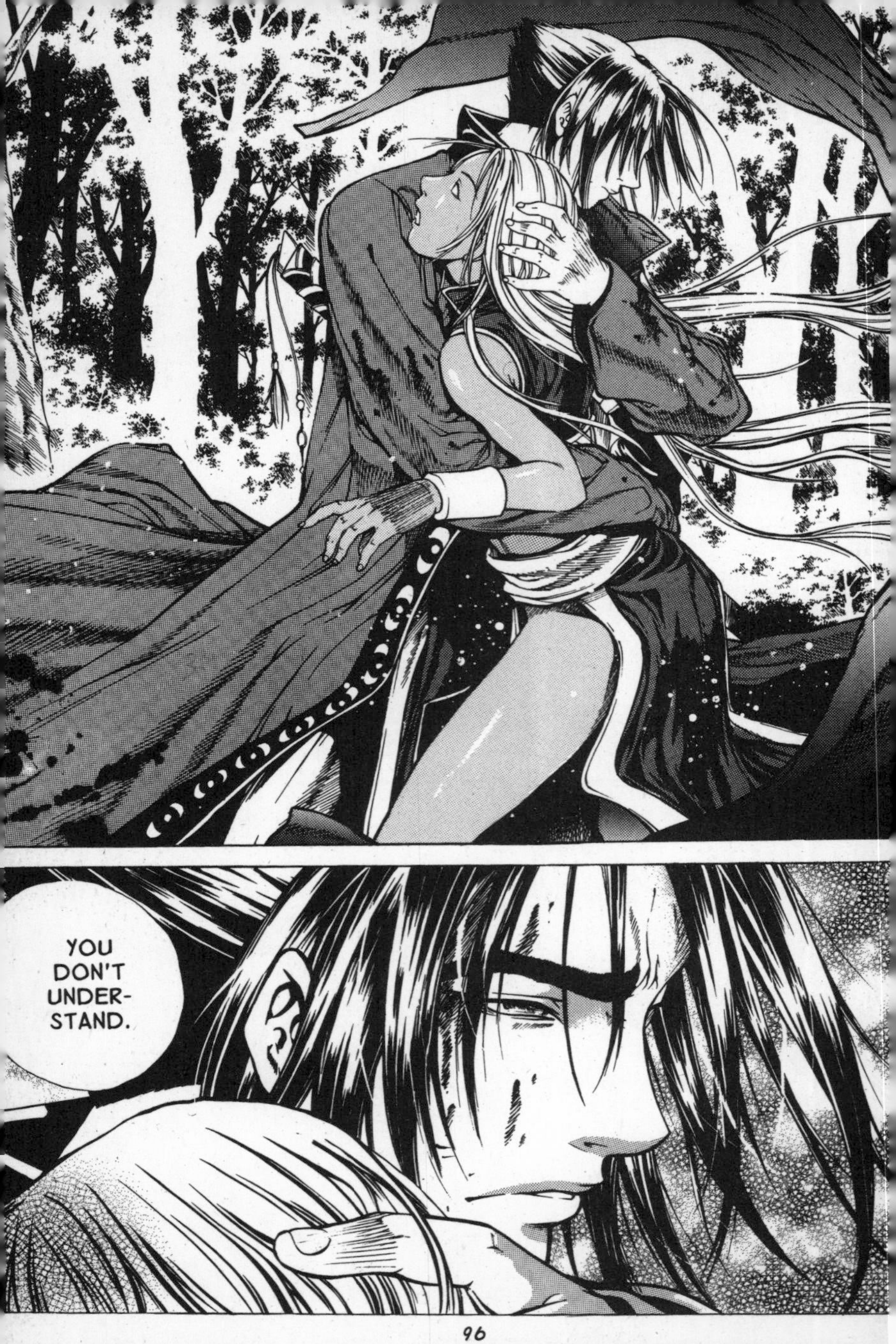
YOU DON'T UNDER-STAND.

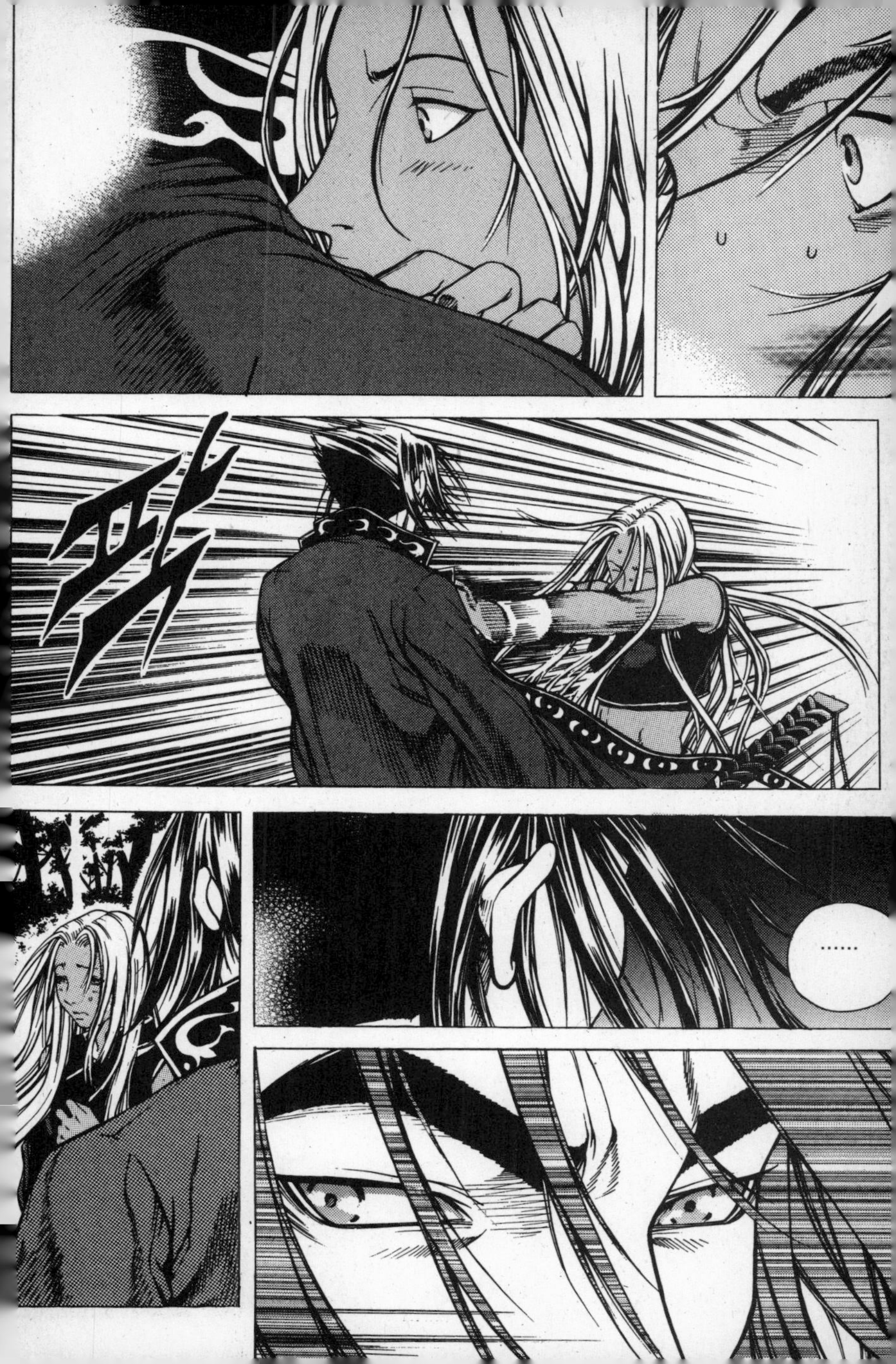
......

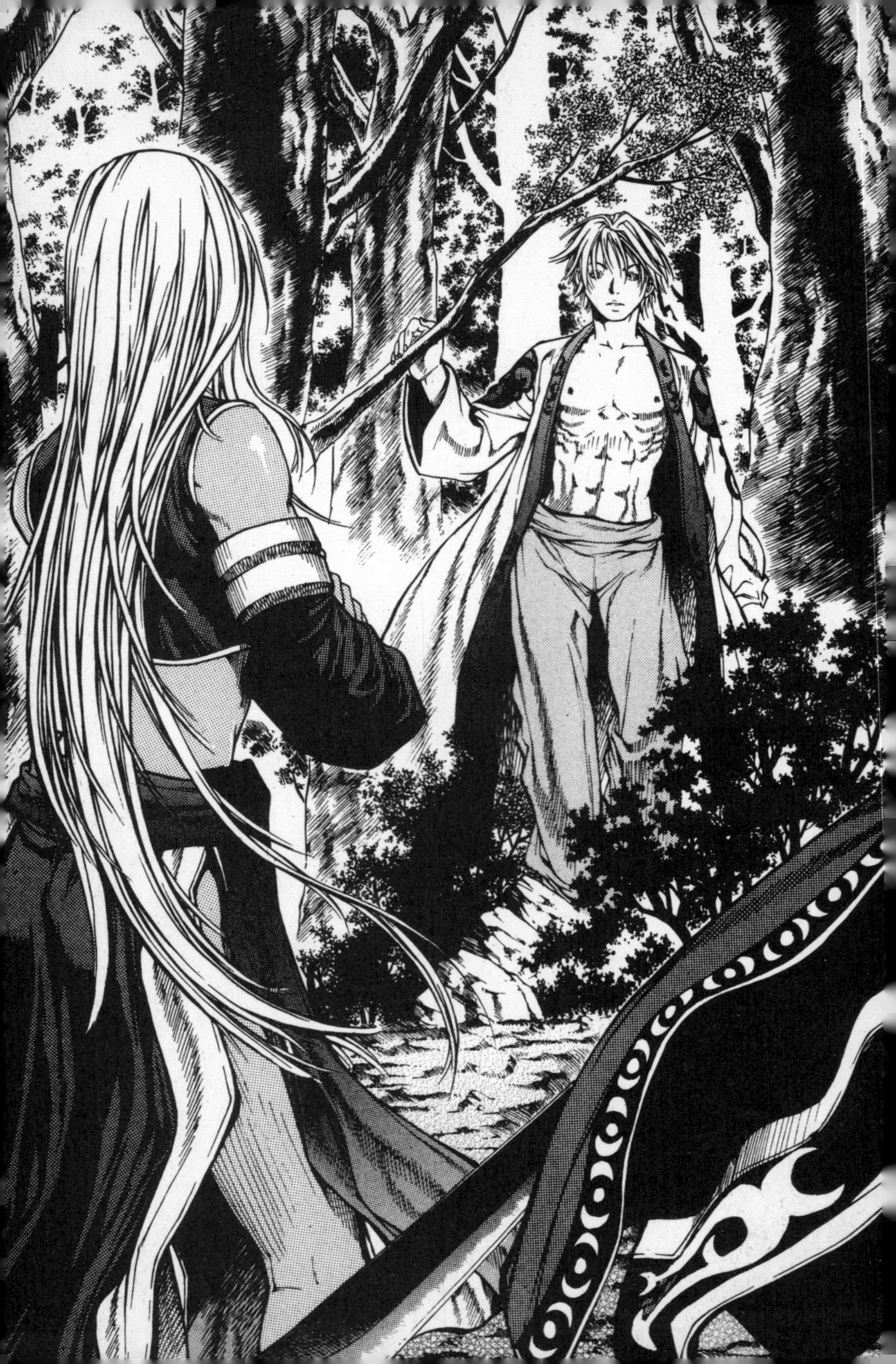

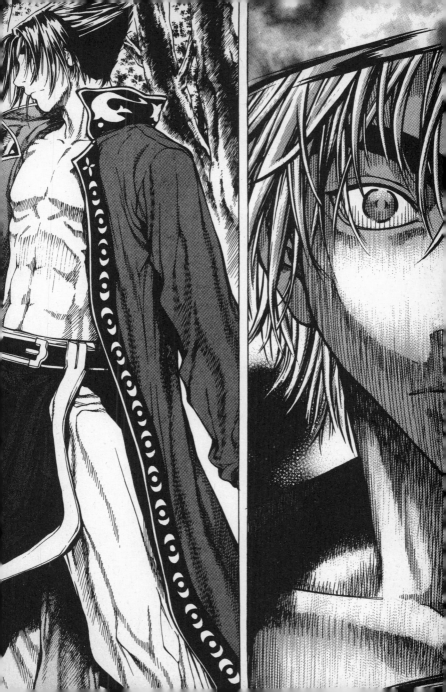

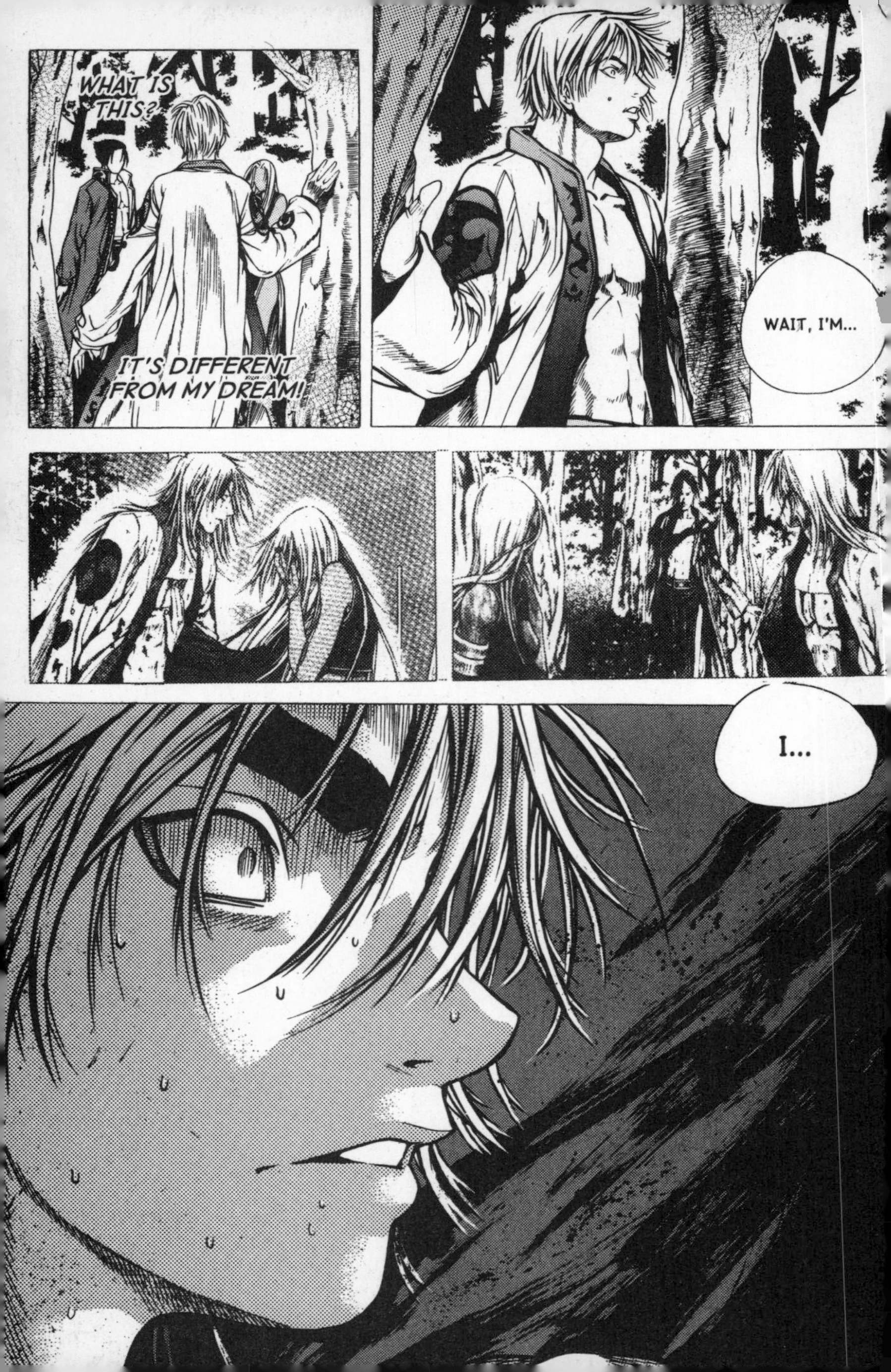
WHAT IS THIS?
IT'S DIFFERENT FROM MY DREAM!
WAIT, I'M...
I...

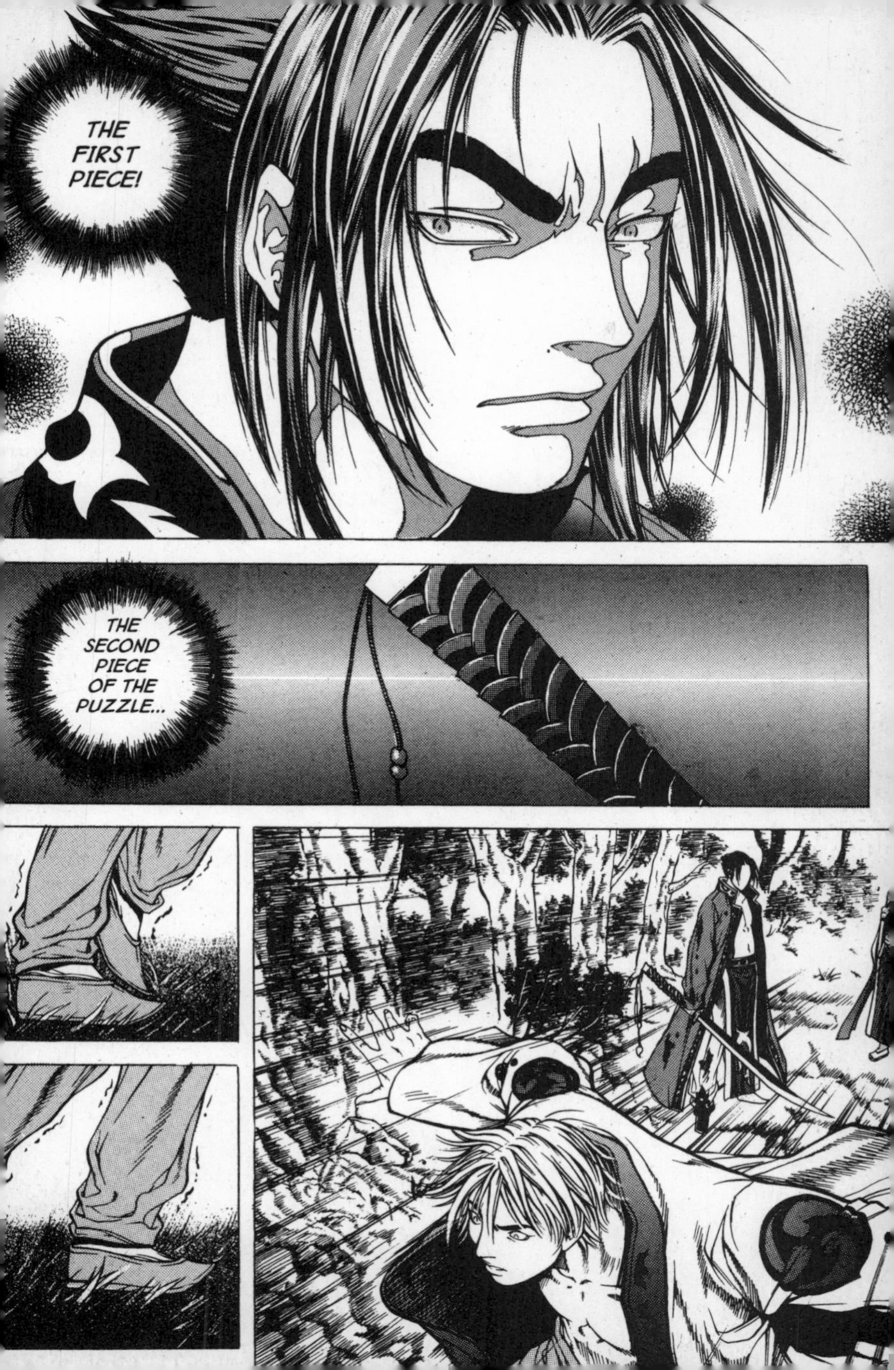
THE FIRST PIECE!
THE SECOND PIECE OF THE PUZZLE...

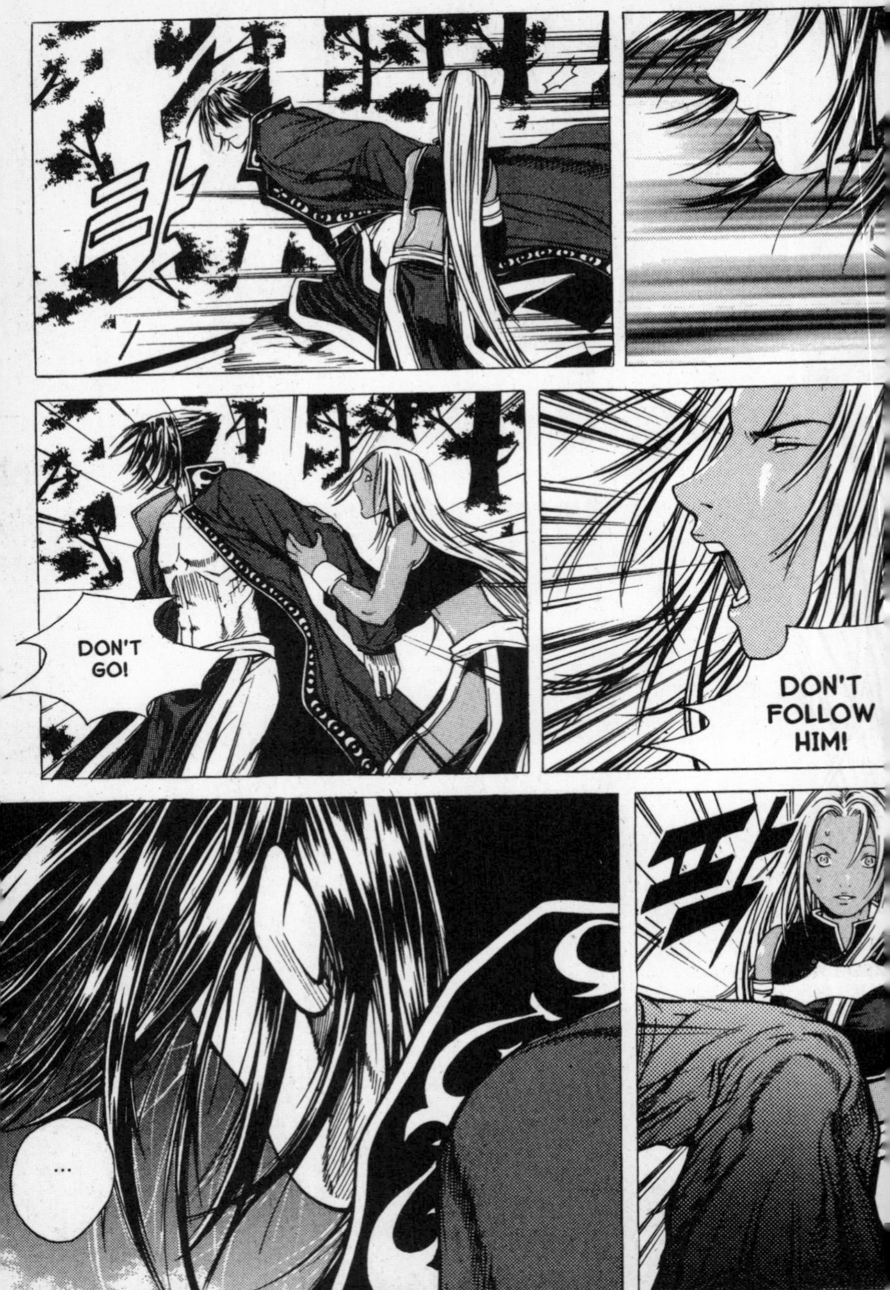
DON'T GO!
DON'T FOLLOW HIM!
...

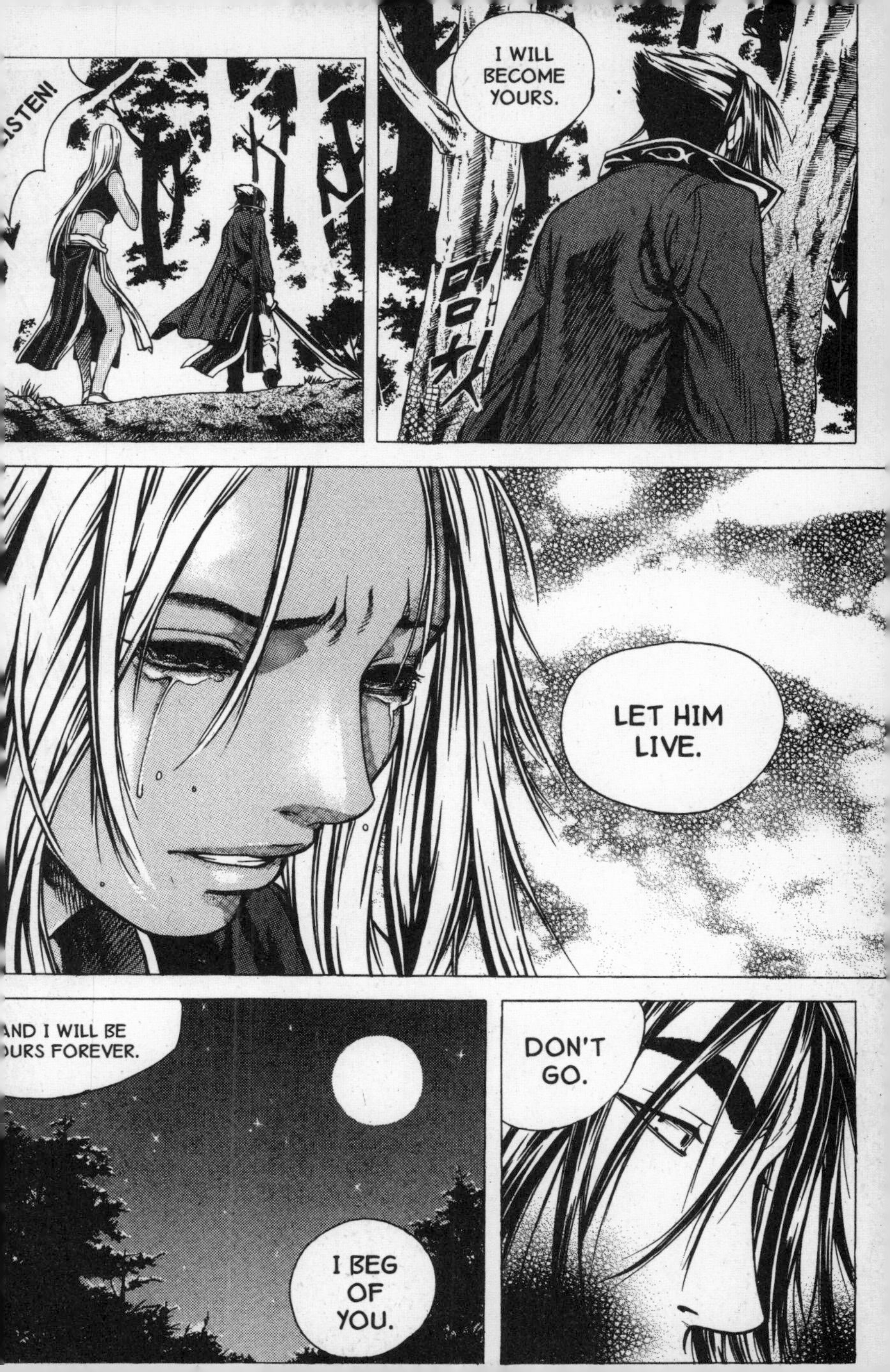
ISTEN!
I WILL BECOME YOURS.
멈칫
LET HIM LIVE.
AND I WILL BE OURS FOREVER.
I BEG OF YOU.
DON'T GO.

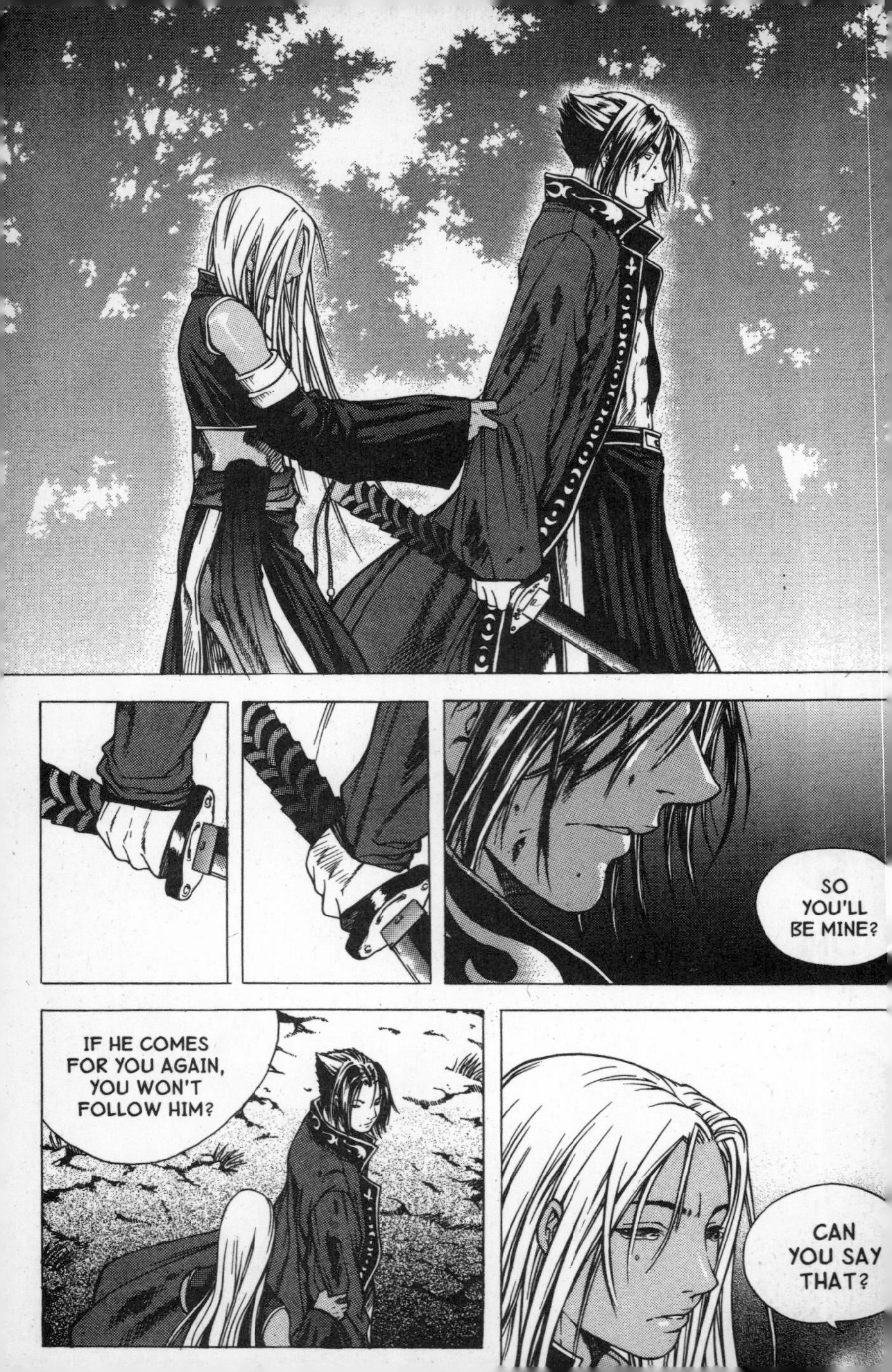
SO YOU'LL BE MINE?
IF HE COMES FOR YOU AGAIN, YOU WON'T FOLLOW HIM?
CAN YOU SAY THAT?

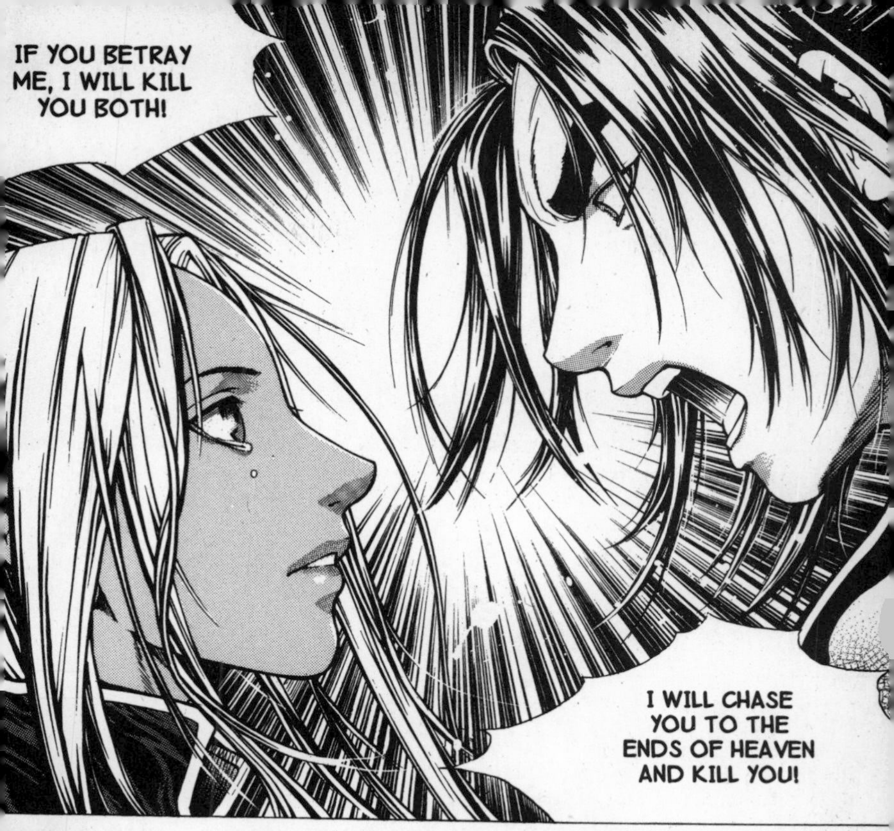
IF YOU BETRAY ME, I WILL KILL YOU BOTH!
I WILL CHASE YOU TO THE ENDS OF HEAVEN AND KILL YOU!
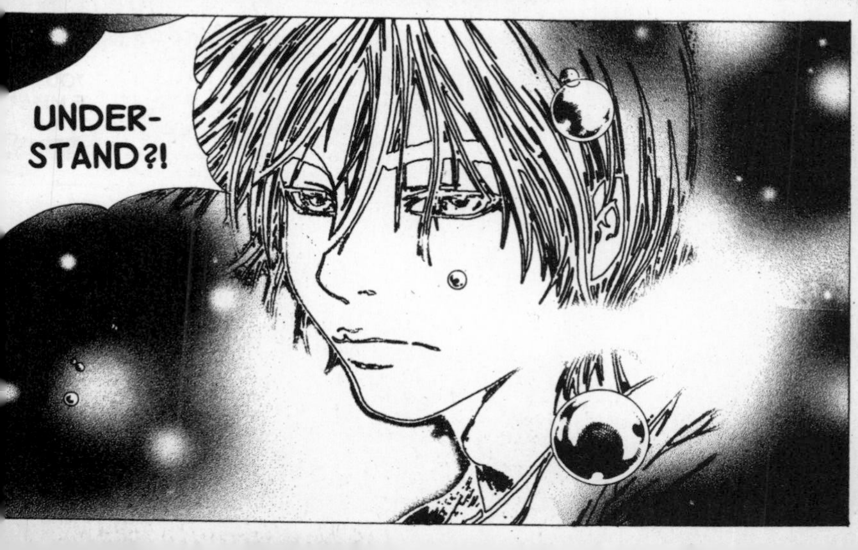
UNDER-STAND?!

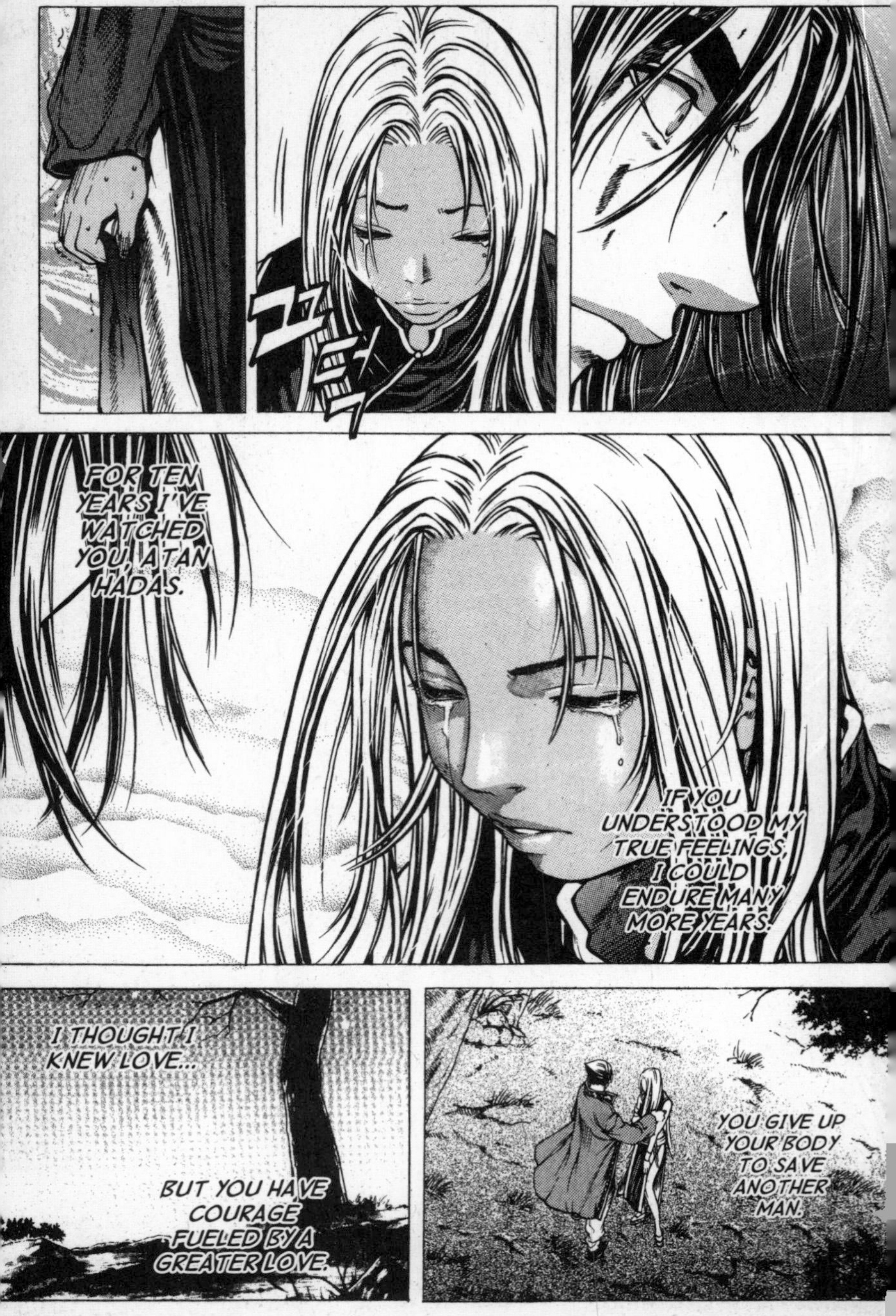
FOR TEN YEARS I'VE WATCHED YOU, ATAN HADAS.
IF YOU UNDERSTOOD MY TRUE FEELINGS, I COULD ENDURE MANY MORE YEARS.
I THOUGHT I KNEW LOVE...
BUT YOU HAVE COURAGE FUELED BY A GREATER LOVE.
YOU GIVE UP YOUR BODY TO SAVE ANOTHER MAN.

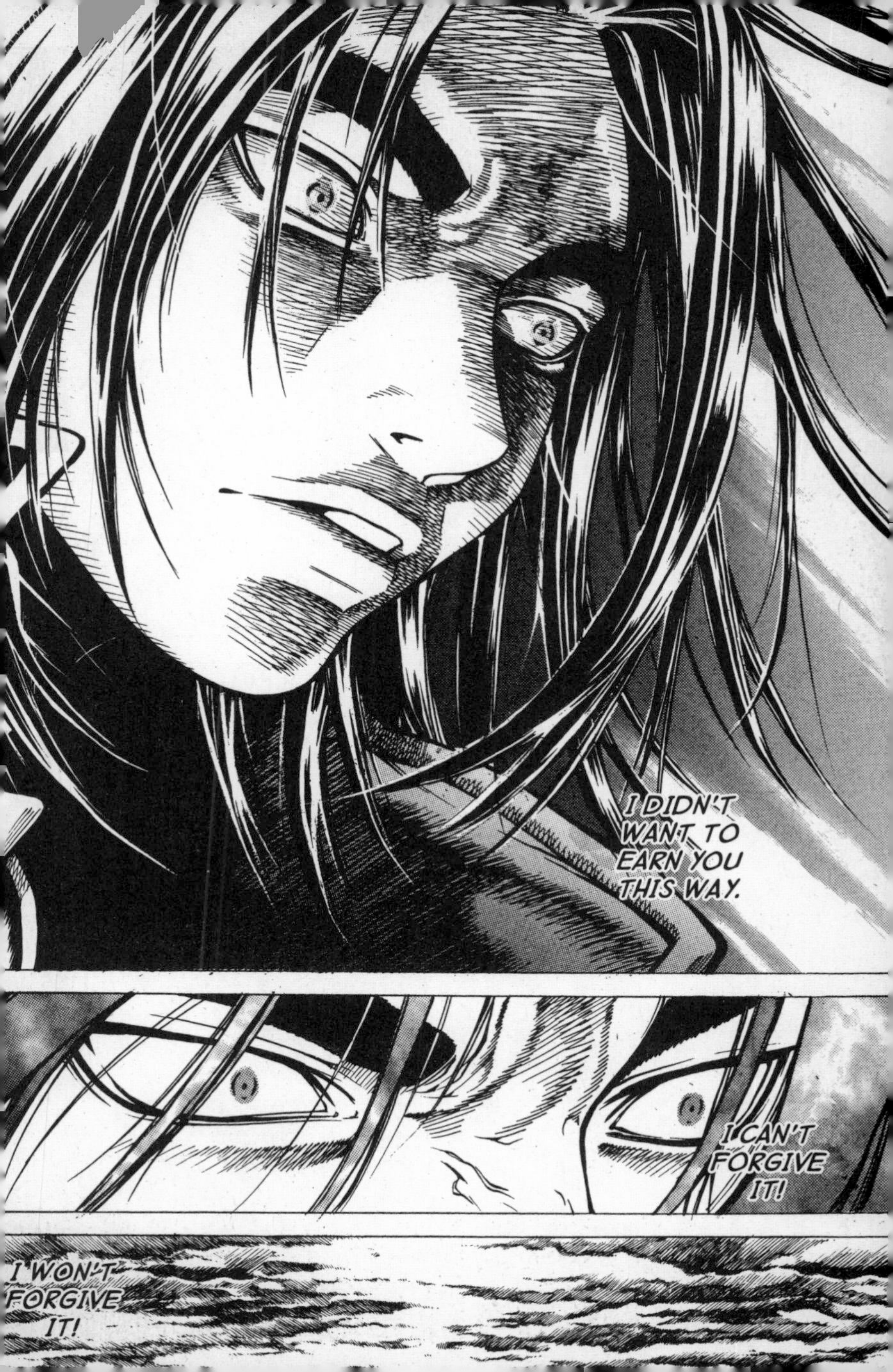
I DIDN'T WANT TO EARN YOU THIS WAY.
I CAN'T FORGIVE IT!
I WON'T FORGIVE IT!

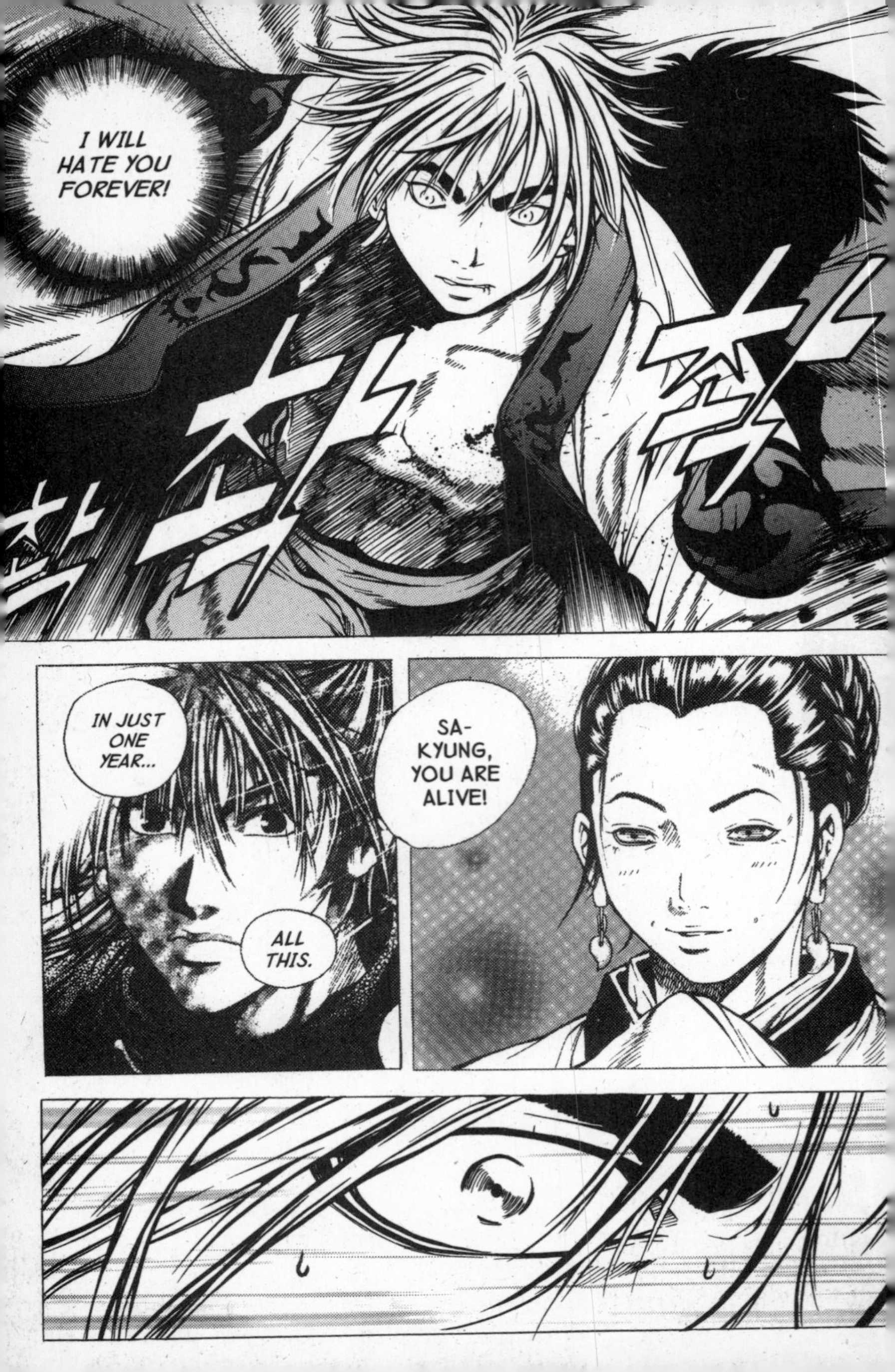

I WILL HATE YOU FOREVER!
IN JUST ONE YEAR...
ALL THIS.
SA-KYUNG, YOU ARE ALIVE!

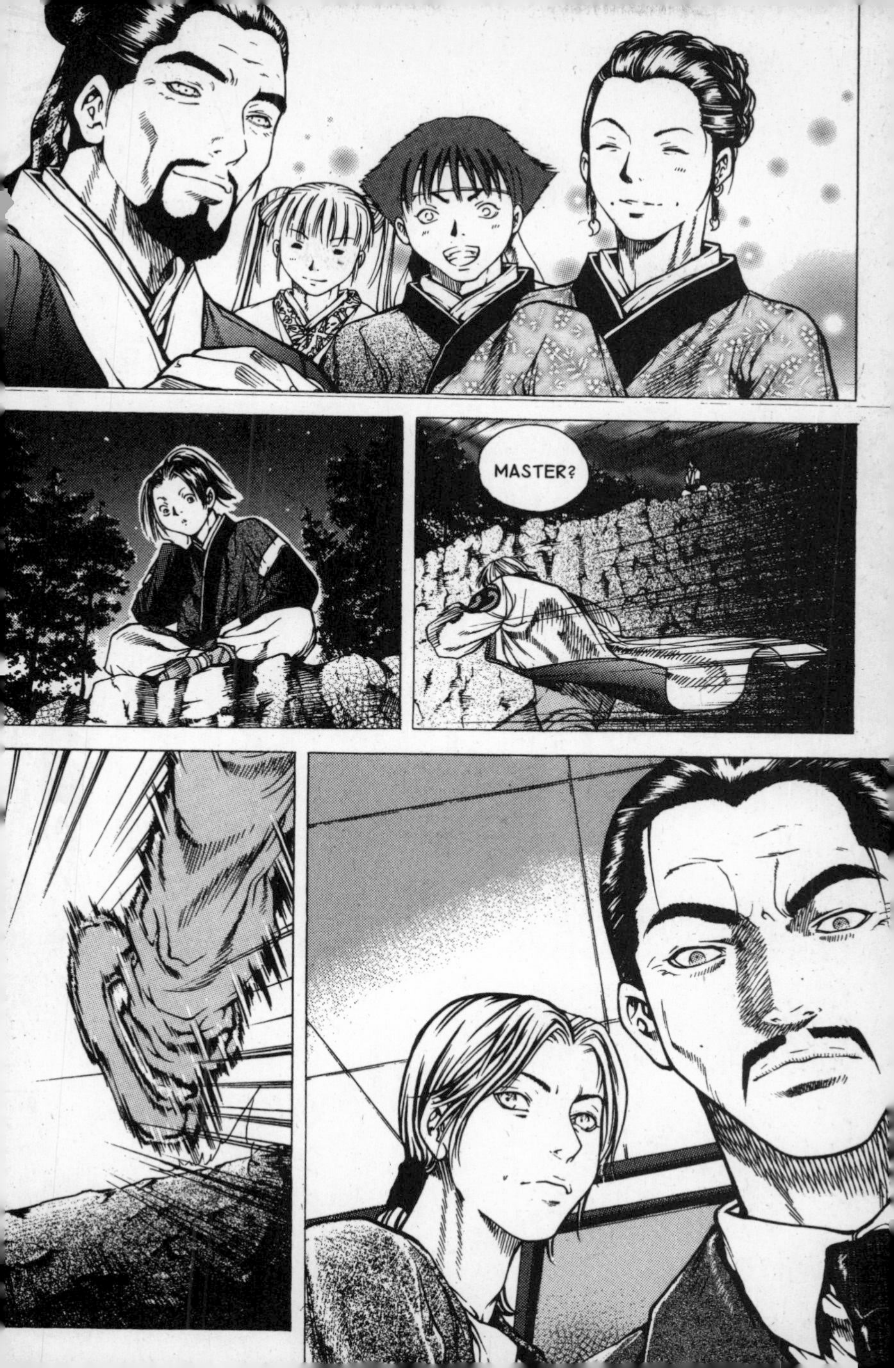
MASTER?

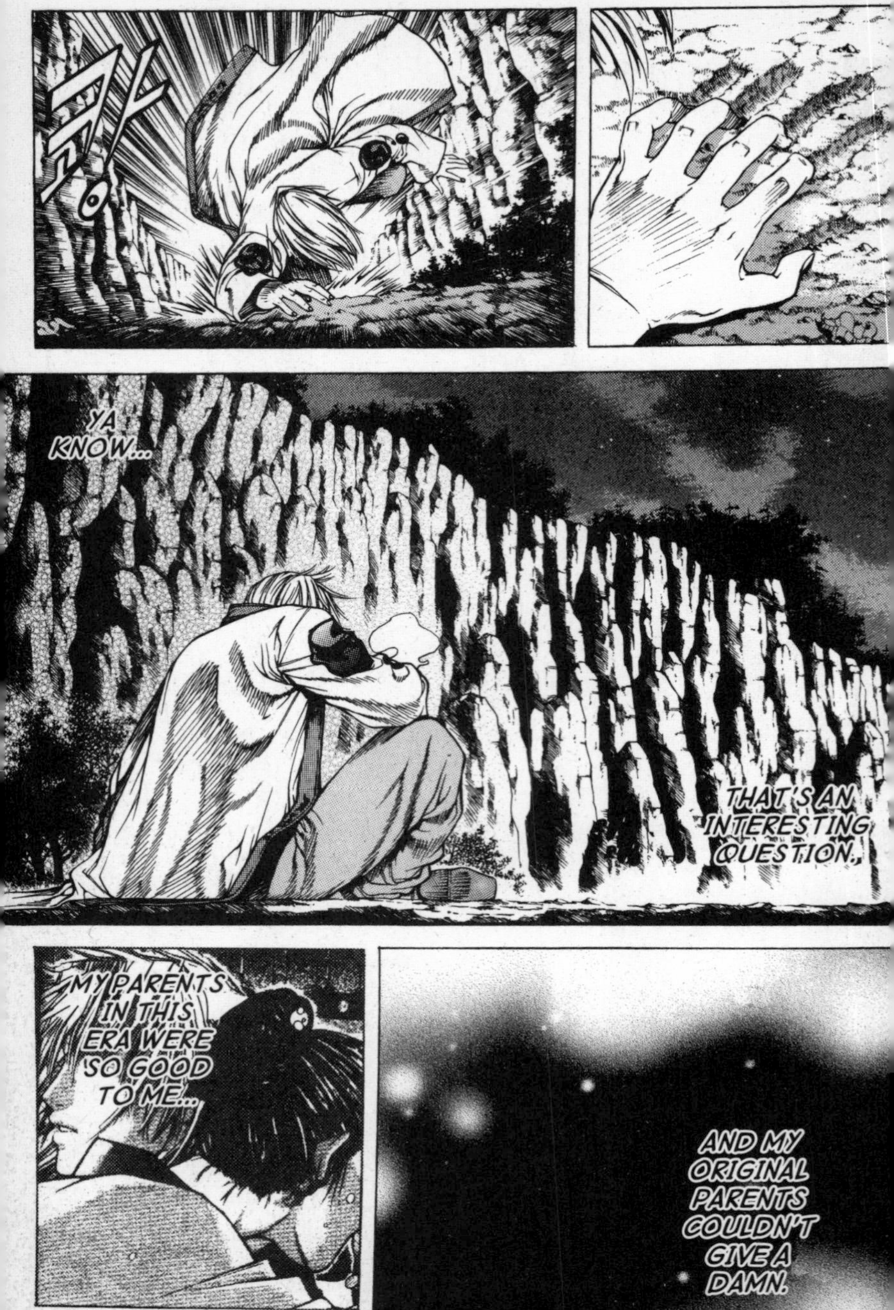
YA KNOW...
THAT'S AN INTERESTING QUESTION.
MY PARENTS IN THIS ERA WERE SO GOOD TO ME...
AND MY ORIGINAL PARENTS COULDN'T GIVE A DAMN.

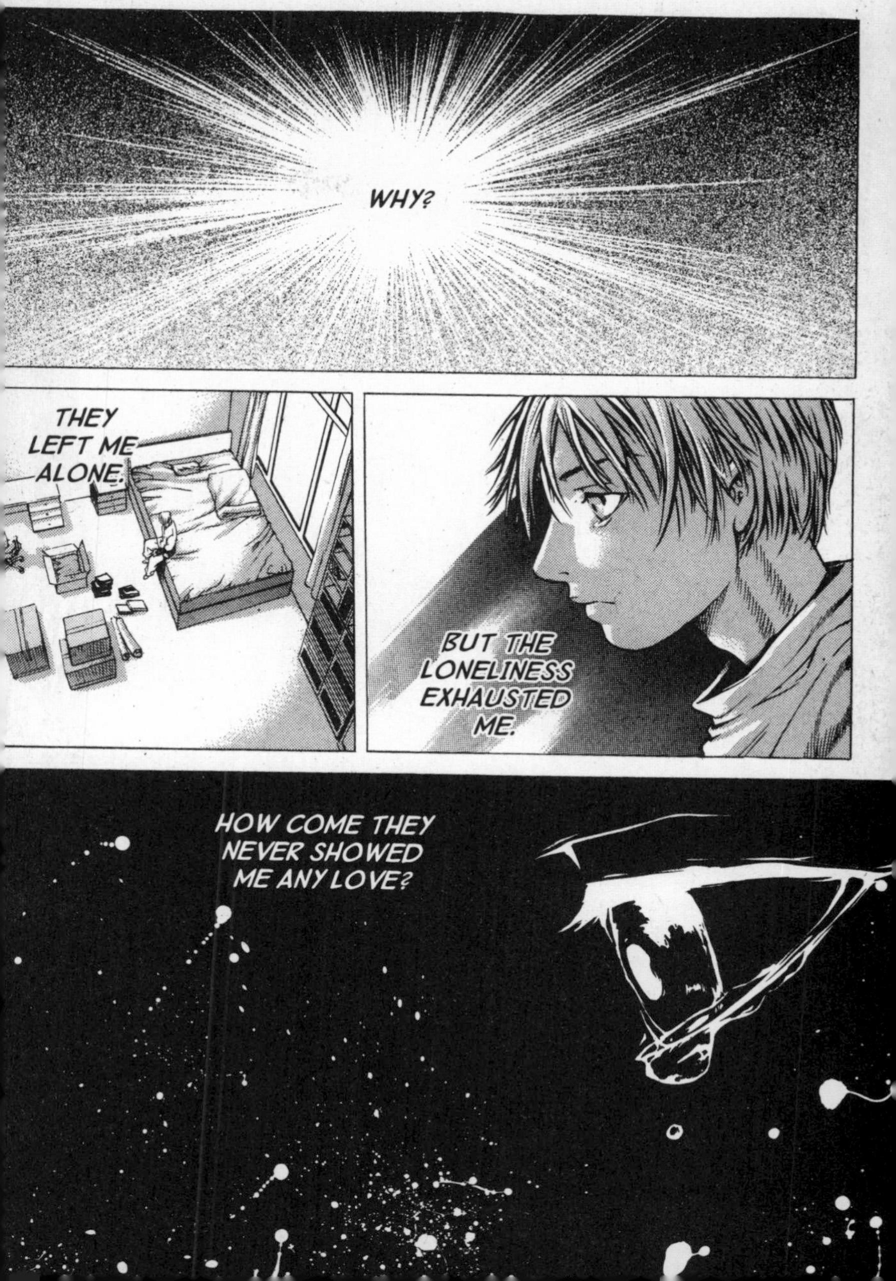
WHY?
THEY LEFT ME ALONE.
BUT THE LONELINESS EXHAUSTED ME.
HOW COME THEY NEVER SHOWED ME ANY LOVE?

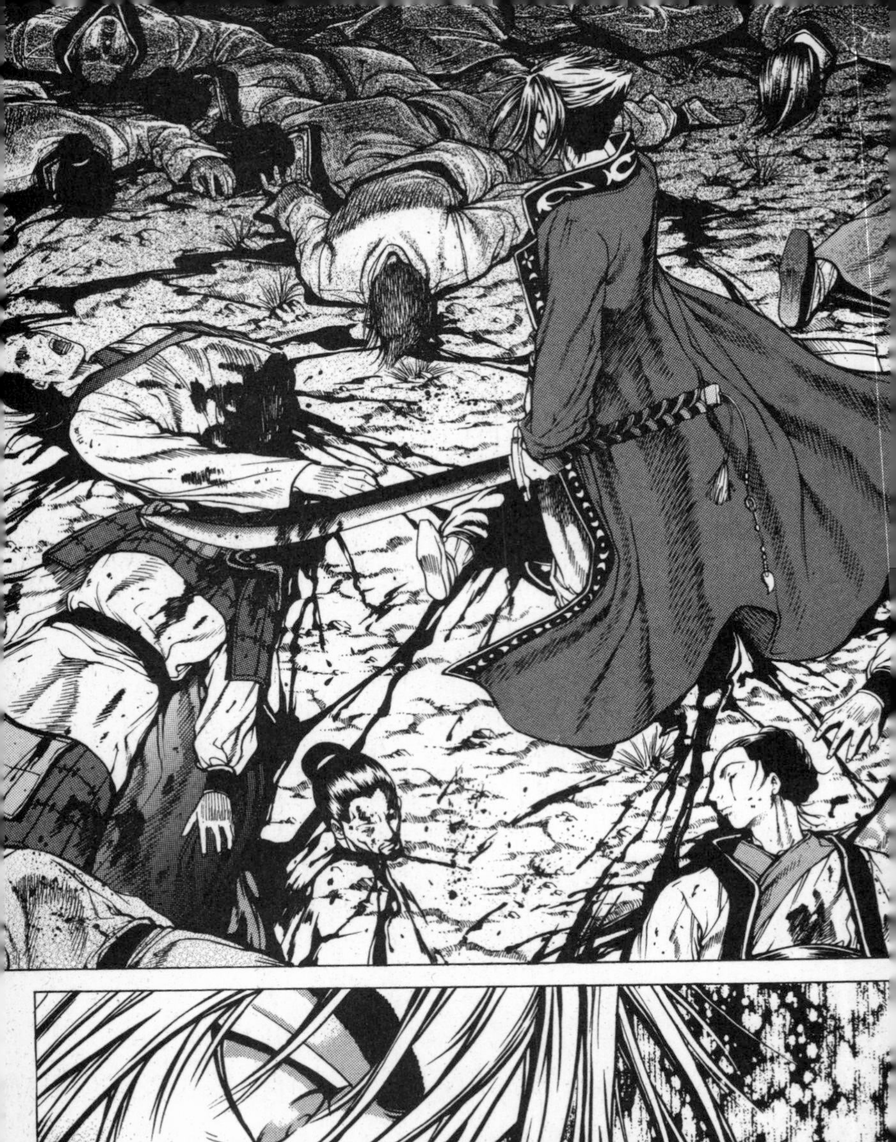
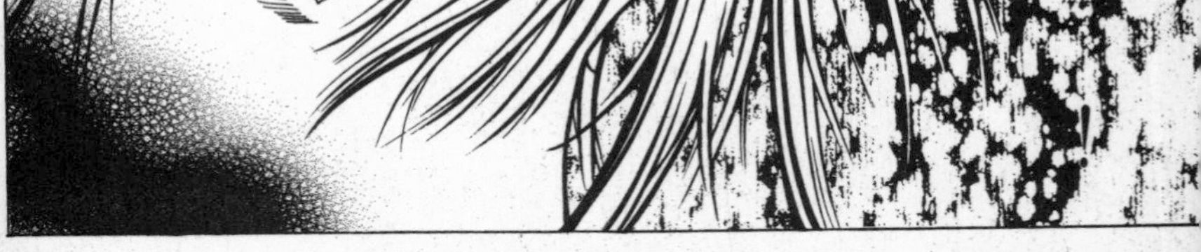

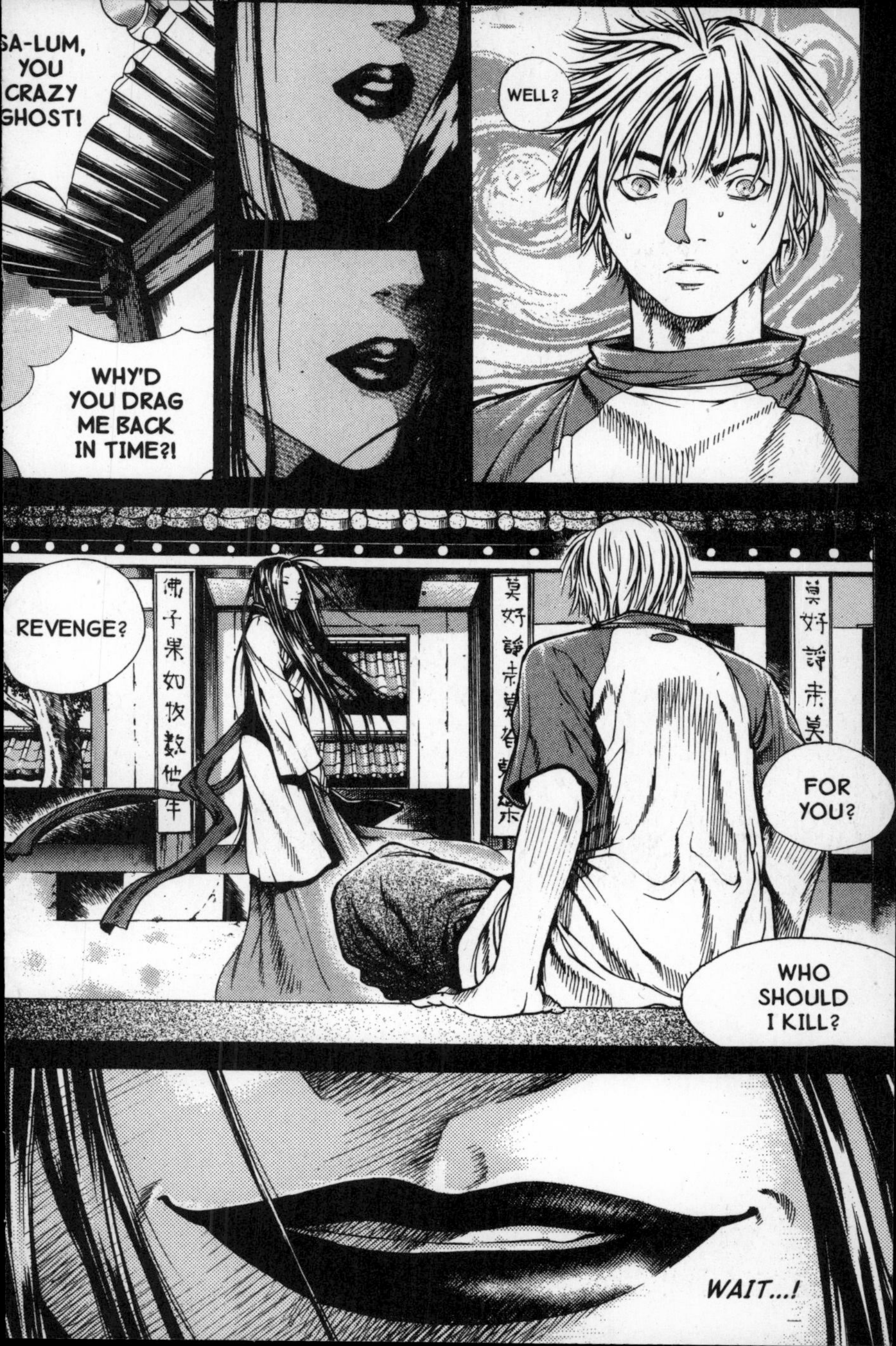
SA-LUM, YOU CRAZY GHOST!
WHY'D YOU DRAG ME BACK IN TIME?!
WELL?
REVENGE?
FOR YOU?
WHO SHOULD I KILL?
WAIT...!

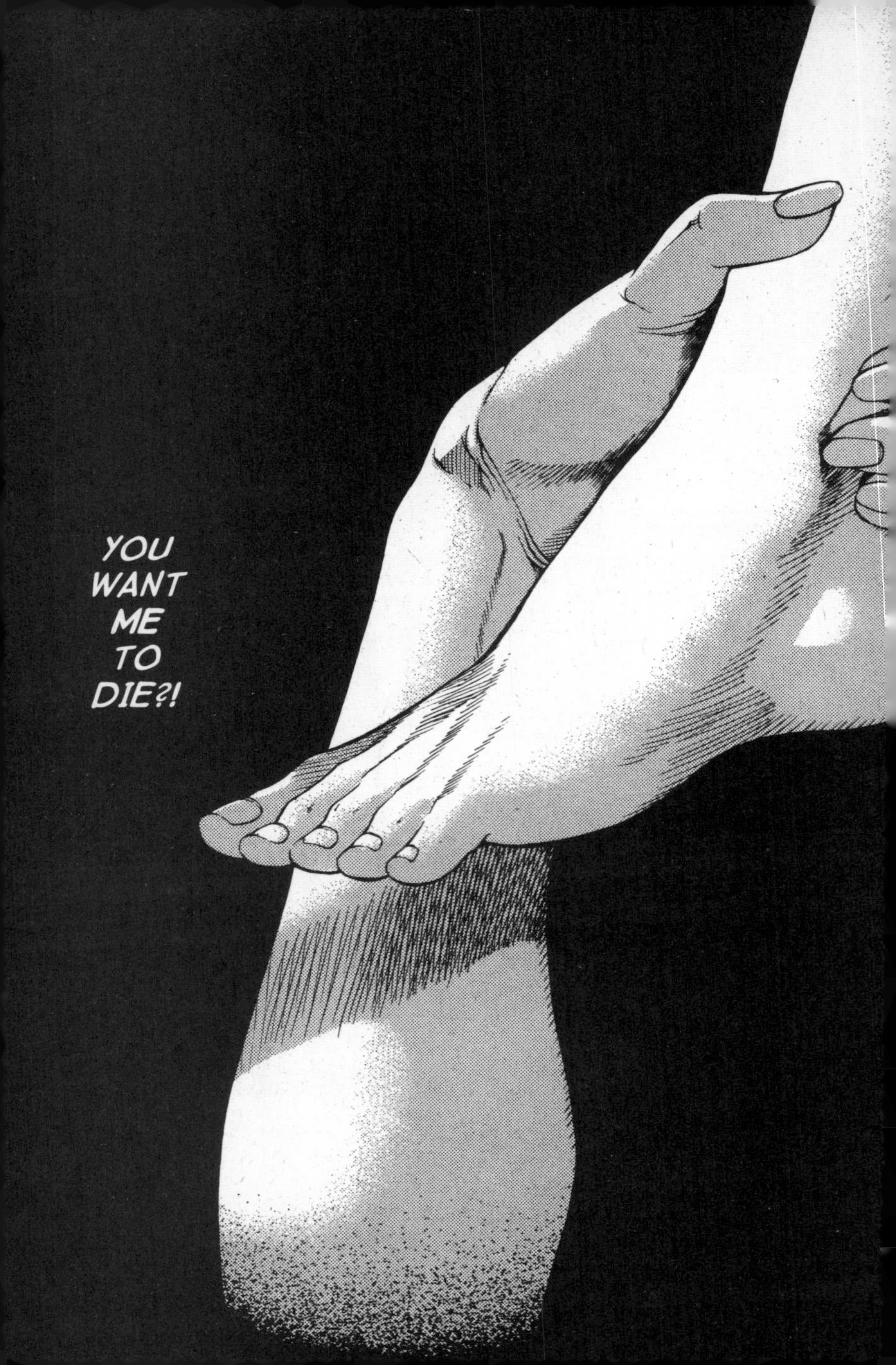
YOU WANT ME TO DIE?!

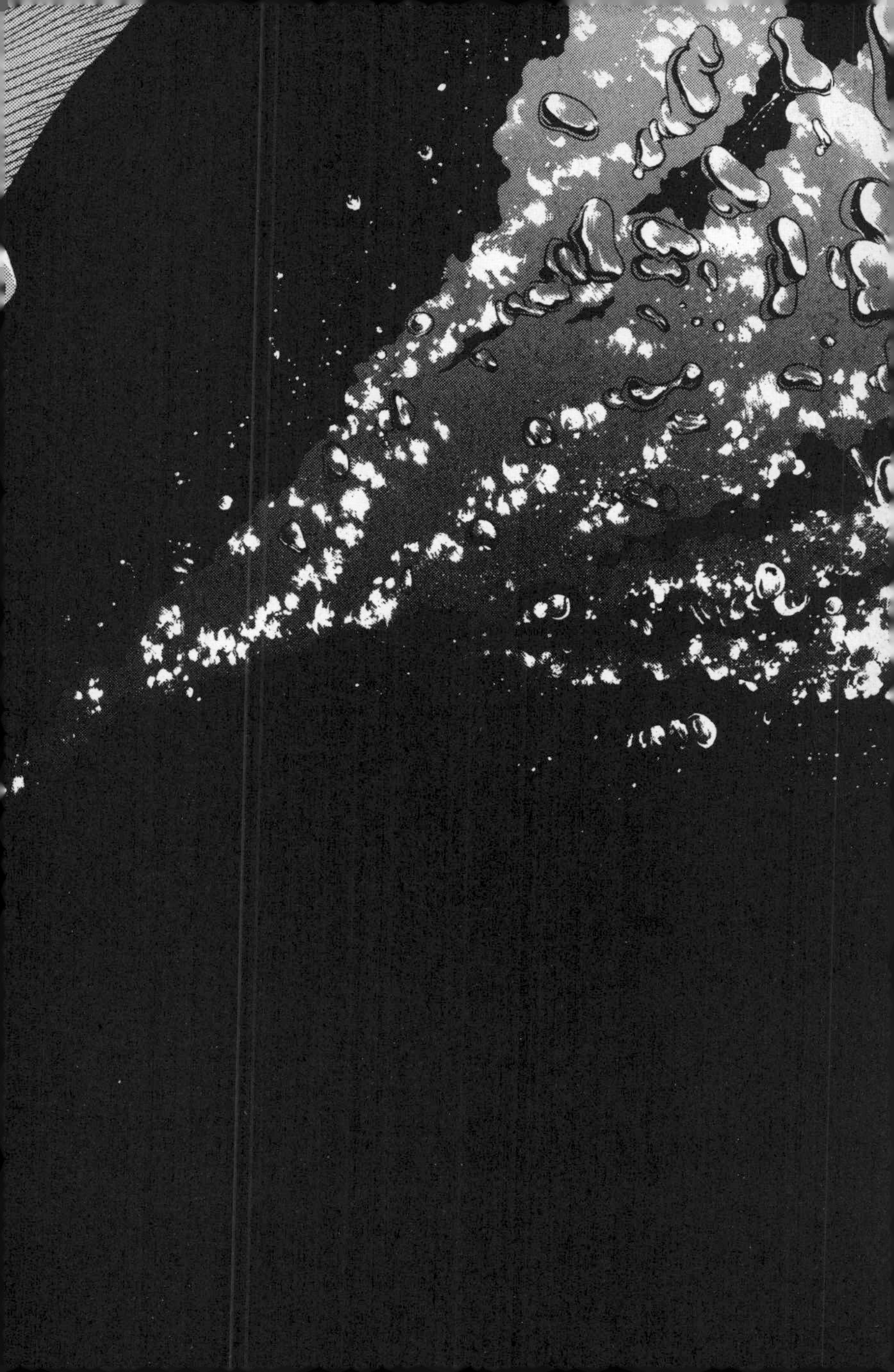

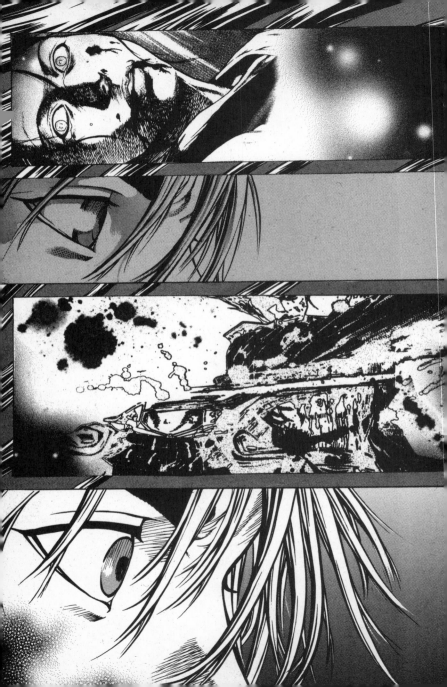

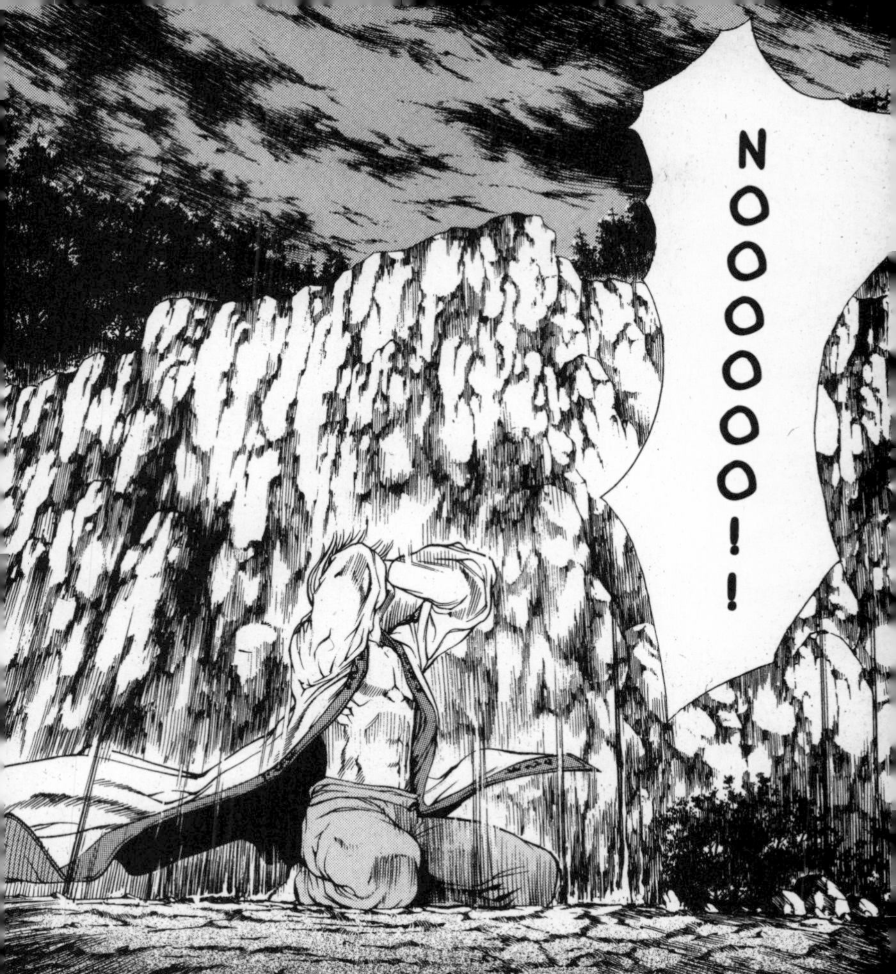
NOOOOOOO!!!
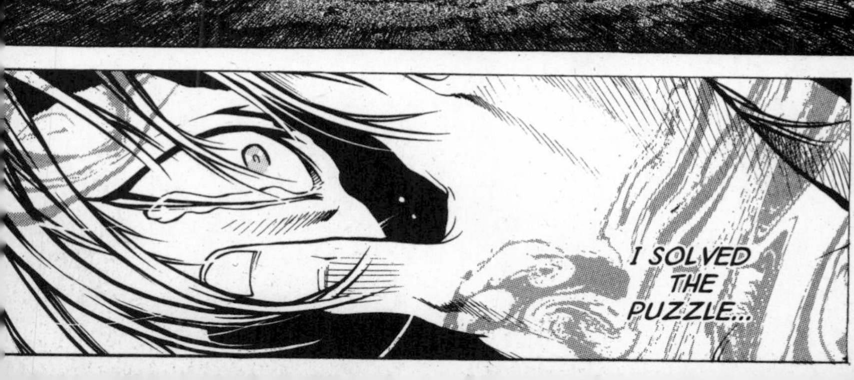
I SOLVED THE PUZZLE...

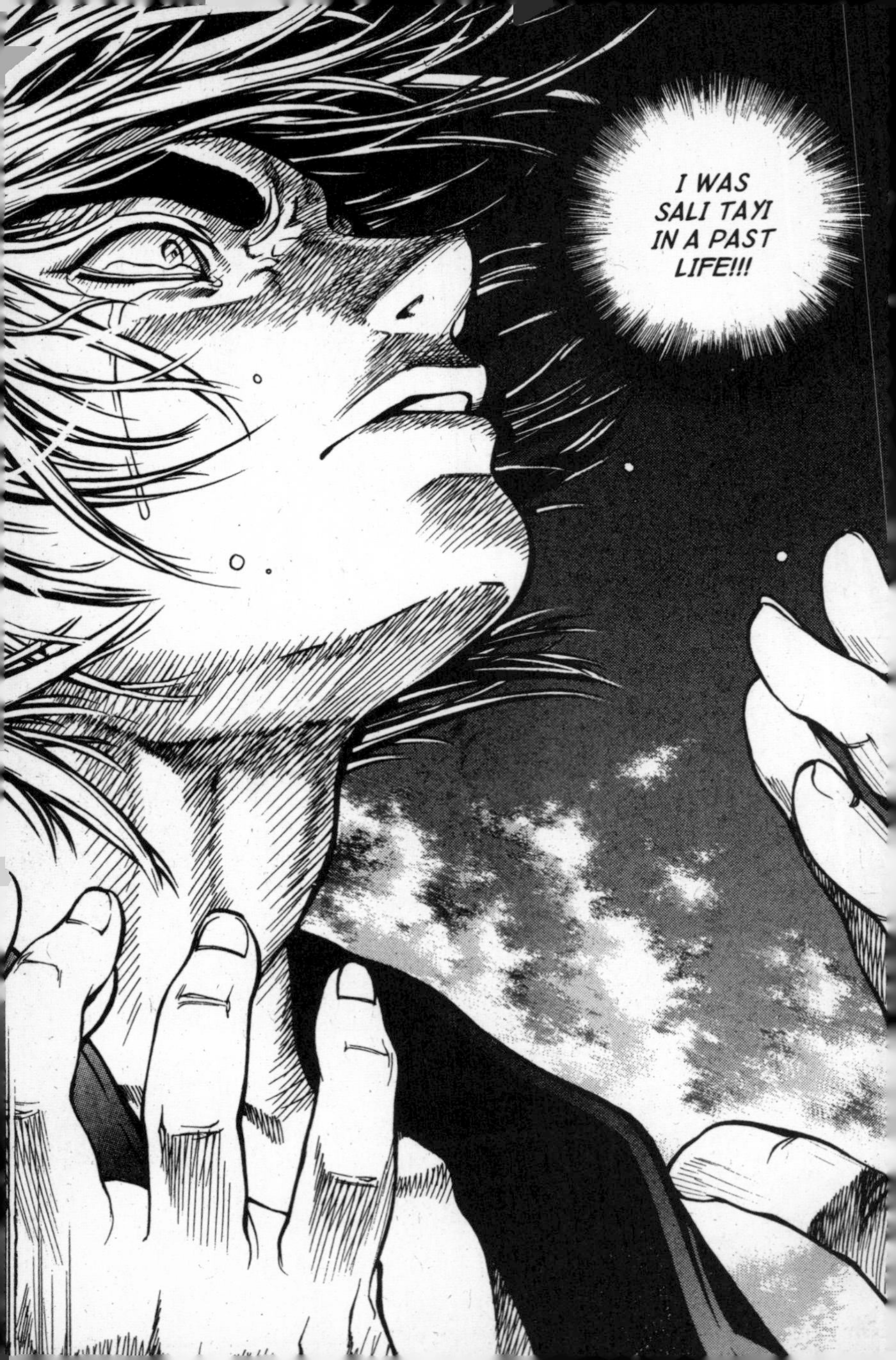
I WAS SALI TAYI IN A PAST LIFE!!!

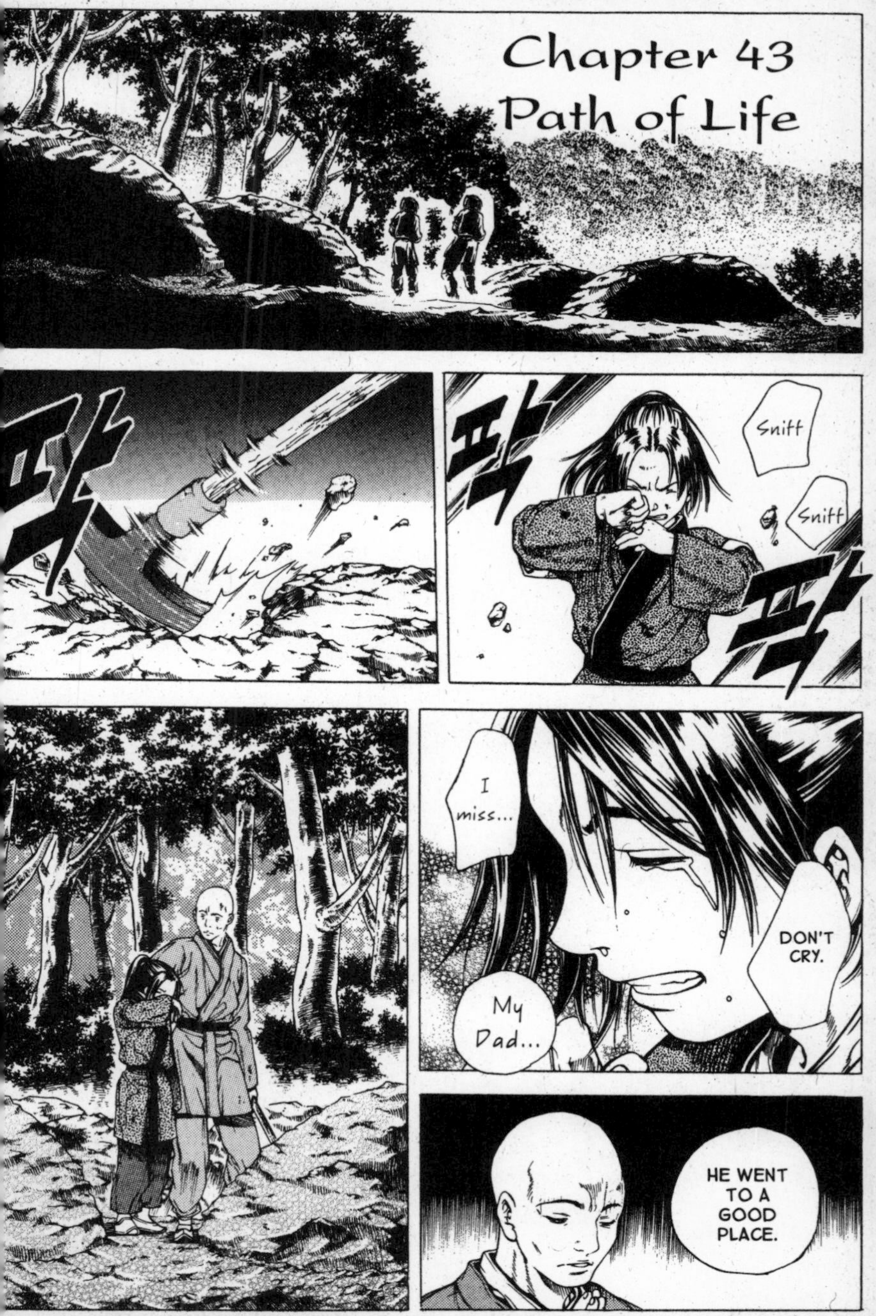
Chapter 43
Path of Life
Sniff
Sniff
I miss...
My Dad...
DON'T CRY.
HE WENT TO A GOOD PLACE.

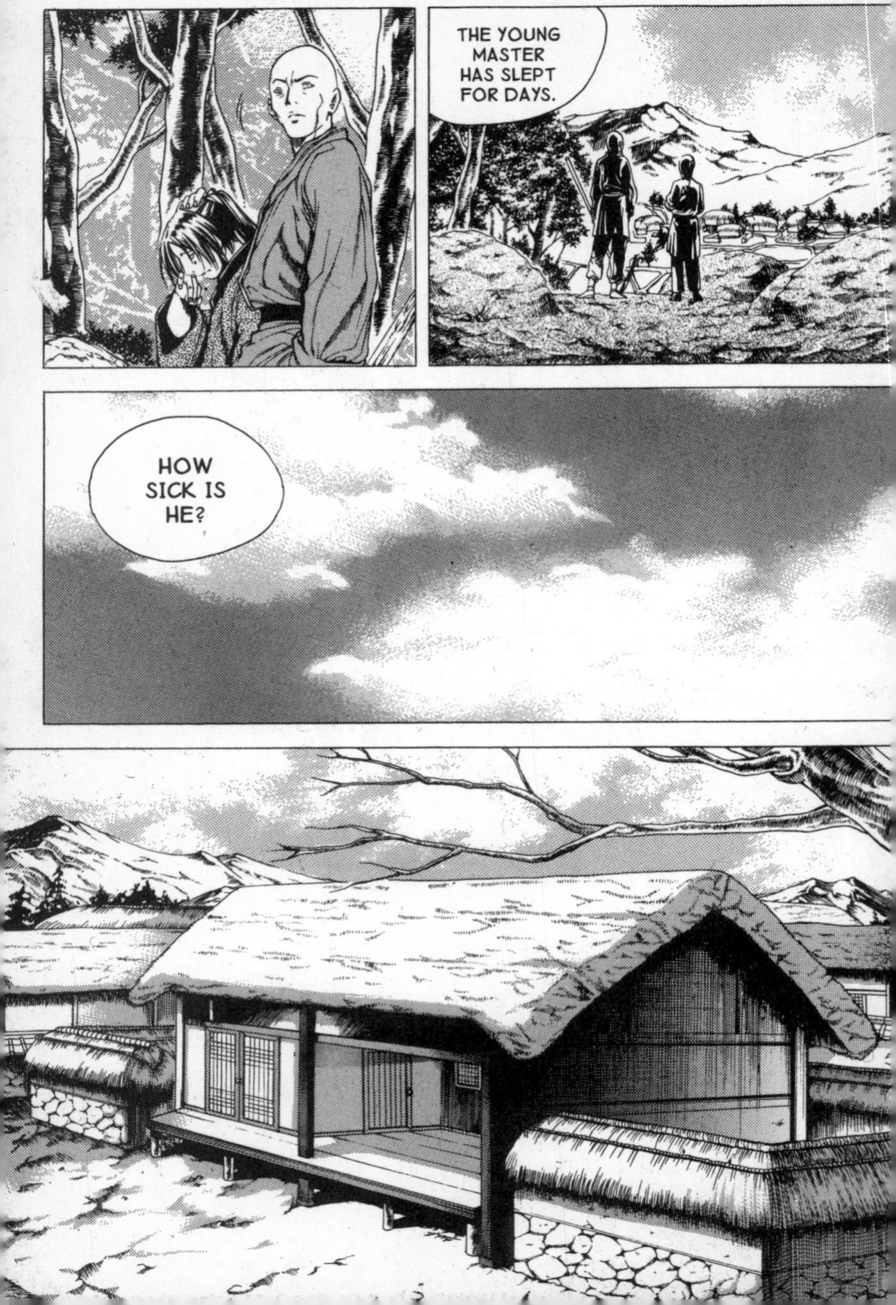
THE YOUNG MASTER HAS SLEPT FOR DAYS.
HOW SICK IS HE?

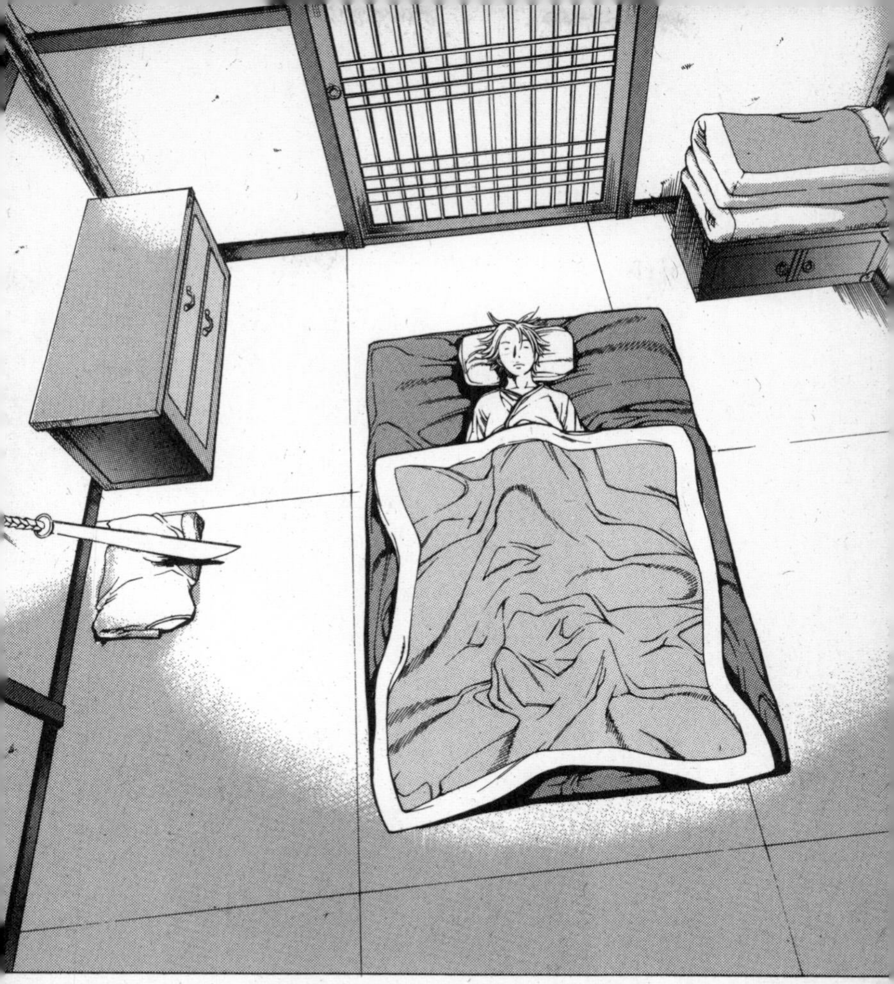
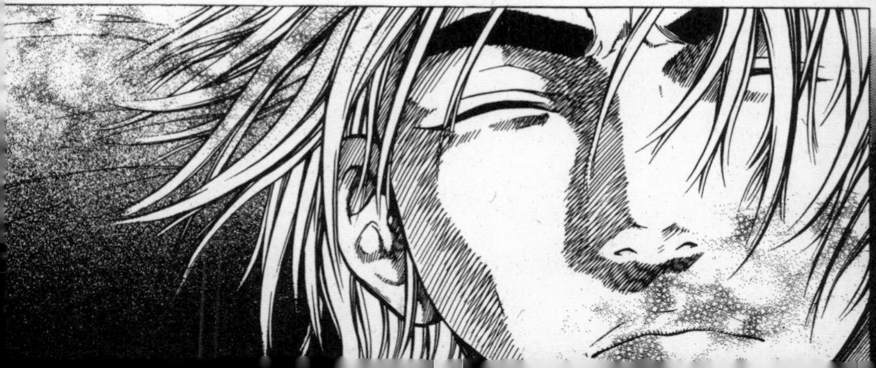

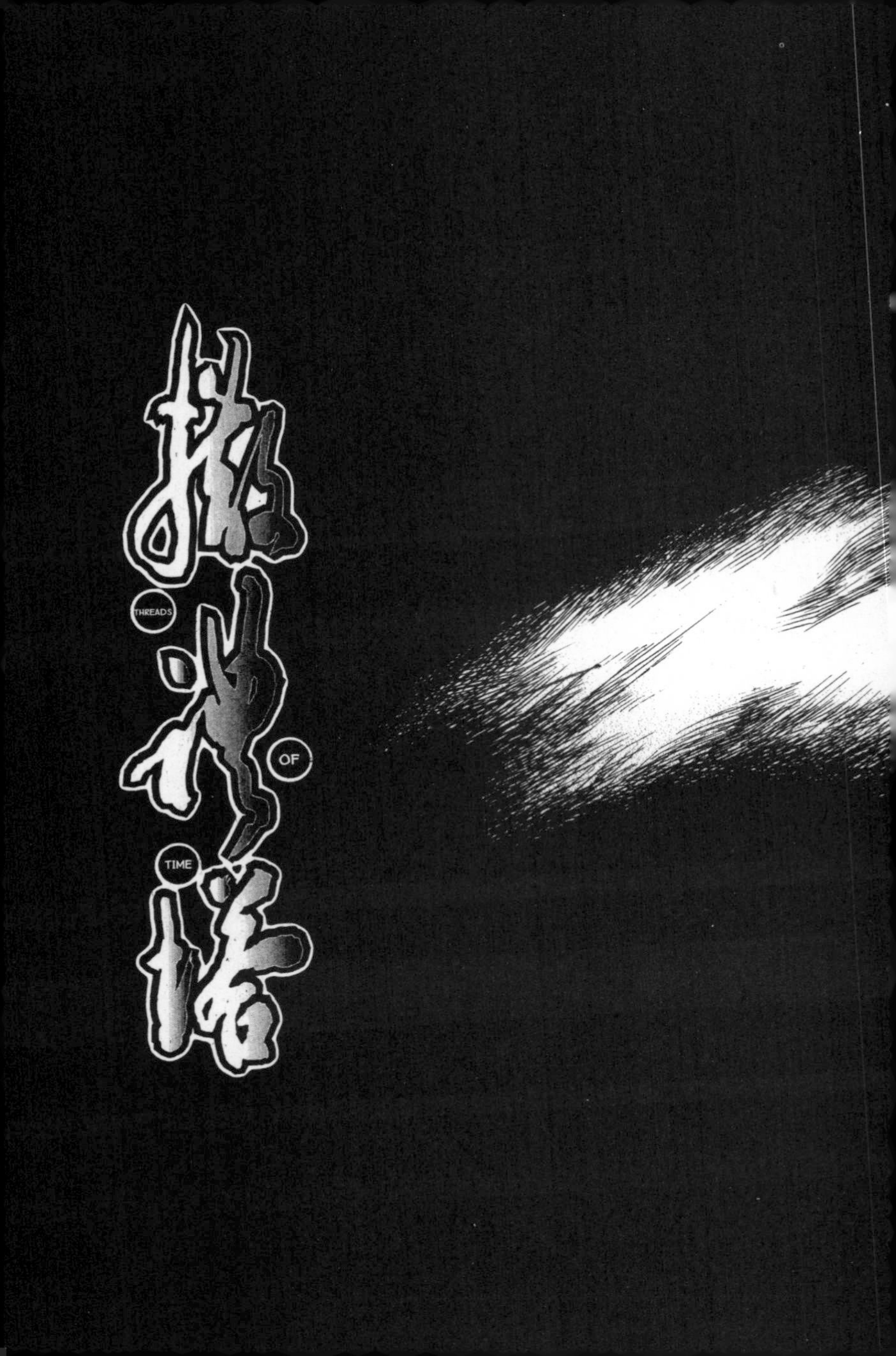
THREADS
OF
TIME

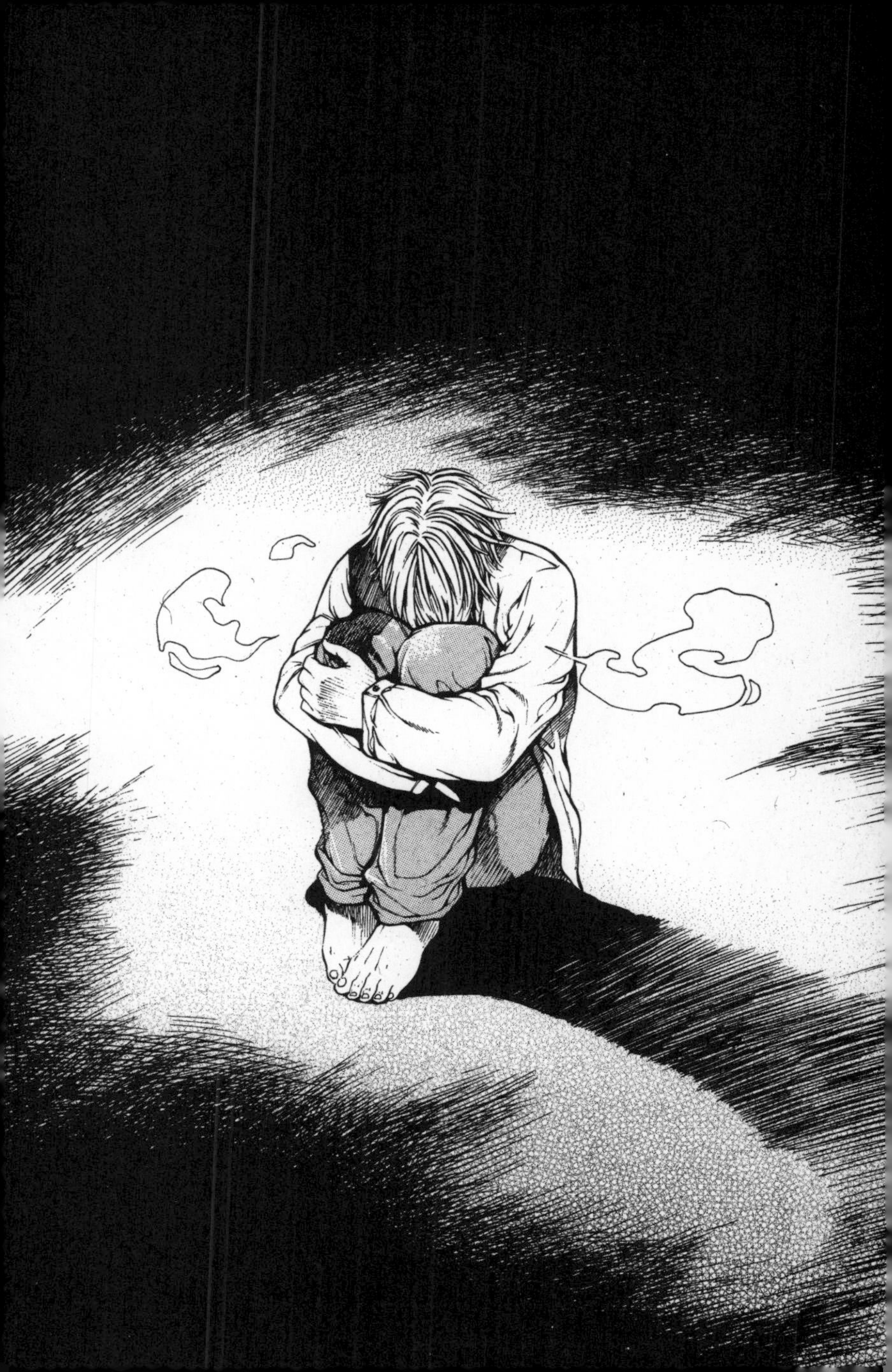

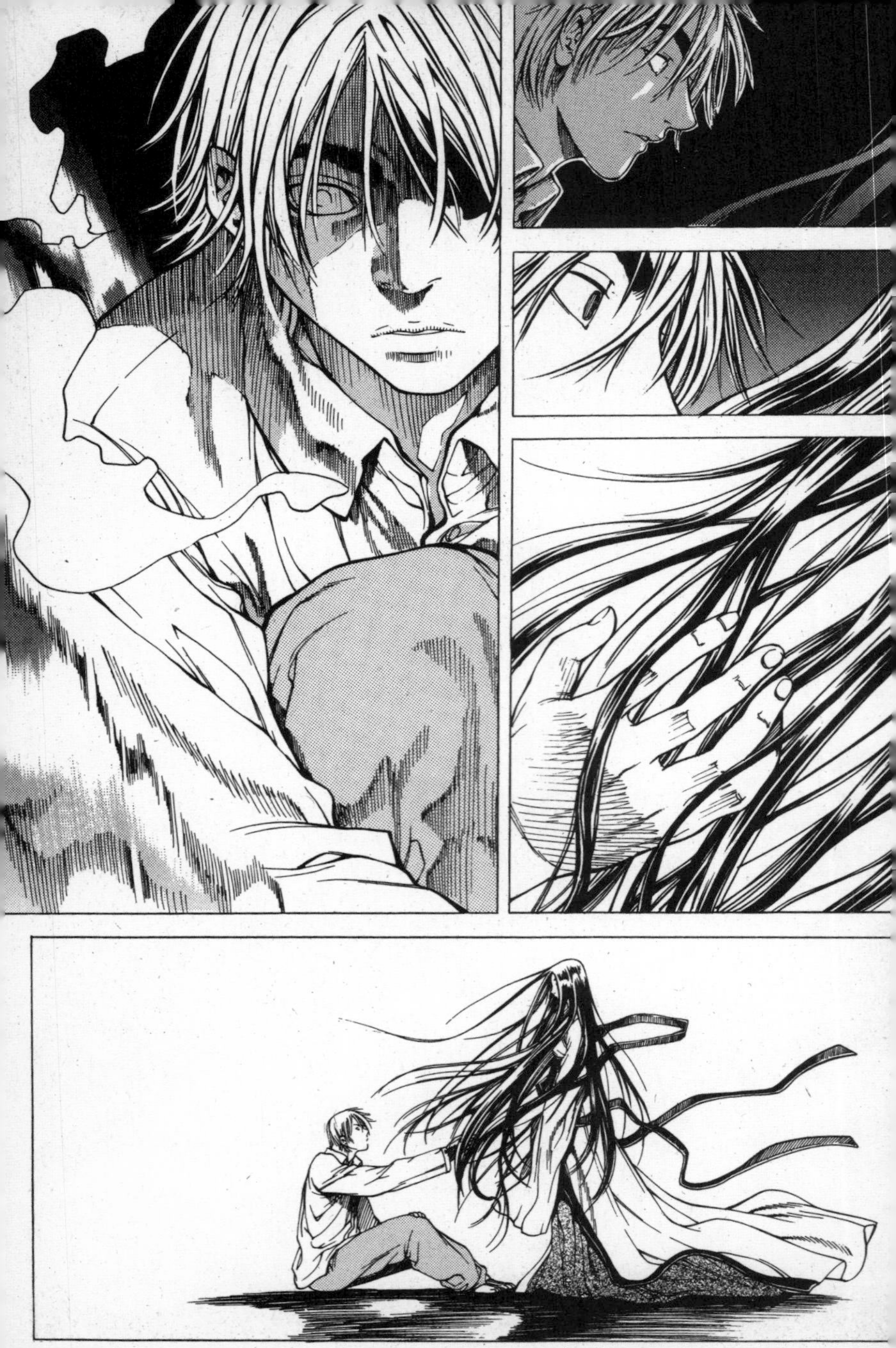

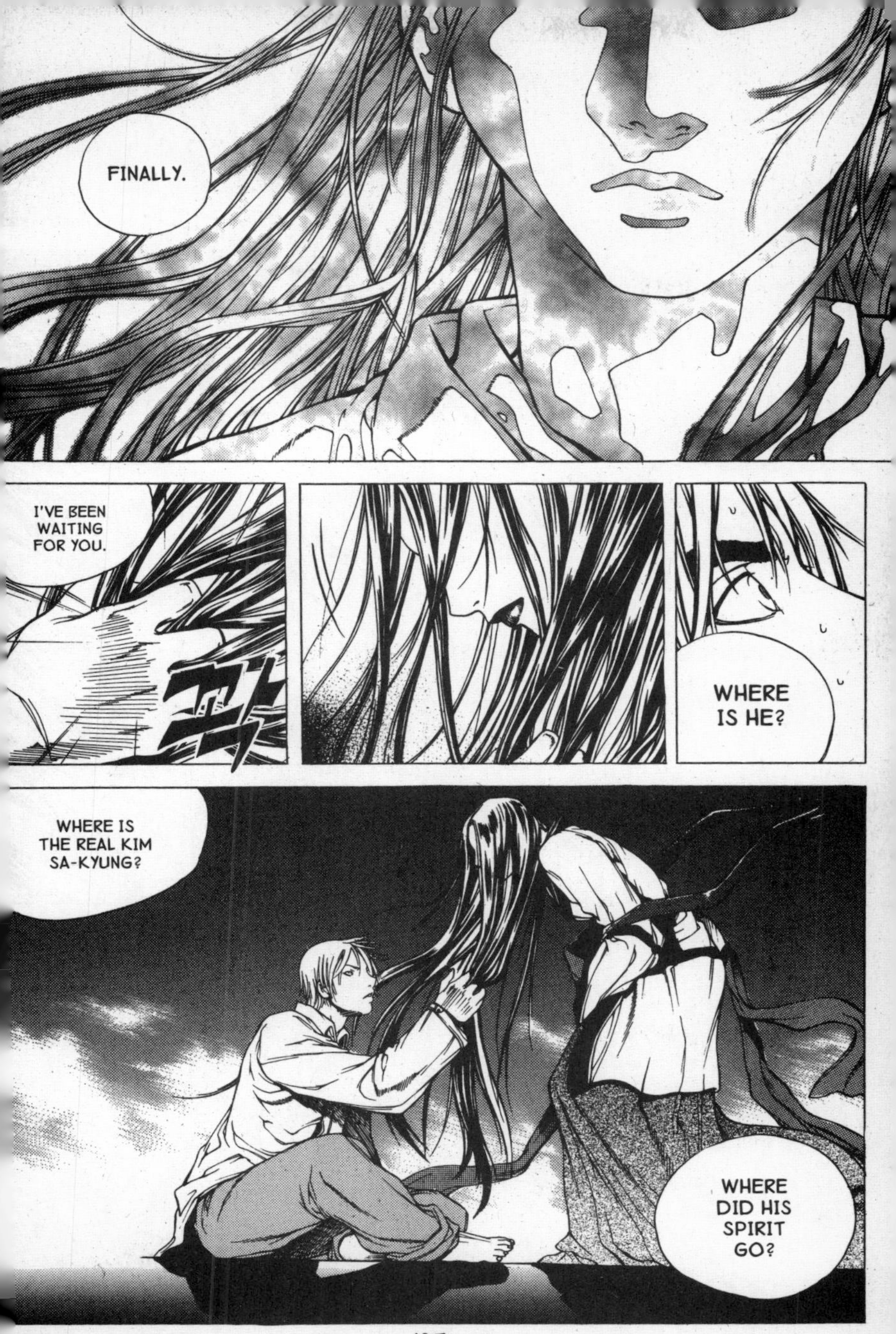
FINALLY.
I'VE BEEN WAITING FOR YOU.
WHERE IS HE?
WHERE IS THE REAL KIM SA-KYUNG?
WHERE DID HIS SPIRIT GO?

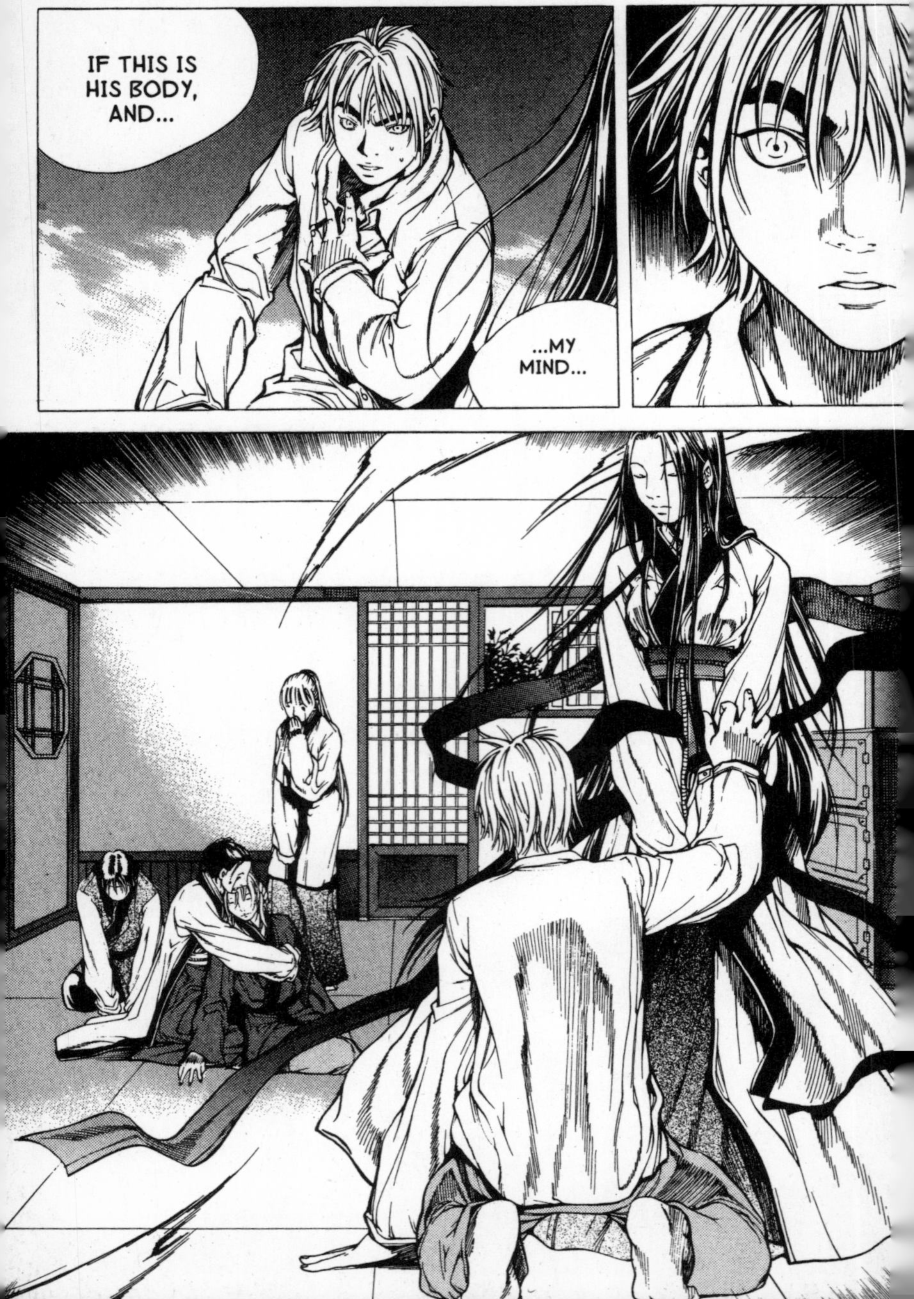
IF THIS IS HIS BODY, AND...
...MY MIND...

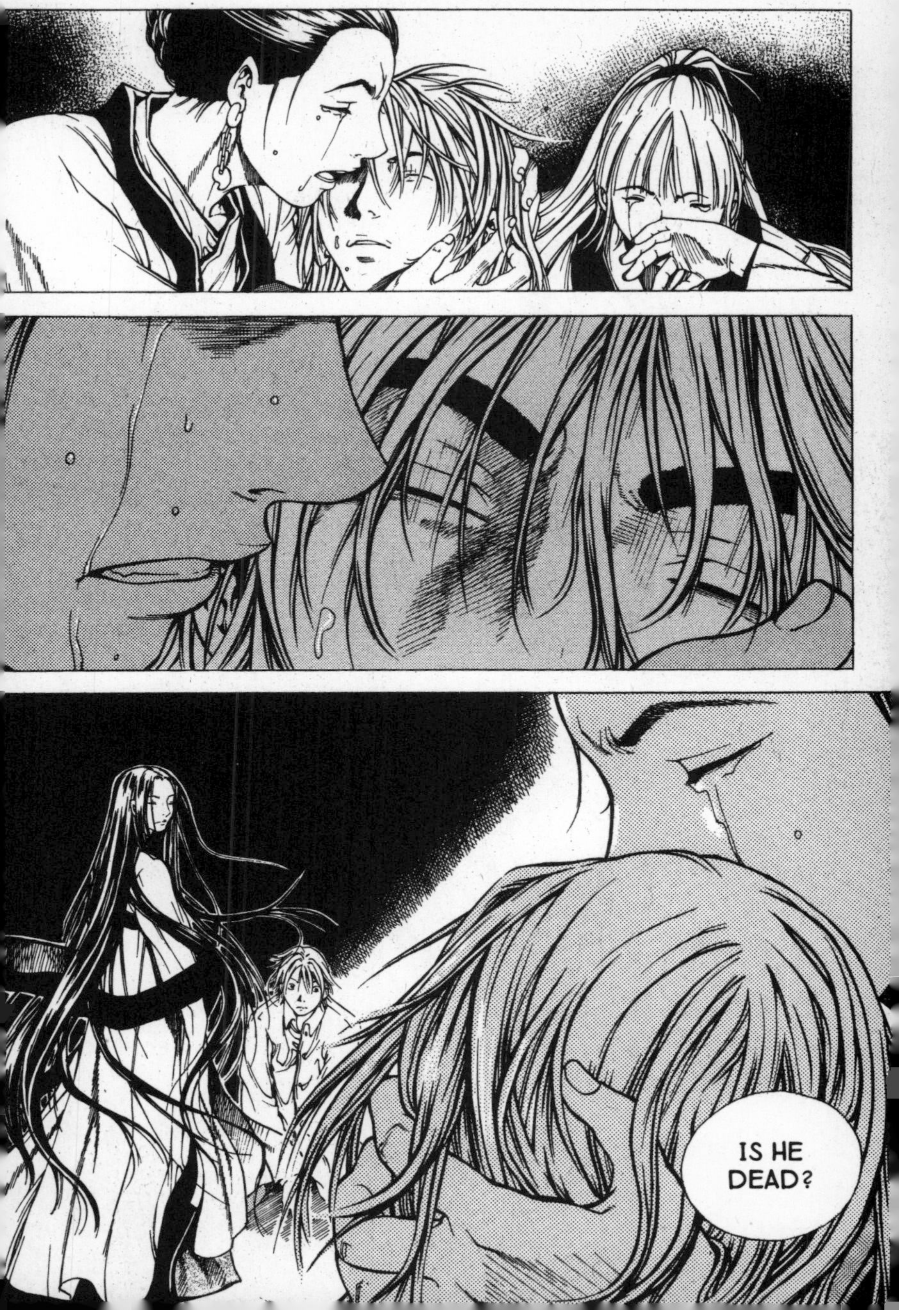
IS HE DEAD?

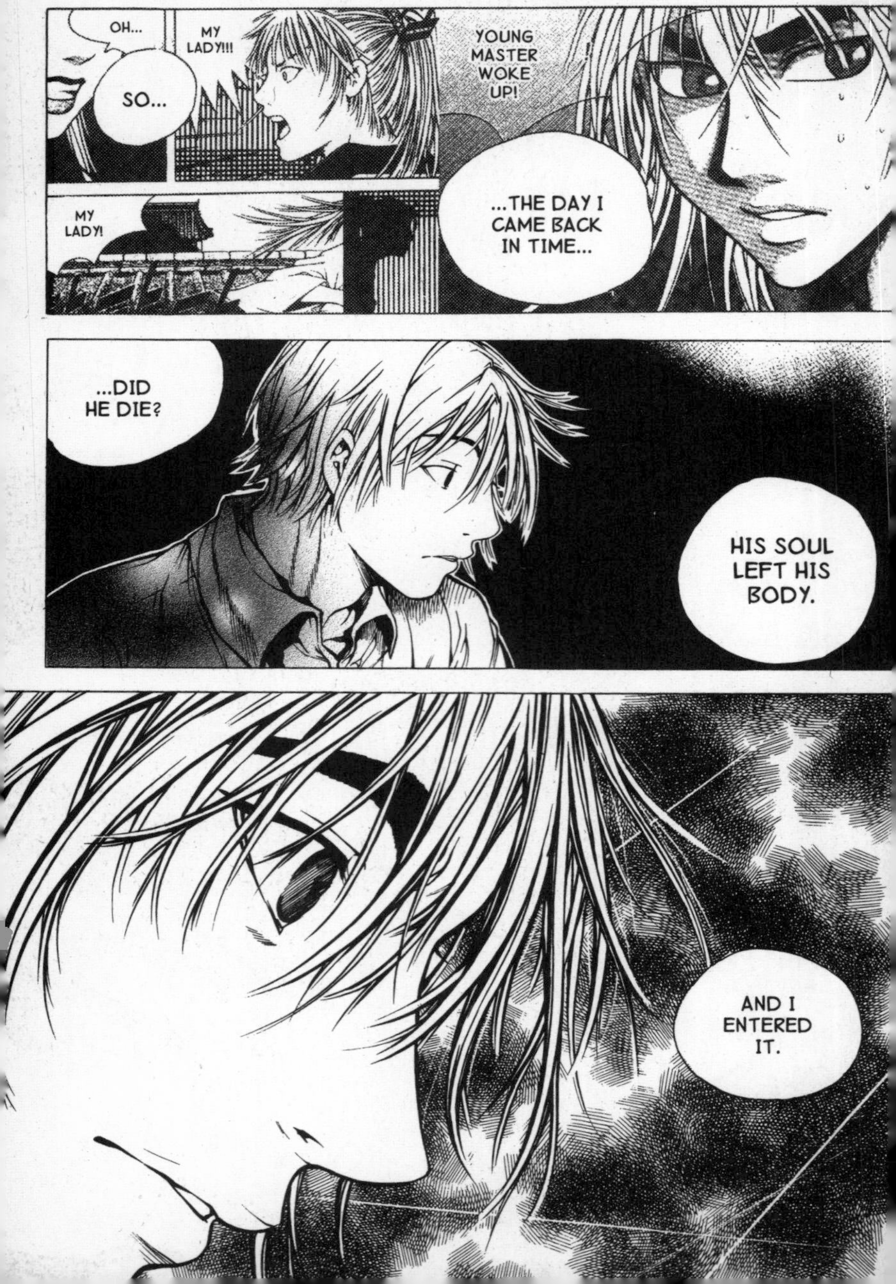
OH...
SO...
MY LADY!!!
MY LADY!
YOUNG MASTER WOKE UP!
...THE DAY I CAME BACK IN TIME...
...DID HE DIE?
HIS SOUL LEFT HIS BODY.
AND I ENTERED IT.

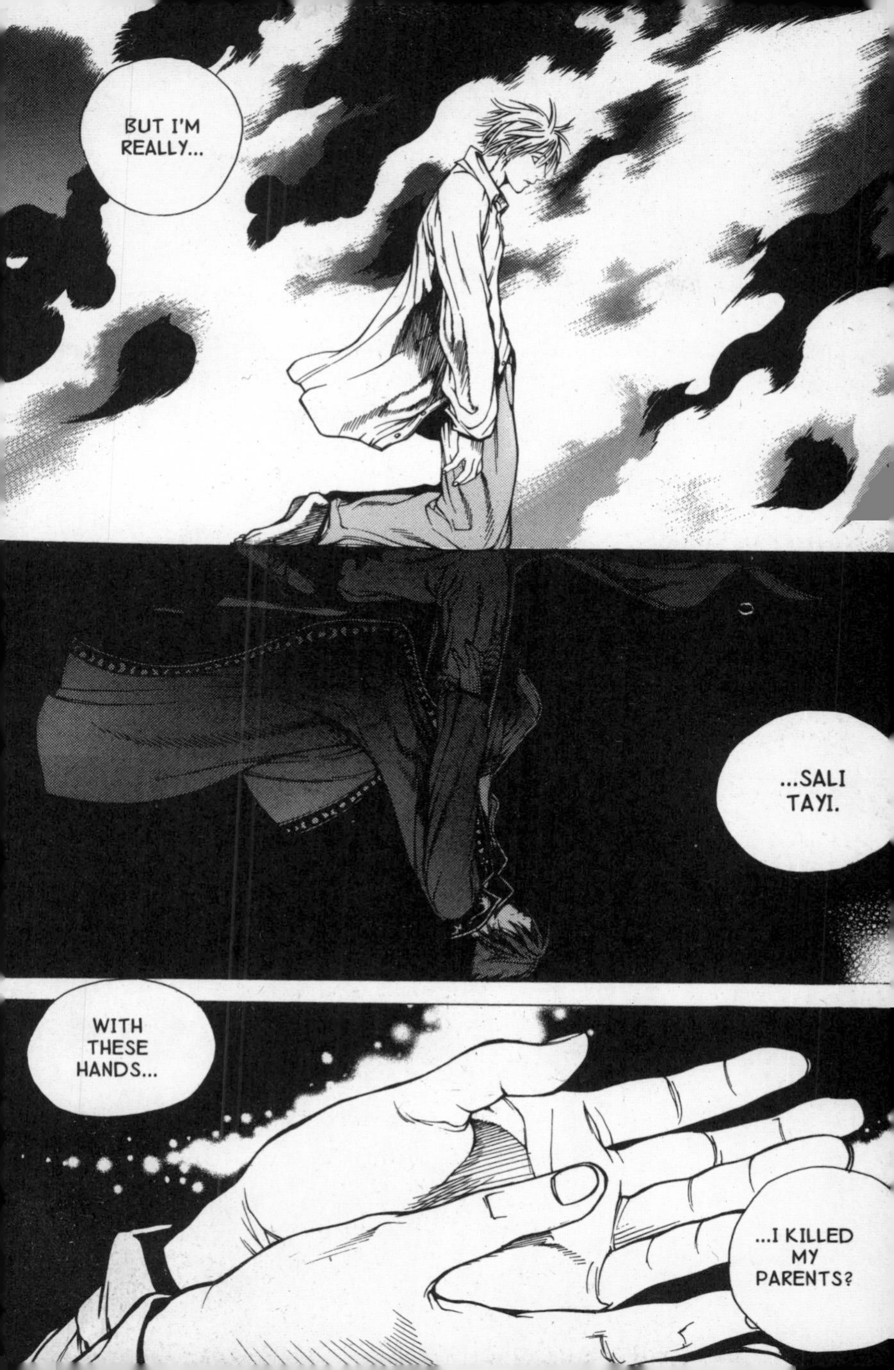
BUT I'M REALLY...
...SALI TAYI.
WITH THESE HANDS...
...I KILLED MY PARENTS?

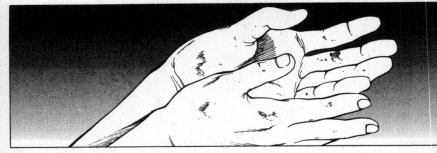

AHHHH!

MOM! I
FELL!

IT
HURTS!

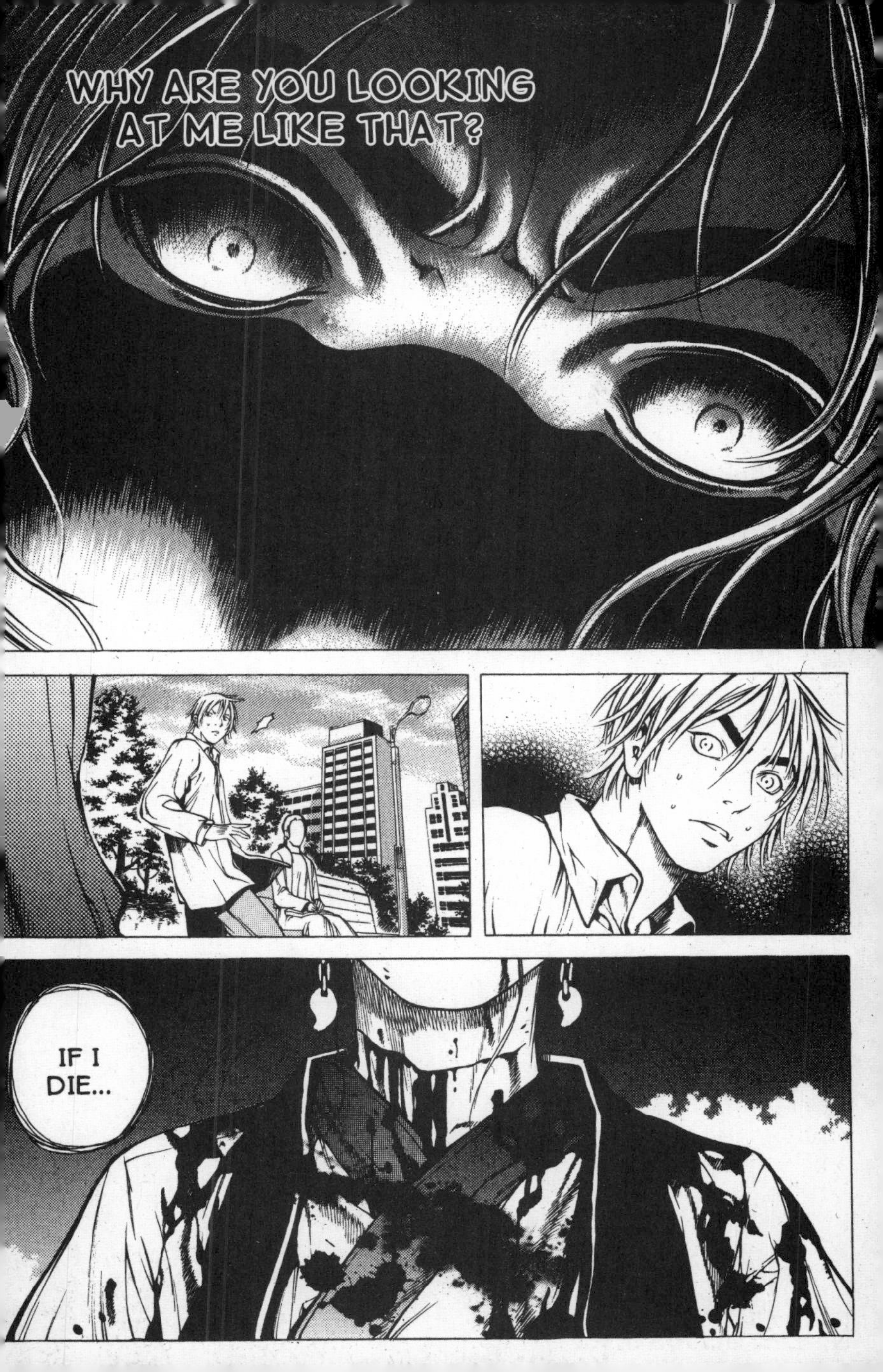
WHY ARE YOU LOOKING AT ME LIKE THAT?
IF I DIE...

...I WILL BECOME AN EVIL SPIRIT THAT PULLS AT YOU FOREVER!!

AHHH!

NO!

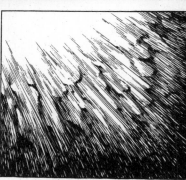

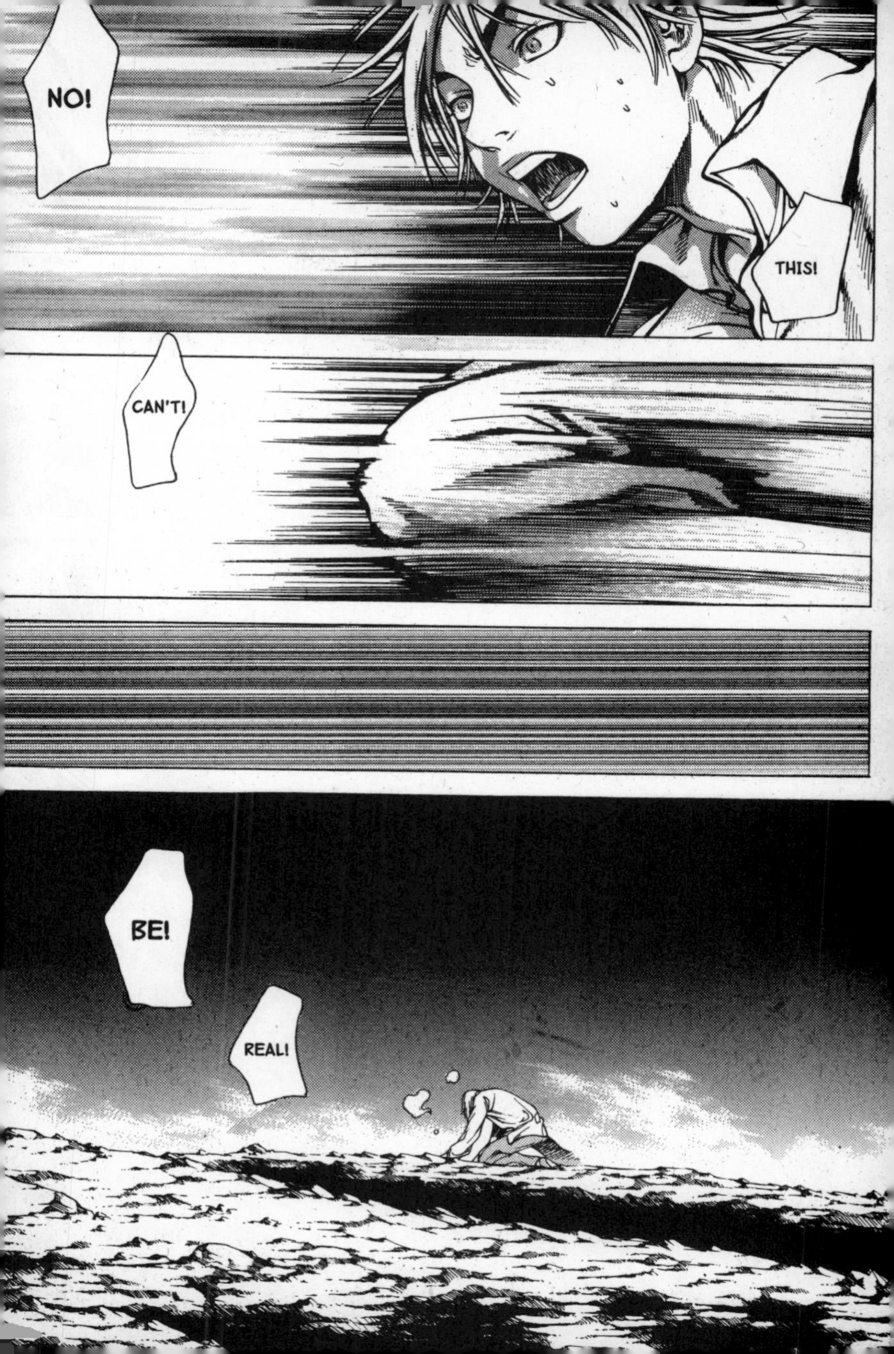
NO!
THIS!
CAN'T!
BE!
REAL!

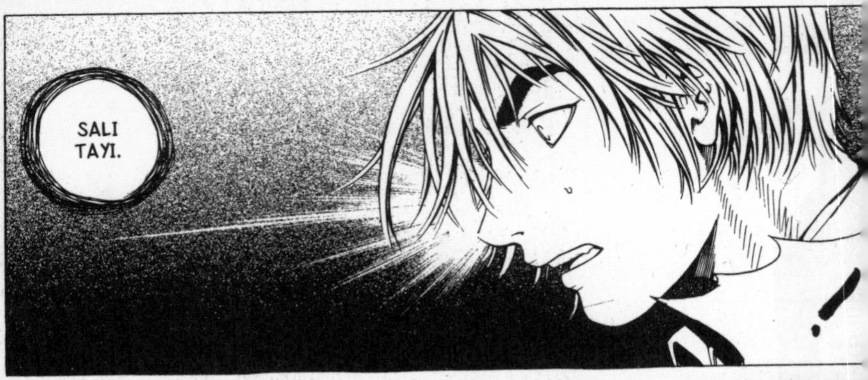
SALI TAYI.
!
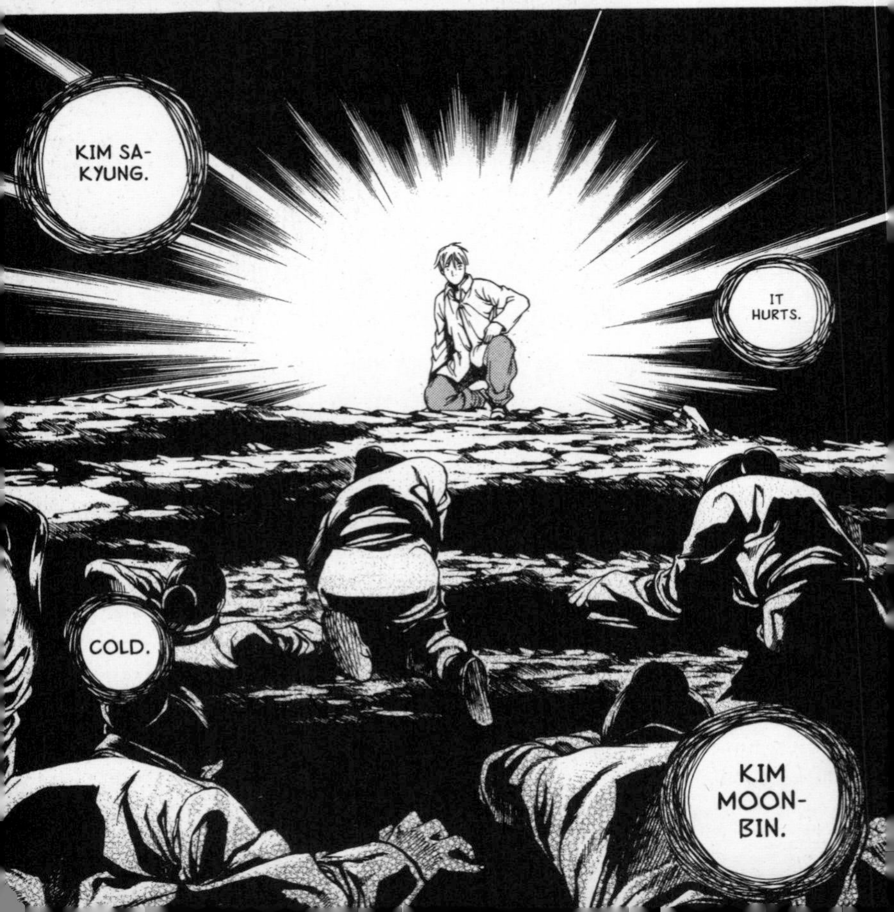
KIM SA-KYUNG.
IT HURTS.
COLD.
KIM MOON-BIN.

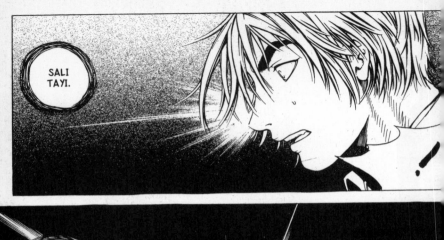

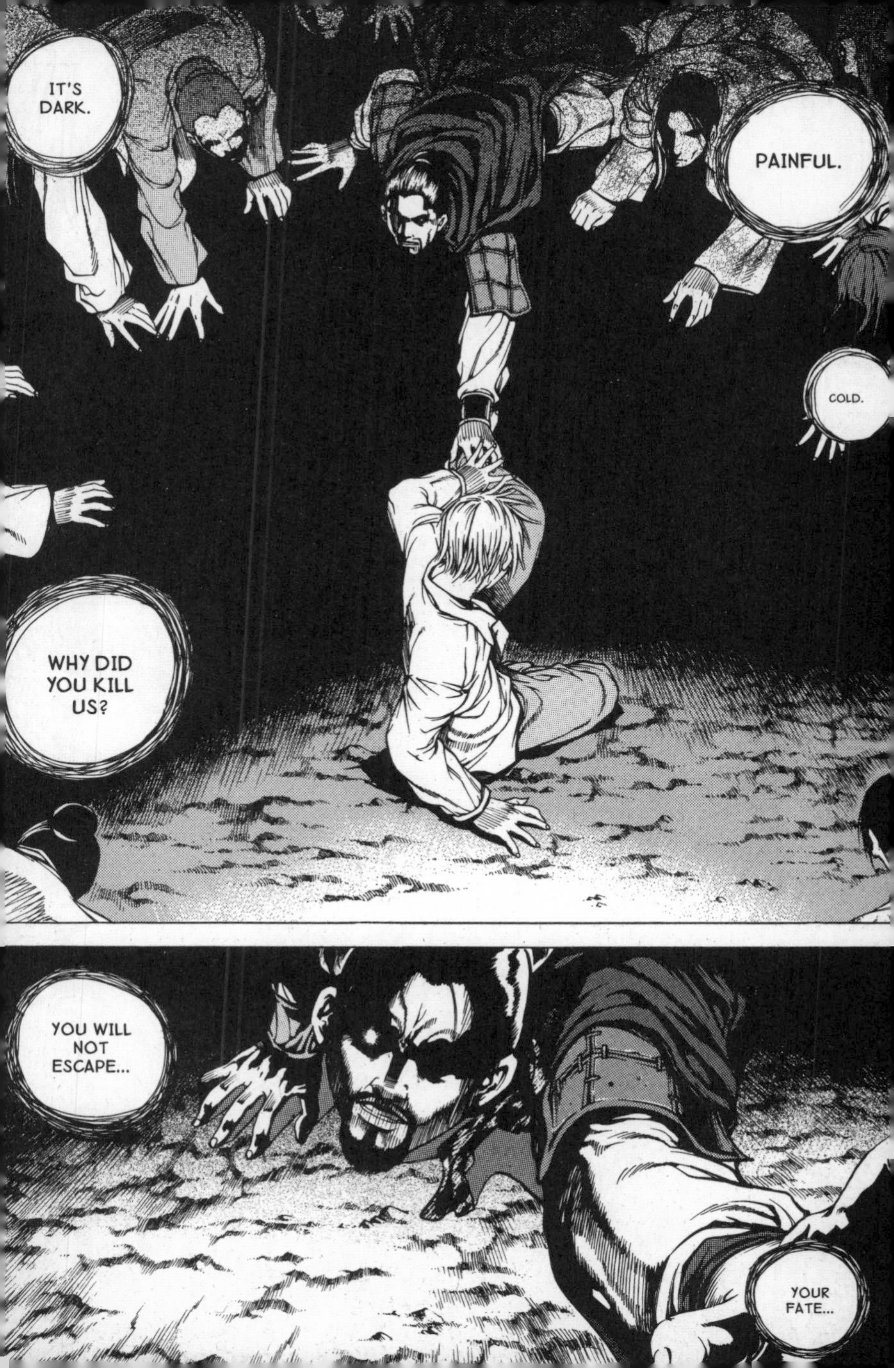
IT'S DARK.
PAINFUL.
COLD.
WHY DID YOU KILL US?
YOU WILL NOT ESCAPE...
YOUR FATE...

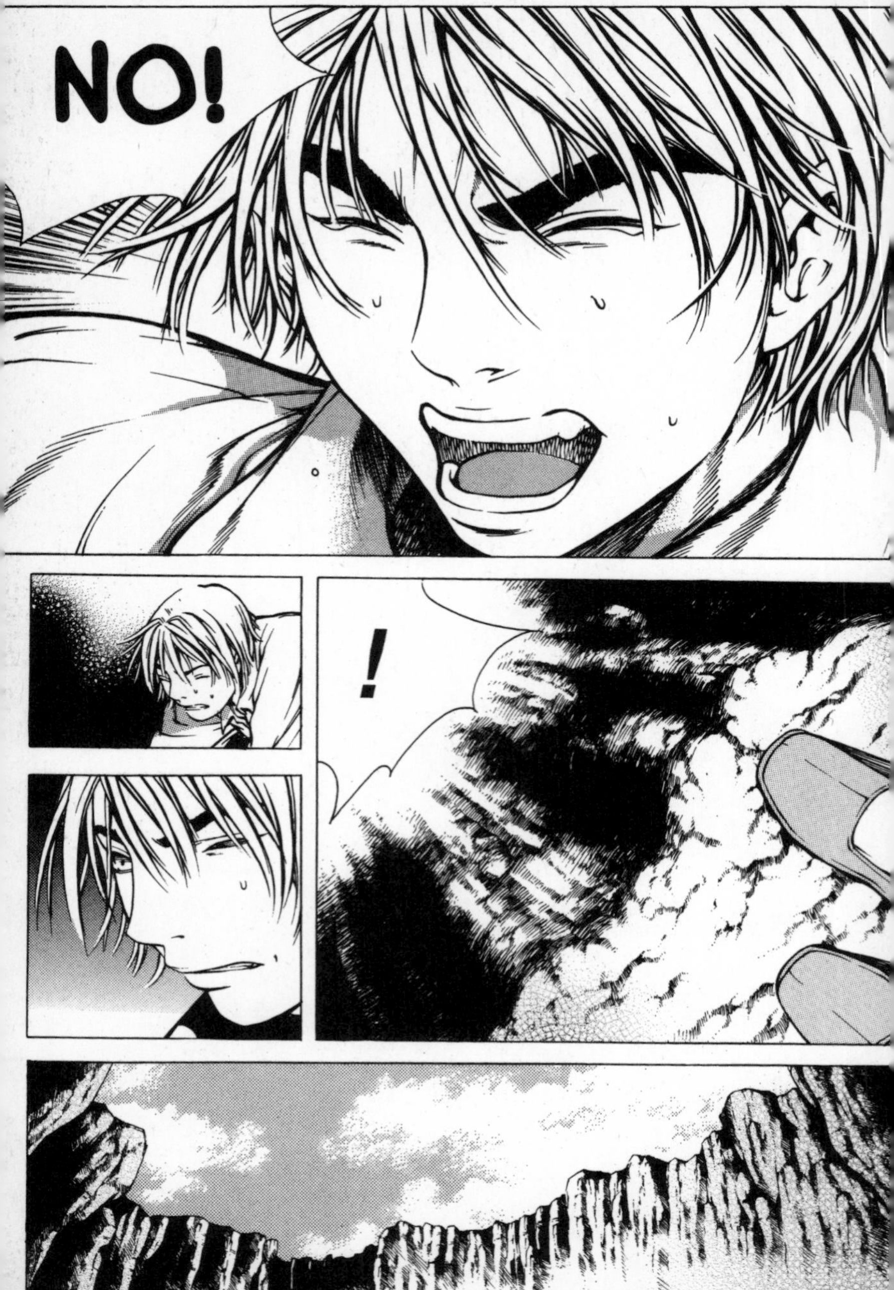
NO!
!

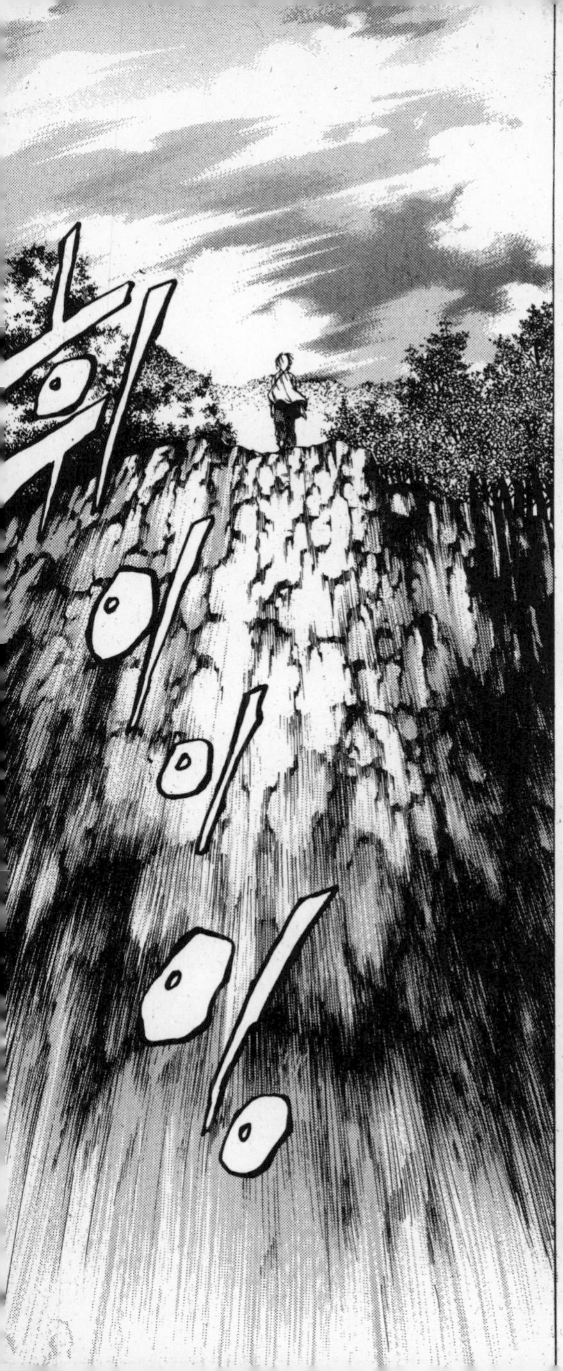
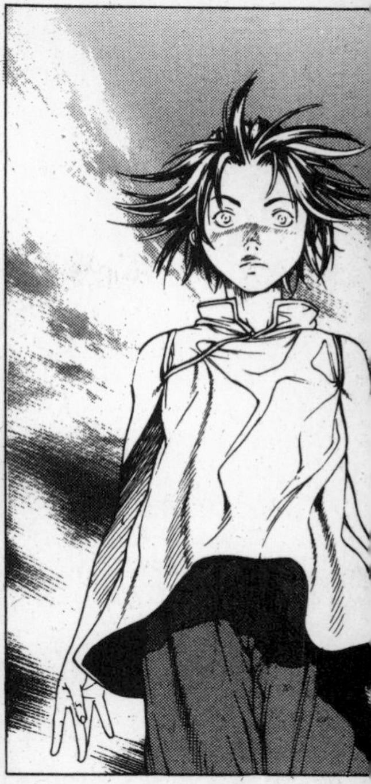
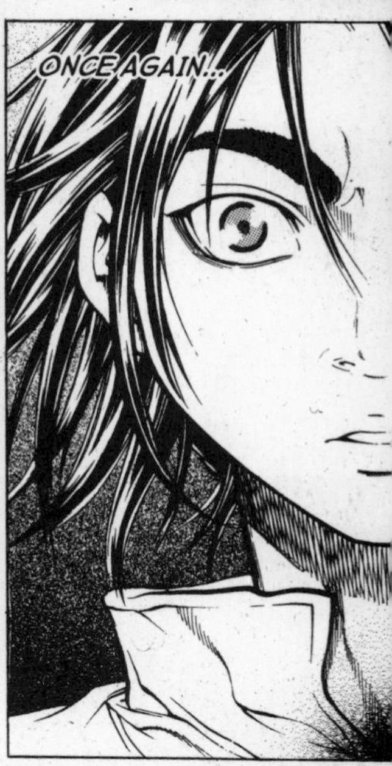
ONCE AGAIN...

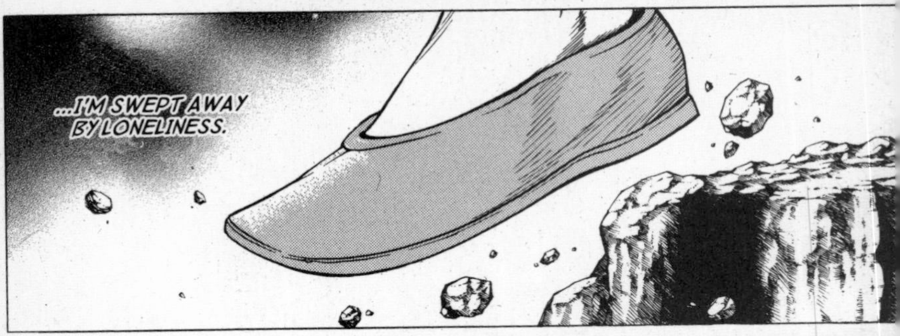
...I'M SWEPT AWAY BY LONELINESS.
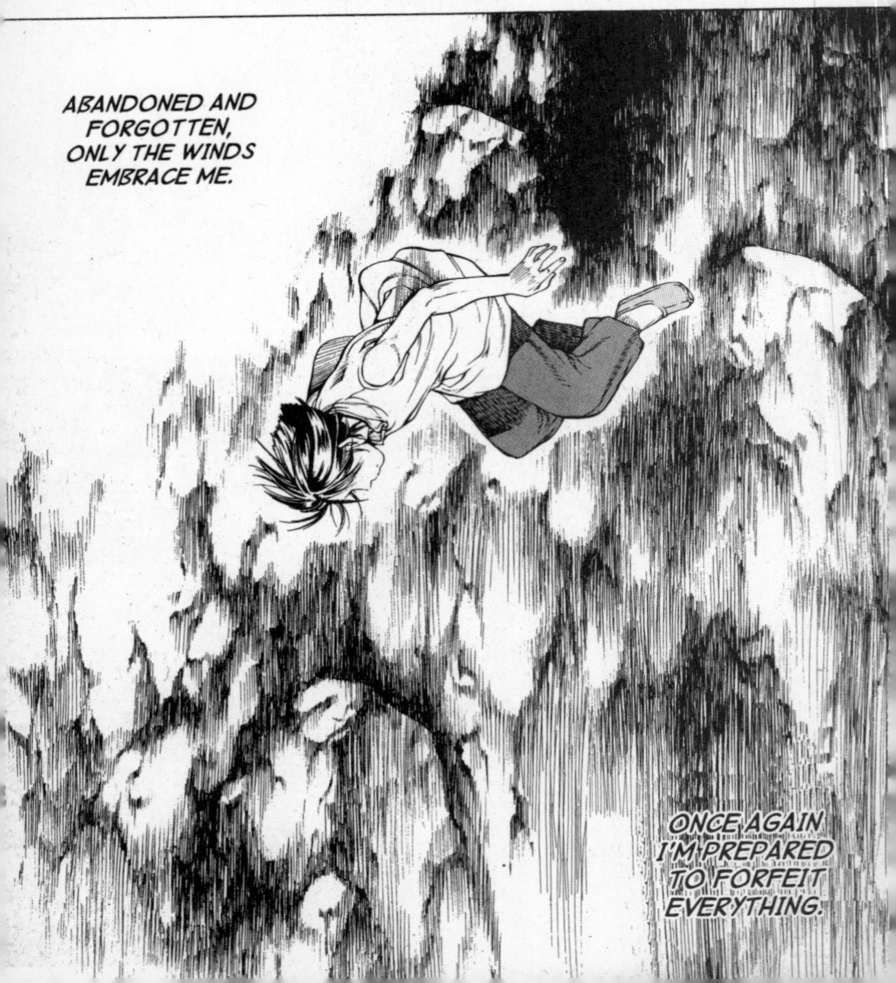
ABANDONED AND FORGOTTEN, ONLY THE WINDS EMBRACE ME.
ONCE AGAIN I'M PREPARED TO FORFEIT EVERYTHING.

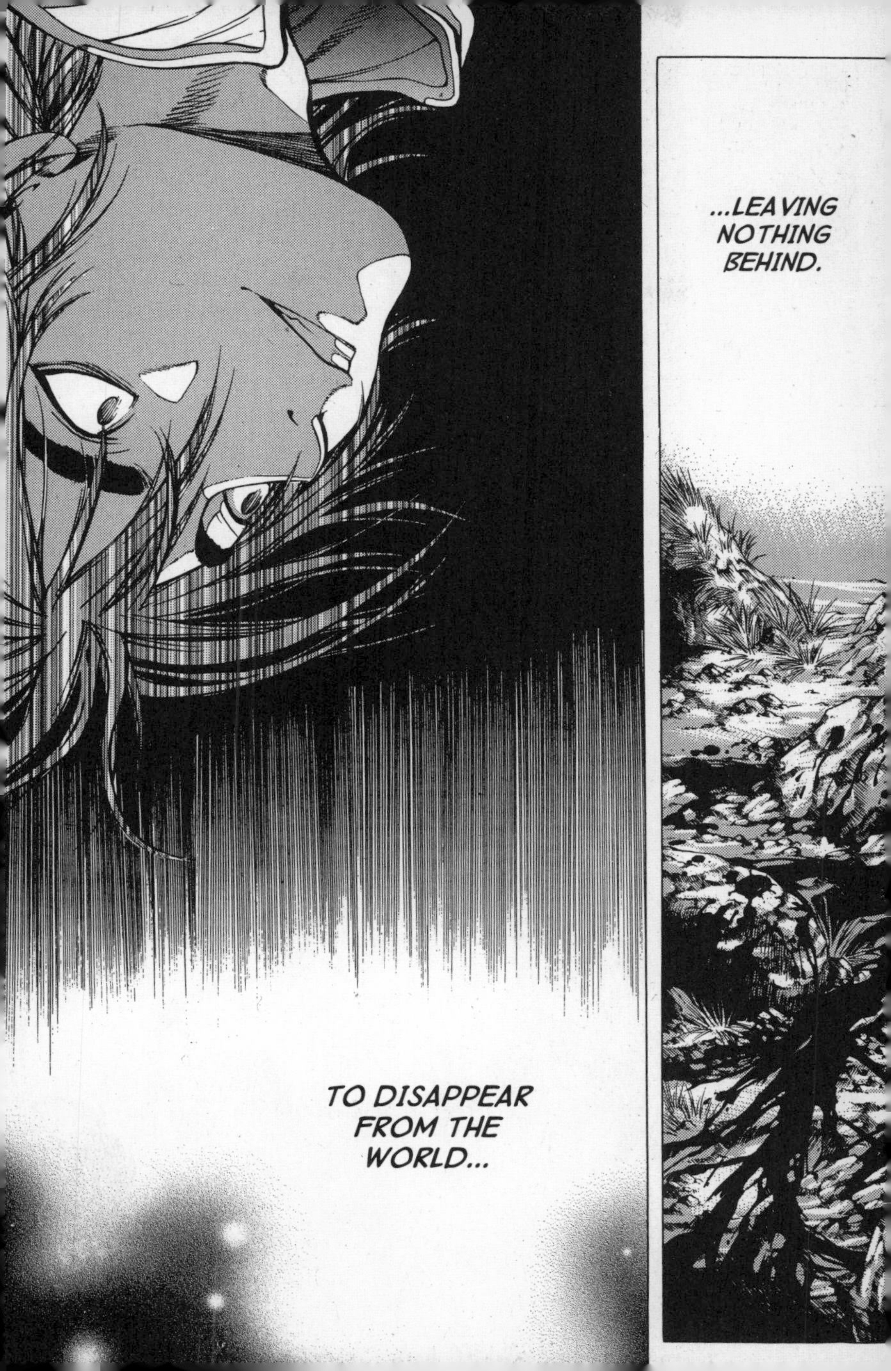
TO DISAPPEAR FROM THE WORLD...
...LEAVING NOTHING BEHIND.

IT
SEEMS
SO
EASY...

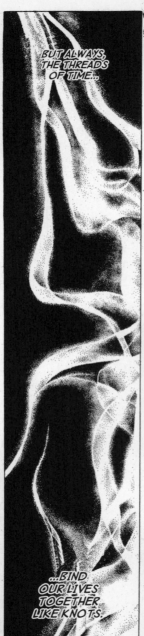

BUT ALWAYS,
THE THREADS
OF TIME...

...BIND
OUR LIVES
TOGETHER
LIKE KNOTS.

MOTHER...

FATHER...

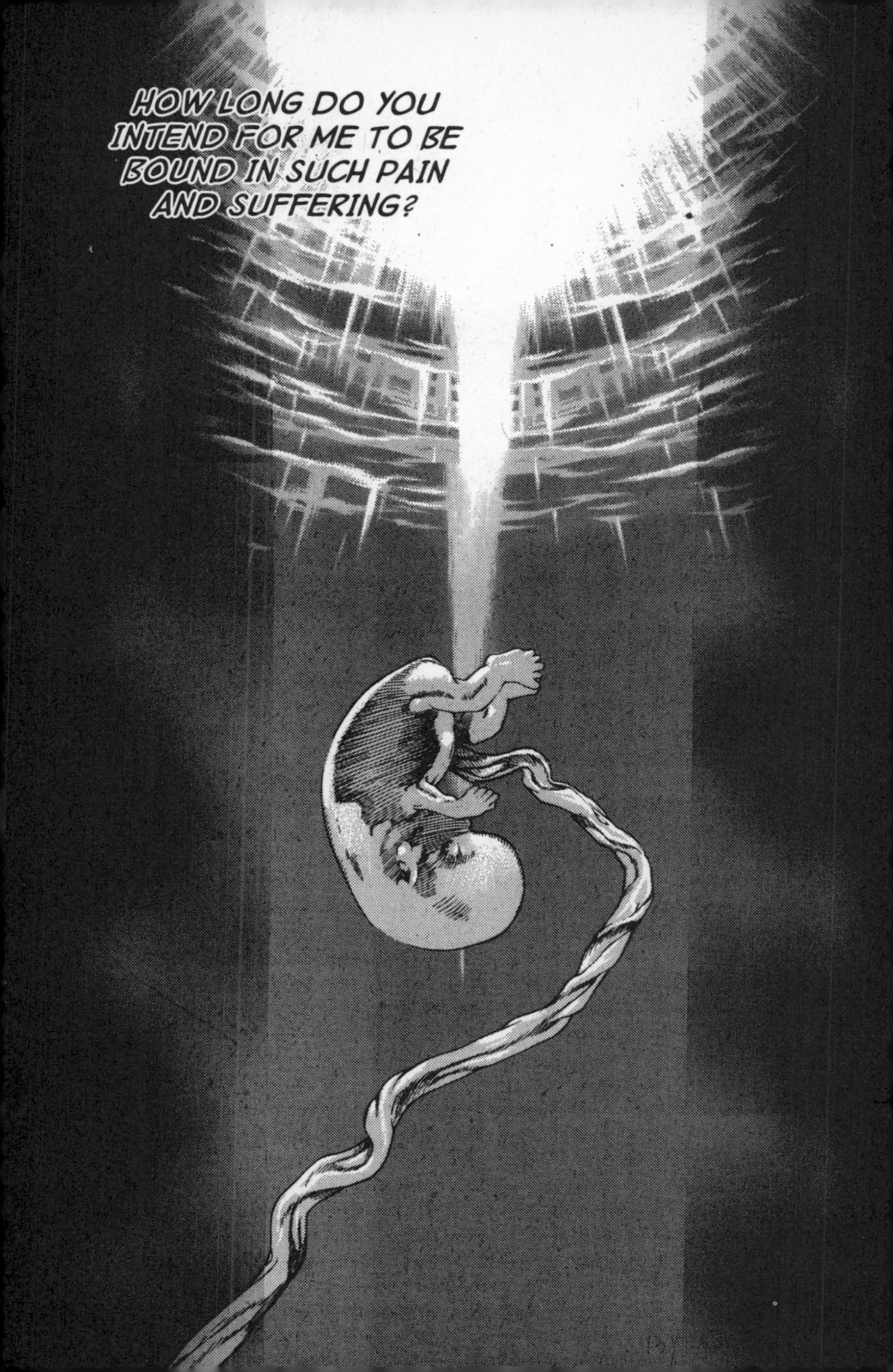
HOW LONG DO YOU INTEND FOR ME TO BE BOUND IN SUCH PAIN AND SUFFERING?

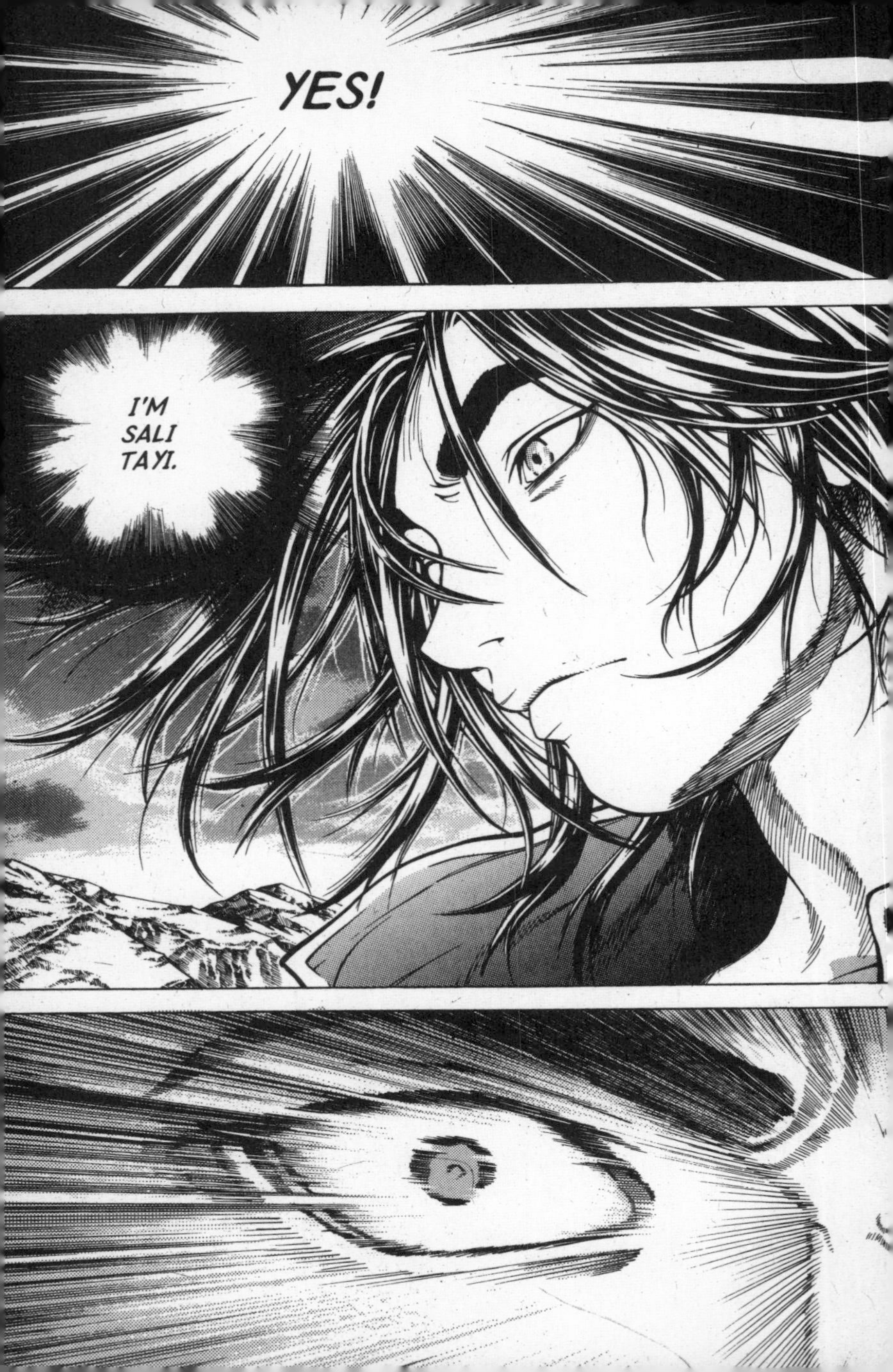
YES!
I'M SALI TAYI.

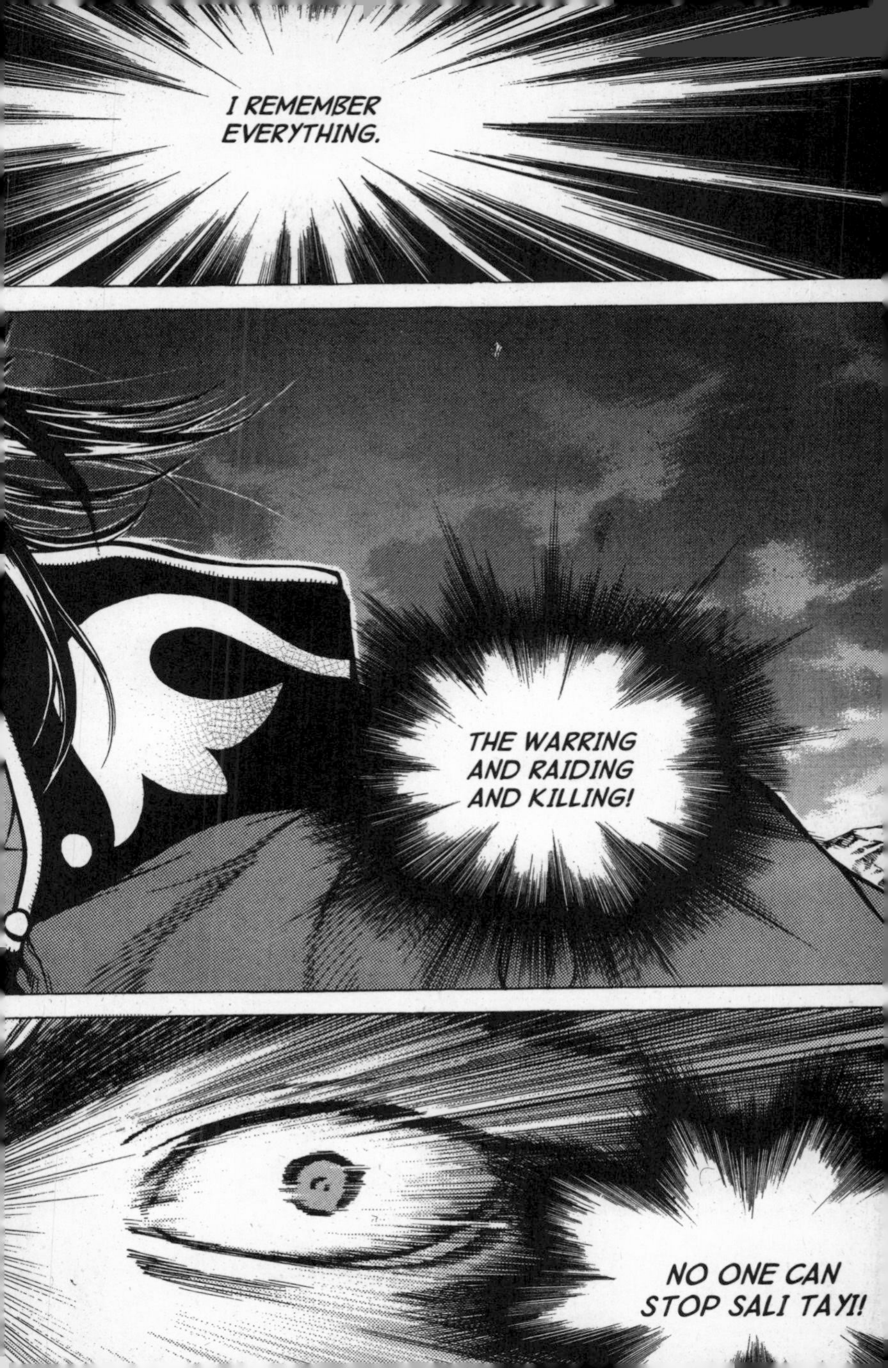
I REMEMBER EVERYTHING.
THE WARRING AND RAIDING AND KILLING!
NO ONE CAN STOP SALI TAYI!

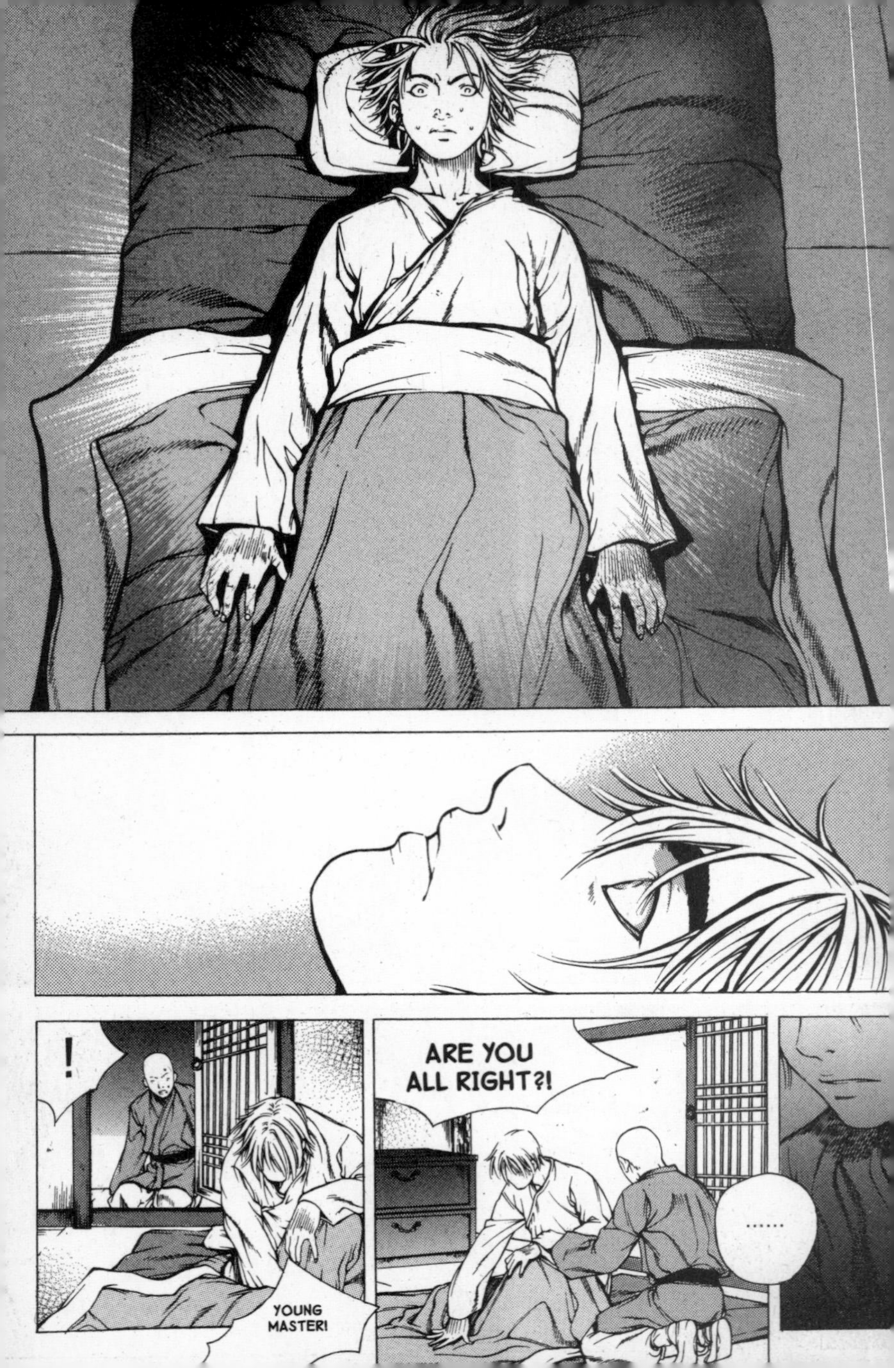
!
YOUNG MASTER!
ARE YOU ALL RIGHT?!
......

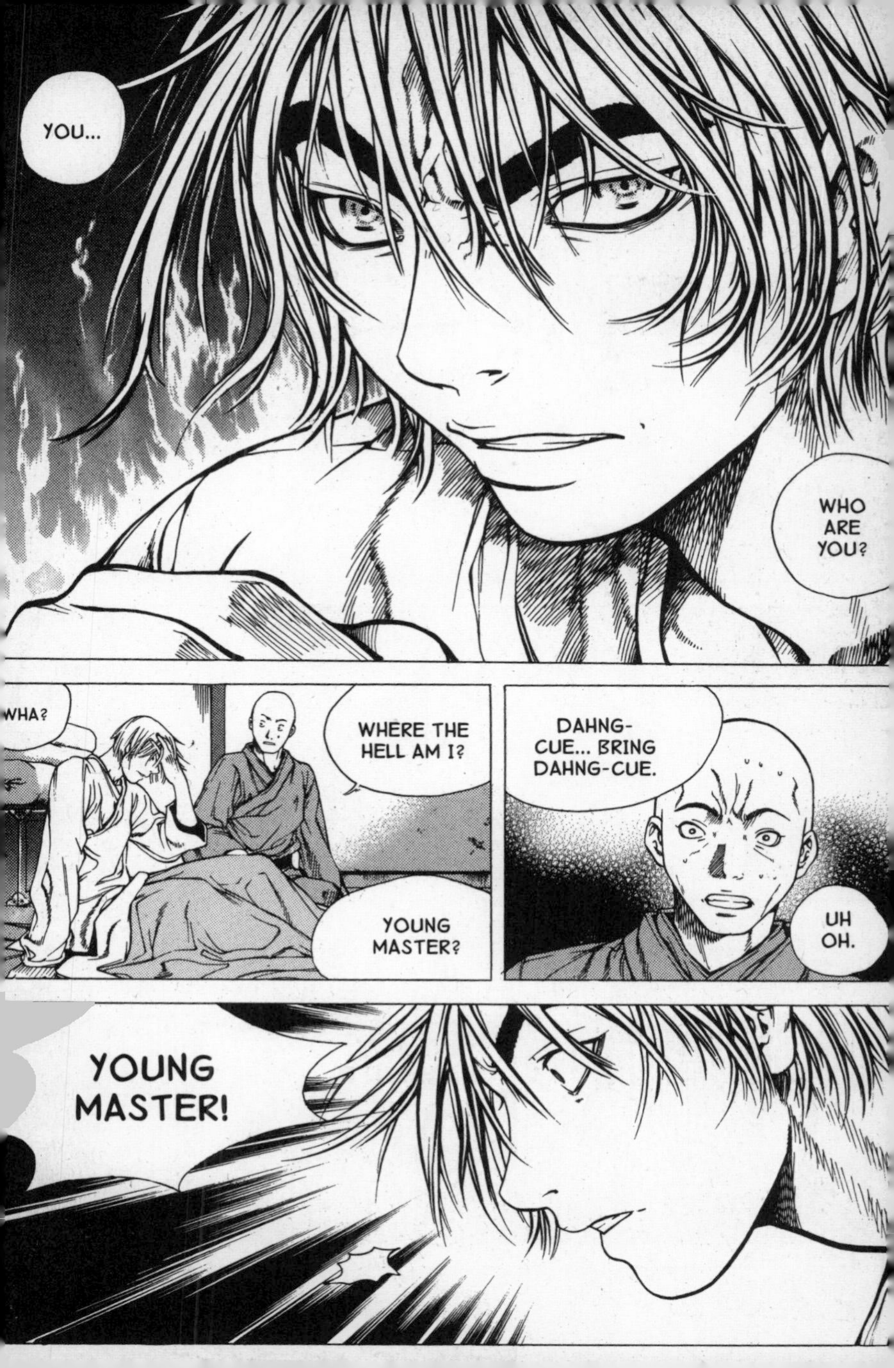
YOU...
WHO ARE YOU?
WHA?
WHERE THE HELL AM I?
YOUNG MASTER?
DAHNG-CUE... BRING DAHNG-CUE.
UH OH.
YOUNG MASTER!

ARE YOU ALL RIGHT?

YOU SOUND UN-WELL.

WHAT IS IT?

I'M JUST...

JUST... CONFUSED

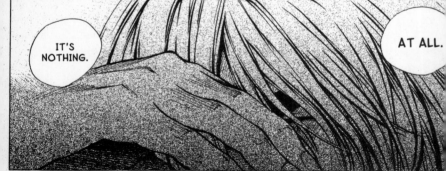

IT'S NOTHING.

AT ALL.

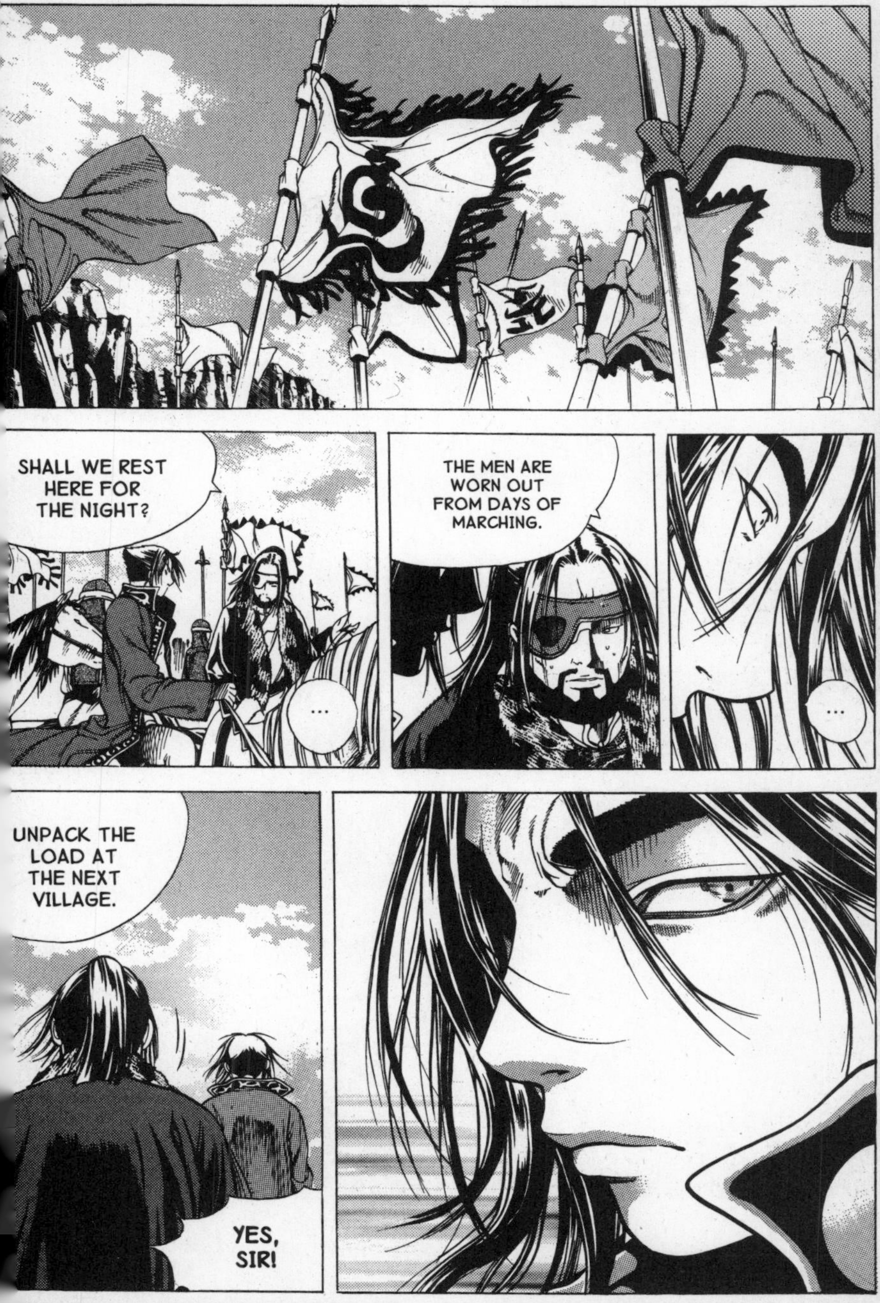
SHALL WE REST HERE FOR THE NIGHT?
...
THE MEN ARE WORN OUT FROM DAYS OF MARCHING.
...
UNPACK THE LOAD AT THE NEXT VILLAGE.
YES, SIR!

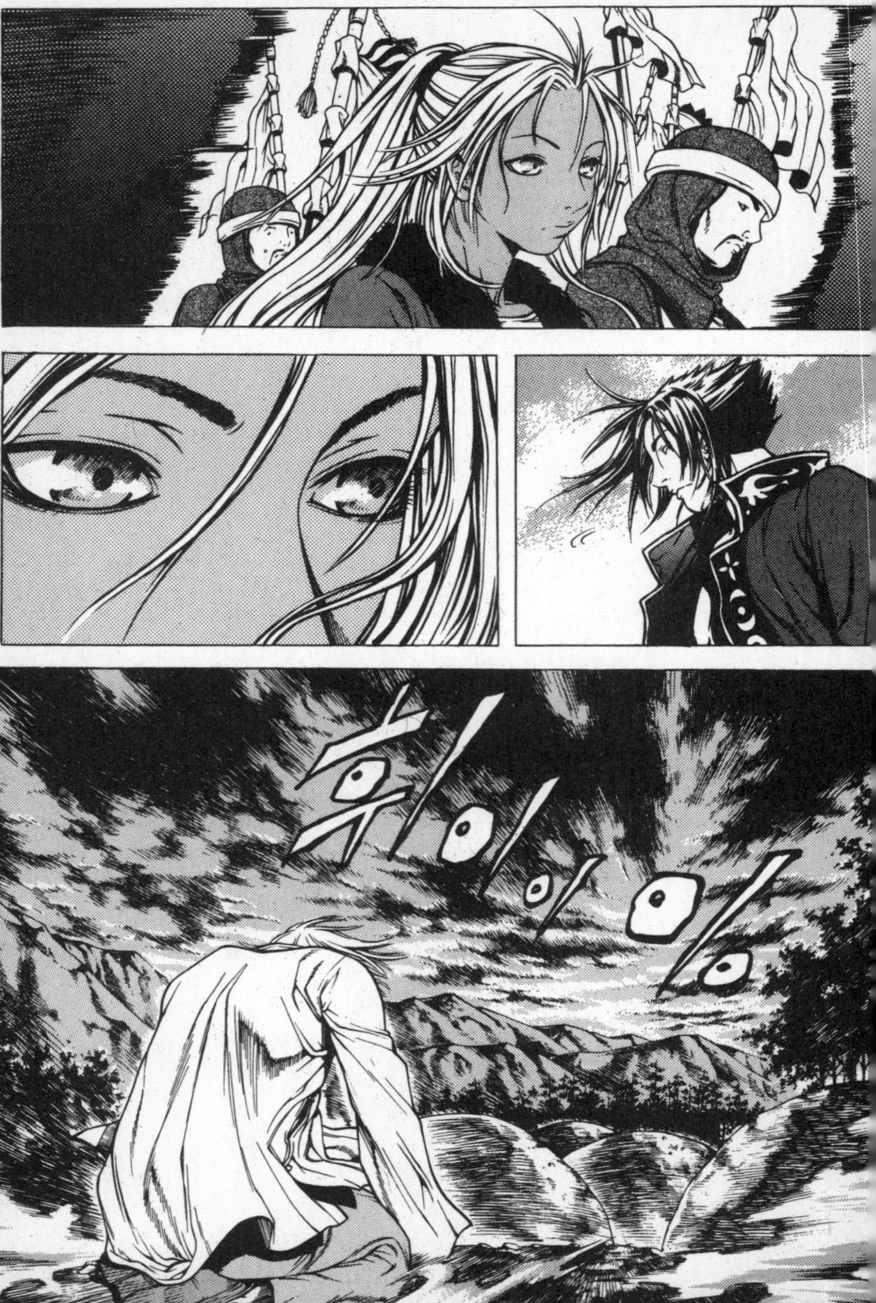
휘이이잉

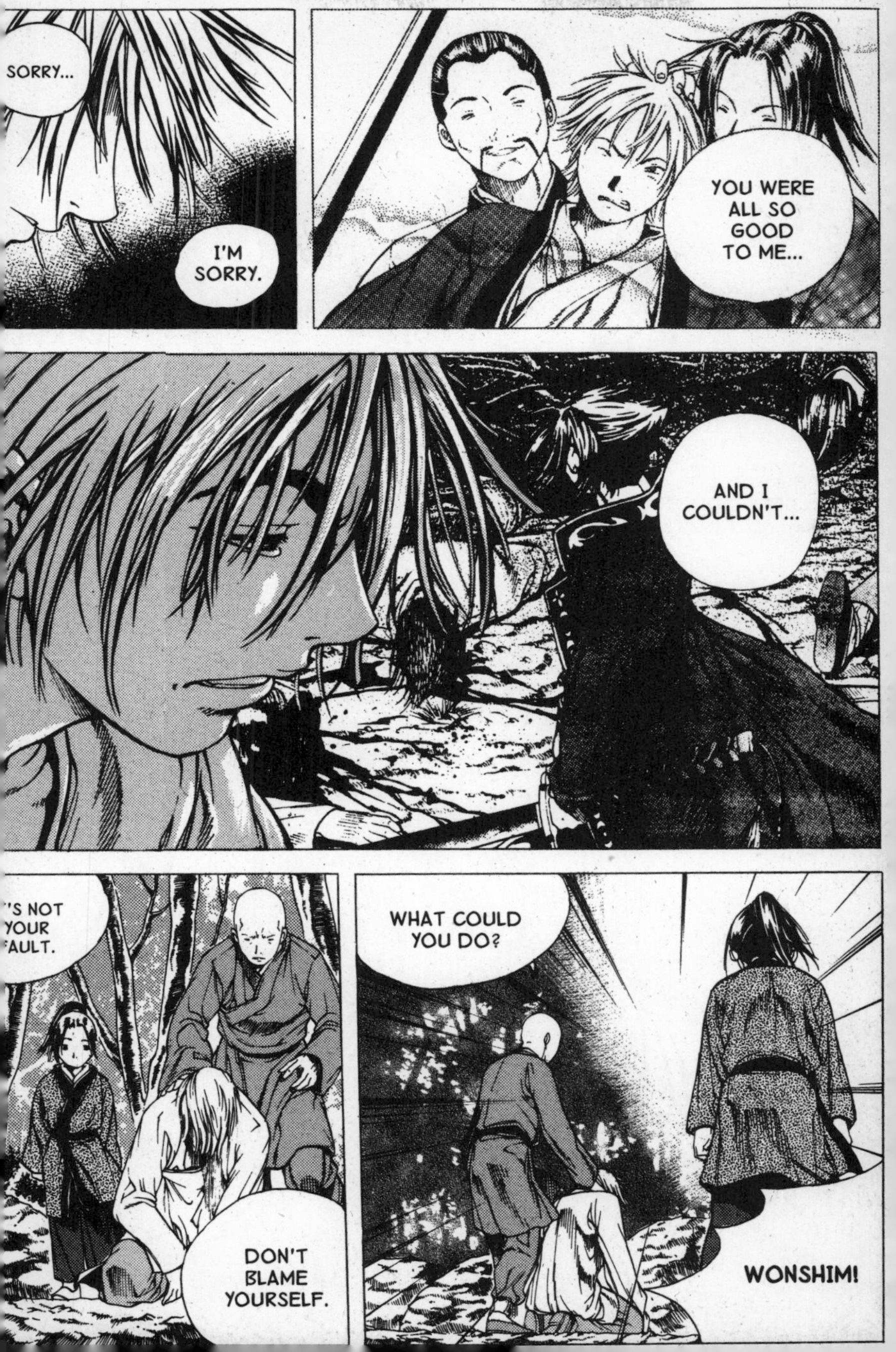
SORRY...
I'M SORRY.
YOU WERE ALL SO GOOD TO ME...
AND I COULDN'T...
'S NOT YOUR FAULT.
DON'T BLAME YOURSELF.
WHAT COULD YOU DO?
WONSHIM!

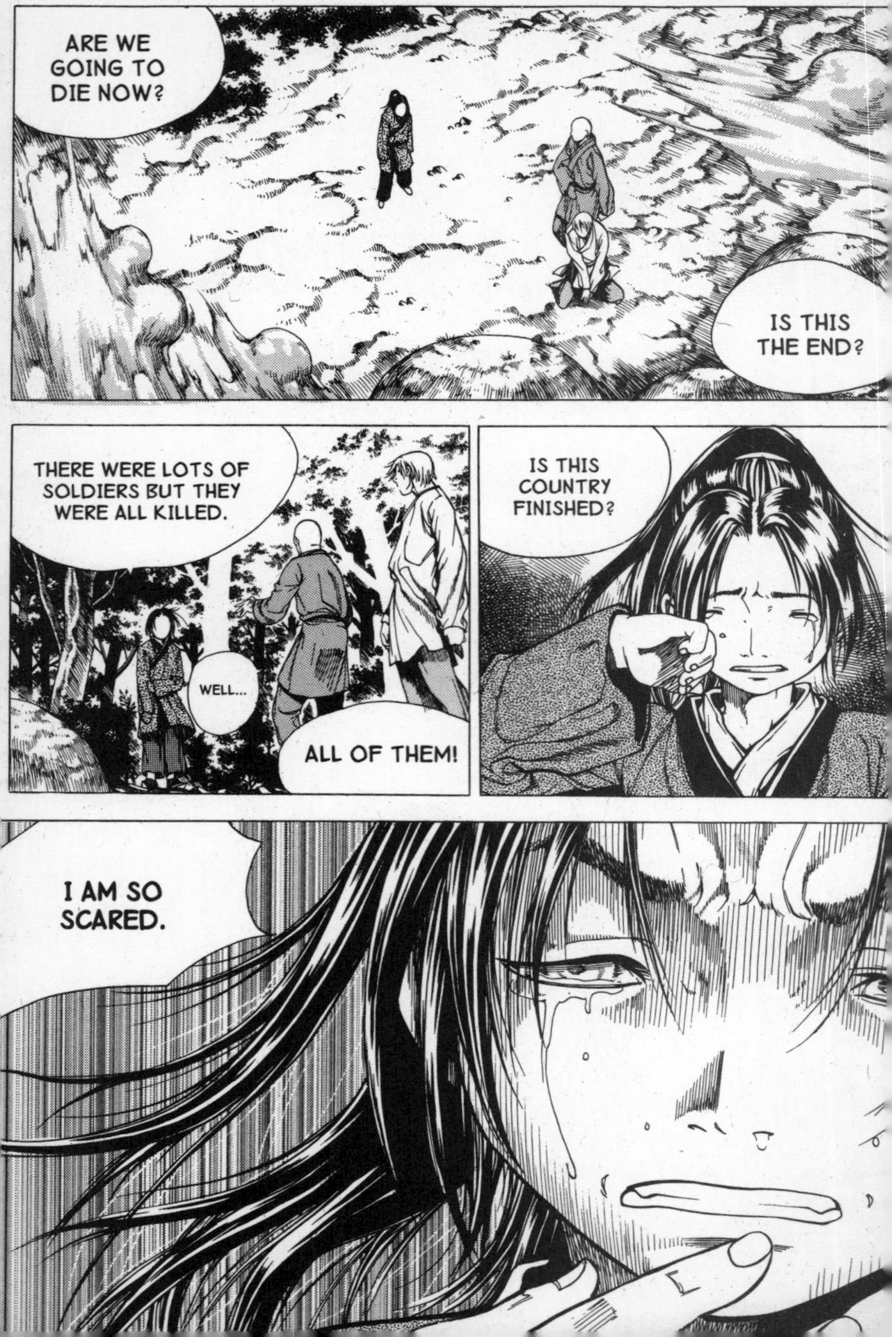
ARE WE GOING TO DIE NOW?
IS THIS THE END?
THERE WERE LOTS OF SOLDIERS BUT THEY WERE ALL KILLED.
WELL...
ALL OF THEM!
IS THIS COUNTRY FINISHED?
I AM SO SCARED.

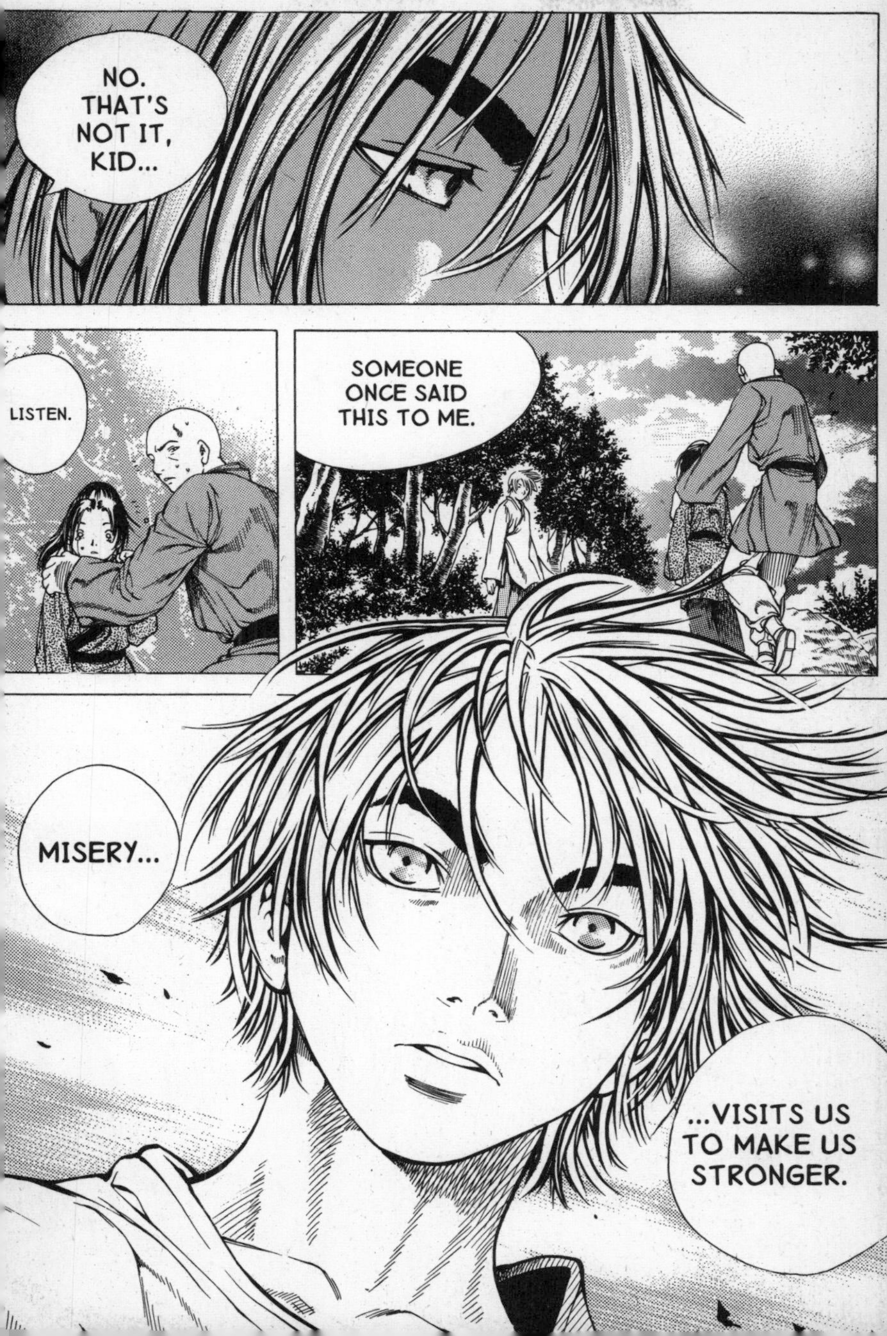
NO. THAT'S NOT IT, KID...
LISTEN.
SOMEONE ONCE SAID THIS TO ME.
MISERY...
...VISITS US TO MAKE US STRONGER.

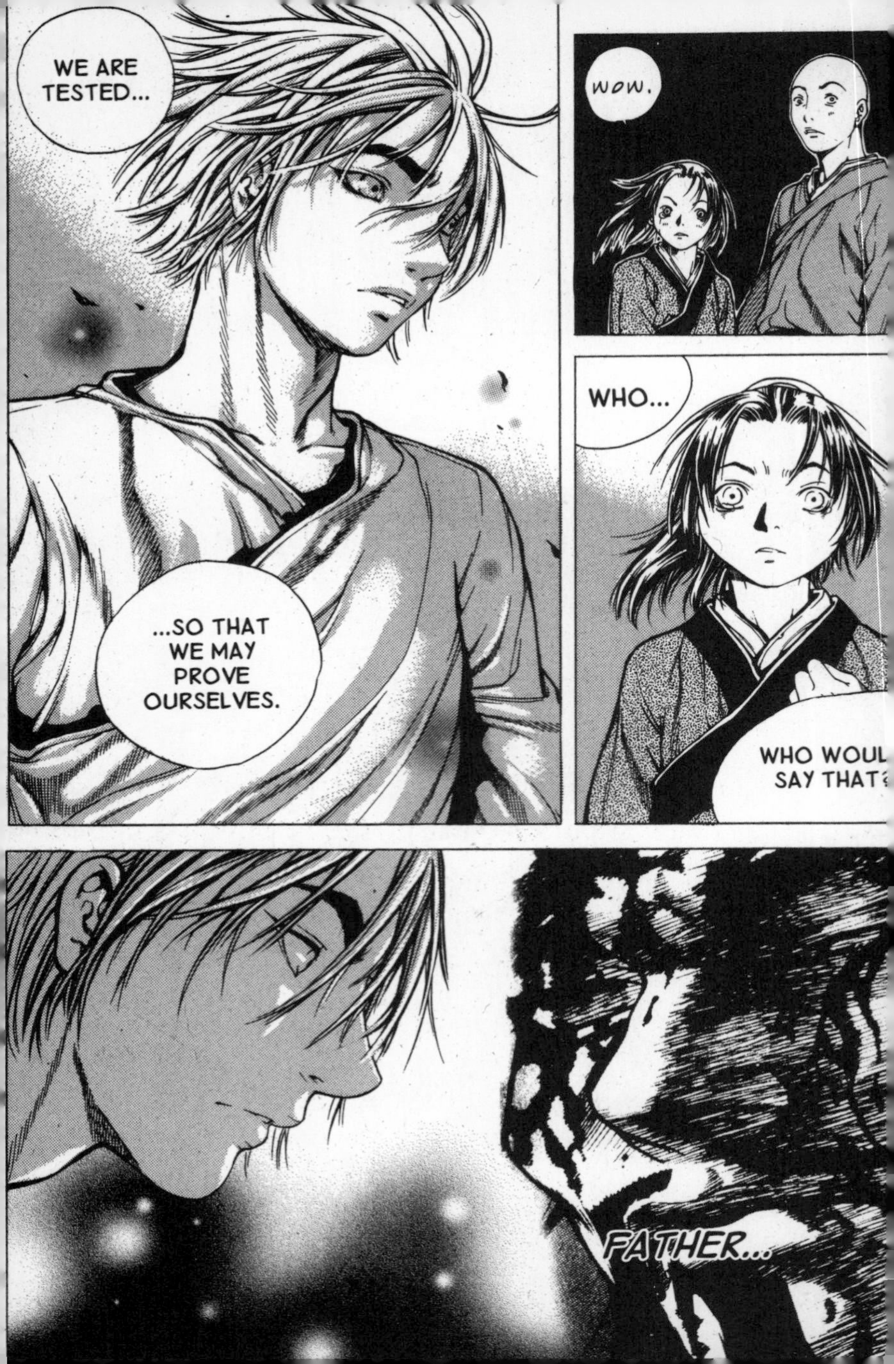
WE ARE TESTED...
...SO THAT WE MAY PROVE OURSELVES.
WOW.
WHO...
WHO WOUL SAY THAT?
FATHER...

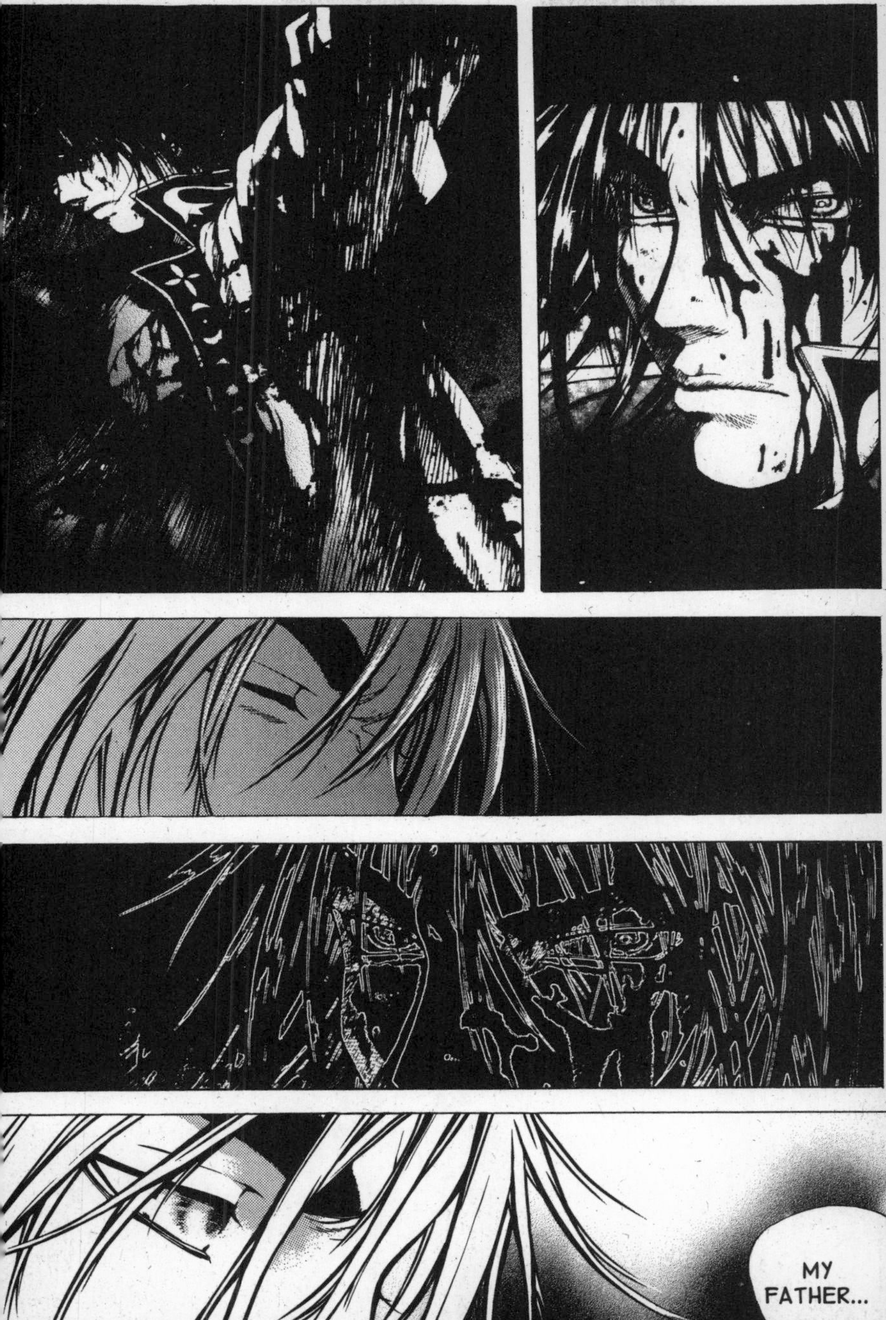
MY FATHER...

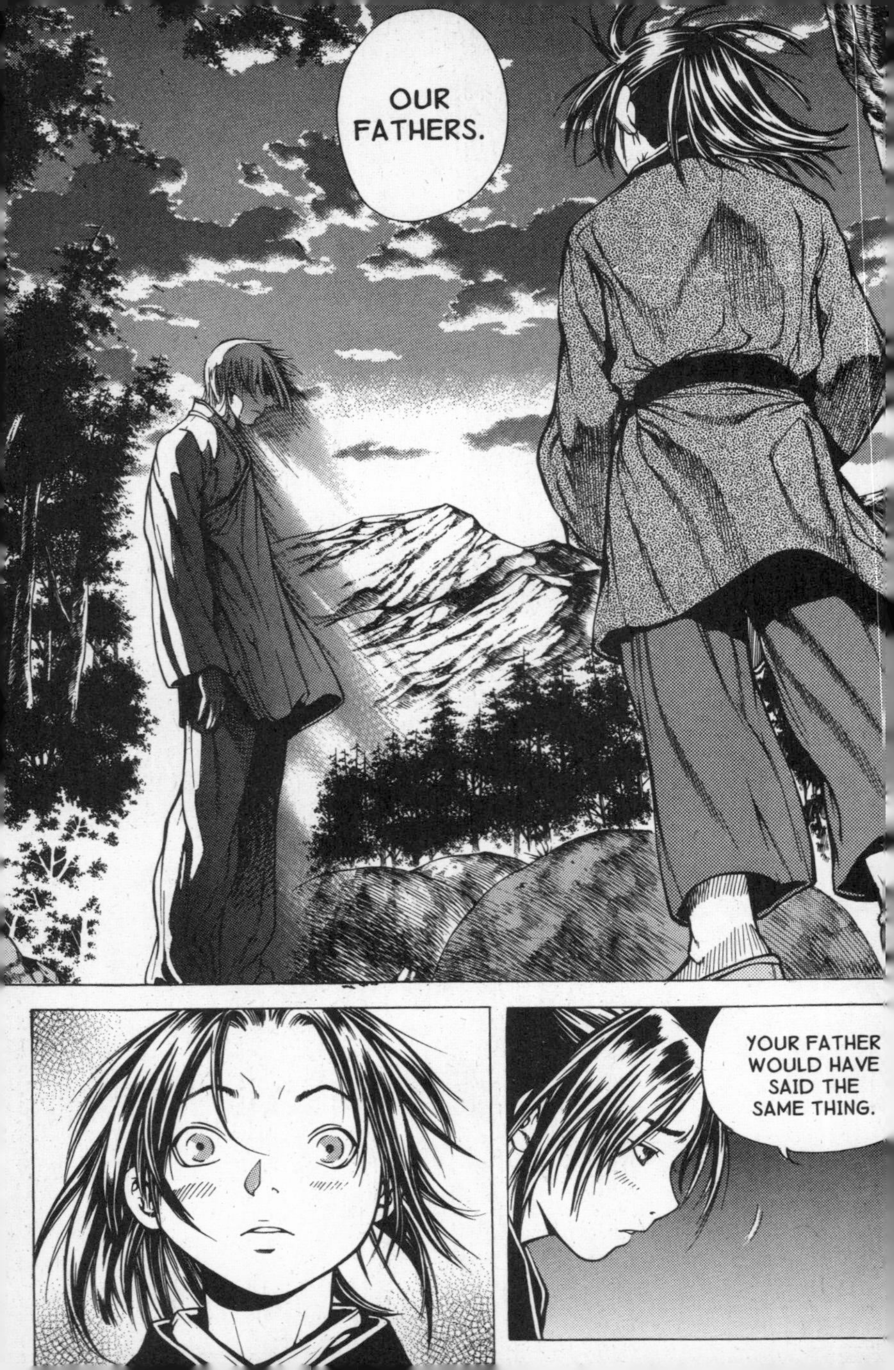
OUR FATHERS.
YOUR FATHER WOULD HAVE SAID THE SAME THING.

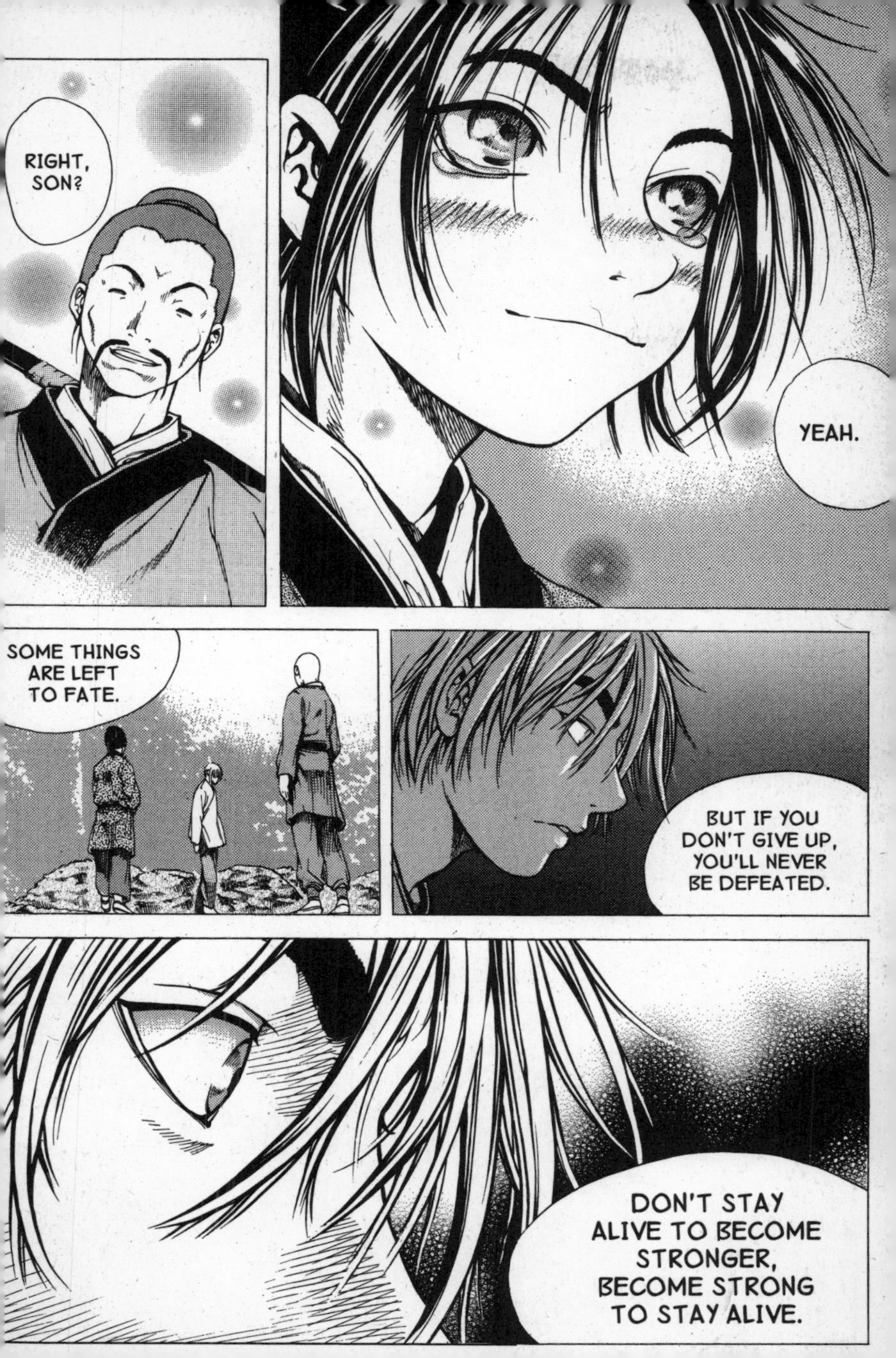
RIGHT, SON?
YEAH.
SOME THINGS ARE LEFT TO FATE.
BUT IF YOU DON'T GIVE UP, YOU'LL NEVER BE DEFEATED.
DON'T STAY ALIVE TO BECOME STRONGER, BECOME STRONG TO STAY ALIVE.

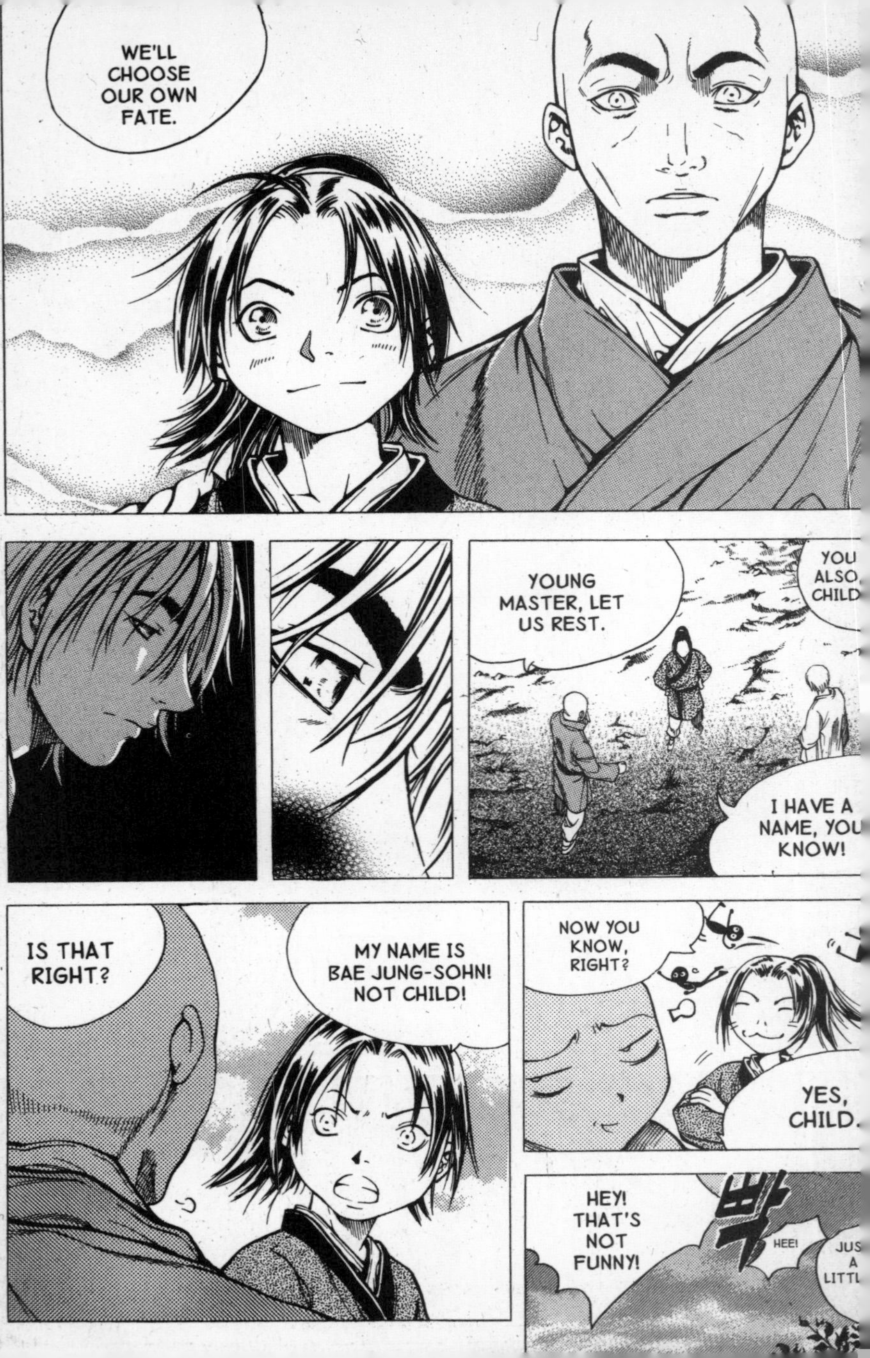
WE'LL CHOOSE OUR OWN FATE.
YOUNG MASTER, LET US REST.
YOU ALSO, CHILD
I HAVE A NAME, YOU KNOW!
IS THAT RIGHT?
MY NAME IS BAE JUNG-SOHN! NOT CHILD!
NOW YOU KNOW, RIGHT?
YES, CHILD.
HEY! THAT'S NOT FUNNY!
HEE!

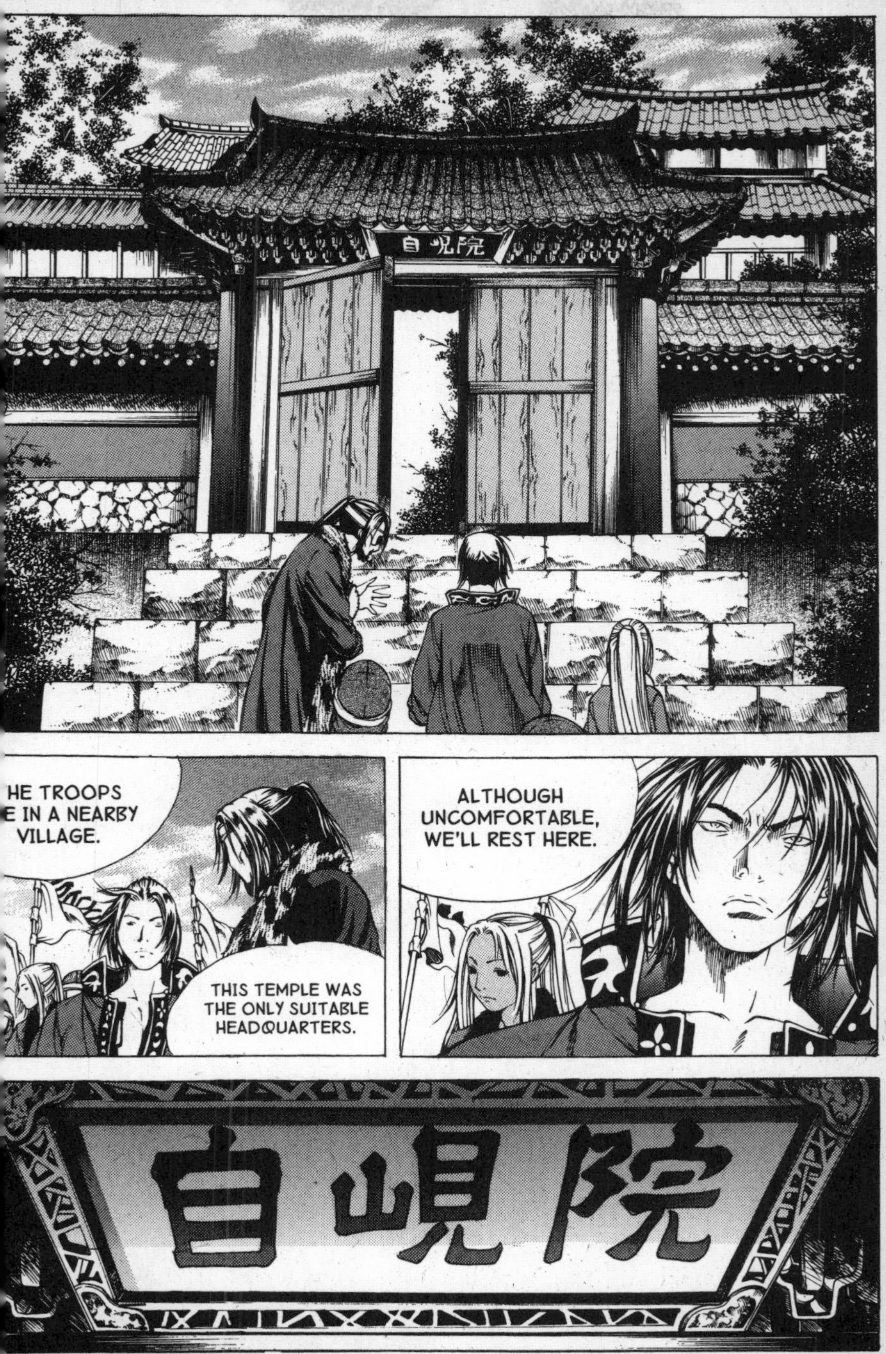
白峴院
HE TROOPS E IN A NEARBY VILLAGE.
THIS TEMPLE WAS THE ONLY SUITABLE HEADQUARTERS.
ALTHOUGH UNCOMFORTABLE, WE'LL REST HERE.
白峴院
YUN WON: A TEMPLE INSIDE CHO-IN CASTLE IN YONGIN.

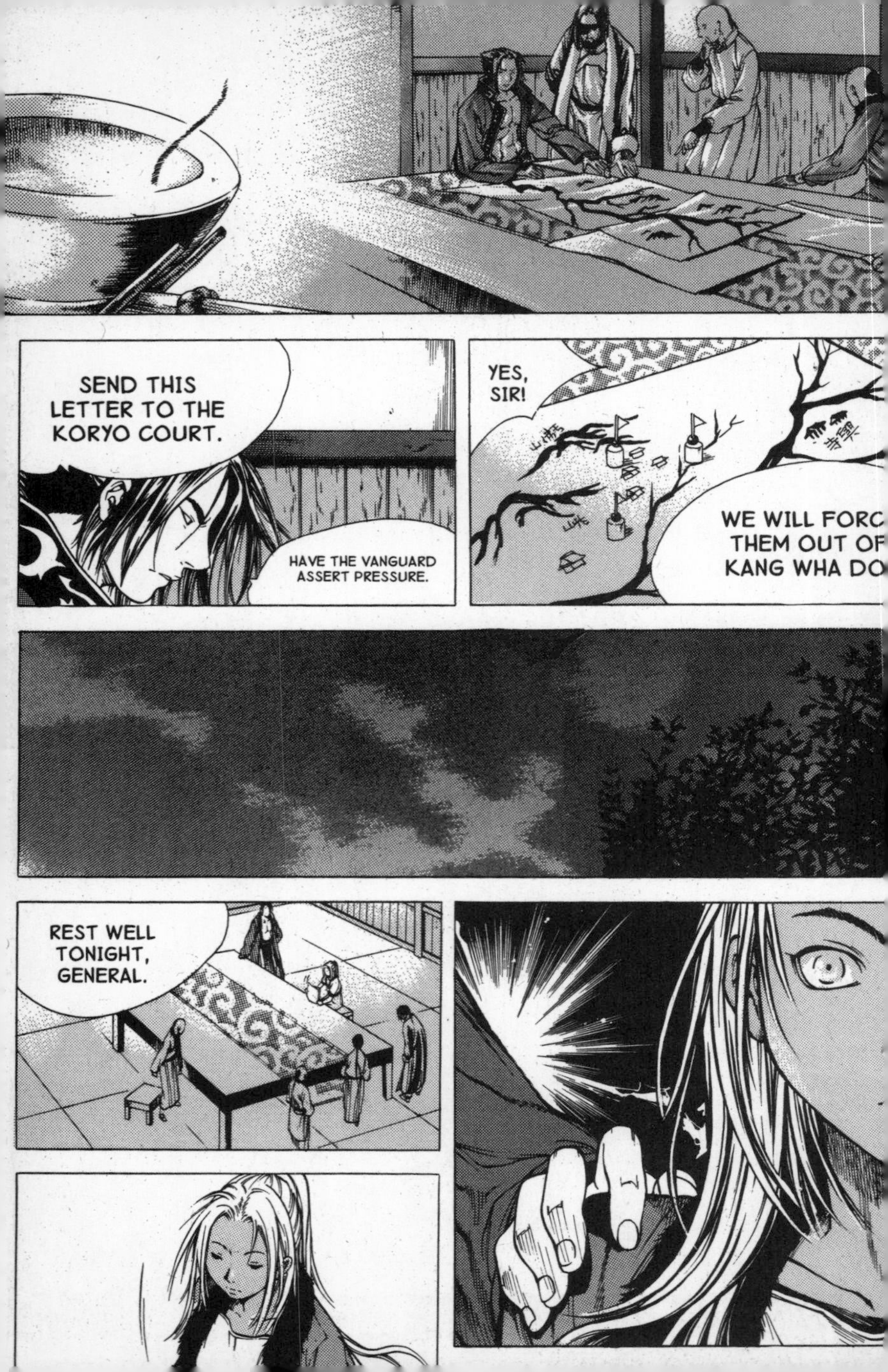
SEND THIS LETTER TO THE KORYO COURT.
HAVE THE VANGUARD ASSERT PRESSURE.
YES, SIR!
WE WILL FORC THEM OUT OF KANG WHA DO
REST WELL TONIGHT, GENERAL.

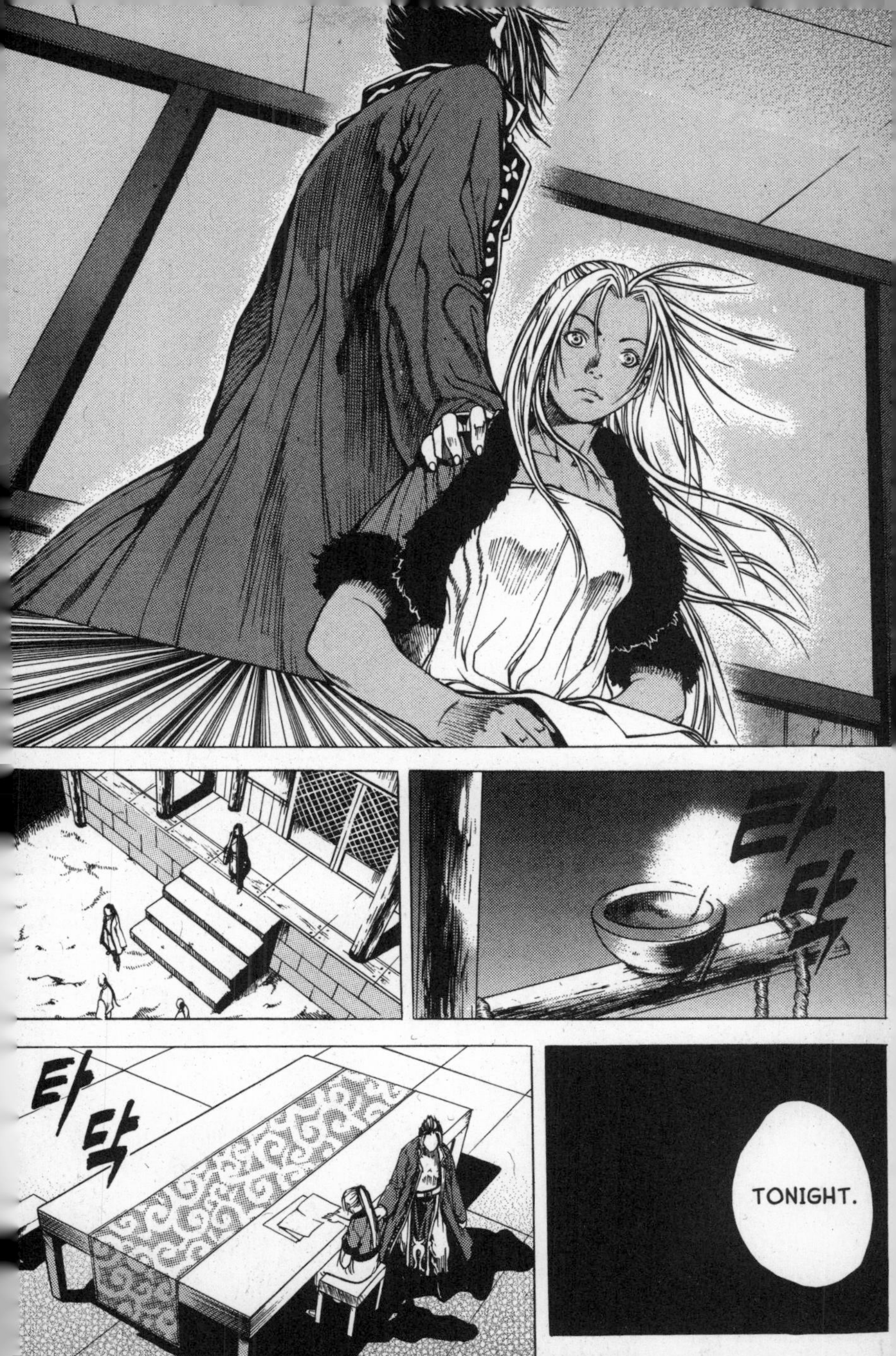
타닥
타닥
TONIGHT.

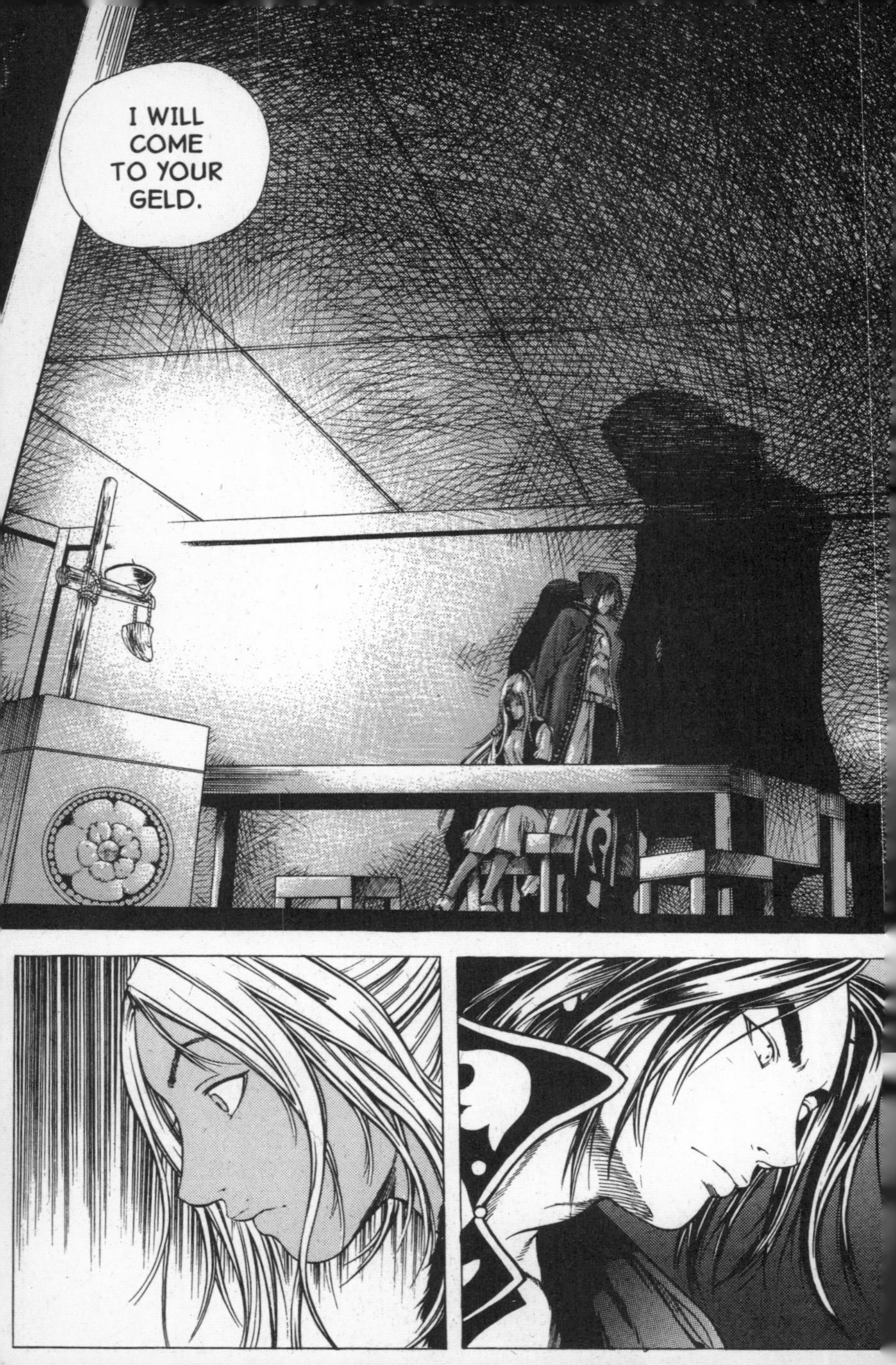
I WILL COME TO YOUR GELD.

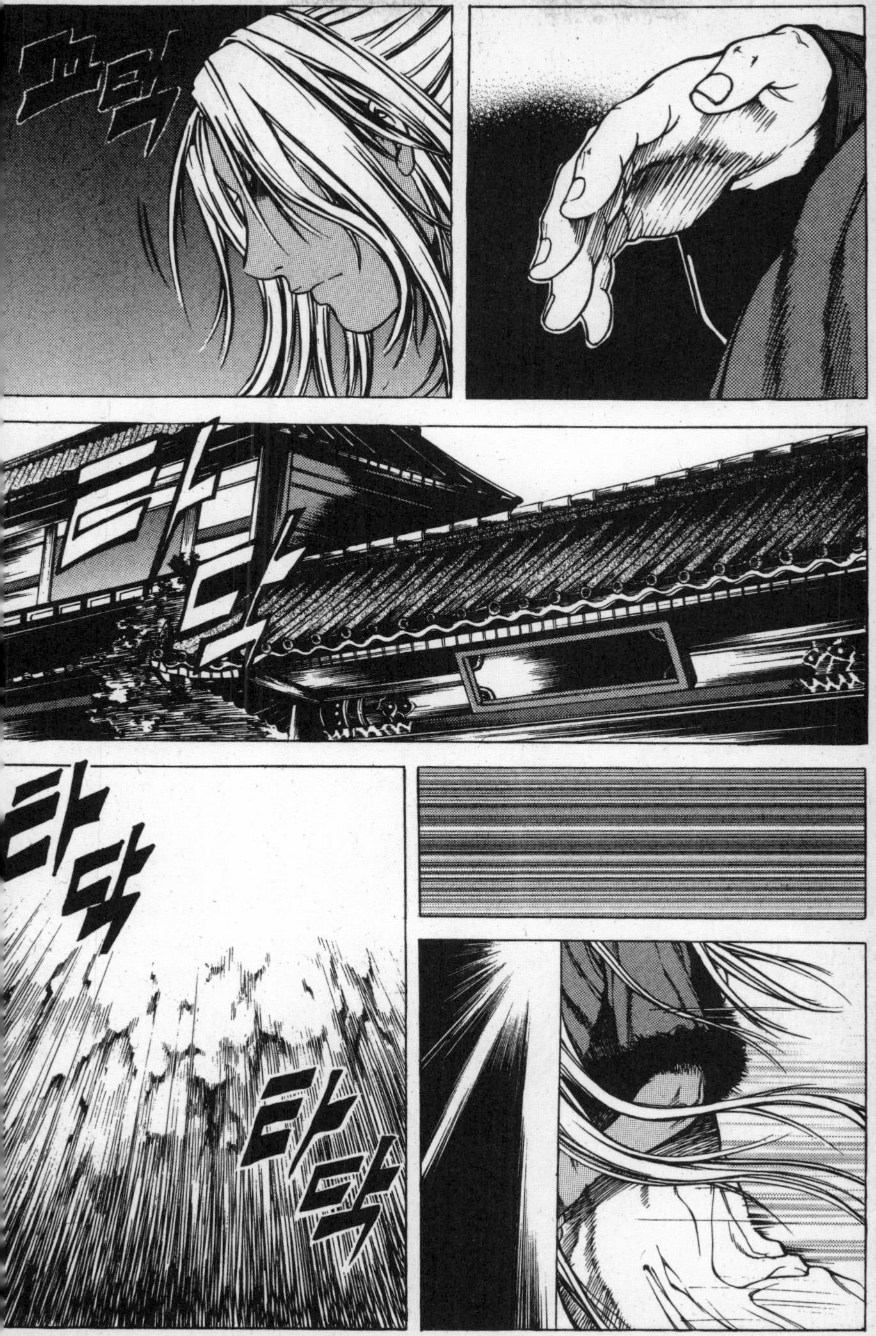
끄덕
타닥
타닥
타닥

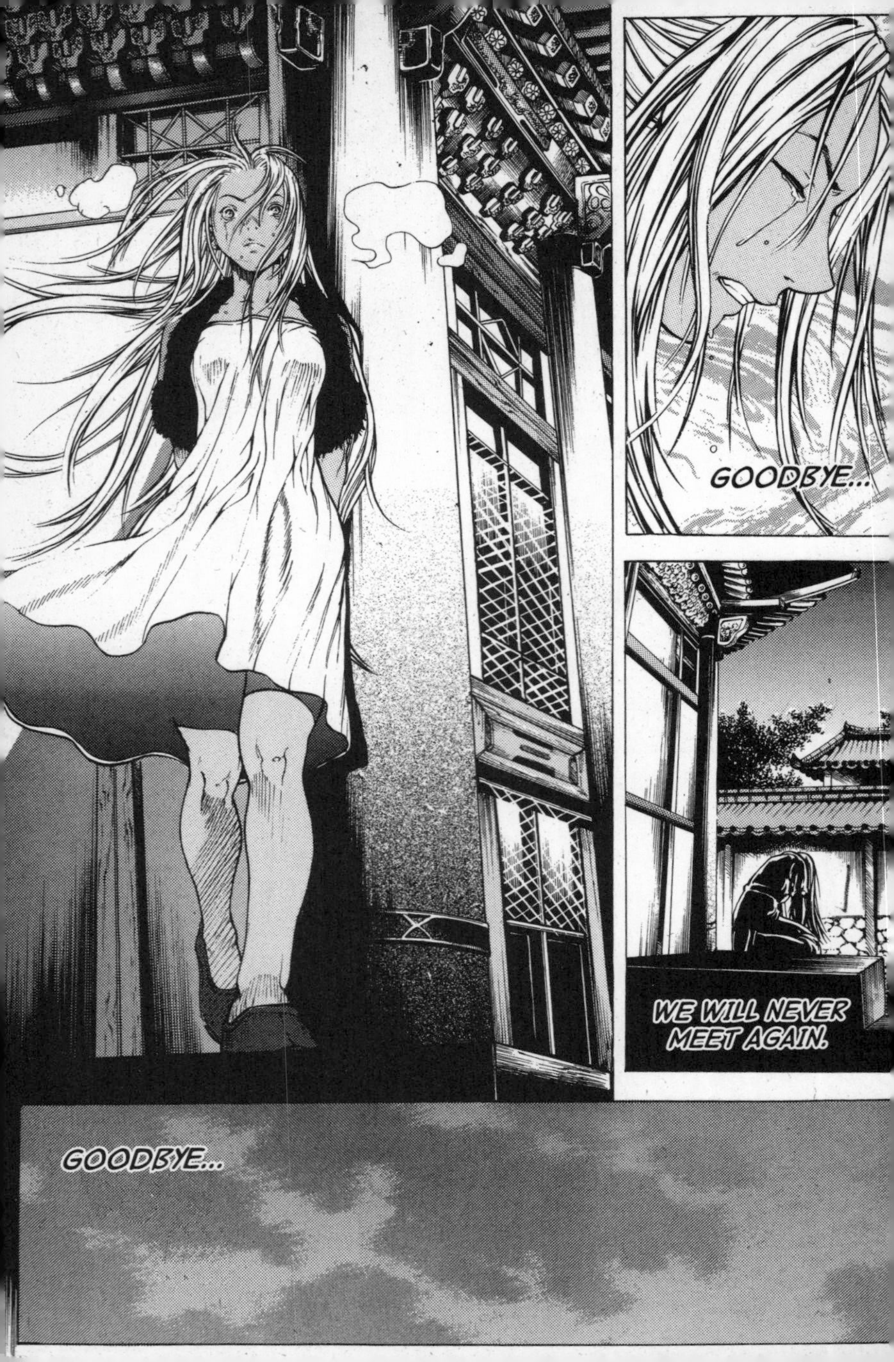
GOODBYE...
WE WILL NEVER MEET AGAIN.
GOODBYE...

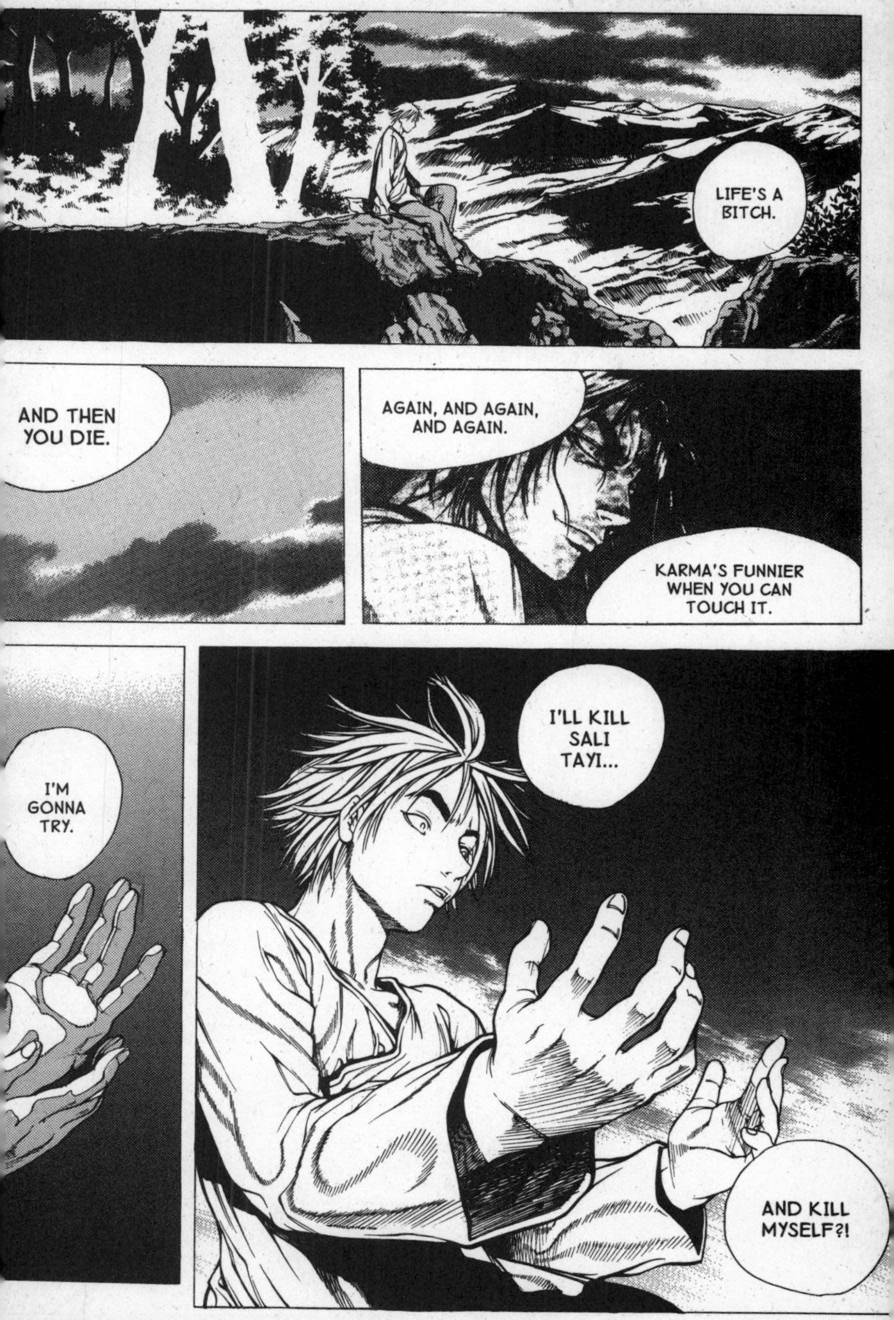
LIFE'S A BITCH.
AND THEN YOU DIE.
AGAIN, AND AGAIN, AND AGAIN.
KARMA'S FUNNIER WHEN YOU CAN TOUCH IT.
I'M GONNA TRY.
I'LL KILL SALI TAYI...
AND KILL MYSELF?!

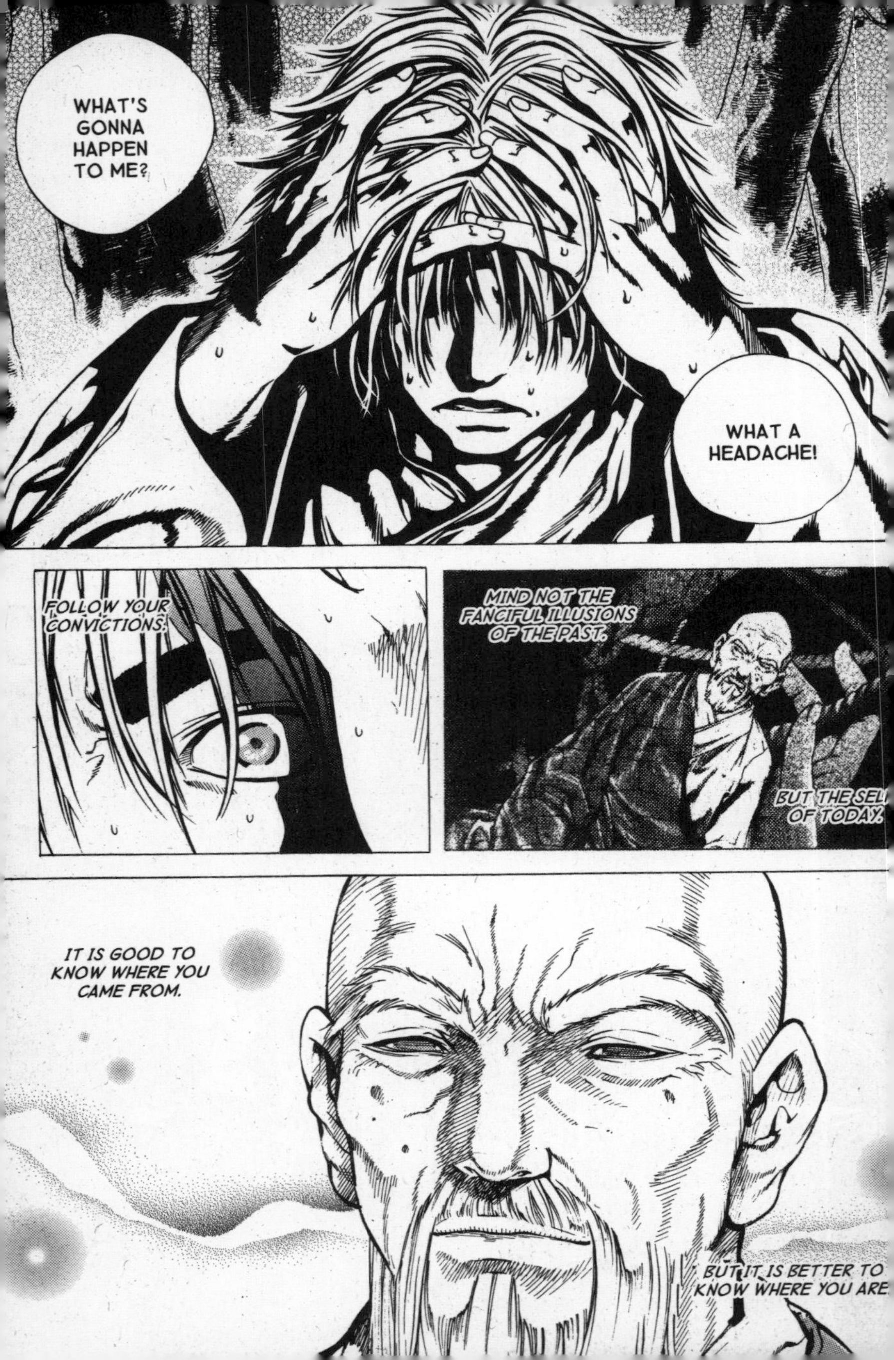
WHAT'S GONNA HAPPEN TO ME?
WHAT A HEADACHE!
FOLLOW YOUR CONVICTIONS.
MIND NOT THE FANCIFUL ILLUSIONS OF THE PAST.
BUT THE SELF OF TODAY.
IT IS GOOD TO KNOW WHERE YOU CAME FROM.
BUT IT IS BETTER TO KNOW WHERE YOU ARE.

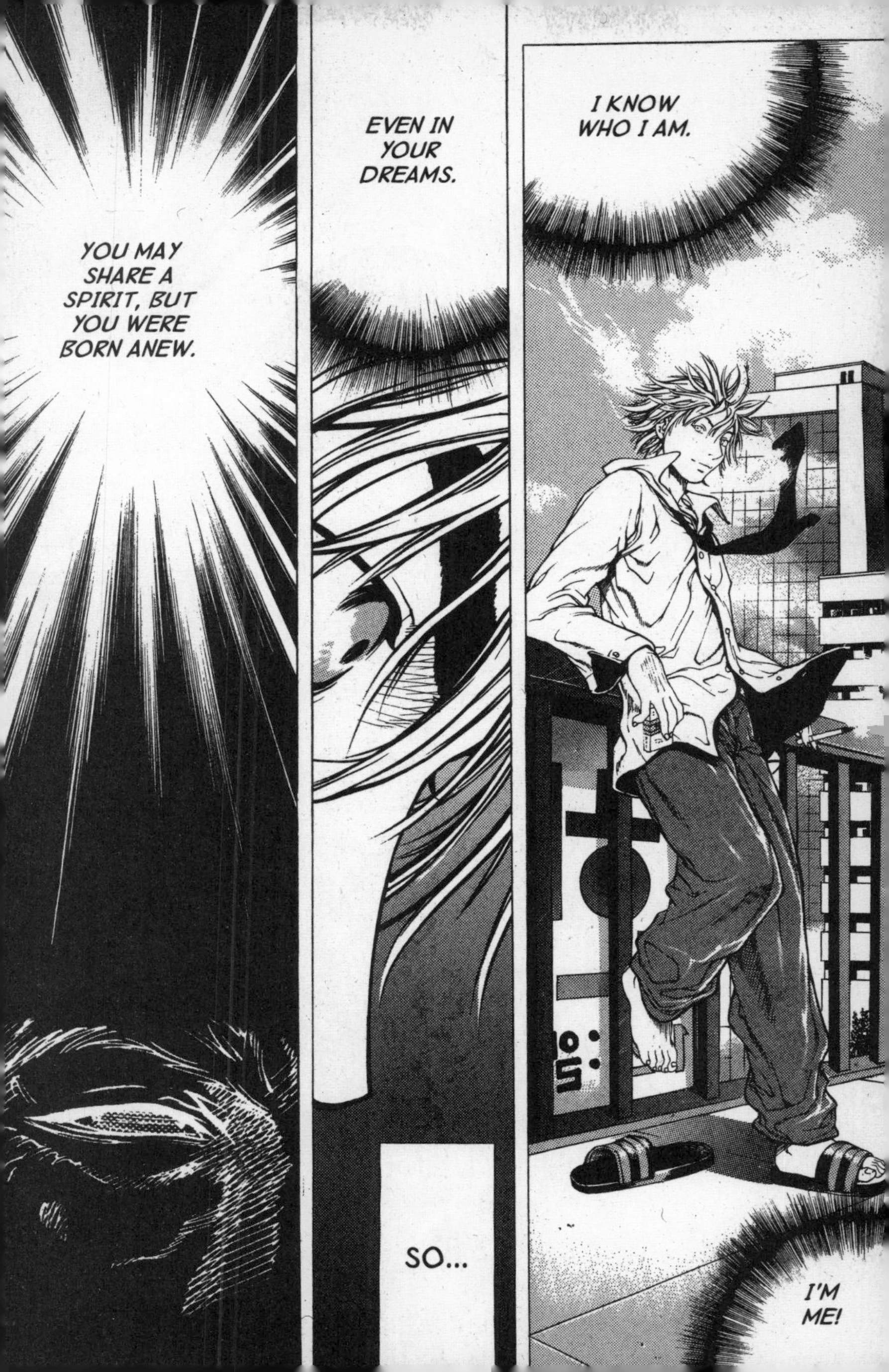
YOU MAY SHARE A SPIRIT, BUT YOU WERE BORN ANEW.
EVEN IN YOUR DREAMS.
SO...
I KNOW WHO I AM.
I'M ME!

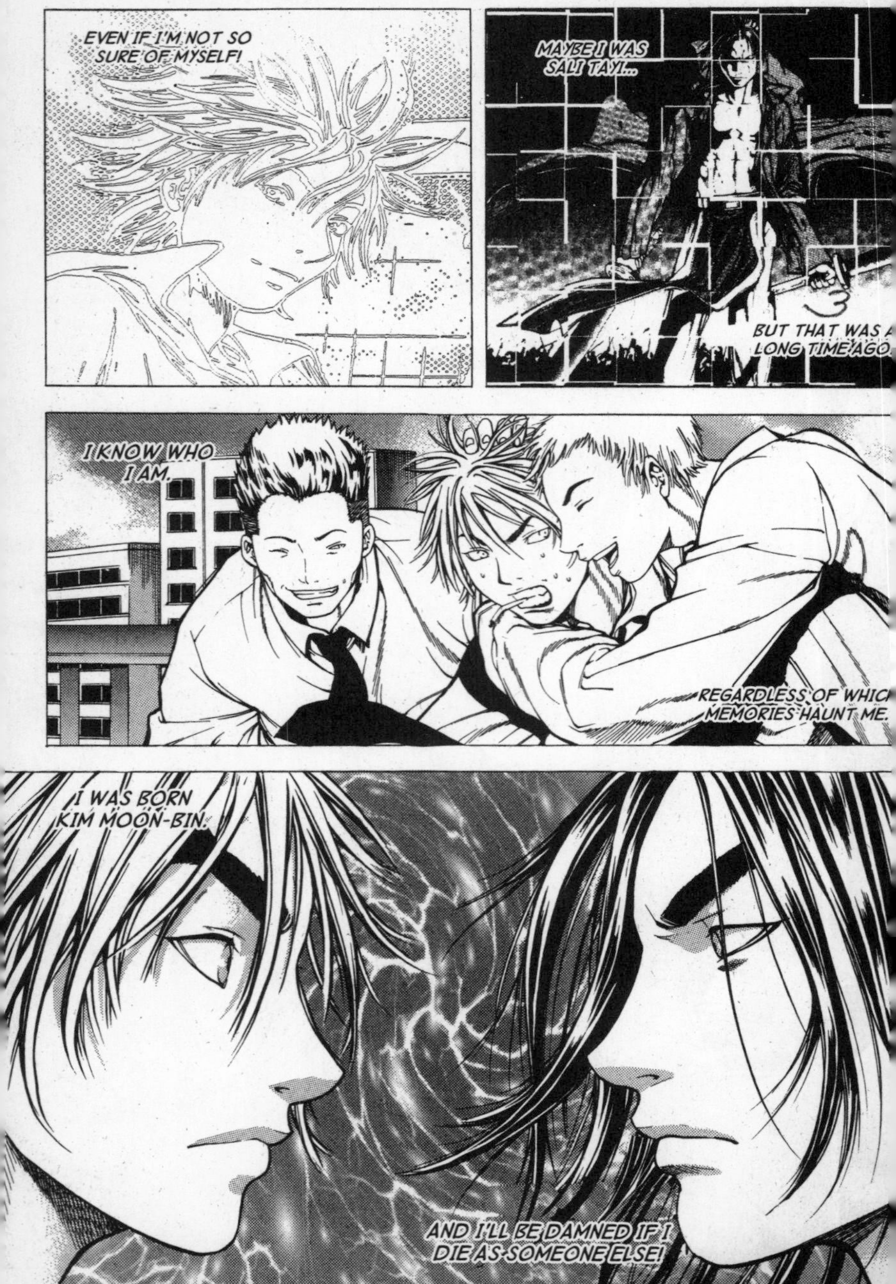
EVEN IF I'M NOT SO SURE OF MYSELF!
MAYBE I WAS SALI TAYI...
BUT THAT WAS A LONG TIME AGO.
I KNOW WHO I AM.
REGARDLESS OF WHICH MEMORIES HAUNT ME.
I WAS BORN KIM MOON-BIN.
AND I'LL BE DAMNED IF I DIE AS SOMEONE ELSE!

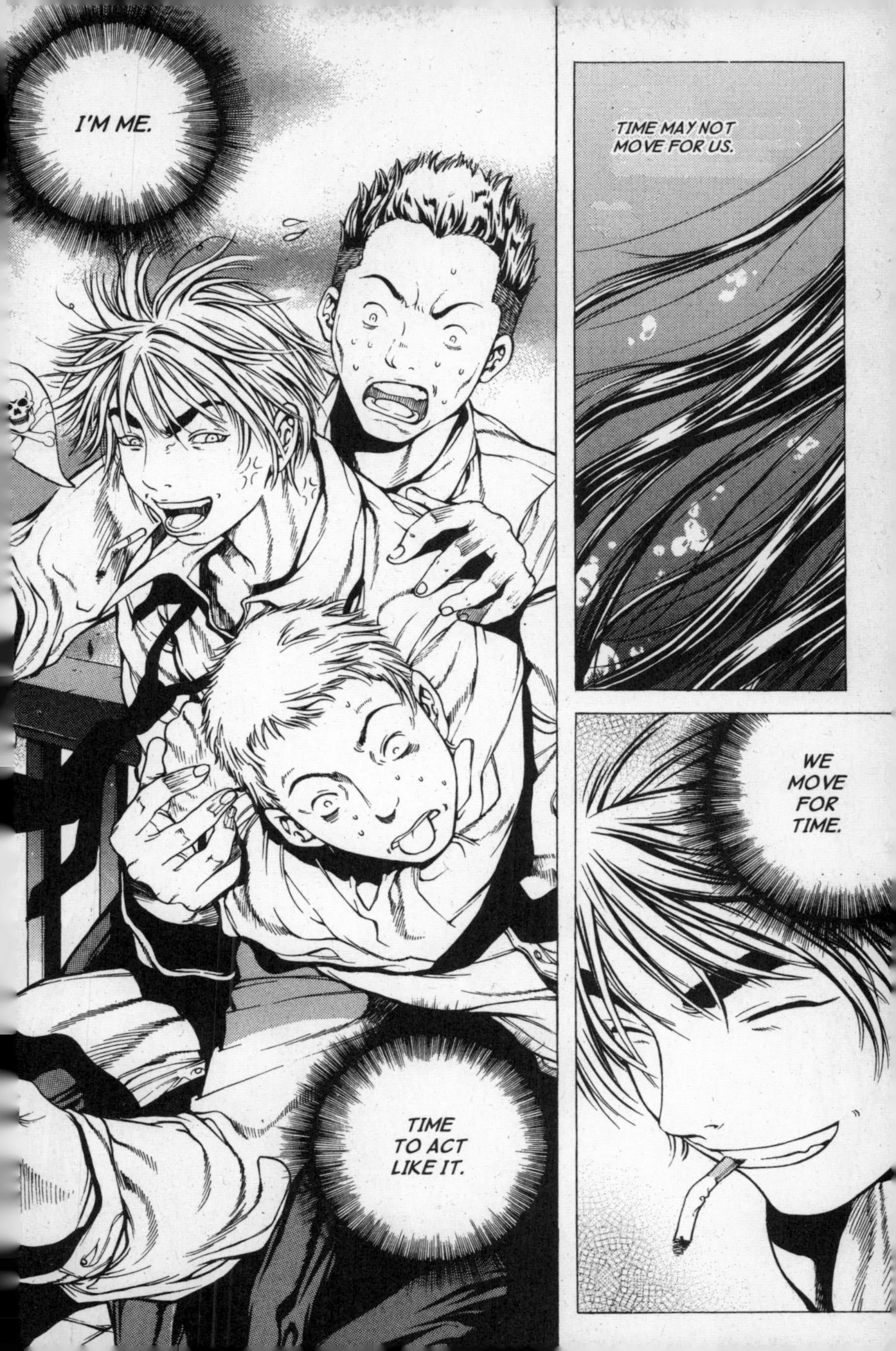
I'M ME.
TIME TO ACT LIKE IT.
TIME MAY NOT MOVE FOR US.
WE MOVE FOR TIME.

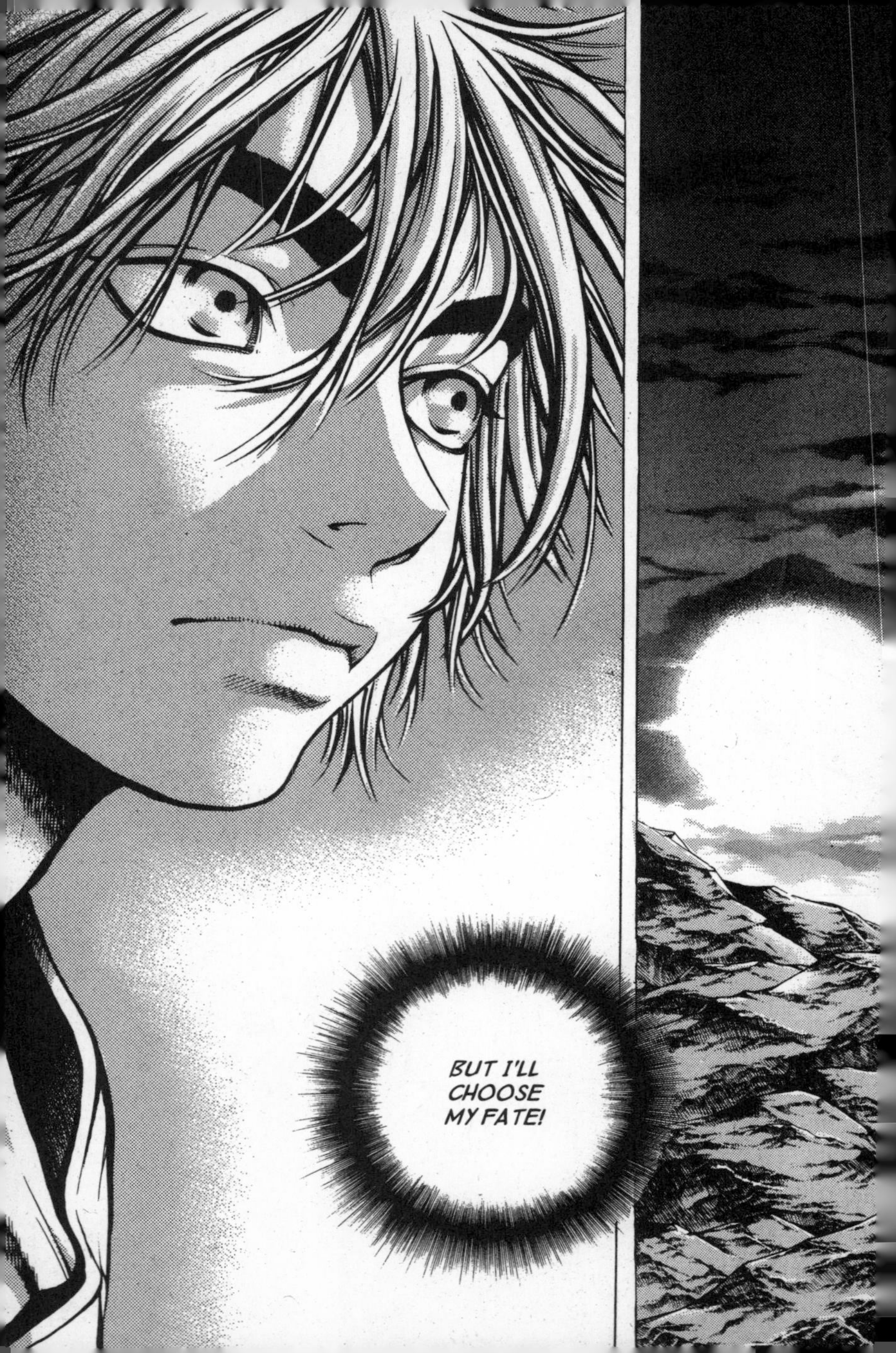
BUT I'LL CHOOSE MY FATE!

끼이이..
슥
탁

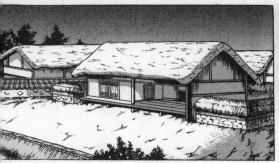

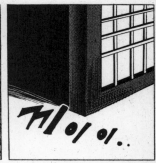

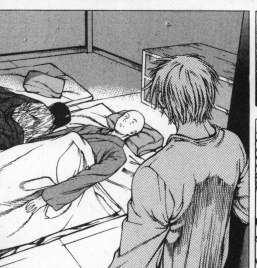

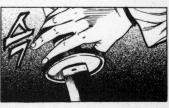

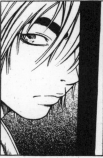

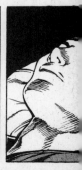

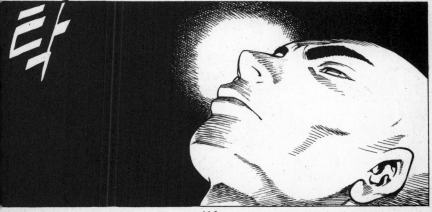

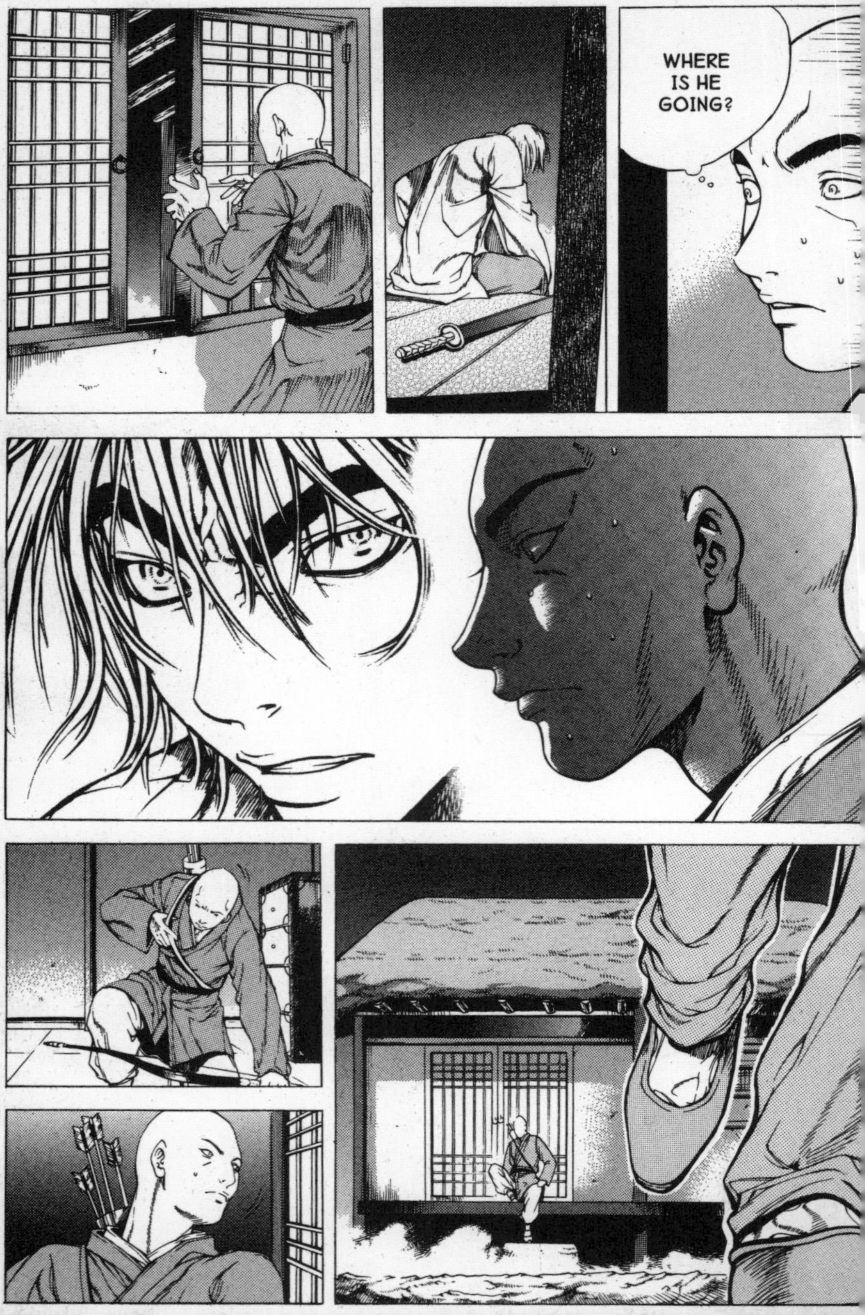
WHERE IS HE GOING?

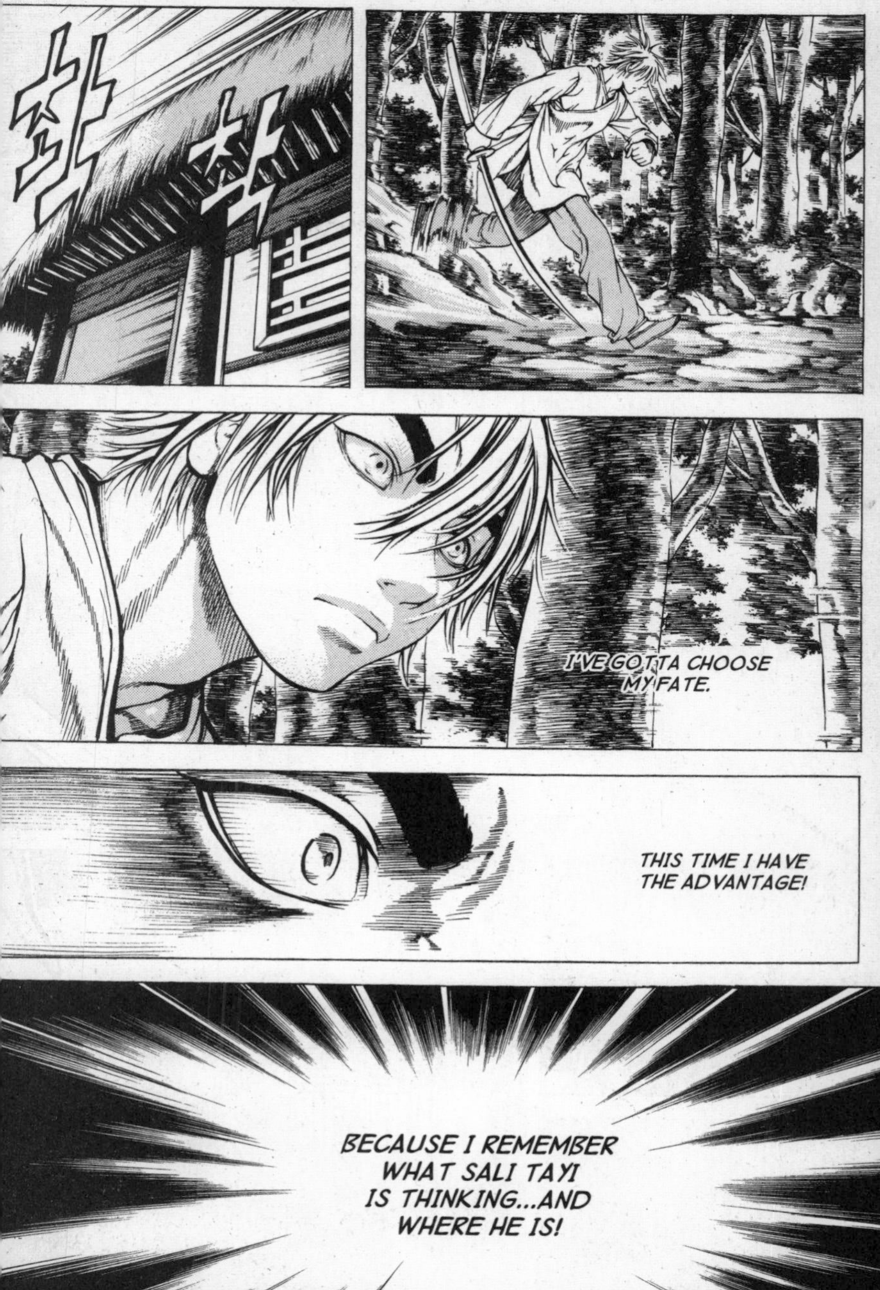
I'VE GOTTA CHOOSE MY FATE.
THIS TIME I HAVE THE ADVANTAGE!
BECAUSE I REMEMBER WHAT SALI TAYI IS THINKING...AND WHERE HE IS!

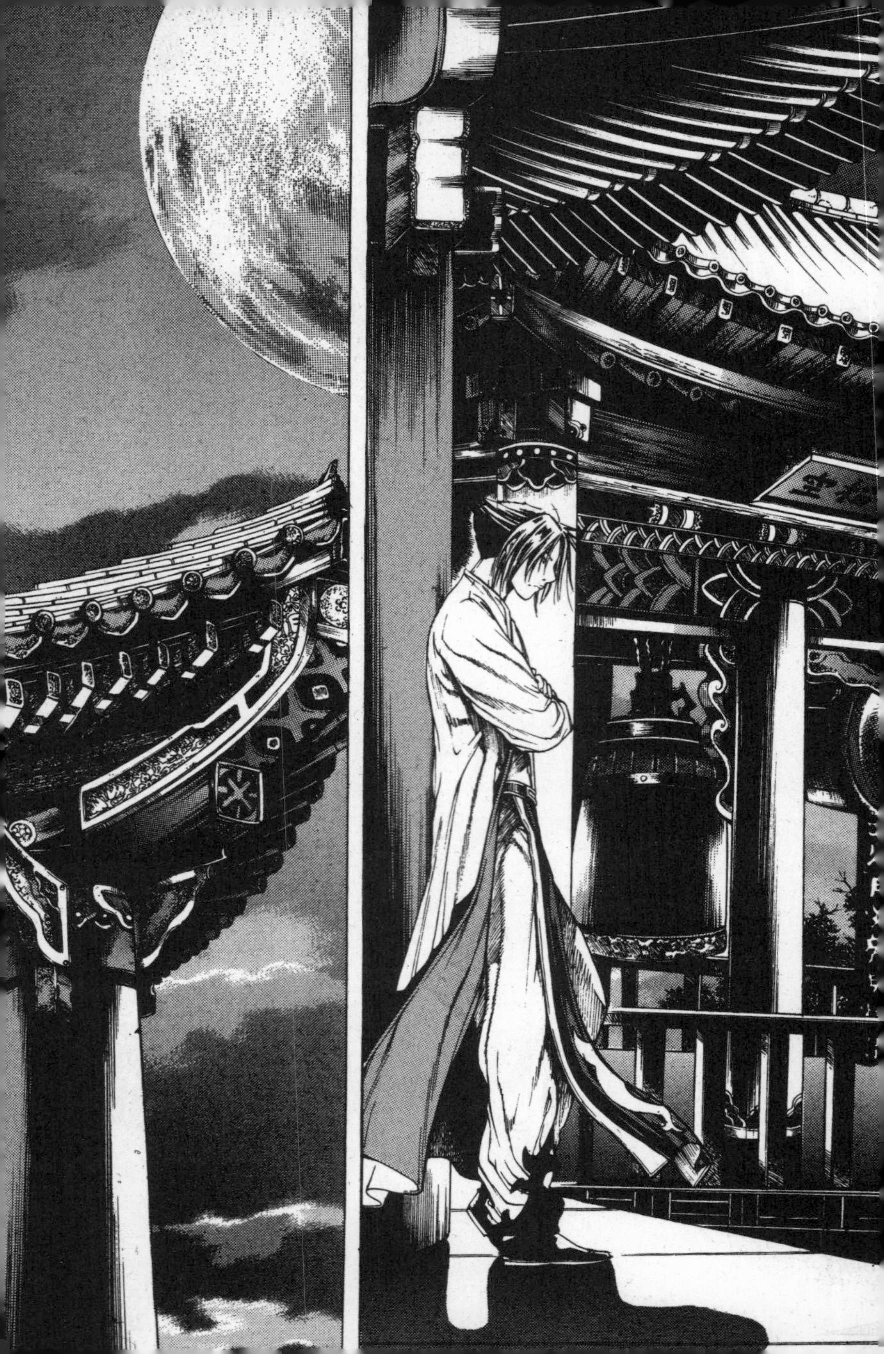

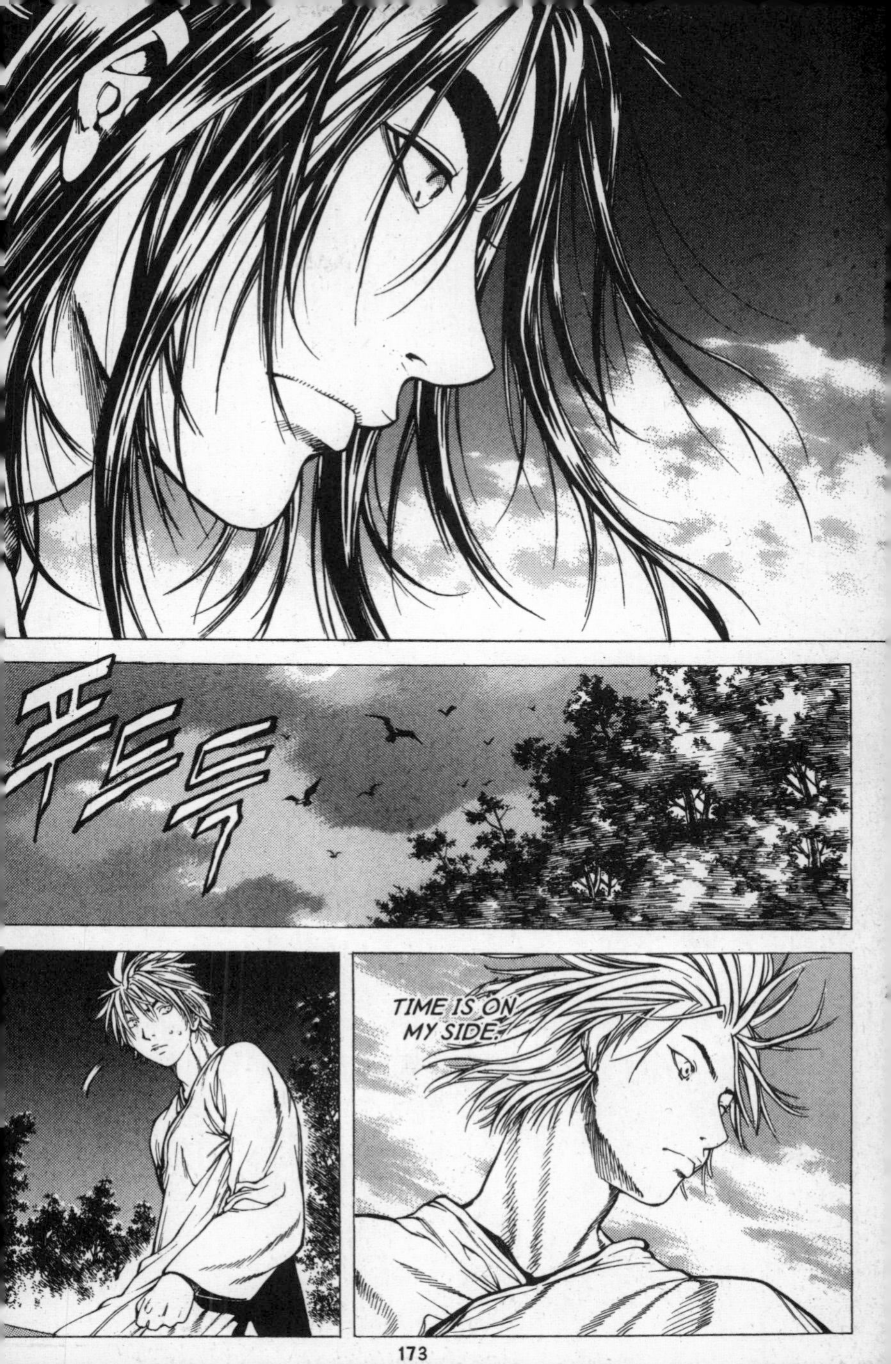
푸드득
TIME IS ON MY SIDE.

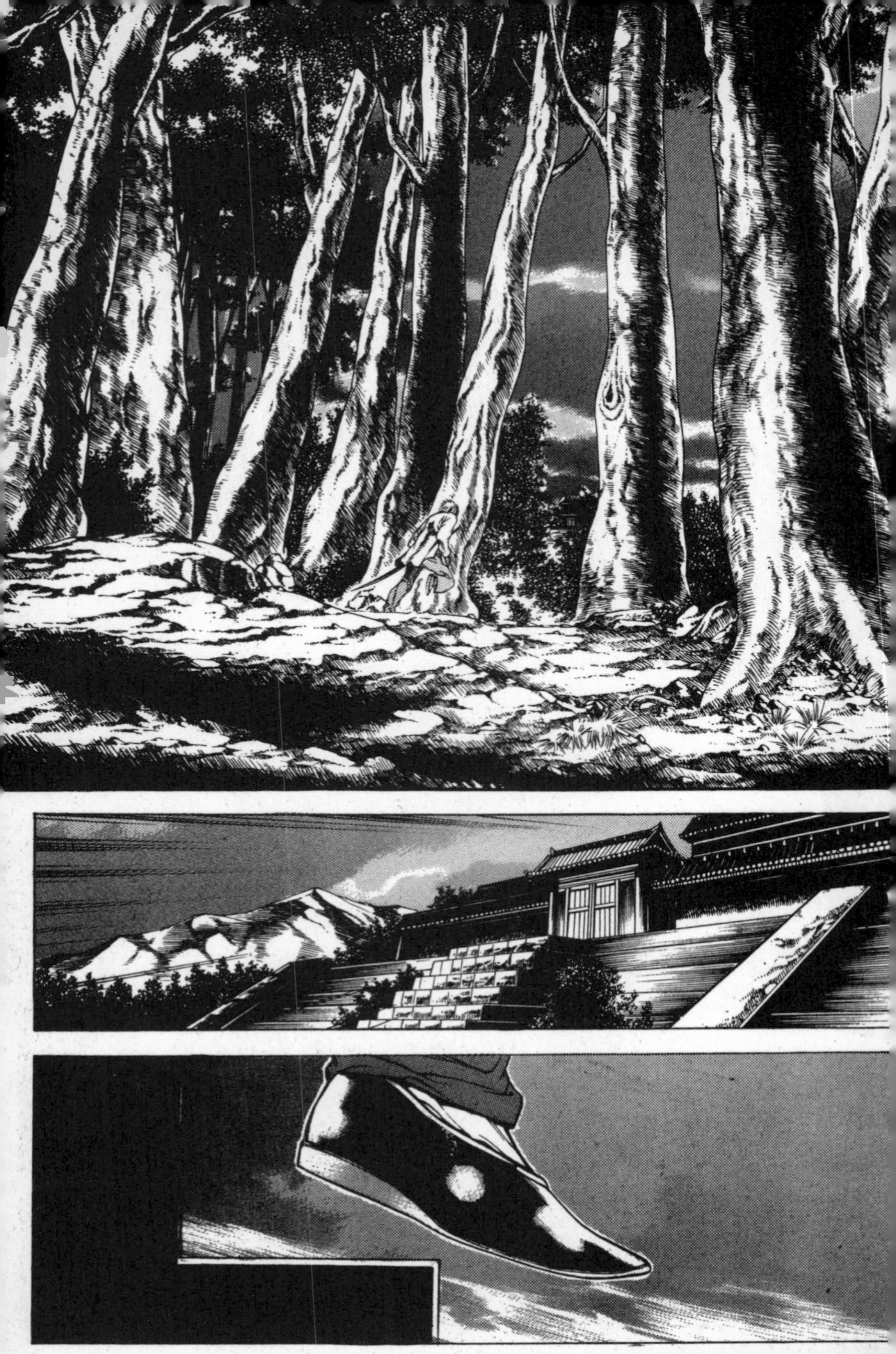

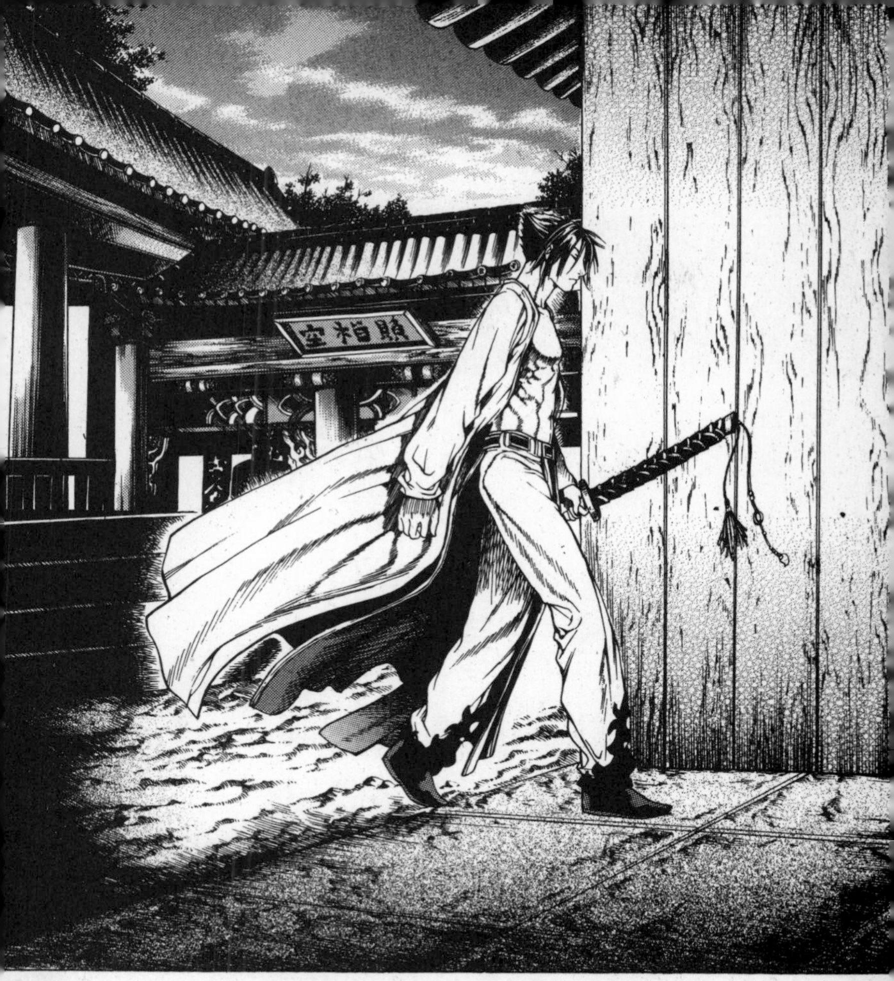
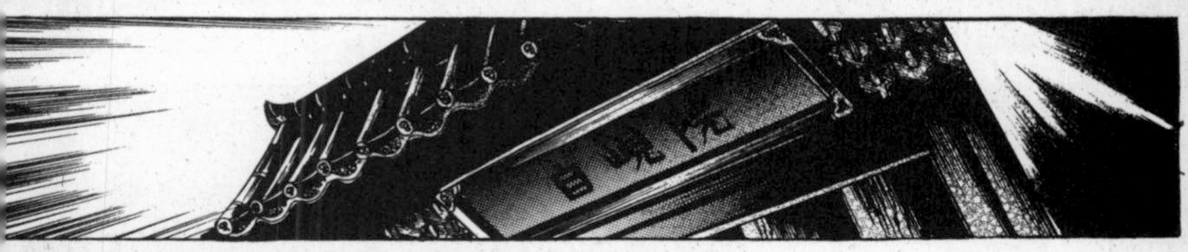
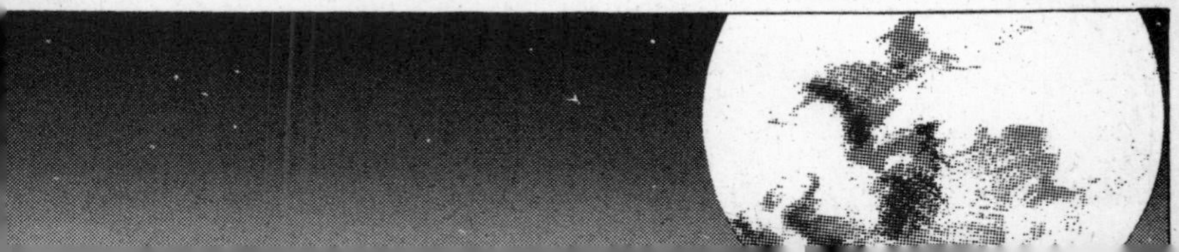

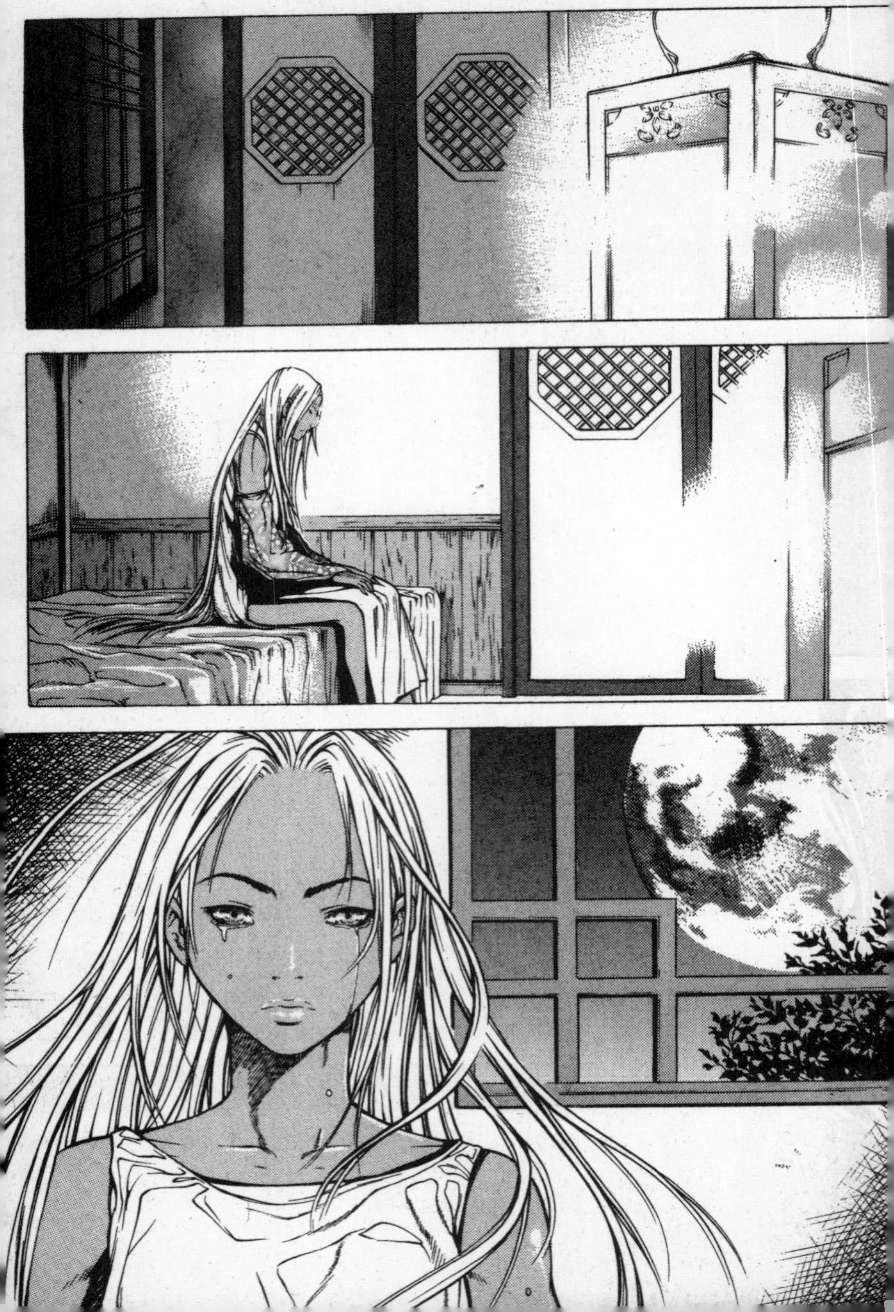

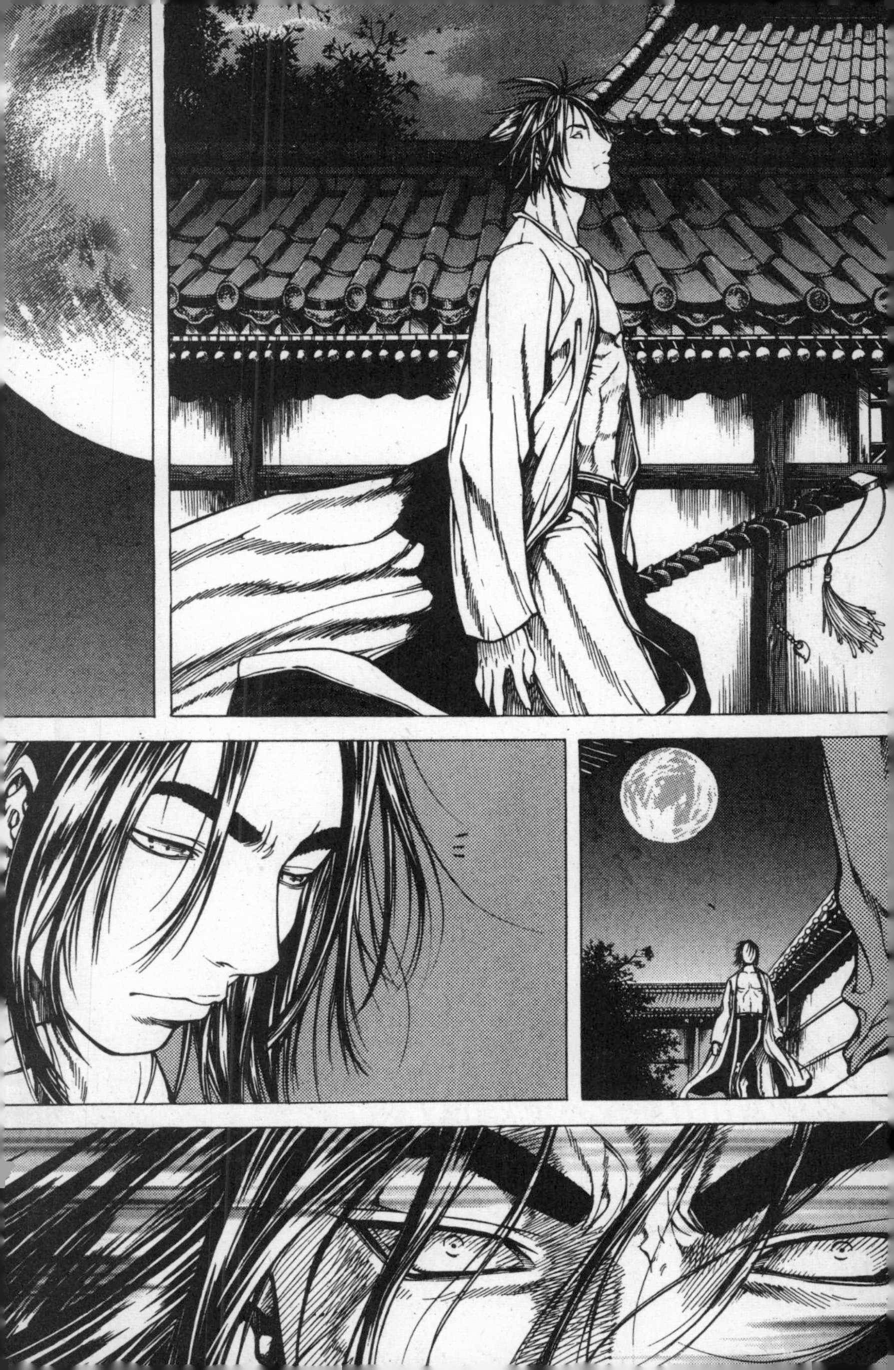

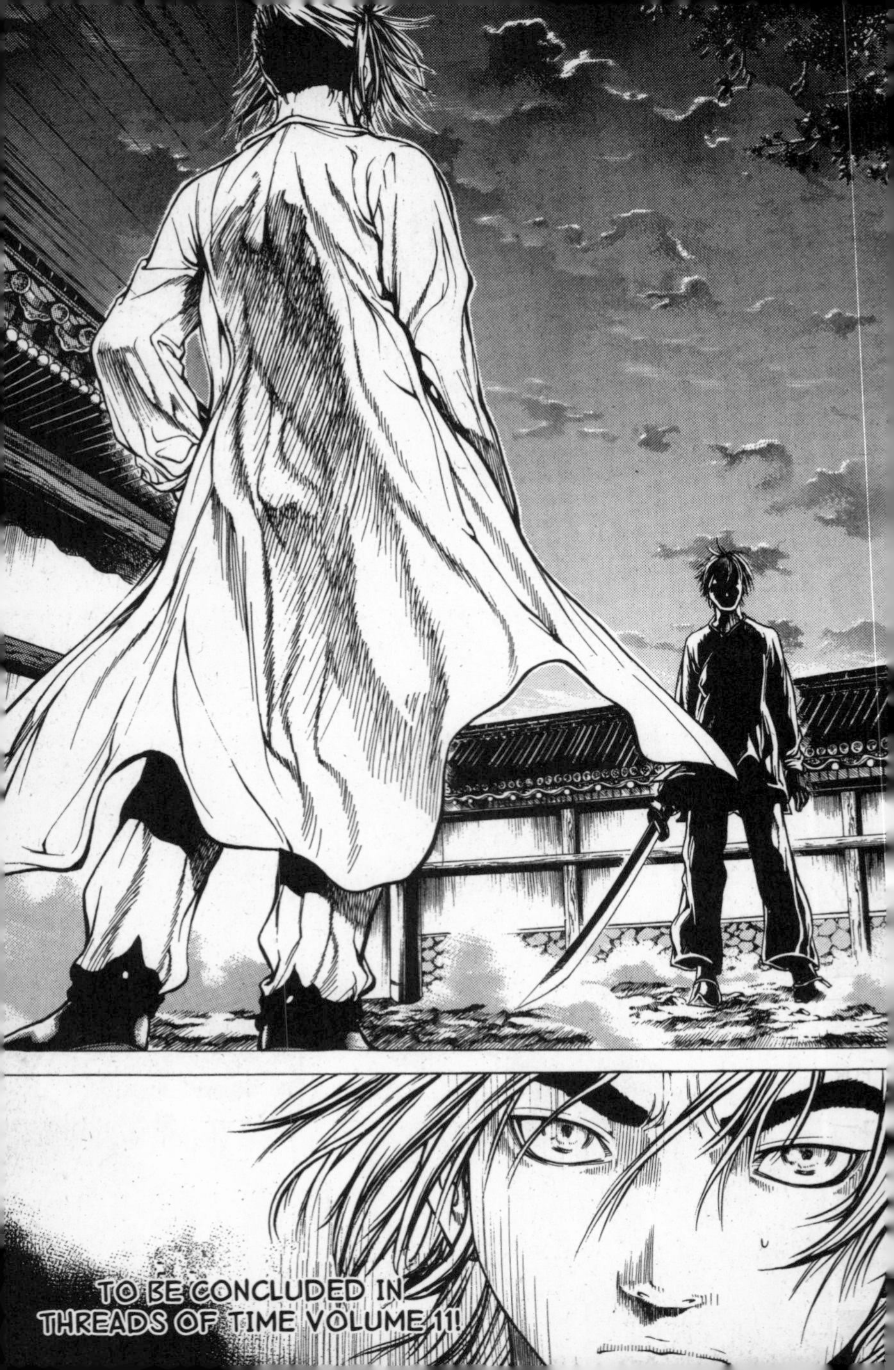
TO BE CONCLUDED IN
THREADS OF TIME VOLUME 11!

MISS K. DAILY HONES HER SKILLS IN THE STUDIO–AS A COOK!

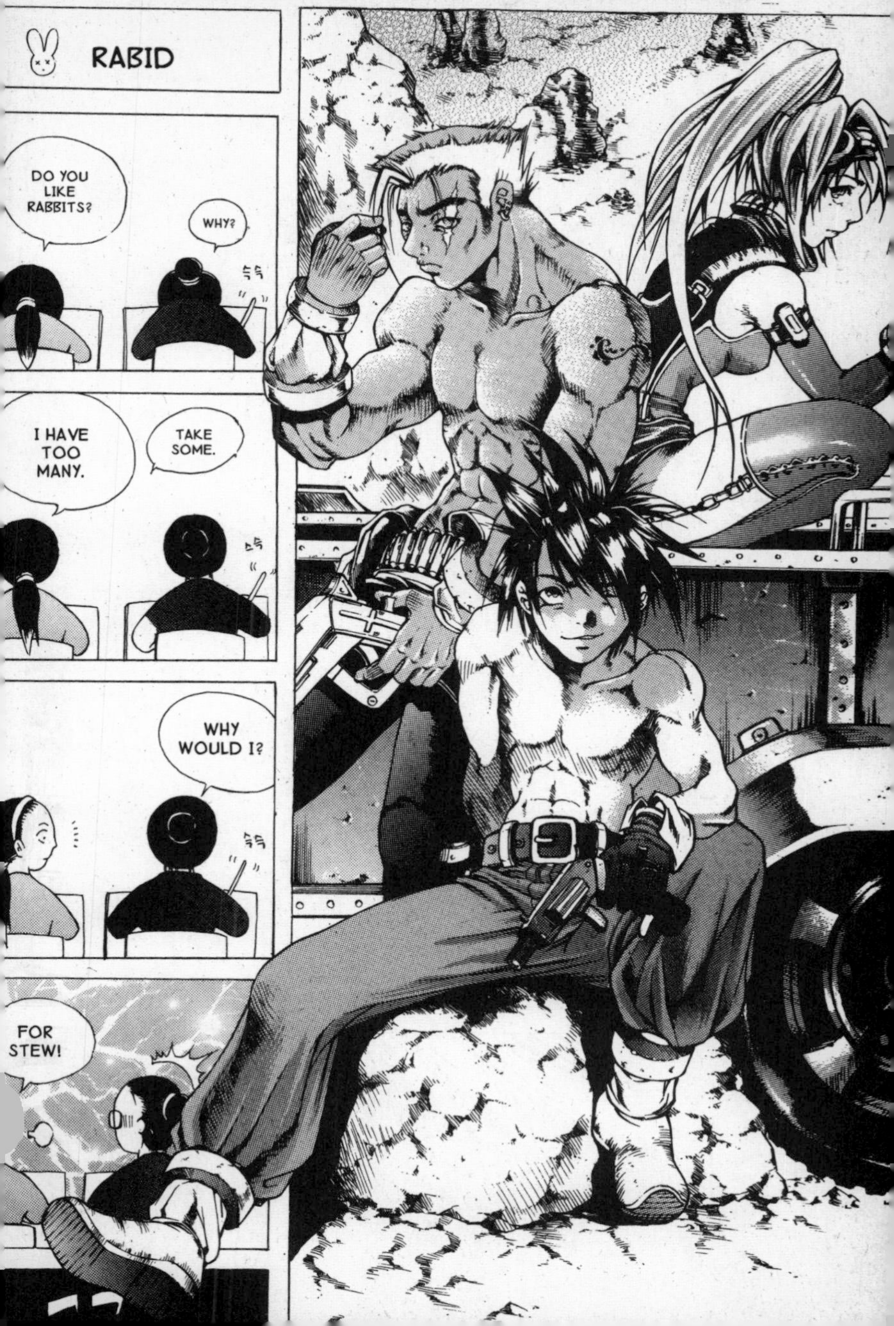
RABID
DO YOU LIKE RABBITS?
WHY?
I HAVE TOO MANY.
TAKE SOME.
WHY WOULD I?
FOR STEW!

MISS L. CONTINUES TO IMPROVE–HER ART AND HER DIET!

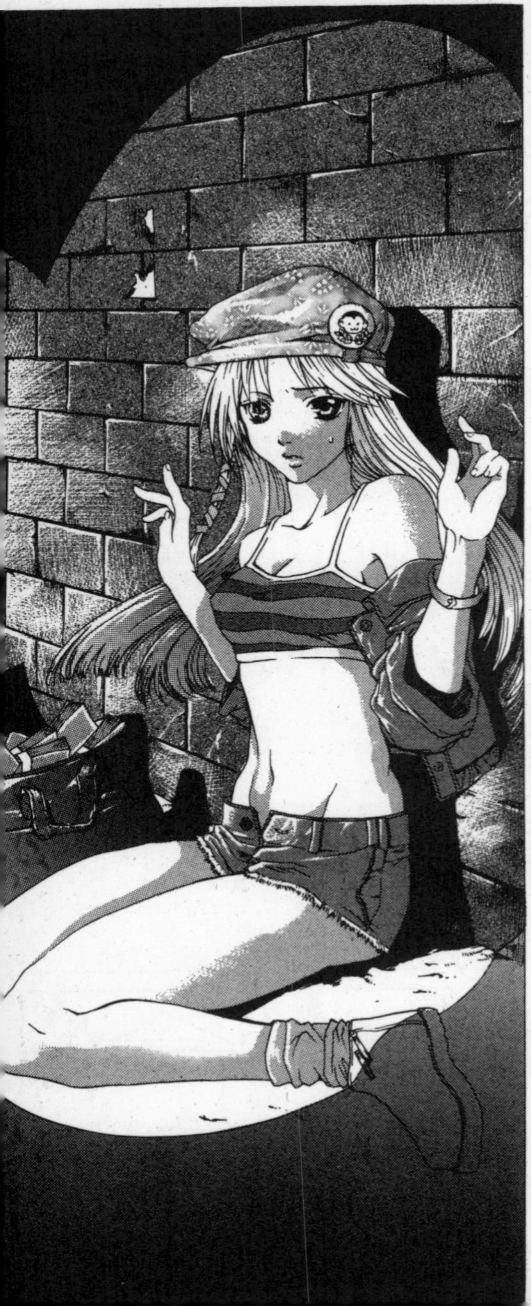

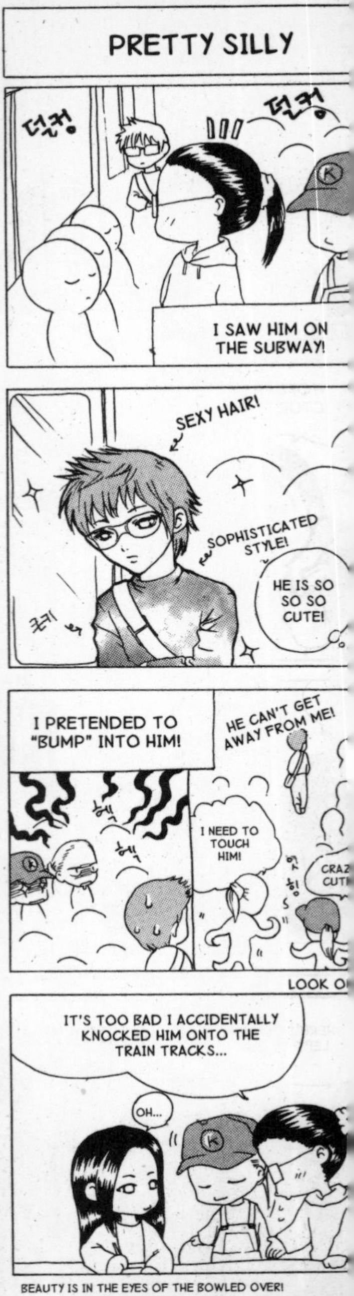
PRETTY SILLY
덜컹
덜컹
I SAW HIM ON THE SUBWAY!
SEXY HAIR!
SOPHISTICATED STYLE!
HE IS SO SO SO CUTE!
I PRETENDED TO "BUMP" INTO HIM!
HE CAN'T GET AWAY FROM ME!
헉
헉
I NEED TO TOUCH HIM!
LOOK O
IT'S TOO BAD I ACCIDENTALLY KNOCKED HIM ONTO THE TRAIN TRACKS...
OH...
BEAUTY IS IN THE EYES OF THE BOWLED OVER!

SING OUT, SISTER!

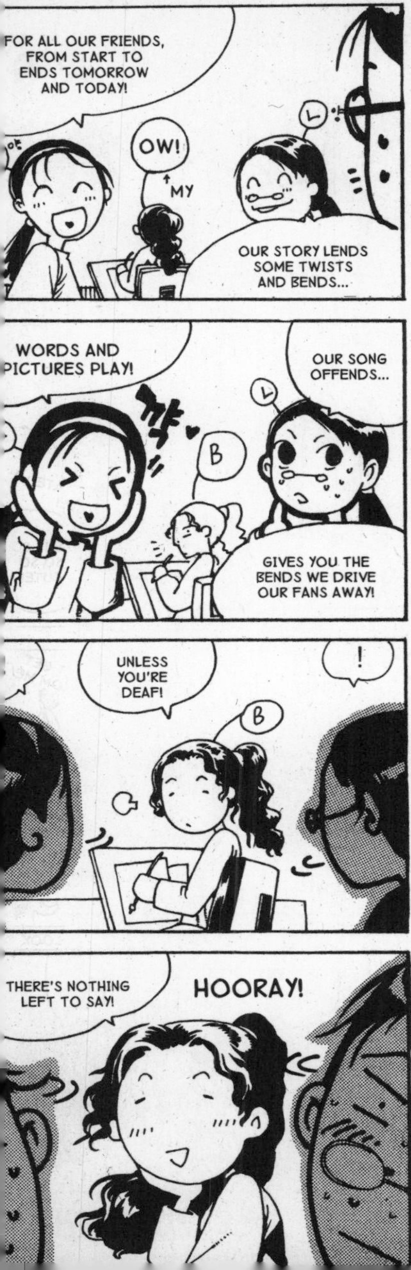

FOR ALL OUR FRIENDS, FROM START TO ENDS TOMORROW AND TODAY!
OW!
MY
L
OUR STORY LENDS SOME TWISTS AND BENDS...
WORDS AND PICTURES PLAY!
꺅
B
L
OUR SONG OFFENDS...
GIVES YOU THE BENDS WE DRIVE OUR FANS AWAY!
UNLESS YOU'RE DEAF!
!
B
THERE'S NOTHING LEFT TO SAY!
HOORAY!

BREAKIN' 'EM

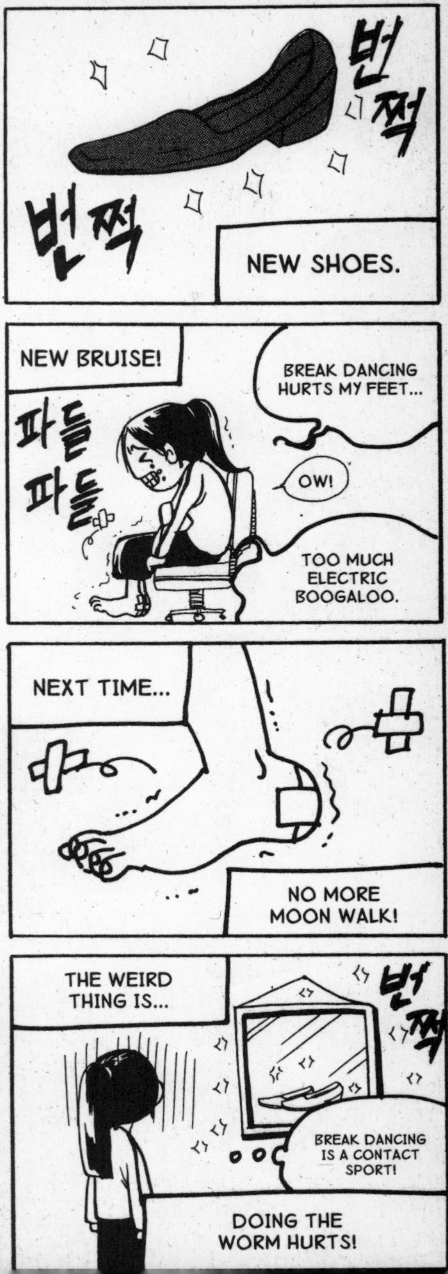

번쩍
번쩍
NEW SHOES.
NEW BRUISE!
BREAK DANCING HURTS MY FEET...
파들 파들
OW!
TOO MUCH ELECTRIC BOOGALOO.
NEXT TIME...
NO MORE MOON WALK!
THE WEIRD THING IS...
번쩍
BREAK DANCING IS A CONTACT SPORT!
DOING THE WORM HURTS!

FUNNY HA HA

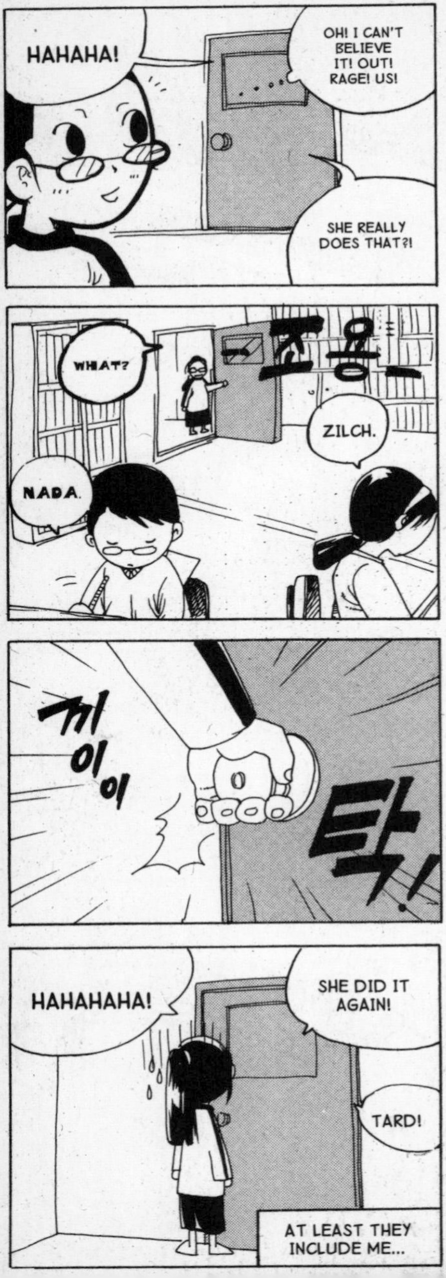

HAHAHA!
OH! I CAN'T BELIEVE IT! OUT! RAGE! US!
SHE REALLY DOES THAT?!
WHAT?
조용-
ZILCH.
NADA.
끼이이
탁!
HAHAHAHA!
SHE DID IT AGAIN!
TARD!
AT LEAST THEY INCLUDE ME...

SET IT TO ELEVEN

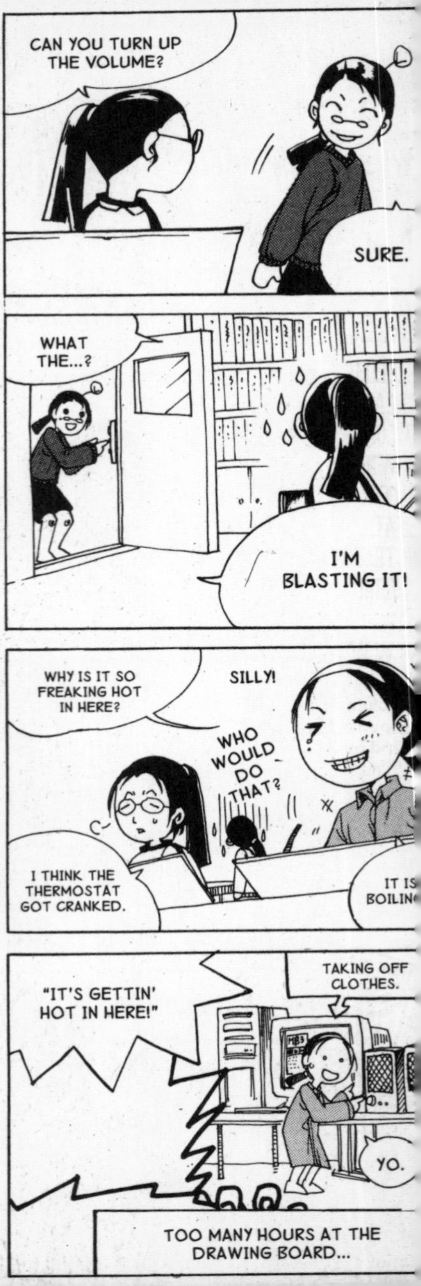

CAN YOU TURN UP THE VOLUME?
SURE.
WHAT THE...?
I'M BLASTING IT!
WHY IS IT SO FREAKING HOT IN HERE?
SILLY!
WHO WOULD DO THAT?
I THINK THE THERMOSTAT GOT CRANKED.
IT IS BOILIN
"IT'S GETTIN' HOT IN HERE!"
TAKING OFF CLOTHES.
YO.
TOO MANY HOURS AT THE DRAWING BOARD...

TOKYOPOP.COM